THE *ENCYCLOPÉDIE* IN EIGHTEENTH-CENTURY ENGLAND

THE *ENCYCLOPÉDIE* IN EIGHTEENTH-CENTURY ENGLAND
AND OTHER STUDIES

John Lough
*Professor of French in the
University of Durham*

ORIEL PRESS

© John Lough 1970
First published 1970

ISBN 0 85362 078 4
Library of Congress Catalogue Card Number 74-112719

AS
25
E6
L66

Published by
ORIEL PRESS LIMITED
32 Ridley Place
Newcastle upon Tyne, England NE1 8LH

Set in 10-pt Baskerville on 12-pt body and printed by
Northumberland Press Ltd. Gateshead

Preface

The studies reprinted here, with additions and corrections, first appeared between 1952 and 1965 in a variety of publications. It has now proved possible to follow up the suggestion made to me from various quarters that they would be easier to consult if assembled in one volume. For permission to reprint them I am grateful to the editors of *French Studies*, the *Modern Language Review* and *Studies on Voltaire and the Eighteenth Century* as well as to the University of Newcastle upon Tyne. I should also like to acknowledge the assistance received from the Research Fund of the University of Durham in carrying out the work on which these articles were based.

J.L.

Durham
November 1969

Contents

Preface	v
List of Abbreviations	viii
I. The *Encyclopédie* in Eighteenth-Century England	1
II. Louis, Chevalier de Jaucourt (1704-1780). A Biographical Sketch	25
III. Two Unsolved Problems	71
IV. Mme. Geoffrin and the *Encyclopédie*	90
V. Luneau de Boisjermain *v.* the Publishers of the *Encyclopédie*	96
VI. The Problem of the Unsigned Articles	159
Bibliography	233
Index	239

List of Abbreviations

AT	Diderot, Œuvres complètes, ed. J. Assézat and M. Tourneux, Paris, 1875-1877, 20 vols.
Bachaumont	L. P. de Bachaumont, Mémoires secrets pour servir à l'histoire de la République des Lettres en France de 1762 jusqu'à nos jours, London, 1777-1789, 36 vols.
Best.	Voltaire, Correspondence, ed. Theodore Besterman, Geneva, 1953-1966, 107 vols.
BN	Bibliothèque Nationale, Paris.
BPUG	Bibliothèque Publique et Universitaire, Geneva.
BSHPF.	Bulletin de la Société de l'Histoire du Protestanisme Français.
Corr. litt.	F. M. Grimm (ed.), Correspondance littéraire, philosophique et critique, ed. M. Tourneux, Paris, 1877-1882, 16 vols.
Essays	J. Lough, Essays on the Encyclopédie of Diderot and D'Alembert, London, 1968.
Gordon & Torrey	D. H. Gordon and N. L. Torrey, The Censoring of Diderot's Encyclopédie and the Re-established Text, New York, 1947.
May	L. P. May, 'Documents nouveaux sur l'Encyclopédie. L'Histoire et les sources de l'Encyclopédie, d'après le registre de délibérations et de comptes des éditeurs, et un mémoire inédit', Revue de Synthèse, 1938.
MLN	Modern Language Notes.
MLR	Modern Language Review.
PAM	Philosophie ancienne et moderne, ed. J. A. Naigeon (in the Encyclopédie méthodique), Paris, 1791-1797, 3 vols.
Perret	J. P. Perret, Les Imprimeries d'Yverdon au XVIIe et au XVIIIe siècle, Lausanne, 1945.
Proust	J. Proust, Diderot et l'Encyclopédie, 2nd edition, Paris, 1967.
RHL	Revue d'histoire littéraire de la France.
Roth	Diderot, Correspondance, ed. G. Roth, Paris, 1955- (in course of publication).
Studies	Studies on Voltaire and the Eighteenth Century.

I The *Encyclopédie* in Eighteenth-Century England[1]

If the obvious pitfall in treating this subject is to assume that the publication of the *Encyclopédie* of Diderot and D'Alembert must necessarily have created a tremendous stir on this side of the Channel and have left an indelible mark on English literature and thought in the second half of the eighteenth century, one is perhaps tempted, after collecting the available material, to go to the opposite extreme and reduce to very small proportions the influence which the work may have exercised. To claim to exhaust the subject in one short chapter would be folly, and it would be presumptuous even to attempt to define with absolute precision the limits of the influence of the *Encyclopédie* in eighteenth-century England. In the pages that follow the main intention is to set forth, as fully as space permits, such evidence on the subject as it has been possible to collect, since the material is not without a certain interest for the history of the diffusion of the *Encyclopédie* outside France.

One must, of course, distinguish between the period before the Revolution and the later period when Jacobinism had brought terror to the ruling classes of this country and obloquy on any work, such as the *Encyclopédie*, which was considered to have contributed in any way to the spread of such a dire disease. Although the third edition of the *Encyclopaedia Britannica* (1788-97) does not contain an article on Diderot, its comments on D'Alembert in the first volume (1788) are on the whole relatively objective, even if it quotes a passage from the *Monthly Review* of 1787 which attacks the treatment of religion in the *Encyclopédie*.[2]

---

[1] First published in *French Studies*, 1952, pp. 289-307.
[2] See below, p. 12.

But the *Supplement* to this edition, which appeared in 1801, contains in the dedication to George III the well-known denunciation of the *Encyclopédie* and all its works:

> The French *Encyclopédie* has been accused, and justly accused, of having disseminated, far and wide, the seeds of Anarchy and Atheism. If the *Encyclopaedia Britannica* shall, in any degree, counteract the tendency of that pestiferous work, even these two Volumes will not be wholly unworthy of Your Majesty's Patronage.

Diderot now receives an article to himself, but one which is inspired by the bitterest prejudice. It is true that the author of the article admits that the parts of the *Encyclopédie* which deal with science, arts and crafts are reasonably well done, but he declares that the great object of the men behind the work was to 'sap the foundation of all religion'. From the very beginning of the article, where the reader is informed that the *Pensées Philosophiques* 'contributed to promote the object of that conspiracy which had been for some time formed against every thing that ennobles human nature' and is at once referred to the article *Jacobins*, it is clear that a great part of it (though not some of the more lurid biographical details, the source of which I have been unable to trace)[3] is taken from the *Mémoires pour servir à l'histoire du Jacobinisme*, published in London in 1797 by the Jesuit Father Barruel, who saw in the *Encyclopédie* one branch of the gigantic conspiracy which had systematically prepared for the coming of the Revolution and had brought to power men like Robespierre.

The reception given to the *Encyclopédie* in this country fifty years earlier was certainly decidedly less hostile. Although it is difficult to trace with any certainty the names of those Englishmen who subscribed to the work from the very beginning,[4] the

---

[3] The author borrowed some of his material from the article on Diderot in Abbé de Feller's *Dictionnaire historique*, 2nd edition, Augsburg-Liège (1791), Vol. III, pp. 530-2.

[4] Charles Burney declared that he was a subscriber to the first edition, according to P. A. Scholes, *The Great Dr. Burney*, Oxford, 1948, 2 vols., Vol. I, p. 76 (see also R. A. Leigh, 'Les Amitiés Françaises du Dr. Burney', (*Revue de Littérature Comparée*, 1951, pp. 162, 167). Samuel Johnson, we know from

presence of the book in so many libraries in this country shows that the first edition must have had a considerable sale here. Moreover, it is often possible to trace the origin of library copies. The British Museum copy, in the Royal Library, belonged to the private collection of George III, while that in the Bodleian, with its inscription 'Joseph Gulston 1768', bears the name of a well-known book-collector of the period. The first edition of the *Encyclopédie* is to be found in four of the five Cambridge libraries where I have sought it. The copy in Trinity College Library was presented in 1775 by four fellows of the college, and that in St. John's College Library was given by the Master, William Craven, who was appointed Professor of Arabic in 1770. The early volumes of the work must have been consulted by Adam Smith at the Advocates' Library in Edinburgh, while we know that in 1759 he had the first seven volumes bought for the University Library at Glasgow.[5] In 1767 the Earl of Findlater, Chancellor of King's College, Aberdeen, presented a copy of the work to the library there.

The interest aroused on this side of the Channel by the publication of the first volume of the *Encyclopédie* in 1751 is reflected in the activity which it provoked among London publishers. Now that some of the papers of the four publishers who brought out the *Encyclopédie* have been published,[6] we know that, when in October 1751 they got wind of the impending publication in London of a pirated edition of the work, they sent two of their number, David and Briasson, post-haste to this country 'pour voir a traiter de maniere ou d'autre pour le proffit de la Comp^e,

the sale catalogue of his library, possessed seven volumes of the work, but there is no evidence that he was a subscriber. In 1766 David Garrick subscribed for the last ten volumes of text and the plates, which he had some difficulty in having sent over to England (cf. his letter to Suard in *The Letters of David Garrick*, London, 1963, 3 vols , Vol. II, p. 524, a letter of D'Holbach in F. A. Hedgcock, *David Garrick and his French Friends*, London, 1912, p. 311, and three letters of Grimm in Garrick's *Private Correspondence*, London, 1832, 2 vols., Vol. II, pp. 465, 475, 479).

[5] See W. R. Scott, *Adam Smith as Student and Professor*, Glasgow, 1937, pp. 116, 179.

[6] By M. Louis Philippe May in the *Revue de Synthèse*, Vol. XV (1938). The text quoted here is taken direct from the manuscript—Archives Nationales, U1051.

Soit pour Cedder un Nombre d'exemplaires a tres bon prix aux Libraires de Londres, soit pour les engager a acheter un Nombre de nos figures pour leur édition'.[7] Unfortunately this document is far from clear as to the outcome of these negotiations, as will be seen from the entry on the subject, dated 25 February 1752:

La Comp^e a donné son Consentement aux affaires traitées en Angleterre en 9bre dernier par les Srs David & Briasson, desquels elle a oui le rapport & paraphés les traités qu'ils ont fait avec les Srs Nourse & Vaillant pour en faire son affaire propre.

frais du Voyage d'angleterre
La Comp^e alloue les frais de Voyage des Srs David & Briasson montant a Quatorze Cent quatre vingt Seize livres dix sols qui seront portés en une seule ligne sur un livre nouveau que le d^t Briasson ouvrira. Sur lequel livre seront portés toutes les depenses concernant cette affaire et l'Impression angloise ainsy que les rentrées dans leur tems.

frais des Transactions
Approuve la Comp^e que led^t Briasson aye fait de la Caisse de la Comp^e les frais et debourcés de l'affaire des transactions Philosophiques dont Il a ouvert un regitre. Elle l'autorise a prendre de la même caisse l'argent necessaire pour se rembourser les depenses du Voyage d'angleterre ainsy que tous les frais a faire pour ces deux affaires a l'avenir. Les depenses de l'une et l'autre affaire seront rendues a la Caisse de la Comp^e des p^{res}. rentrées qui viendront alors quelles seront en valeur. Fait a Paris les jour & an que dessus.[8]

If this agreement seems to have required the London publishers to furnish copies of the *Philosophical Transactions*, what they were to receive in return is not made clear. If one may venture a hypothesis, it might be that Nourse and Vaillant were the

---

[7] Ibid., p. 25.
[8] Ibid., pp. 26-7. There is a further reference to Nourse and Vaillant in these papers on p. 30 (1762) and to Nourse and Saillant on p. 89 (1765), but in both cases the entries concern the price of different volumes of the *Encyclopédie* and throw no light on the agreement entered into in 1751. Nourse and Vaillant (or Saillant) are the only English booksellers mentioned in these accounts, which contain no information about the number of English subscribers to the work.

publishers mentioned in the *Gentleman's Magazine* of January 1752,[9] who, 'having agreed with the French authors for their copy and plates, defer their work till the French is so far advanced, that they may make their English alphabet regular'. Whether this hypothesis be correct or not, the fact remains that the names of Nourse and Vaillant do not appear on the title-page of any of the English publications known to have been inspired by the *Encyclopédie*, and it would therefore seem that nothing came of their project.

However, that a pirated edition of the first volume of the work did actually appear in London in 1752 is made clear by an item in the accounts of the French publishers for that year, which reads: '809. un to. 1er. Encyclopedie 4°, tiré de Londres p. la societe 20.'[10] The appearance of this first volume is confirmed by a passage in a letter of Jean François de Boissy, written from Leyden in July 1752: '*L'Encyclopédie* a été imprimée à Londres in 4°, mais il ne paraît pas que cette édition soit fort recherchée. On préfère celle de Paris comme originale'.[11] If none of the English newspapers of the time which I have been able to consult contains any reference to this quarto edition, there are a certain number of allusions to it in the reviews of the period. Thus the *Gentleman's Magazine* for January 1752 states that 'an exact copy of the French edition is also in the press; undertaken by some London booksellers',[12] while the *London Magazine or Gentleman's Monthly Intelligencer* gives in its catalogue of books for March and April 1752 the following item: 'Encyclopaedie, ou, Dictionnaire Raisonné des Sciences, des Arts & des Metiers. Tome Premier, 4to, pr. 18s. in Boards, Innys, &c.'[13] Curiously enough, although these pieces of evidence leave no doubt as to the appearance of the first volume of this pirated edition of the

---

[9] Vol. XXII, pp. 46-7.
[10] May, p. 64.
[11] J. F. de Boissy, *Lettres*, ed. C. E. Engel, Neuchâtel, 1941, p. 99. See also the *Lettre de M. Dutens à M. De *** sur les différentes éditions de l'Encyclopédie* (*Journal encyclopédique*, 15 June 1771, p. 446): 'La contrefaction que l'on commença d'en faire à Londres, il y a environ 14 [sic] ans, fut bientot discontinuée en conséquence d'arrangemens pris entre les Libraires'.
[12] Vol. XXII, pp. 46-7.
[13] Vol. XXI, p. 194, no. 48.

Encyclopédie, one seeks in vain for a copy of it in the British Museum, Cambridge University Library, Bodleian Library and National Library of Scotland; nor has an inquiry through the National Central Library led to any result.

Fortunately the British Museum[14] possesses a copy of the work the title of which precedes the item just quoted in the *London Magazine*: 'A Translation of the Plan of the French Encyclopaedia. pr. 2s. 6d. Innys &c.' The fact that these two works were brought out by the same group of publishers would lead one to suppose that the translation of D'Alembert's *Discours Préliminaire* was intended as a sort of prospectus for the reprint of the French text, an impression which is borne out by the *Monthly Review* of July 1752[15] which, after speaking of 'a translation publish'd here (in *Octavo.* Price 2s. 6d.) of the *preface* to, or *plan* of the work', goes on:

> An edition in quarto of the *Encyclopaedia* is undertaken by the book-sellers of *London [which they offer to sell at* half the price *of the* Paris *edition]*, who have published one volume, printed *verbatim* from the *Paris* edition, price 18s. half bound. But their reprinting the other *nine* volumes will depend upon the reception of the *first.*

Compare this with the *Advertisement* of *The Plan of the French Encyclopaedia, or Universal Dictionary of Arts, Sciences, Trades and Manufacturers, being an Account of the Origin, Design, Conduct and Execution of that Work. Translated from the Preface of the French Editors, Mess. Diderot and Alembert*[16]—a monument to the publishing ethics of bygone days, which is worth reproducing in full:

> The first Volume of the French *ENCYCLOPAEDIA,* herewith published, is reprinted verbatim from the Paris Edition; and was carefully corrected by two ingenious Gentlemen, Natives of

---

[14] 1158.k.15.
[15] Vol. VII, pp. 69-70.
[16] The publishers responsible for this edition are stated on the title page to be: W. Innys, T. Longman, C. Hitch and L. Hawes, J. and P. Knapton, S. Birt, J. Ward, J. Hodges, R. Hett, J. and J. Rivington, M. Senex, D. Browne and A. Millar.

France. The Proprietors have engaged in a Design of Reprinting the Whole at London, with a View to serve their country, by encouraging Arts, Manufactures, and Trades; and keeping large Sums at Home, that would otherwise be sent Abroad. They offer their work at Half the Price of the Paris Edition; and hereby promise, in case they meet with no Discouragement, to proceed regularly in printing the subsequent Volumes. But, if they should be obliged to stop short, it is hoped that no Blame will fall upon them, for declining to sacrifice their private Fortunes, upon finding too few to join them in their real Design of promoting the Public Good.

This appeal to the self-interest and patriotism of potential subscribers appears to have fallen on deaf ears, since there is no evidence that this pirated edition was carried beyond the first volume.

Another project of London publishers in 1752 was the production of a translation of the *Encyclopédie* in ten volumes (eight quarto volumes of text and two of plates), to be published in parts by Christmas 1756 at a total cost to the subscribers of nine guineas. It was the work of Sir Joseph Ayloffe (1709-81), a well-known antiquarian of the time. The first part is announced in the January 1752 number of the *Gentleman's Magazine*:

> Encyclopaedia Nº. I, or, a rational dictionary of arts, sciences, and trade; by several eminent hands. Methodized, digested, and now publishing at Paris, by M. Diderot, fellow of the royal academy of sciences and belles-lettres in Prussia; and, as to the mathematical part, by M. D'Alembert, member of the royal academy of sciences at Paris and Berlin, and fellow of the royal society.—Translated from the French, with improvements; in which will be included a great variety of new articles, tending to explain and illustrate the antiquities, history ecclesiastical, civil and military, laws, customs, manufactures, commerce, curiosities, etc. of Great Britain and Ireland. By Sir Joseph Ayloffe, Bart., fellow of the royal society of antiquaries, London, and author of the Universal Librarian.[17]

In announcing this work, the review waxes sarcastic on the alleged improvements and additions promised in this translation:

[17] p. 46.

Why these various additions should be made, and how they can be called improvements is a mystery. The room that Abingdon takes up, is well enough in a geographical dictionary, but as they have placed it on the river Ouse instead of the Thames, we have a strange instance of their improvements.

According to the *Dictionary of National Biography* the first number of Ayloffe's translation 'obtained such scanty support, and was so severely handled in the *Gentleman's Magazine* (xxii, 46) that the project was immediately abandoned', but this is no more accurate than the statement in the same article that this first number appeared on 11 *June* 1752. The *Daily Advertiser* of 11 January contains the following advertisement:

This day is Published, Numb. 1. To be continued Weekly, Price Six-Pence, of ENCYCLOPAEDIA: OR, A RATIONAL DICTIONARY OF ARTS, SCIENCES, and TRADE . . . Translated from the *French*, with Additions and Improvements . . . By Sir JOSEPH AYLOFFE, Bart.[18]

The same advertisement appeared in the *Daily Advertiser* of 16 January, and subsequent advertisements in this paper make it clear that the project did not immediately collapse, since the number of 29 February advertises the publication of the eighth part. As each sixpenny part of Ayloffe's translation was to consist of three sheets, at least twenty-four sheets of the first volume must have appeared; yet, like the first volume of the London pirated edition of the *Encyclopédie*, they appear to have left no trace whatever in the libraries of this country.

Twenty years later an attempt to translate the five volumes of the *Esprit de l'Encyclopédie* (Geneva-Paris, 1768) was little more successful. The first volume appeared in 1772 with the following title-page: 'Select Essays from the Encyclopedy, being the Most Curious, Entertaining, and Instructive Parts of that Very Extensive Work, Written by Mallet, Diderot, D'Alembert, and Others, the Most Celebrated Writers of the Age. London, Printed for Samuel Leacroft, opposite to Spring-Gardens, Charing Cross, M,DCC,LXXII.'[19] Nothing more of this work appears to have been translated.

[18] British Museum, Burney Collection, Vol. 443.
[19] British Museum, 721.g.2.

If the London publishing world showed considerable interest in the publication of the first volume of the *Encyclopédie*, the same cannot be said of such reviews as existed at that time, or indeed during the whole period of the publication of the work. Thus the *Gentleman's Magazine* contains only the half column, already quoted, on the subject of Ayloffe's translation and other projected publications of a similar type, and does not directly mention the appearance of the *Encyclopédie*, while the *London Magazine* merely lists the translation of the *Discours Préliminaire* and the first volume of the quarto edition of the French text. Among the reviews founded at a later date which might have been expected to discuss subsequent volumes of the work, neither the *Critical Review* (1756-) nor the *Annual Register* (1758-) appears even to mention the work. It is true that bombing destroyed some of the sets of periodicals in the British Museum which might contain references of interest: only a few odd volumes of the *Royal Magazine* (1759-) have been left undestroyed, while the complete set of Smollett and Goldsmith's *British Magazine* (1760-67), which is not to be found in the *Union Catalogue of Periodicals*, has gone.

Of the contemporary periodicals which it has been possible to consult, only one, the *Monthly Review*, can be said to have devoted any space to a serious discussion of the *Encyclopédie*. The account of the work offered by a series of reviewers over a period of nearly forty years,[20] is worth some study, as, although often critical of certain aspects of the *Encyclopédie*, this journal, Whig and Nonconformist in outlook, gave the *Encyclopédie* sympathetic consideration. Its mention of the work begin with a review[21] of the first two volumes in the number of July 1752.[22] This review consists mainly of extracts from the *Discours Préliminaire* on the aims and objects of the enterprise, and

---

[20] The Bodleian Library possesses a set of this review, which gives the initials of the reviewers in the handwriting of the proprietor, Ralph Griffiths. (Cf. B. C. Nangle, *The Monthly Review. First Series, 1749-1789: Index of Contributors and Articles*, Oxford, 1934).
[21] By William Bewley (1726-85), a Norfolk surgeon and apothecary, and friend of Joseph Priestley and Dr. Burney (see Nangle, op. cit., p. 4).
[22] Vol. VII, pp. 66-71.

concludes with a discussion as to whether the work, 'which was some time since suppressed at Paris (for reasons best known to the government there)', is likely to resume publication, a point on which the reviewer 'can give no satisfactory intelligence'.

Sixteen years passed before another review of the *Encyclopédie* appeared in the *Monthly Review*. The first of the two articles on the subject in 1768 was a short notice of the *Esprit de l'Encyclopédie*, followed by a summary of Voltaire's article HISTOIRE.[23] Much more interesting are the pages devoted to a discussion of the work itself, now that the seventeen volumes of text had appeared. This review was written by Owen Ruffhead (1723-69), a well-known political pamphleteer of the time.[24] It begins with a discussion of the opposition which the work had encountered in the course of its publication, and especially the role of the Jesuits in the matter. The reviewer rejoices in the triumph of 'the bold spirit and acknowledged merit of the writers against whom they directed their attacks', and declares that the opposition of the Jesuits 'certainly contributed to accelerate their ruin'. Of the merits of the work the reviewer has certain doubts, since by its very nature its articles are of unequal value, many of them being 'so exceedingly diffusive as to become tedious', a defect which also prevents the reader from taking in what he has read. On the other hand he has high praise for the *Discours Préliminaire*, and concludes his review very eulogistically: 'We do not scruple however to recommend it, with all its imperfections, as one of the most extensive and valuable treasures to be found within the whole circle of literature.'

The most interesting part of this review is undoubtedly the paragraph devoted to the treatment of political questions in the *Encyclopédie*. It is generally held today that the political ideas, the criticism of the abuses of the Ancien Régime, and the projects for reforms set forth in the *Encyclopédie* are extremely timid.

---

[23] Vol. XXXVIII, pp. 523-31. The author was Dr. William Rose (see Nangle, op. cit., p. 37). The opening words of the article ought perhaps to be quoted: 'As there are very few persons who have an opportunity of consulting the *Encyclopédie*, the work before us can scarce fail of being acceptable to the public.'

[24] Vol. XXXIX, pp. 543-5 (see Nangle, op. cit., p. 39).

Ruffhead takes a very different view, since he finds that 'the same manly freedom of sentiment which is observable in the philosophical and other departments of this work, is eminently conspicuous in the political'. Indeed, as a patriotic Englishman, writing shortly after the end of the Seven Years' War, he is almost alarmed by the prospect of his country's chief rival enjoying one day similar political freedom:

> In short, whoever takes the trouble of combining the several political articles, will find that they form a noble system of civil liberty; and however, as Englishmen, we may have no reason to rejoice at the prospect of a gradual establishment of such a system among our rivals, yet as friends to the rights of mankind, we are delighted to see such a generous system every where expanding its influence.

The prevailing view of the political theories of the contributors to the *Encyclopédie* has no doubt much to justify it, and yet it is interesting that a very different gloss should have been put upon them by a contemporary who was perhaps in a better position than we are today to interpret that mixture of submission to authority, irony and veiled criticism which is to be found in the political articles of the work.

The 1780s brought further interesting references to the *Encyclopédie* in the *Monthly Review*. In 1780 there appeared an account of the *Table analytique* to the work, which contains some general reflections on the value and aims of the *Encyclopédie*. The reviewer[25] has several criticisms to offer, though he considers it 'a valuable work' which, with all its faults, 'contains a great treasure of knowledge'. Yet he also declares that, from the technical point of view, 'it embarrasses instead of enlightening uninstructed readers', and that the articles are too often 'pieces of eloquence, and so far they depart from the plain and didactic tone, that belongs to a dictionary'. But his most serious criticisms fall on the underlying ideas of the work, which

[25] Archibald Maclaine, D.D. (1723-1805) who was Minister of the English Church at The Hague for about fifty years and who composed nearly all the reviews of foreign literature for the *Monthly Review* between 1775 and 1788 (see Nangle, op. cit., p. 28).

appear to him to be dangerous. He accuses the authors of the *Encyclopédie* of having

> usurped a kind of despotism in the republic of letters, introduced a spirit of cabal and faction into the temple of Science and attempted alternately to assail and undermine those truths that are the great support of society and morals, and which even the authority of human government should render respectable, to those who are so unhappy as to look no higher.[26]

Seven years later the same author returned to the charge in a review of the *Histoire de l'Académie Royale des Sciences* for 1783 which contains Condorcet's *Eloge de d'Alembert*. While he praises highly D'Alembert's *Discours Préliminaire*—'one of the most capital productions of which the philosophy of the present age can boast', he says of it—and is willing to admit that 'the masterbuilders of this new and stupendous *temple* of Science, for the worship of NATURE, had also really in view the advancement of human knowledge and the improvement of the arts and sciences', he shows that he has no doubt as to the attitude towards religion of its editors and principal collaborators, when he goes on:

> This, no *true*, no candid philosopher will call in question. But that in the *inner court* of this temple, there was a confederacy formed against all those who looked higher than *nature*, for the principal object of their veneration and confidence, is a fact too palpable, nay too boldly avowed, to stand in need of any proof.[27]

Though put forward here with moderation, this was a view of the *Encyclopédie* which a few years later, after the outbreak of the Revolution, was to receive great prominence; it is interesting therefore to note that this passage was reproduced in the article on D'Alembert which appeared in the third edition of the *Encyclopaedia Britannica* in 1788.[28]

It is instructive to compare the attitude to the *Encyclopédie* of these anonymous and relatively obscure reviewers with the

[26] Vol. LXIII, pp. 137-8.
[27] Vol. LXXVI, pp. 242-3.
[28] It may be that it was the reviewer who contributed the article on D'Alembert.

opinions of the work expressed by some of the more famous writers of the period. Here some disappointments are in store for anyone investigating the question. David Hume, for instance, does not appear to have committed himself to an opinion of the work, either in public or in private, even though he was on familiar enough terms with D'Alembert, one of its editors, to remember him in his will and to leave him a legacy of £200. Although Dr Johnson had seven volumes of the *Encyclopédie* in his library, neither in his writings nor in Boswell is there any hint of his verdict on the work (it was no doubt highly unfavourable).[29]

We have indeed to cross the border into Scotland to find the most interesting contemporary comment on the *Encyclopédie* to come from this side of the Channel. In a letter published anonymously in the *Edinburgh Review* of 1756,[30] Adam Smith called upon his compatriots to give their attention, not only to the literary, philosophical and scientific writings of their own country, but also to those of England and especially France. He urges them to study in particular the works of Voltaire, Rousseau, Buffon and Réaumur, and also the volumes of the *Encyclopédie* as they appeared. This work, he declares, 'promises to be the most compleat of the kind which has ever been published or attempted in any language', and quoting Voltaire's praise of the undertaking in the *Siècle de Louis XIV*, he declares that 'it promises indeed to be in every respect worthy of that magnificent eulogy'. Speaking of the delays brought about in the publication of the work by the opposition of Church and State, he states, interestingly enough, that to neither did 'the authors seem to have given any just occasion of suspicion'.

His article is not without criticisms of such volumes of the *Encyclopédie* as had so far appeared. Thus he finds the articles very unequal in merit and many of them too declamatory in tone, while some of them might well have been left out, 'since their

---

[29] L. F. Powell in his article, 'Johnson and the *Encyclopédie*', in the *Review of English Studies*, Vol. II (1926), p. 337, also notes the absence of all mention of the work in Johnson's writings.
[30] In the volume covering July 1755 to January 1756, pp. 63-79.

insertion can serve only to throw ridicule upon a work calculated for the propagation of every part of useful knowledge'. The example which he gives in the following lines is amusingly chosen and presented: 'The article of *Amour*, for example, will tend little to the edification either of the learned or unlearned reader, and might, one should think, have been omitted even in an Encyclopaedia of all arts, sciences and trades.' The pages of this article[31] which concern the *Encyclopédie*, end with the suggestion that future volumes of the work should receive detailed attention in the coming volumes of the *Edinburgh Review*, and if Adam Smith's letter appeared in what was to be the last number of that periodical, it did contain what was undoubtedly the most eulogistic account of the *Encyclopédie* to be published in this country in the eighteenth century.

There seems little doubt that part of the famous chapter on the division of labour at the beginning of the *Wealth of Nations* was inspired by Adam Smith's reading of the *Encyclopédie*. The example which he uses to illustrate the advantages of a division of labour—the various processes in the manufacture of pins, carried on by eighteen different workmen, each of whom can produce 2,000 pins a day—seems to have been taken from the article ÉPINGLE which appeared in the fifth volume of the *Encyclopédie* in 1755.[32]

The *Encyclopédie* seems to have aroused considerable interest in Scotland. Not only was the work acquired by various libraries at that time, but it was from Edinburgh that there issued forth in 1768 the first parts of the *Encyclopaedia Britannica*, which was perhaps partly inspired by the publication of the *Encyclopédie*. It is interesting that in 1766 an obscure teacher of French, who ran a school first in Edinburgh and later in Aberdeen, should have considered that it would help the sales of his collection of texts entitled *Nouveau recueil de pièces choisies des meilleurs auteurs françois*, if he dedicated the book to 'Monsieur Diderot,

---

[31] pp. 66-70.
[32] The illustration was already used in his lectures as taken down by a student in 1763 (cf. *Lectures on Justice, Police, Revenue and Arms*, ed. E. Cannan, Oxford, 1896, p. 164) and also in an early draft of the *Wealth of Nations*, composed about the same time (cf. W. R. Scott, op. cit., pp. 328-9).

auteur de l'Encyclopédie'.[33] In 1781 Diderot, along with Buffon, was elected an honorary member of the Society of Antiquaries of Scotland, which caused him to compose a letter of thanks in English, which has recently been published.[34]

Similar interest was shown in the *Encyclopédie* by a number of well-known English writers of the period. In his autobiography Gibbon tells us that his first work, his *Essai sur l'étude de la littérature* (1761), was in part an answer to D'Alembert's slighting remarks about scholars:

> I was provoked to hear (see M. d'Alembert, *Discours Préliminaire à l'Encyclopédie*) that the exercise of the memory, their sole merit, had been superseded by the nobler faculties of the imagination and the judgment. I was ambitious of proving, by my own example, as well as by my precepts, that all the faculties of the mind may be exercised and displayed by the study of ancient literature.[35]

At the outset of his career, Goldsmith, in his *Enquiry into the Present State of Polite Learning* (1759), speaks with praise of Diderot and D'Alembert, but very slightingly of 'those monsters of learning, the Trevoux, Encyclopédies and Bibliotheques of the age'. Their compilers consist of 'men of every rank in literature . . . Wits and dunces contribute their share, and Diderot, as well as Desmarets, are candidates for oblivion. The genius of the first supplied the gale of favour; and the latter adds the useful ballast of stupidity'. There follows a colourful passage about the boredom which such works inspire in the reader: 'Woe to the reader, who, not daunted at the immense distance between one great pasteboard and the other, opens the volume, and explores his way through a region so extensive, but barren of entertainment . . .'[36] Yet curiously enough, we know that in 1762 Goldsmith borrowed from his bookseller eight

[33] Cf. my note entitled 'The *Encyclopédie* in Eighteenth-Century Scotland,' MLR, 1943, pp. 38-40.
[34] See H. Dieckmann, 'Diderot, membre honoraire de la Société d'Antiquaires d'Écosse', *Cahiers Haut-Marnais*, 1951, no. 24, pp. 23-25.
[35] 'Everyman' edition, p. 93. The *Essai* (p. 12) contains references to both the *Discours Préliminaire* and the article ERUDITION.
[36] *Works*, ed. J. W. M. Gibbs, London. 1884-86, 5 vols., Vol. III, pp. 495-8.

volumes of the *Encyclopédie* (presumably the first seven volumes of the text and the first volume of the plates, which appeared in that year), and that the catalogue of his books, published after his death in 1774, contains the following item: 'Encyclopédie, ou Dictionnaire universal raisonné, 1770, 25 vol. in 4°,'[37] i.e. a substantial part of De Félice's *Encyclopédie d'Yverdon*.

Moreover, modern detectives have shown that Goldsmith's borrowings from Diderot's *Encyclopédie*, both in articles and in various compilations for which he was responsible, began in the very year 1759 when he spoke so sneeringly of the work![38] It is also significant that, shortly before his death, Goldsmith planned and even began work on the prospectus of a *Universal Dictionary of the Arts and Sciences*, to which such celebrities as Johnson, Burke, Reynolds, Gibbon, Adam Smith, Garrick and Burney were to contribute.[39] It is amusing to speculate as to how far his sarcastic comments on the *Encyclopédie* and similar works were a mere cloak for his numerous borrowings from it.

A more admiring note is struck by Arthur Young in his references to the *Encyclopédie*. In his *Political Arithmetic* (1774)[40] he mentions with approval the articles FERMIER and GRAINS contributed by Dr. Quesnay, and in a footnote to his translation of Hirzel's *Socrate rustique*, published as an appendix to his *Rural Oeconomy* (1770), he says of the *Encyclopédie*: 'I have read the memoirs of that work on the subject of agriculture; they are extremely sensible, and call aloud for a translation into English.'[41]

Dr. Burney is another writer of the age who consulted the work with profit in his own special field. Towards the end of his life, when the first English encyclopaedia of any magnitude—that

---

[37] A. Lytton Sells, *Les sources françaises de Goldsmith*, Paris, 1924, pp. 32, 213.

[38] For details see Joseph E. Brown, 'Goldsmith's Indebtedness to Voltaire and Van Effen', *Modern Philology*, 1926, pp. 273-5, and R. S. Crane and A. Friedman, 'Goldsmith and the *Encyclopédie*', *The Times Literary Supplement*, 11 May 1933, p. 331.

[39] *Works*, Vol. I, p. 37.

[40] pp. 74, 209, 219.

[41] p. 506 (cf. the footnote to p. 430 which, although not marked with an asterisk, appears to be by the translator; it contains extracts from the article ARBRE.)

edited by Abraham Rees under the title of *The Cyclopaedia; or, Universal Dictionary of Arts, Sciences and Literature* (1802-20, 45 vols.)—was in course of preparation, Burney was asked to contribute the articles on music. As he was by that time over seventy, he sometimes contented himself with translating articles which Jean-Jacques Rousseau had written for the *Encyclopédie* and later brought together in his *Dictionnaire de musique*. On occasion he even forgot to translate the French title of the article, so that it must be sought under the French word, and now and again one actually finds two articles on the same subject—one under the English word, the other under the French![42]

Perhaps more important is the problem of the influence exercised by the *Encyclopédie* on English encyclopaedias and dictionaries of arts and sciences published between 1751 and the end of the century. It would clearly be impossible, without long and arduous researches, to follow out, encyclopaedia by encyclopaedia, the exact influence of the French work on its English successors. For one thing, the problem is complicated by the existence of common sources for all these works. The prospectus of the *Encyclopédie* informs us that the work is 'recueilli des meilleurs auteurs et particulièrement des dictionnaires anglois de Chambers, d'Harris, de Dyche, etc.'[43] It would obviously be an extremely tricky business to draw the line between what English encyclopaedias and dictionaries owed to the *Encyclopédie*, and what they derived from the English sources on which Diderot and his collaborators had drawn before them. The question is further complicated by uncertainty as to how much of the material in the *Encyclopédie* and its English successors was drawn from other sources—English, French and also German.

One can, however, say that, with few exceptions, the encyclopaedias and dictionaries of arts and sciences published in this country between 1751 and 1800 claim to have made use of (and, of course, to have improved upon) the material contained in the

[42] Cf. Scholes, op. cit., Vol. II, pp. 188-9.
[43] The English (and German) sources of the *Encyclopédie* are dealt with at some length by R. Loyalty Cru in *Diderot as a Disciple of English Thought*, New York, 1913.

Complete Dictionary of Arts and Sciences, published in three folio volumes between 1764 and 1766 by three principal editors, Temple Henry Croker, Thomas Williams and Samuel Clarke. In the *Advertisement* the editors solemnly assure the reader that 'Everything valuable in Mr. Chamber's Cyclopaedia, and the other Works of that Kind, particularly the Encyclopédie published at Paris, shall be contained in this Dictionary, augmented with the Discoveries and Improvements made since these works were completed'. This claim aroused the sarcasm of the author of a long article in the *Monthly Review,* who asked how all this mass of material was to be crammed into 'three small volumes in folio'.[47]

The same writer goes further in his criticisms of the work. What he has to say about the plates of the *Encyclopédie*—it is most unfavourable—has a certain interest:

> The authors of the Encyclopaedia have given elegant cuts of every common utensil, according to the pompous manner of French writers. It should appear as if that grand work was cautiously prepared against some expected general desolation, which like another deluge is to destroy all traces of every mechanical art; when the Encyclopaedia, happily preserved, will teach a new race of men to restore them.

Ignoring all the highly valuable illustrations of complex industrial processes which the work contains, he continues:

> They give not only common tools, as files, hammers, and shears, but a perspective view of tradesmen's shops, where perhaps you see the maker trying a pair of shoes on the feet of the wearer, or a boy turning a wheel for grinding razors; all which may do very well to amuse children.[48]

Given his poor opinion of the plates of the *Encyclopédie,* it is not surprising that the reviewer should be highly critical of the fact that some of them[49] had been copied in the English work—'with what propriety, we leave our readers to determine', he adds. He

[47] Vol. XL, p. 3.   [48] P. 5.
[49] Four volumes of the plates of the *Encyclopédie* were published between 1762 and 1765.

is able to make great play with one of these borrowings, since the printer had reversed the plate, with rather unfortunate consequences:

> In plate 55 we are amused with a group of scholars in a drawing school or academy; and though the editors say in their prefatory advertisement that 'the bare view of an object often conveys more information than whole pages of words', this plate contains no information excepting that it is better to draw with the left hand than with the right; all the scholars having their pencils in their left hands.[50]

Curiously enough, although the reviewer[51] devotes nearly twenty pages to a merciless criticism of the mistakes and other short-comings of the dictionary, he could have made much more of the editors' borrowings from the *Encyclopédie*, since these are by no means limited to a certain number of such of its plates as had appeared in the middle of the 1760s. Thus the paragraph in the *Advertisement* which deals with the difficulties which the treatment of mechanical arts presents for the editors of an encyclopaedia, is merely a summary of the passage on this subject in the Prospectus and *Discours Préliminaire* of the *Encyclopédie*.[52]

If one turns next to the preface of this dictionary, which is followed by a table entitled *A Systematical View of Human Knowledge*, one makes some curious discoveries. A rapid glance at the table shows that, except for its title and a few insignificant changes, it is virtually identical with the table attached to the 1752 translation of the *Discours Préliminaire*. It is therefore less surprising to discover that the editors had taken the liberty of copying the whole of their preface straight from the English translation of the *Discours Préliminaire*.[53] It is true that they omitted a number of short passages, and also took the precaution

---

[50] p. 6.
[51] The Bodleian set of the *Monthly Review* gives 'N' as the author of this article. This might possibly stand for Nugent, but Nangle (op. cit., p. 30) refuses to commit himself on this point.
[52] Cf. pp. 130-1 of the 1752 translation.
[53] pp. 3-57.

of changing the word-order in the first sentence of a number of paragraphs; but otherwise their preface simply reproduces all that part of the *Discours Préliminaire* which D'Alembert devoted to the history of the origin of our ideas, leading to the formation of a general system of all the sciences and arts. No doubt a detailed study of the articles of this dictionary would lead to some equally interesting discoveries.

None of the dictionaries of arts and sciences published later in the century offers quite such blatant examples of plagiarism. It is true that the preface to *A New Royal and Universal Dictionary of the Arts and Sciences*, edited by M. Hinde, W. Squire, J. Marshall and the Rev. Thomas Cooke, which appeared in two folio volumes in 1771-72, does little more than summarize fairly briefly and freely D'Alembert's account of the development of thought since the Renaissance and his classification of the arts and sciences, based on memory, reason and imagination, while, in addition, one or two of the plates seem strangely familiar. On the other hand, the *Modern Dictionary of Arts and Sciences; or Complete System of Literature*, edited by the Rev. Percival Proctor, William Casteliau and others, which appeared in London in 1774 in four octavo volumes, has no preface, and such plates as it contains, do not appear to have a French source. The title-page of *A New Complete Dictionary of Arts and Sciences; or, An Universal System of Useful Knowledge*, edited by the Rev. Erasmus Middleton and others, and published in London in 1778 in one folio volume, claims to have preserved in that somewhat limited compass 'the Marrow and Quintessence of every other Dictionary and Work of the Kind', including '*The Encyclopédie*, printed at Paris'. Once again, one or two of 'the masterly and superb Set of Copper-plates' offered in this volume, strike one as being familiar. The greatly enlarged edition of Chambers' *Cyclopaedia*, published in five volumes between 1778 and 1786 under the editorship of Abraham Rees, contains no reference to the *Encyclopédie* and at least no obvious borrowings.

What of the relationship between the *Encyclopédie* and the first work of the kind, apparently, to be called an 'encyclopaedia' in this country, the *Encyclopaedia Britannica*? Although this was ultimately to become the largest work of this type published in English, it must be remembered that, to begin with, it was a very modest affair. The first edition, published in parts between 1768 and 1771, formed only three quarto volumes and is today extremely rare.[54] Moreover, the distribution of the articles over these three volumes seems to show that it was originally planned on a much more lavish scale than it was later found possible to carry out, since the letters A and B, which have the whole of the first volume to themselves, occupy 697 pages, while the whole of the rest of the alphabet is crammed into just under 2,000 pages in the remaining two volumes. As it appeared just after the whole of the text of the French work had at last come on the market, its editors were able to make use of what is described in the list of books consulted as 'Le Grand Encyclopédie'. The preface claims, however, that this new enterprise has an advantage over all previous works of the kind, including 'even the voluminous French Encyclopédie', in that it devotes long articles to the different sciences, instead of scattering the information about each branch of knowledge in short articles arranged in alphabetical order. Like the *New and Complete Dictionary of Arts and Sciences*, published by Owen in 1754, the *Encyclopaedia Britannica* quotes the *Encyclopédie*'s definition of 'cyclopaedia'. It is also noticeable that its articles on *Fortification* and *Foundry* are surprisingly similar to those given by Temple Croker, which no doubt indicates a common source.

The second edition of the *Encyclopedia Britannica* appeared in parts between 1777 and 1784, but by this time the work had swollen from three to ten quarto volumes. The preface claims that this edition contains a new feature in its biographical articles—'a department which is not to be found in any other collection of the same kind, except in the French Encyclopédia'. This last assertion is somewhat strange, although it is true that in the *Encyclopédie* biographical data are hidden away in such places as geographical articles. Perhaps because both were still alive

[54] Whereas copies of the *Encyclopédie* are quite common in Cambridge, I have been unable to find one of the first edition of the *Encyclopaedia Britannica*.

when the earlier volumes of this edition were prepared, neither Diderot nor D'Alembert is honoured with an article, though Voltaire, Montesquieu and Jean-Baptiste Rousseau (but not Jean-Jacques!) are. Finally between 1788 and 1797 there appeared in Edinburgh the eighteen quarto volumes of the third edition of the *Encyclopaedia Britannica,* followed four years later by the two volumes of the supplement with their violent diatribes against Diderot and the *Encyclopédie.*

The conclusions to be drawn from this account of the main facts concerning the diffusion of the *Encyclopédie* in this country in the eighteenth century must be, as was indicated at the outset, extremely cautious. In both England and Scotland the work appears to have had quite a wide circulation considering its size and cost, which is not surprising when we bear in mind that a knowledge of French was widespread among the cultured classes and especially that it was not until half a century had passed that any similar work of comparable bulk appeared on this side of the Channel. If attempts to reprint the French text or to translate it broke down at an early stage, the appearance of the *Encyclopédie* no doubt helped to stimulate the publication of other works to replace the earlier attempt at an encyclopaedia made by Ephraim Chambers; and there can be no question that these later works owed some of their material to Diderot and D'Alembert. As we have seen, some prominent writers of the period consulted the *Encyclopédie* with profit, and in addition to praising the work in public, derived from it either information or the stimulus to new ideas.

One may therefore conclude that from the purely technical point of view the influence of the *Encyclopédie* in eighteenth-century England was considerable. On the other hand, the ideas which its editors and their principal collaborators attempted, not without caution, to disseminate among the general public—their rationalist, secular outlook and their demand for religious, civil and perhaps even political liberty—would seem to have had scant effect on this side of the Channel. Given the very different social, political and religious atmosphere in England and France in the eighteenth century, this is scarcely surprising. It is significant that in 1769 a writer in the *Monthly Review*[55] expressed the opinion that 'the plan on which the French Encyclopaedia was undertaken, promised fair for satisfying public opinion, *had it been executed under a more liberal form of government*'. To an Englishman such an enterprise, carried out under an absolute monarchy which denied to its editors and their collaborators freedom to discuss political, philosophical and religious questions, must have seemed to have its wings clipped from the very start. And if many of the ideas which the *Encyclopédistes* were attempting to disseminate in France, seemed timid, others, particularly their views on religion, appeared too radical, even before the Revolution and the Jacobin scare, for at least the majority of their contemporaries in England.

[55] Vol. XL, p. 2.

II Louis, Chevalier de Jaucourt (1704-1780.) A Biographical Sketch[1]

In April 1766, when the last ten volumes of the text of the *Encyclopédie* had made their way into the world, Voltaire wrote from Ferney to Damilaville: 'En lisant le Dictionnaire, je m'aperçois que le chevalier de Jaucourt en a fait les trois quarts. Votre ami [Diderot] était donc occupé ailleurs?'[2] Other contemporaries were similarly impressed by the magnitude of the contribution which the Chevalier made to the *Encyclopédie*. Three years later *La France Littéraire*[3] made much the same comment: 'Il a fait près de deux tiers du grand dictionnaire de l'Encyclopédie.' The researches recently carried out by Professor R. N. Schwab[4] show that, although greatly exaggerated, such contemporary statements were not altogether false. Although Jaucourt wrote nothing for the first volume and only seven articles for the second, so great was his contribution to the remaining volumes—especially the ten which appeared together in 1765—that he composed twenty-eight per cent of the total number of articles contained in the seventeen volumes and twenty-four per cent of the text. Without help on such a massive scale, it is unlikely that Diderot could ever have succeeded in bringing the whole undertaking to a triumphant conclusion.

[1] First published in *Essays presented to C. M. Girdlestone*, Newcastle upon Tyne, 1960, pp. 195-217. Pp. 60-68 first appeared in *French Studies*, 1961, pp. 350-357.
[2] Best. 12361.
[3] By J. Hébraïl and J, de La Porte, Paris, 1769, 2 vols, Vol. 1, p. 298.
[4] 'The Extent of the Chevalier de Jaucourt's Contribution to Diderot's *Encyclopédie*', *MLN*, 1957, pp. 507-8.

Yet, except for a brief article by Professor Schwab,[5] the student of the *Encyclopédie* can find nothing more recent on the life and career of Jaucourt than what is offered by such works of reference as the *Biographie universelle* of Michaud and the *Nouvelle Biographie générale* of Hoefer, by an article of Christian Bartholmess in the *Encyclopédie des Gens du Monde* and by Haag's *La France Protestante*. All these sources are at least a hundred years old, and while they occasionally offer valuable information, it seemed possible to supplement this by researches in the printed and manuscript material which has become available in the interval and, with the co-operation of librarians and archivists in London and Paris, Stockholm and Bordeaux, Geneva and Leyden, to piece together a somewhat fuller account of the life and career of the Chevalier.[6]

According to the *Biographie universelle* Louis de Jaucourt was born in Paris on 26 September 1704: it is unfortunately impossible to confirm this date from the *État civil reconstitué* of the Archives de la Seine. He was born into an old aristocratic family from Burgundy which had been converted to Protestantism in the sixteenth century. Indeed members of other branches of the family had been driven abroad by the persecution of the Huguenots which culminated in the Revocation of the Edict of Nantes.[7] One of the fourteen children of Pierre Antoine de Jaucourt, Marquis d'Espeuilles, and of his wife, Marie de Monginot, the Chevalier belonged technically to the class of *nouveaux convertis*. One of his sisters, Marie Josèphe, presumably spent most of her life abroad, as she married an officer of dragoons in

---

[5] 'The Chevalier de Jaucourt and Diderot's *Encyclopédie*', *Modern Language Forum*, 1957, pp. 44-51. Since the above lines were written in 1959, the same author has produced an important article entitled 'Un encyclopédiste huguenot: le Chevalier de Jaucourt', *BSHPF*, 1962, pp. 46-75, which has been taken into account in revising my original articles on Jaucourt.

[6] I am particularly indebted to the Marquis de Jaucourt for permission to consult the archives of his family which are deposited in the Archives Nationales (86 AP).

[7] Copies of letters written by exiled members of these other branches of the family are preserved in the library of the Société de l'Histoire du Protestantisme Français in Paris (MS. 790)

the British army, named John Carmichael.[8] However, the d'Espeuilles branch of the family did not emigrate *en bloc*. In order to pursue *the* aristocratic career as officers in the armed forces Louis's brothers, nephews and great-nephews (among the latter was one of the leading figures of French Protestantism after the Revolution, Arnail François, Marquis de Jaucourt) had no choice but to conform, at least outwardly.

Some light is cast on Louis's family and early upbringing by a passage in the memoirs of Dupont de Nemours, both of whose parents were Protestants. His mother, whose family claimed relationship with the Jaucourts and whose father lived in the Burgundy château of Brinon-les-Allemands as agent for the estates of the d'Espeuilles branch, was brought up by Louis's mother to whom Dupont de Nemours pays this tribute:

> Mme d'Espeuilles qui élevait ses enfants elle-même voulut bien aussi élever ma mère.
> Jamais on ne fut mieux élevé. De là sont sortis le marquis de Jaucourt, grand-père de ceux d'aujourd'hui, homme d'une bonté et d'une loyauté dont on révère encore le souvenir; le chevalier de Jaucourt, qui fut en Hollande étudier la médecine sous Boerhaave, préférant les sciences à la vanité, et qui depuis a tant travaillé à l'*Encyclopédie*; Mlle de Jaucourt, célèbre par le nerf et le sel de son esprit; et ma mère à laquelle je dois tout le peu que je vaux.[9]

Louis's Protestant sympathies can be deduced fairly clearly from his contributions to the *Encyclopédie*. Le Breton, the self-appointed censor of the last ten volumes, struck out the whole of the following article:

RELIGION PROTESTANTE, (*Théolog. chrétienne*). 'C'est cette religion raisonnable et sainte, qui loin d'abrutir l'homme, l'ennoblit et l'élève, qui ne favorisant ni l'impiété ni le fanatisme, permet d'être sage et de croire, d'être humain et pieux tout-à-la-fois.'

---

[8] 'Partage entre les Sieurs et Dam^{elles} de Jeaucourt, 26 May 1740' (Minutier Central, I. 399). I am indebted to Me Robert Morel d'Arleux for permission to consult this document.
[9] *L'Enfance et la jeunesse de Du Pont de Nemours racontées par lui-même*, ed. H. A. Du Pont de Nemours, Paris, 1906, p. 52.

Voilà la définition que M. J. J. Rousseau donne de cette religion dans ses ouvrages (D.J.).[10]

It was not only abroad, but at Geneva itself that the Chevalier received his early education. According to the *Biographie universelle* he was sent to school there from the age of eight. While it seems impossible to confirm this statement, there is perhaps some reminiscence of the playground in his reference, in a letter written in 1758 to the wealthy Genevan banker, Jean Louis Labat (1701-1775), to 'l'amitié que je vous ai vouée, depuis l'ancien tems où je vous regardois dans le lointain, pour le plus grand polisson de la République'.[11] There is, however, no doubt that on 15 May 1719, in his fifteenth year, he was admitted to the University of Geneva, for his name appears on that date as 'Louis de Neufville Parisiensis' in the *Livre du Recteur de l'Académie de Genève*.[12] Among students in the same year were several who were later to achieve fame, either in Geneva or further afield, for instance François Tronchin (1704-1798), who was to be a member of the *Petit Conseil* of Geneva from 1753 to 1768 and is chiefly remembered today for his relations with Voltaire and other *philosophes*.[13]

It was, however with François's cousin, Théodore, the famous doctor, that Jaucourt was to strike up an enduring friendship. It is not easy to say when this began; Théodore was five years younger than the Chevalier and did not enter the University of Geneva until 1723. According to the *Biographie universelle* Jaucourt, after leaving Geneva, studied for three years at Cambridge. This would seem to be confirmed by Théodore Tronchin's biographer,[14] who states that the latter came to England at some

[10] Gordon & Torrey, p. 78.

[11] For further details about all letters to and from Jaucourt quoted in this chapter see the appendix (pp. 68-70) which contains a list of such fragments of his correspondence as it has proved possible to track down.

[12] Information supplied by Professor Bernard Gagnebin when he was Conservateur des Manuscrits, Bibliothèque Publique et Universitaire, Geneva.

[13] See Henry Tronchin, *Le Conseiller François Tronchin et ses amis Voltaire, Diderot, Grimm*, etc. Paris, 1895, and especially Voltaire. *Lettres inédites aux Tronchin*, ed. B. Gagnebin, Geneva-Lille, 1950, 3 vols.

[14] Henry Tronchin, *Un Médecin du XVIIIe siècle, Théodore Tronchin*, Paris, 1906, p. 5.

date in the 1720s and proceeded to study at Cambridge:

> Tronchin eut le joie de retrouver sur les bancs de cette Université un compagnon d'enfance, le chevalier Louis de Jaucourt, élevé comme lui à Genève, et auquel il resta toujours uni par la plus solide affection. Les deux jeunes gens suivaient les leçons du célèbre critique et philosophe Bentley qui, touché du zèle et du progrès de ses disciples, les admit bientôt dans son intimité.

In the same work[15] there is an amusing account—derived from the *Éloge de M. Tronchin* delivered in 1782 at the Académie Royale de Chirurgie by the surgeon, Antoine Louis—of how Tronchin arrived in Leyden from Cambridge, armed with a letter of introduction from Bentley to Peter Burmann, the Professor of Greek, who was furious, on opening the letter, to discover that it contained nothing but insulting remarks.

It comes as a decided cold douche to discover that there is no trace of the names of either Jaucourt or Tronchin in Venn's *Alumni Cantabrigienses*. Is one then to strike out the Cambridge years from the Chevalier's career? When consulted on this point the late J. A. Venn wrote: 'As promised, when you were here recently, I have looked fully into the case of the Chevalier de Jaucourt. I can assure you that he was never admitted a member of any College, that he did not matriculate as a member of the University, and that, of course, he took no degree'. He went on, however, to point out that in this period quite a number of people resided in Cambridge and attended lectures without going through the formalities of matriculating or being admitted to a college. That the Chevalier did spend some time in Cambridge—though not three years—is proved by a letter recently brought to light by Professor Schwab.[16] As it throws considerable light both on Jaucourt's outlook at this stage in his career and on the state of the University at this period in its long history,

---

[15] pp. 9-10. This *éloge* is not reproduced in A. Louis, *Éloges lus dans les séances publiques de l'Académie royale de Chirurgie de 1750 à 1792*, ed. E. F. Dubois, Paris, 1859; but there is apparently a copy of it in the Archives Tronchin (BPUG).

[16] *BSHPF*, 1962, pp. 51-2. The MS. of the letter which is in the Archives Tronchin (Vol. 210, ff. 6-8), is in rather poor condition.

it deserves to be reproduced in full. The letter was addressed to Jean Tronchin (1662-1761), soon to be *procureur général* of the Republic of Geneva.

Monsieur
Ayant appris par ma Chere Soeur que vous eties à Paris, j'ai cru que ce seroit manquer à mon devoir que de ne pas profiter de l'occasion qui se [pre]sente pour avoir l'honneur de vous écrire, conservant pour vous toute [la c]onsideration possible et en particulier une tres sensible reconnoissance [pou]r toutes les bontes dont vous m'avez honoré dans mon sejour à Geneve, [d]ont mon depart plus que precipité m'a privé de l'honneur de vous dire adieu. [Ce n]'est pas que dans les deux jours que j'eûs pour faire mon bagage, je ne fus deux [fo]is chez vous pour avoir l'honneur de vous voir, mais j'eûs le malheur de ne vous pas trouver. J'arrivai à Paris fort heureusement où je n'ai pas resté une Semaine. Je partis de là avec mon Beau-frere[17] pour Londres où j'ai sejourné un mois à parcourir un peu les diverses Curiosités de cette grande ville. De là par avis de mes parens j'ai choisi l'Université de *Cambridge* pour apprendre l'anglois où je suis depuis 6 Semaines sans y avoir fait de fort grands progres. Cette langue est si abondante, la difficulté de la pronontiation si grande par raport à un françois qui n'y est pas des l'age de 10 ans au moins, que je deffie le plus habile de pouvoir jamais atraper le vrai ton. Pour ce qui est en particulier de l'Université de *Cambridge* que je ne connoissois auparavant que de reputation, en gros et méme d'une maniere à lui faire honneur, je ne saurois assez vous marquer à present que je l'examine, que je la vois de mes yeux en *detail*, combien de mepris j'en fais. Elle est composée de quinze où Seize grandes maisons qu'ils nomment *Colleges* dans chacun desquels il y a 200, 100 plus ou moins d'Ecoliers et 40 où 30 à proportion de Maitres qui sont *Associez* dans les colleges pour l'instruction de ces Jeunes Ecoliers, c'est a dire depuis l'age [de?] 17 ans car je n'en ai point vû de plus Jeunes. La Vie de ces maitres c'est de tirer le plus d'argent qu'ils peuve[nt] des Ecoliers et du reste s'en embarassent tres peu. Ils font leurs Parties où tout leur plaisir pendant des jours entiers c'est de boire et de fumer. Gens pour la pluspart ignorans du moins à proportion de l'habileté qu'ils devroi[ent] avoir, Contents de savoir leu[r]s *auteurs*, leur *Sophistiquerie*, et leur Breviai[re]. Des qu'ils sont une fois parvenus à etre associez du College, comme cela leur aporte une rente fixe, ils ne pensent plus à pousser leurs etudes,

[17] John Carmichael.

mais à s'atirer des Ecoliers pour amis, à dormir, à boire, à raisonner de politique, et à se partager en Whigs et en Torys dont nous avons ici (je parle des derniers) une bonne quantité. Apres qu'on a demeuré un certain tems dans l'Université, on donne des *degrez*, c'est a dire de certains avancemens. Ces degrez ne se donnent pas au merite, à l'habileté comme vous pourriez vous l'imaginer. C'est premierem[en]t au tems que l'on a demeuré dans l'Université, ensuite pour obtenir ces degrez, il faut une somme d'argent moyennant quoi quelque leger que soit vôtre savoir, vous etes assuré d'êre *Bachelier, maitre es arts Docteur*, en un mot tout. P[ou]r moi quand je reflechis sur tout cela, je ne saurois m'empecher de benir le Ciel, qui m'a fait etudier dans une ville où si je n'ai pas fait les progrcz que je devois, c'est à mes maladies et à ma negligence que j'en dois seuls atribuer la Cause, ville où le merite et l'habileté sont du moins estimez et honorez s'ils ne sont pas recompensez par les biens de la fortune. Ici c'est [tout?] autrement. C'est *l'argent, la Cabale* qui ont le dessus. Sur tout un françois qui ne sçait pas parler leur langue, qui n'entre pas avec fureur d[an]s le Whigisme et le Torisme, qui ignore l'art de Bien boire et de bien fumer est dans cette Université tres mal venu. Vous jugez bien M^r que moi qui suis imbu d'autres maximes, je ne recherche pas la Compagnie de Semblables gens. Mon occupation est de tacher d'aprendre la langue Angloise, et de lire des livres en cette langue. J'en trouve beauc[ou]p et d'admirablement beaux qui me font écouler mes heures avec plaisir. Apres quoi je penserai a prendre les ordres, abandonnant le reste aux bons Soins [de l]a providence. Je pense que vous en avez bien voulu raisonner avec Mon Pere et Ma Mere; etant de retour à Geneve je me persuade que vous aurez la bonté d'en parler à M^rD . . . et à Mr Caze et me faire part la dessus de Vos Conseils, d'une maniere libre et franche desquels j'aurai soin de [pro]fiter, considerant infiniment tout ce qui vient de votre part, et etant avec tout le respect, la reconnoissance et la consideration possible.

                Votre tres humble et tres obeissant Serviteur
De Cambrige (*sic*) ce 24 Avril   L. de Neufville
   1727 V.S.
The address runs: à Monsieur
                       Monsieur J. Tronchin Ancien
                       Procureur de la Republique de
                       Geneve.

Resisting the temptation to examine how far such a gloomy view of Cambridge in the 1720s was well founded, we can glean some information from this letter about this period of the Chevalier's career. It will be noted that it contains no mention of Théodore Tronchin and that it makes it clear both that Jaucourt did not arrive in Cambridge until early in March 1727 and that he had still been in Geneva down to the end of January of that year. Of his protracted studies in Geneva we learn disappointingly little, except that they had been held up to some extent by spells of ill health. An intriguing glimpse into the Protestant conscience of the Chevalier is provided by his intention, at this stage of his career, to go into the church. Such a step would inevitably have made considerable difficulties for him in France. Some echoes of his family's agitation at the news of his intentions can be found in a letter of his sister-in-law, the Marquise de Jaucourt, to his sister Isabelle, preserved today in the Archives Nationales among the family papers: [18]

Vous vous étes amusée à La moutarde ma chere enfant avec vôtre Anglois. Vous vous êtes contentée de lui tendre de petits gluaux, a present qu'il a Laile forte il vous échape. Il auroit été pourtant bien jolli dêtre Mad^e. Levechesse. Ce penchant que vous vous santez nouvellement pour la devotion, ne proviendroit-il point de votre vocation pour Lépiscopat. Vous vous en aviseriez un peu tard, examinez vous. On a souvent des penchans dont on ygnore La source. J'ai été dévote autre fois et je croyois L'être de bonne foi. Cependant on a voullu que ma devotion fut accidentelle. Je n'ai pas encore bien decidé Le cas avec moi même. Je ne scai si mr de N. est sa propre dupe sur ce fait la, ou s'il se sert du pretexte de La religion pour suivre son inclination. Je croi qu'il seroit a propos que vous Lui fissiez sentir qu'il s'expose a de grands inconvenians, et qu'un jour avenir on ne seroit peut etre pas maistre de lui conserver son bien, quelques bonnes intentions qu'on put avoir; le pauvre garçon auroit bien mauvaise opinion de ma pieté si vous lui raportiez mot a mot ce que je viens de vous dire. Il sécriroit de bon coeur. ô tems ô meurs, est il possible qu'on attribüe a des motifs de corruption ce que produit le Zele le

---

[18] 86 AP 6, 8 (part of the letter is quoted in *BSHPF*, 1962, p. 52). The letter begins with the words: 'A paris ce 30 7bre 1728', but it is addressed to the 'rüe tarane fauxbourg S^t. germain A paris' and appears to have been written from the provinces. The date cannot be right as by that time the Chevalier had gone to Leyden to study medicine.

plus pur. Je plains son sort de toutte mon ame, faittes lui je vous prie bien des amitiez de ma part.[19]

However, the Chevalier changed his plans. How long he remained in Cambridge after April 1727 and whether he was joined there by Théodore Tronchin we do not at present know. What is certain is that on 13 September 1728 both men were inscribed together on the matriculation register of the University of Leyden, 'la premiere de l'Europe' as Jaucourt was to declare in his article LEYDE in the *Encyclopédie*:

Neuvil de Jaucourt Gallus, 23. M.
Theodorus Tronchin Genevensis, 20. M.[20]

What drew them to the Faculty of Medicine was the reputation of the great Dutch physician, Hermann Boerhaave (1668-1738), the most famous clinical teacher of his age. In the *Encyclopédie* Jaucourt was to devote six columns to his former master in the article VOORHOUT, this little village being Boerhaave's birthplace. Although the article owes much to Fontenelle's *Éloge de Boerhaave*, it contains some personal touches which could only be supplied by one of Boerhaave's own students. One passage throws considerable light on Jaucourt's own career and on his outlook on the world:

Tous mes éloges n'ajouteront rien à sa gloire: mais je ne dois pas supprimer les obligations particulieres que je lui ai. Il m'a comblé de bontés pendant cinq ans, que j'ai eu l'honneur d'être son disciple. Il me sollicita long-tems avant que je quittasse l'académie de Leyde, d'y prendre le degré de docteur en Médecine, & je ne crus pas devoir me refuser à ses desirs, quoique résolu de ne tirer de cette démarche d'autre avantage que celui que l'homme recherche par humanité, j'entends de pouvoir secourir charitablement de pauvres malheureux. Cependant Boerhaave estimant trop une déférence, qui ne pouvait que m'être honorable, voulut la reconnoitre, en me faisant appeler par le stadhouder à des conditions les plus flatteuses comme gentilhomme & comme

---

[19] I am no longer convinced that the passage in a letter of the Marquise dated 22 September 1728 (86 AP 6, 26) refers to our Chevalier and accordingly have not reproduced it here.
[20] *Album Studiosorum Academiae Lugduno Batavae*, The Hague, 1875, col. 918.

médecin capable de veiller à la conservation de ses jours. Mais la passion de l'étude forme naturellement des ames indépendantes. Eh! que peuvent les promesses magnifiques des cours sur un homme né sans besoins, sans desirs, sans ambition, sans intrigue; assez courageux pour présenter ses respects aux grands, assez prudent pour ne les pas ennuyer, & qui s'est bien promis d'assûrer son repos par l'obscurité de sa vie studieuse? Après tout, les services éminens que M. Boerhaave vouloit me rendre étoient dignes de lui, & sont chers à ma mémoire. Aussi, par vénération & par reconnoissance, je jetterai toute ma vie des fleurs sur son tombeau.

Medical studies could be disposed of rapidly in those days; on 9 August 1730, less than two years after matriculating, 'Ludovicus a Neufville, Parisiensis' sustained his doctoral thesis, being admitted to the degree twelve days later, Tronchin's progress was equally speedy: he sustained his thesis two days after Jaucourt and was admitted to his degree on the day after him.[21] The Chevalier's doctoral dissertation, *De Allantoide humana*, was published at Leyden in the same year and was reprinted, together with Tronchin's thesis, in 1736.

At this point the two men appear to have gone their separate ways, for while Tronchin began to practise in Amsterdam in 1730, when he was just twenty-one, Jaucourt is known to have remained in Leyden until at least February 1733.[22] This fits in with his statement that he studied under Boerhaave for five years. However, Tronchin and he were certainly together in Amsterdam on various occasions. At the beginning of 1732 he wrote to Jean Tronchin at Geneva:

Je suis, Monsieur, trop sensible à l'honneur de vôtre Souvenir pour ne pas saisir l'occasion de vous en marquer ma reconnoissance, et vous remercier en même tems du profond de mon coeur de vôtre obligeante lettre. Je puis vous assurer que je conserverai toujours precieusement la memoire de toutes les bontés et politesses dont vous m'avez honoré pendant mon sejour dans vôtre ville, et je desire avec la plus forte ardeur de trouver les occasions de vous en marquer mon ressentiment. Ma situation ne

[21] Information supplied by Miss Hulshoff Pol of the Department of Manuscripts, the University Library, Leyden.
[22] Information supplied by Miss Hulshoff Pol.

se trouve pas encore assurée. mes Parens se trouvent actuellement accables d'un Procez qui leur coute beaucoup de depense et de soucis.[23] ils m'assurent chaque jour de leur attention à mes interests, et de leur dessein de regler leurs affaires avant leur mort, d'une maniere dont j'aurai lieu d'être content. En attendant je vis dans ce pays depuis pres de quatre ans, continuellement attaché à diverses Etudes, mais en particulier à celle de la Medecine qui occupe une assez grande partie de mon tems : Je passe le reste à l'amusement de lectures diversifiees en tout genre. je coule ainsi mes jours, je ruine ma santé dont je fais peu de cas, et apres bien du travail je me trouve toujours dans le même cercle d'ignorance. Je ne dois pas oublier de mettre au rang de mes plaisirs celui que je goute dans la compagnie de M^r vôtre Neveu, qui (mis a part toute mon amitié,) est un garçon d'un génie des plus elevés, d'un grand merite, et doué de ces talens necessaires pour former ces hommes dont nous admirons le gout et la profonde erudition, d'ailleurs fort estimé, et chargé d'une profession où il reünit l'honnete homme, et l'homme entendu dans son metier, qualités assez rares, et qui ne se rencontrent gueres dans ces sortes detats où l'on cherche à vivre d'industrie : Vous savez que dans les grandes villes et en particulier dans celle ci des gens de ce calibre sont peu communs, et si jamais il y eût du merite à n'être pas singe, c'est assurement dans ce cas : je suis ravi de la continuation de la santé de Mr Caze, il me fait l'honneur de m'ecrire de tems en tems, et j'ai grand soin d'entretenir un commerce qui m'est si precieux. Je forme souvent le desir d'y substituer des entretiens de bouche, je voudrois bien que ma fortune me permit d'executer ce dessein, et d'avoir l'occasion de vous prouver la consideration et l'attachement avec lequel je suis
                   Monsieur

Vous voulez bien me permettre
de presenter mes tres humbles
respects à Madame votre Epouse
Amsterd. le 3 Janvier 1732
              Votre tres humble et tres
                Obeissant Serviteur
                   Neuville
    A Monsieur
    Monsieur Tronchin Conseiller
    d'Etat
      à Geneve.[24]

---

[23] For details about this lawsuit see *BSHPF*, 1962, pp. 68-9.
[24] BPUG, Archives Tronchin, Vol. 211, 65.

Later that same year, on 20 November they addressed a joint letter, written in Latin in the Chevalier's hand, to Sir Hans Sloane, President of the Royal Society, thanking him for a copy of his *Voyage to the Islands of Madera*.

While in Leyden, the Chevalier devoted himself to various literary pursuits. According to *La France littéraire*[25] 'il a travaillé à la Bibliothèque raisonnée, depuis le commencement de ce Journal, jusques en 1740'. The *Bibliothèque raisonnée des Ouvrages des Savans de l'Europe* began publication at Amsterdam in 1728, the year of his matriculation at Leyden. According to Barbier Jaucourt, along with S'Gravesande, Barbeyrac and Desmaiszeaux, was among the nine people who contributed to this periodical. What form his collaboration took it is not possible to say, as the reviews as well as the *Nouvelles littéraires* are unsigned.

It was in 1734 that the Amsterdam publisher, François Changuion, brought out Jaucourt's edition of Leibniz's *Théodicée*, prefaced by a life of the author and a chronological catalogue of his works. On the title page the editor bears the name of 'L. de Neufville'. When the same publisher produced a new edition in 1747, the preface states:

La *Vie de Leibnitz*, qui précède ici la Théodicée, est un morceau connu depuis longtems par le débit qu'il a eu, & par la Traduction Latine qu'on en a faite en Allemagne. Nous avons mis à cette Edition le vrai nom de l'Auteur de cette Vie qu'il seroit inutile de cacher aujourd'hui. Il l'a composée en 1734, pendant le séjour qu'il a fait dans les Provinces-Unies, séjour où les Arts et les Sciences, la Physique, l'Histoire-Naturelle, la Médecine, la Politique, l'étude des Langues, remplissoient tous ses momens. Il a préféré dès sa jeunesse la culture des Lettres au tumulte des Armes, qui semblent être la seule Profession de la Noblesse de France. S'il n'est pas nécessaire que tous les Savans soient nobles, il seroit du mons à desirer que tous les Nobles fussent savans.[26]

It is not clear why Jaucourt should have used the name Louis de Neufville in the first half of his life; perhaps the spectacle of the scion of an old aristocratic family disporting himself in such

[25] Vol. I, p. 298.
[26] A third edition appeared at Lausanne in 1760.

Protestant territories as Geneva and Holland was one to be hidden from the French authorities.

According to the *Biographie universelle* it was in 1736 that the Chevalier finally returned to France. His mother died in November 1732 and his father in October 1736. When their estate was divided up in 1740, it was stated that this had not been done earlier 'attendu l'absence dudit Sieur Louis de Jaucourt dans les pays étrangers'.[27] Three letters of Voltaire[28]—recently identified by M. J. D. Candaux as being addressed to the Chevalier,[29] one of them to 'Monsieur de Neufville à Amsterdam' —show that Jaucourt was still in Holland in February and March 1737. However, two of his letters to Tronchin which have come down to us from the year 1738, show that he returned to France before July of that year.[30] Down to 1756 he seems to have lived in Paris in his brother's house in the Rue de Grenelle, and before and after that date he spent part of the year on the family estates, either at Brinon-les-Allemands in Burgundy or more frequently at Chantôme, near Beaugency in the Loire valley.

Glimpses of his life and interests at this period can be obtained from four of his letters to Tronchin which have survived.[31] In the first of these (July 1738) the future author of a fiery denunciation of negro slavery in the article TRAITE DES NEGRES

---

[27] Minutier Central, I. 399 (28 May 1740).
[28] *Studies*, Vol. IV, pp. 191-2 and Vol. X, pp. 445-8.
[29] *BSHPF*, 1962, pp. 254-5.
[30] Professor Schwab (*BSHPF*, 1962, p. 72, n. 51) quotes an interesting extract from a letter of Rémond de Montmort to President Bouhier, written on 28 December 1738: 'Mr le m. de Jaucourt m'emmena hier un frère nouvellement reconnu par sa famille et rendu à sa patrie. Il s'est toujours appelé en Hollande Neuville et j'ai veu de lui la vie de Mr. de Leibniz. C'est un garçon aussi aimable par son caractère et par son esprit que laid de figure. Ses connoissances sont justes et étendues.' (BN, MS. fr. 24416, f. 344). The extract comes from G. E. Guhrauer, *Gottfried Wilhelm Freiherr von Leibnitz*, Breslau, 1842, 2 vols., Vol. I, p.x. I do not see, however, that this passage gives the impression that the Chevalier had been 'temporairement déshérité par sa famille'.
[31] Though the whereabouts of not a single letter of Tronchin to Jaucourt appears to be known, twenty-one letters from Tronchin to the Marquise de Jaucourt, his nephew's wife, are preserved in the Jaucourt family papers (86 AP 6, 374-377, 381, 385).

in the *Encyclopédie*, already shows interest in the question when he describes a lawsuit which was pending:

On va plaider à l'Amirauté une cause Nouvelle, où le Droit Naturel, le genie et l'Eloquence auront une ample matiere à discussion. C'est la cause d'un Negre qu'un habitant des Iles Françoises a amené à Paris, et sur lequel il pretend pouvoir exercer le même droit de Severité que dans son habitation. Le Negre a bientot trouvé un illustre Avocat pour sa defence qui a entrepris la cause de la franchise du Negre, contre un autre Avocat qui defendra celle du Maitre. Voila un morceau d'addition pour un nouveau volume des Causes Celebres.[32]

Another letter to Tronchin (September 1738) refers to the last illness of Boerhaave who died later that month. 'Je plains', exclaims the Chevalier, 'les soufrances d'une longue maladie que la mort termine lentement.'[33] He also makes several references to Voltaire and Mme du Châtelet which show considerable intimacy with the Cirey *ménage*.

The three letters mentioned above as being addressed to Jaucourt by Voltaire in February and March 1737 throw fresh light on the relations between the two men. The first, written from Amsterdam to ask Jaucourt for a reference needed for the *Éléments de la Philosophie de Newton*, was composed while the author was in Holland seeing to the publication of this work. The other two letters, written from Cirey at the beginning and end of March, reveal that Jaucourt was acting as an intermediary between Voltaire and Ledet, the printer of his *Éléments*; and the third contains a pressing invitation from both Voltaire and Mme du Châtelet to pay them a visit at Cirey.

The letter from Jaucourt to Tronchin of September 1738 shows that he had received from the author a copy of the *Éléments de la Philosophie de Newton*; he also expresses regret that he has been unable to visit Cirey during the summer. We catch another glimpse of relations between Jaucourt and Voltaire in a letter of

---

[32] *Causes célèbres et intéressantes* by Gayot de Pitaval (Paris, 1734).
[33] H. Tronchin (*Un Médecin du XVIIIe siècle*, pp. 16-17) quotes from an 1851 sale catalogue a letter written by Tronchin to Jaucourt in February 1739 in which he describes his last interview with Boerhaave.

his sister Isabelle of 9 June 1747: 'Le ch^{er}. soupa jeudy chez Melle de Th—(?) avec M^e du ch. et V. Je n'ai pas nuir (*sic*) a cet exces de gloire, mais helas V. fut froid et le ch^{er}. ne le preconisoit pas le lendemain.'[34] A note from Voltaire in 1749 thanking him for his letter of condolence on the death of Mme du Châtelet is the only other evidence of relations between the two men in this period of Jaucourt's life. This same letter to Tronchin, written from Brinon-les-Allemands, contains some more personal touches; he asks, for instance, to be remembered to some friends and adds: 'Je bois leurs santés in *Petto* avec de l'excellent Vin de Bourgogne tous les jours, et à tous mes repas, dans un lieu charmant que la Nature a pris plaisir d'embellir et d'egayer'.

The next letter to Tronchin (November 1743) was written in the midst of a European war. 'Vous' has now given place to the more intimate 'tu', and the Chevalier's reproaches about Tronchin's failure to answer letters show how well he was acquainted with his correspondent's family:

Tu me laisses dans l'ignorance de tant d'evenemens domestiques, particuliers, auxquels je prends un si vif interêt, ta vie, ta Santé, tes projets, tes occupations, l'Etat de mon Amie,[35] de tes deux garçons, les nouvelles de ton Pere, Mere, Soeurs, en un mot que de détails à me mander qui se renouvellent chaque jour?

The last of these letters to Tronchin (1 January 1747) is mostly given up to news of the war; it also contains some interesting remarks on the frivolity of the French and concludes:

Je t'envoye pour echantillon une de nos chansons pour le 1er jour de l'an. Nous sommes des Maitres pour attraper en ce genre des Portraits dans la perfection. L'air même et la Musique quadre toujours aux paroles et aux choses. Tu en jugeras en faisant déchiffrer l'air de celle-ci que ma belle-soeur a noté en ta faveur.

The Chevalier's interest in society verse, shown elsewhere in these letters to Tronchin by the trouble which he took to copy

---

[34] I owe the reference (86 AP 6, 334) to Professor Schwab (*BSHPF*, 1962, p. 72, n. 55).
[35] Tronchin had married in 1740.

out various poems of Voltaire, is also reflected in the family papers; they contain two pages in his own hand with thirty-six alexandrines headed 'Logogriphe. *Patrouille.* 1742 à Chantome par Louis de Jaucourt, qui le fit sous le nom du Baron de Bezenval'.[36] Not all the references in the inventory of these papers to the Chevalier Louis de Jaucourt are of interest to his biographer. If a *Réponse au nouveau mémoire de Mr. de Buffon*[37] is accurately described as being 'entièrement écrite de la main du chevalier de Jaucourt', it turns out to be merely an attack on Buffon by a fellow member of the Académie des Sciences which the Chevalier took the trouble to copy out. Again, a series of essays on such varied topics as punctuation, education, free will, sensibility, the origins of society, the abuses of pleasure and the origin of the universe (these are contained in a folder on which is written in a modern hand 'Études diverses—papiers du Chevalier de Jaucourt, encyclopédiste'[38]) are not in his very characteristic hand nor is there any reason to think that they were composed by him.

However, a number of letters to and from the Chevalier are preserved in this collection and supplement the fragments of his correspondence to be found in the Bibliothèque Victor Cousin at the Sorbonne. Among the latter collection is one from his cousin, Caze, at Geneva (October 1747) which offers some interesting gossip about the impending appearance of the *Esprit des Lois*:

On imprime aussi actuellement icy un autre livre d'un tout autre genre sous le titre *Esprit des Loix &* que l'on attribue a un de vos plus beaux esprits, quand il paroitra il sera aisé de connoitre s'il vient effectivement de lui.

Jaucourt certainly knew Montesquieu. In the latter's correspondence there is a short note, dated 1753, addressed to him which

[36] 86 AP 7(1), 47ter.
[37] 86 AP 7(1), 47.
[38] 86 AP 7(1), 47 bis.

mentions his sister, Isabelle,[39] as does a letter of Montesquieu to the Chevalier de Vivens.[40] What is more, Jaucourt is mentioned by Mme d'Aiguillon as being amongst those present during Montesquieu's last illness.[41]

Among the letters preserved are two from Gilly, at one time director of the Compagnie des Indes, whose daughter married the Chevalier's nephew, Louis Pierre, Marquis de Jaucourt. Among the family letters is one dated 1752, in which this nephew thanks Louis for the interest which he had shown in his recent marriage. It concludes: 'Madame de Jaucourt vous donne une jolie main à baiser et vous fait mille complimens. Je crois qu'il ne tiendra qu'a vous d'etre son medecin de Confiance'.[42] It is a disappointment to find that this collection includes only one letter to the Chevalier from his unmarried sister, Isabelle, and not a single letter from the Chevalier to her. Louis endorsed her letter, which is dated 1743:[43] 'Lettre de ma Soeur à garder. Elle voudroit se dispenser de contribuer à l'entretien de Mr Pr. notre Oncle. Repondu le 11 et démontré que son idée ne pouvoit avoir lieu. Cy joint est copie à garder de ma Reponse' (unfortunately his reply has been lost). Again if thirty-one of Isabelle's letters to her sister-in-law, the Marquise de Jaucourt, have been preserved,[44] they offer us no information about Louis; nor—except for the passages quoted earlier[45]—do the sixty-two letters which she received from the Marquise.[46]

Fortunately we do catch an occasional glimpse of Jaucourt in the letters which the Marquise wrote to his nephew, Louis Pierre, an officer in the French army. In 1743 she wrote to her son, then a young *cornette* with the French armies in Germany:

Si tu allois au cartier general il te faudroit rendre une visite a Mr. de Silhoüette qui demeure chez Mr. le m$^{al.}$ de Noailles, tu lui dirois que tu est le neveu de Mr. le Ch$^{er.}$ de Jaucourt avec qui

---

[39] *Oeuvres complètes*, ed. A. Masson, Paris, 1950-55, 3 vols., Vol. III, p. 1458.
[40] Vol. III, p. 1290.
[41] Vol. III, p. 1550.
[42] 86 AP 7(1), 26.
[43] 86 AP 6, 333.
[44] 86 AP 6, 334-364.
[45] See above, pp. 32-33.
[46] 86 AP 6, 8-69.

il est en relation et a qui il a eu la bonté d'envoyer le detail de la Journée du 27 juin.[47] Mr. de Silhoüette possede la confiance de Mr. le M^al. et il a deja rendu de bons offices a quelques personnes que ton oncle lui a recommendée. C'est a sa protection que le frere de Mr. le Gai doit l'emploi qu'il a obtenu dans une Comp^ie. franche, et il pouroit te presenter a Mr. le M^al.[48]

It is interesting to see that the Chevalier was on such terms with the future *Contrôleur général*, who was already well known in the world of letters.

We obtain a closer view of Louis from a letter written in 1747 by the Marquise to her son, now *enseigne de gendarmerie*, in an effort to cheer him up:

Pour calmer les furieux (je te le repette) je ne connois que l'occupation. Je te citerai un trait de son utilité; ton Oncle aprit par les dernieres lettres que nous reçumes, que le feu du Ciel avoit consumé en entier une grange qui lui appartenoit avec toute la recolte qu'on venoit d'y renfermer. La perte est considerable pour son peu de fortune, il en fut frappé, mais depuis ce tems la, il a repris un Ouvrage sur la medecine qu'il a entrepris depuis qu'il est ici, et il paroit avoir oublié le tonnerre et la grange. Je ne te propose pas de faire des livres, je me contenterois que tu voulû en lire.[49]

What the book in question was is not clear. The great calamity of an apparently uneventful life was the Chevalier's loss of the manuscript of a vast medical dictionary when it was on the way to the printer's. The most precise account of this misfortune is to be found in *La France littéraire*: 'Tous les manuscrits de son *Lexicon Medicum Universale*, prêts à être imprimés en six vol. *in fol.* à Amsterdam, sont péris dans un naufrage sur les côtes de la Nort-Hollande.'[50] The exact date of this calamity is unknown,[51]

[47] The Battle of Dettingen.
[48] 86 AP 6, 104.
[49] 86 AP 6, 177.
[50] Vol. I, pp. 298-9.
[51] Professor Schwab (*BSHPF*, 1962, pp. 72-3) has drawn attention to a reference to Jaucourt's presence in Amsterdam in 1750. See *Lettres sur l'Angleterre, la Hollande et l'Italie* in *Recueil des Œuvres de Madame du Boccage*, Lyons, 1770, 3 vols., Vol. III, p. 96 (30 June 1750): '. . . J'ai eu le

but it must have occurred some time before the appearance of the second volume of the *Encyclopédie* in January 1752, for in the *avertissement* the editors speak of Jaucourt's articles as 'les débris précieux d'un Ouvrage immense, qui a péri dans un naufrage, & dont il n'a pas voulu que les restes fussent inutiles à sa patrie'.

It was not through his own independent writings that the name of the Chevalier was destined to reach posterity, but through his part in the production of the *Encyclopédie*. He did not join the team of contributors until after the publication of the first volume in June 1751. Three months later Diderot wrote to thank him for his offer of collaboration, declaring 'Je n'ignore pas ce que notre dictionnaire y gagnera'. The preface to the second volume introduces the new contributor thus:

M. le Chevalier de Jaucourt, que la douceur de son commerce & la variété de ses connoissances ont rendu cher à tous les gens de Lettres, & qui s'applique avec un succès distingué à la Physique & à l'Histoire Naturelle, nous a communiqué des articles nombreux, étendus, & faits avec tout le soin possible. On en trouvera plusieurs dans ce volume, & nous avons eu soin de les désigner par le nom de leur Auteur.

The pleasure which these words gave to the Chevalier is shown by a passage in a letter written by the Marquise de Jaucourt to her son in December 1752: 'La tante et l'encyclopediste sont dans leur trou où ils passent les journées entieres. L'approbation des Srs. Diderot et d'Alembert a fait un signalé plaisir'.[52] Presumably similar gratification was felt by the Chevalier when in the following year he read in the *avertissement* to the third volume of the *Encyclopédie* the following lines:

La Medecine . . ., la Physique générale, & presque toutes les
bonheur de rencontrer trois hommes de mérite en divers genres: MM. de
S. Sauveur, Consul de notre Nation, Tronchin, fameux Médecin, & le chevalier de Jaucour, aussi connu par son savoir que par sa naissance. Il voyage
sans faste, & n'en est que plus respecté. Ces sages daignerent sacrifier un de
leurs moments à nous montrer le cabinet de M. Brankam . . . : les manufactures de soieries, la belle maison de campagne de M. Pinto . . . , &
l'hôtel de ville . . .'
[52] 86 AP 6, 152.

parties de la Littérature, doivent dans ce volume un très-grand nombre de morceaux à M. de Jaucourt. Ils seront un témoignage de l'étendue & de la variété de ses connoissances; & nous croyons pouvoir en présager le succès par celui des excellents articles qu'il avoit déjà insérés dans le second volume. M. de Jaucourt s'est livré à ce travail pénible avec un amour du bien public, qui ne peut trouver sa récompense que dans lui-même. Mais l'Encyclopédie lui appartient de trop près, pour ne pas du moins lui donner ici de foibles marques de sa reconnoissance. En célébrant les talens, elle ne doit pas laisser les vertus dans l'oubli.

The Chevalier's literary pursuits seems to have proved infectious in his family even though such occupations still appeared faintly disreputable to members of the aristocracy; in 1754 we find the Marquise mentioning to her son a work which she herself had written: 'Je suis sortie de la bonne compagnie de vos ancêtres, le ch^{er}. fait copier mon ouvrage pour l'impression, nous serons tous sous la presse, et j'en aurai l'honneur'.[53] There is a possible explanation of the mysterious 'ouvrage' in the *Avertissement* of Volume VI of the *Encyclopédie*,[54] which states that 'une Femme que nous n'avons pas l'honneur de connoître, nous a envoyé les articles FALBALA, FONTANGE, & autres'. With this we must combine the following letter, reproduced in the *Correspondance littéraire* of 15 April 1756[55] as being addressed to Diderot by an unknown woman. From the text of the letter she must be identified as the sister-in-law of that indefatigable contributor, the Chevalier de Jaucourt:

Vous serez surpris, Monsieur, qu'une femme qui n'a pas l'avantage de vous connoître, qui n'a aucune prétention à l'esprit, encore moins à la science, vous envoie un article pour votre *Encyclopédie*. Mais il ne faut que du bon esprit pour aimer cet ouvrage, et une femme, sans savoir lire, peut traiter mieux l'article *Fontange* que le plus habile médecin. Je sais combien celui qui s'en est chargé a de connoissances en tous genres; mais il n'a, je vous assure, jamais vu de *fontanges*, d'assez près pour les bien définir, et je ne crois pas qu'Aristote, Hippocrate ou Galien lui aient

---

[53] 86 AP 6, 177.
[54] P. vi.
[55] *Corr. litt.*, Vol. III, p. 203 (see Roth, Vol. I, pp. 207-208).

Encyclopédie. An early example of these attempts to exploit the interest aroused in this country by the publication of such an enormous work is provided by an advertisement which appeared in various London newspapers throughout the year 1752.[44] The publishers of *A New and Universal Dictionary of the Arts and Sciences*, published in parts to form altogether one folio volume, endeavoured to attract custom by appending the following note to each of their advertisements:

> N.B. A Translation of all the Discoveries and Improvements, contained in the *Encyclopédie*, now publishing at Paris, by M. Diderot, will be inserted in the New Dictionary of Arts and Sciences.

How they proposed to solve the age-old problem of putting a quart into a pint bottle, they did not, of course, inform the public.

Another dictionary of the same type—*A New and Complete Dictionary of Arts and Sciences*—appeared in 1754 in four octavo volumes.[45] In the introduction[46] the editors claim that their 'Table or Scheme of Knowledge' is constructed on a very different plan from that of Chambers, and 'even that of the great Bacon, with all the improvements of the ingenious authors of the French Encyclopaedia', which they reject as 'too complicated, inasmuch as it blends the consideration of the human soul with that of the objects of its knowledge'. In this dictionary there are other signs of familiarity with such volumes of the *Encyclopédie* as had appeared by 1754. Thus the brief article *Cyclopaedia or Encyclopaedia* contains the following *sentence*: 'A cyclopaedia, say the authors of the French Encyclopaedia, ought to explain, as much as possible, the order and connection of human knowledge.'

Such debts as this work may have contracted towards the *Encyclopédie* are certainly less obvious than those of *The*

---

[44] See the *General Evening Post* for 4 January, the *Daily Advertiser* for 18 January and the *London Gazette* for 7-11 January and later dates down to the end of the year. (British Museum, Burney Collection, Vol. 446b.)

[45] The title-page states that the dictionary was the work of 'a Society of Gentlemen'. The publisher was W. Owen. In 1763-64 appeared a second edition 'with many additions and other improvements'.

[46] pp. iv-v.

donné des lumières sur cet important sujet. Si ma *fontange* a le bonheur de vous plaire, je pourrai vous fournir des articles du même genre. Si vous la trouvez mal nouée, dénouez-la, et renouez-la. Si vous préférez celle du docteur, je croirai que l'on peut bien parler des choses que l'on n'entend pas; et je vous enverrai un article de médecine qui ne serait peut-être pas mauvais.

If a few fragments of the article submitted by this female contributor appeared in the unsigned FONTANGE in Volume VII of the *Encyclopédie*, it would seem that the Marquise's hand is also to be seen in the unsigned article FALBALA in the previous volume.

In another letter of the Marquise (December 1756) we sense again how odd it appeared to some of the Chevalier's contemporaries that this scion of an old family of the *noblesse d'épée* should be not only a scholar and a writer, but even a qualified doctor. We also learn that the Chevalier had recently left his brother's house in the Rue de Grenelle and had gone to live elsewhere in Paris:

Tu as fort bien repondu sur ce qui regarde ton Oncle, je suis la même routte, j'ai mandé à Mde de Broglie que le public n'avoit rien a dire de sa sortie d'avec nous, puisque nous ne nous en plaignions pas, et que nous n'en étions pas moins bons amis; qu'ayant passé sa jeunesse avec un homme qui s'etoit distingué par tout ou il avoit vecû, qui professoit une science a la qu'elle le Ch^{er} s'étoit adonné, il n'y avoit rien de fort étrange qu'il allat vivre avec lui, que de professer la medecine pouvoit être un ridicule, mais que ce n'etoit point un vice, &c.[56]

In 1761 the Chevalier was living in the Rue de Condé, but who the doctor was with whom he went to live is not clear. Although his old friend, Théodore Tronchin, visited Paris in 1756 in order to inoculate the children of the Duc d'Orléans against smallpox,[57] he left in June for Geneva and did not finally settle in Paris until ten years later. However, the two old friends were certainly in close contact during this period. Rousseau records in his *Confessions* that when Tronchin arrived in Paris in 1756, he

---

[56] 86 AP 6, 196.
[57] According to Collé, it was Jaucourt who had first suggested that Tronchin should be sent for from Geneva (see H. Tronchin, *Un Médecin du XVIIIe siècle*, p. 112).

came to visit him, accompanied by Jaucourt;[58] and according to a letter which Tronchin wrote to the Marquise de Jaucourt, his nephew's wife, it was the Chevalier who bullied him into publishing in the following year his treatise, *De Colica Pictonum*, a work which encountered a good deal of hostile criticism in medical circles.[59] It was later to be defended in the pages of the *Encyclopédie*: Jaucourt who had written for an earlier volume the article COLIQUE DE POITOU inserted a sixteen-lined article POITOU, COLIQUE DE, in which he came to his friend's defence.

There are further references to the *Encyclopédie* in the letters of the Marquise de Jaucourt to her son. On 30 October 1757— shortly before the publication of the seventh volume—she wrote: 'Nous n'avons pas l'encyclopédie, mais ton frere s'est fort rejoui du fragment de la preface que ta tante lui a envoyé, c'est un petit . . .'[60] fort drole'.[61] The meaning of this is far from clear. There are, however, two other letters which refer to the violent controversy which raged round the *Encyclopédie* in 1760, in the midst of the disasters of the Seven Years War. On 12 June, shortly after Palissot's satirical comedy, *Les Philosophes*, had finished its sensational run at the Comédie Française, the Marquise wrote to her son:

La guerre entre les philosophes beaux esprits et les devots politiques continue vivement, passe pour celle la, il n'y aura que de l'ancre repandue . . . Le memoire de mr. de P. au Roy[62] assortit tres bien a son discours accademique. Le ch^er n'est pas epargné dans la preface, s'il l'a été dans la piece des philosophes.[63]

---

[58] *Oeuvres complètes*, ed. B. Gagnebin and M. Raymond, Paris, 1959, Vol. I, p. 397.
[59] H. Tronchin, *Un Médecin du XVIIIe siècle*, pp. 86-92.
[60] One illegible word.
[61] 86 AP 6, 209.
[62] *Mémoire présenté au roi, le 11 mai 1760* by Lefranc de Pompignan, published along with the *discours de réception* which he delivered at the Academy on 10 March. In both he attacked the *philosophes*.
[63] 86 AP 6, 261.

In a letter of the following month[64] the Marquise again referred to the controversy:

> On ne dit pas trop de bien de nos affaires des indes, Mr. de Bussi tué dans une deroute, Mr. de Lailly fait prisonnier par les Anglois, ont rendu les actions de nulle valeur. Ton oncle le ch$^{er.}$ en a bien quelques unes, mais son nom qui s'immortalise dans les Brochures du tems le console des pertes pecuniaires.

She then proceeds to quote two very eulogistic references made by Voltaire to the Chevalier:

> Voici ce qui est imprimé dans une Note du *Russe à Paris* 'Mr. le ch^{er} de J. homme d'une gr^{de} naissance, auteur de cent excellents articles, qui enrichissent le dict. Encyc.'[65]

> Volt . . . dans sa lettre a Palis: qui court imprimée, a mis ce qui suit: 'Vous m'assurés que vous n'avez point accusé mr le ch; de J. Cepend^t c'est lui qui est l'auteur de l'article Gouvernem^t. Son nom est en grosses lettres à la fin de cet article. Vous en defferés plusieurs traits qui pourroient lui faire gr$^{d.}$ tort dépoüillés de tout ce qui les precede, et de ce qui les suit; mais qui remis dans leur tout ensemble, sont dignes des Cicerons, des Grotius, et des de Thou. Vous n'ignorés pas d'ailleurs que mr le ch^{er} de Jaucourt, homme de tres gr^{de} maison, et beaucoup plus respectable par ses moeurs que par sa naissance &c.'[66]

After quoting these passages, the Marquise continues:

> Ne crois tu pas que le ch^{er} a pû se moucher en lisant cela? . . . En tout on aime a voir son nom honoré dans les fastes de sa Nation, n'importe a quel titre, soit par les lettres ou par l'épée.

---

[64] 86 AP 6, 235. Although this letter is headed 'Ce d^r. juillet 1759', the date should obviously read '1760' as both the quotations from Voltaire which it contains come from works published in 1760 and refer to Palissot's *Les Philosophes* and its preface.

[65] See Voltaire, *Oeuvres complètes*, Vol. X, p. 125.

[66] The Marquise ends her quotation with 'par sa naissance', cutting out the following words: 'est dans des circonstances délicates qui exigent de tout honnête homme le plus grand ménagement'. (Best. 8257.) The precise meaning of the last remark is not clear. Diderot's words in the passage quoted on p. 49—'Avec quelle constance ne s'est-il pas refusé à des sollicitations tendres & puissantes qui cherchoient à nous l'enlever?'—would seem to imply that Jaucourt was under pressure from some members of his family to give up writing for the *Encyclopédie*.

It is a curious fact that, in 1771, in his *Mémoires pour servir à l'histoire de notre littérature*, Palissot devoted several pages to Jaucourt and praised his writings and, in particular, his character:

> Mais ce qui caractérise, surtout, les Ecrits de Mr. de Jaucourt, c'est que l'honnête homme n'est jamais éclypsé par l'Auteur. Il ne prêche point la vertu avec cette fausse chaleur à laquelle l'imagination a plus de part que le sentiment; mais il la fait aimer, en imprimant à ses moindres Ouvrages le caractère d'une ame sensible & honnête. Aussi n'a-t-il jamais été mêlé dans aucune de ces querelles scandaleuses qui ont déshonoré, parmi nous, tant de prétendus sages. Il vit en paix, sans ambition, sans prétentions, avec un amour noble & désintéressé pour les sciences, vrai Philosophe au milieu des Charlatans qui s'en arrogent le titre.[67]

While the controversy raged, preparations were going on in secret for finishing the *Encyclopédie*, despite the withdrawal of its *privilège* in March 1759. In a letter written to Grimm on 1 May Diderot describes a dinner attended by D'Alembert, D'Holbach, Jaucourt and himself to discuss with the four publishers plans for continuing the work. When the disgruntled D'Alembert kicked up a row, the Chevalier, he notes, 'ne disoit mot. Il avoit la tête baissée et il paroissoit abasourdi'.[68] Writing to Sophie Volland in November of the following year, in a mood of disillusionment at the slow progress of the last ten volumes of text, he exclaims:

> Mes collègues n'ont presque rien fait. Je ne sçais plus quand je sortirai de cette galère. Si j'en crois le chevalier de Jaucourt, son projet est de m'y tenir encore un an. Cet homme est depuis six à sept ans au centre de quatre à cinq secrétaires, lisant, dictant, travaillant treize à quatorze heures par jour, et cette position là ne l'a pas encore ennuyé.[69]

A glimpse of the indefatigable Chevalier at work on the *Encyclopédie* is provided by another letter written later in the same month:

[67] *La Dunciade*, London, 1771, 2 vols., Vol. II, pp. 136-7.
[68] Roth, Vol. II, p. 120.
[69] Roth, Vol. III, p. 248.

Le chevalier de Jaucourt?—Ne craignez pas qu'il s'ennuie de moudre des articles; Dieu le fit pour cela. Je voudrois que vous vissiez comme sa physionomie s'allonge quand on lui annonce la fin de son travail, ou plutôt la nécessité de le finir. Il a vraiment l'air désolé.[70]

In contrast to these not very flattering references to Jaucourt there is the eloquent tribute which Diderot paid to him when the last ten volumes of the work were launched on the world:

Si nous avons poussé le cri de joie du matelot, lorsqu'il apperçoit la terre, après une nuit obscure qui l'a tenu égaré entre le ciel & les eaux, c'est à M. le Chevalier de Jaucourt que nous le devons. Que n'a-t-il pas fait pour nous, sur-tout dans ces derniers tems? Avec quelle constance ne s'est-il pas refusé à des sollicitations tendres & puissantes qui cherchoient à nous l'enlever? Jamais le sacrifice du repos, de l'intérêt & de la santé ne s'est fait plus entier & plus absolu. Les recherches les plus pénibles & les plus ingrates ne l'ont point rebuté. Il s'en est occupé sans relâche, satisfait de lui-même, s'il pouvoit en épargner aux autres le dégoût. Mais c'est à chaque feuille de cet Ouvrage à suppléer ce qui manque à notre éloge; il n'en est aucune qui n'atteste & la variété de ses connoissances & l'étendue de ses secours.[71]

More in line, alas, with Diderot's true feelings on the subject of Jaucourt's contribution to the *Encyclopédie* is a passage in a document brought to light by Luneau de Boisjermain in his lawsuit against the publishers of the *Encyclopédie*.[72] In a memoir composed by Diderot when Panckoucke was trying to bring out a revised edition of the *Encyclopédie*, he included a comment which, as M. Jean Meyer has pointed out,[73] can apply only to Jaucourt's massive contribution to the work: 'J'oubliois de dire qu'il y a dans tout genre au moins quatre volumes in-folio du ***, dont il y a très-peu de choses à conserver. Il n'en peut rester que la nomenclature.' That this reference was to the Chevalier is made absolutely clear by a passage in a letter of Diderot to Catherine the Great where he speaks of his plan for a new edition

[70] Roth, Vol. III, p. 265.
[71] Vol. VIII, *Avertissement*.
[72] See Chap. V, p. 142.
[73] *Diderot homme de science*, Rennes, 1959, p. 37n.

of the *Encyclopédie* in which he would be able to 'réparer les sottises de l'abbé Chappe et de M. le chevalier de Jaucourt'.[74]

The reputation of Jaucourt seems to have stood higher with Voltaire than with the *philosophes* of Paris. He continued to refer to him in public in the most eulogistic terms, for instance in the article *Figure* in his *Questions sur l'Encyclopédie* where he describes him as 'homme au-dessus des philosophes de l'antiquité, en ce qu'il a préféré la retraite, la vraie philosophie, le travail infatigable, à tous les avantages que pouvait lui procurer sa naissance, dans un pays où l'on préfère cet avantage à tout le reste, excepté à l'argent'.[75] Similar praise is also to be found in his correspondence. One ought not perhaps to take at its face value the postscript which he added to a letter to the Chevalier's nephew, the Marquis de Jaucourt:

Je lis actuellement tous les articles de M. le chevalier de Jaucourt. Vous ne sauriez croire combien il me fait aimer sa belle âme, et comme je m'instruis avec lui.[76]

Yet in an earlier letter to the publisher Panckoucke who was proposing to bring out a new edition of the *Encyclopédie*, he had expressed himself in scarcely less enthusiastic terms:

Quant à votre entreprise de la nouvelle Encyclopédie, gardez-vous encore une fois de retrancher tous les articles de M. le chevalier de Jaucourt. Il y en a d'extrêmement utiles, et qui se ressentent de la noblesse d'âme d'un homme de qualité et d'un bon citoyen, tels que celui du Labarum.[77]

Such eulogies form a striking contrast with the condescending and often sneering terms in which other *philosophes* spoke of Jaucourt in their writings. Of his contribution to the *Encyclopédie* Grimm wrote in 1771:

---

[74] Roth, Vol. XIV, p. 84 (13 Sept. 1774).
[75] *Oeuvres complètes,* Vol. XIX, pp. 125-6 (see also *Honnêtetés littéraires,* Vol. XXVI, p. 127, and *Lettres à S. A. Mgr. le Prince de* . . . , Vol. XXVI, p. 513).
[76] Best. 15319 (April/May 1770).
[77] Best. 14320 (Oct./Nov. 1768). About half of the article LABARUM comes from the *Essai sur les moeurs.*

Un grand nombre d'articles de toute espèce et des plus essentiels fut abandonné à M. le chevalier de Jaucourt, homme d'un grand zèle et d'un travail infatigable, mais compilateur impitoyable, qui n'a fait que mettre à contribution les livres les plus connus et souvent les plus médiocres.[78]

Of the literary articles contributed by Jaucourt to the last ten volumes Marmontel wrote: 'Un laborieux compilateur, le chevalier de Jaucourt, s'étoit chargé de la partie littéraire, et l'avoit travaillée à sa manière, qui n'étoit pas la mienne'.[79] The same sarcastic tone is adopted by Naigeon in a note criticizing the Chevalier's *Vie de Leibnitz*, where he speaks of him as 'ce compilateur, qui, en général, connaissoit assez bien les bonnes sources, et dont la plupart des articles d'*Encyclopédie* sont copiés mot pour mot de nos auteurs les plus célèbres'.[80] A similar unfavourable impression was picked up at second hand by the Italian writer, Alessandro Verri, who wrote from Paris in 1766 to his brother, Pietro:

Vi ricordate che nella Enciclopedia vi sono moltissimi articoli del cavaliere di Jaucourt? Ebbene, questo uomo veramente esiste, è disprezzato, passa per un solenne seccatore e mi dicono che, se lo avessero lasciato fare, avrebbe voluto far tutto lui. E un compilatore spaventoso. No lo conosco ancora.[81]

One point, however, on which contemporaries agreed was that the Chevalier was ruthlessly exploited by the publishers of the *Encyclopédie*. Palissot, for instance, wrote:

On est effrayé du contingent immense que lui seul a fourni à l'Encyclopédie. On assure que plus de dix volumes de cette vaste collection lui appartiennent. Mais ce qu'on doit le plus admirer en lui, c'est un désintéressement dont peut-être on n'a pas d'exemple. Qui ne croiroit qu'après avoir tant concouru à l'Encyclopédie, Mr. de Jaucourt en eût du moins retiré quelque avantage? Point du tout; on s'est contenté de lui en donner un exemplaire,

---
[78] *Corr. litt.*, Vol. IX, p. 206.
[79] *Mémoires*, ed. M. Tourneux, Paris, 1891, 3 vols., Vol. II, p. 364.
[80] *PAM*, Vol. III, p. 114n.
[81] *Carteggio di Pietro e di Alessandro Verri*, ed. F. Novati and others, Milan, 1923-1942, 12 vols., Vol. I, Part I, p. 46.

&, à l'égard du reste, les généreux Editeurs crurent lui sauver l'embarras d'un refus.[82]

In 1766, just after the appearance of the last ten volumes of text, Grimm had commented scathingly on the contrast between the profits of the publishers and their meanness towards the contributors:

> M. le chevalier de Jaucourt, qui, après M. Diderot, a le plus contribué à mettre fin à cet ouvrage immense, non seulement n'en a jamais tiré aucune récompense, mais s'est trouvé dans le cas de vendre une maison qu'il avait dans Paris afin de pouvoir payer le salaire de trois ou quatre secrétaires, employés sans relâche depuis plus de dix ans. Ce qu'il y a de plaisant, c'est que c'est l'imprimeur Le Breton qui a acheté cette maison avec l'argent que le travail du chevalier de Jaucourt l'a mis à portée de gagner. Aussi ce Le Breton trouve que le chevalier de Jaucourt est un bien honnête homme.[83]

The story of Jaucourt selling a house to Le Breton was confirmed by the discovery of the contract of sale which was on show at the exhibition 'Diderot et l'Encyclopédie' held at the Bibliothèque Nationale in 1951.[84]

The house in question was 'une maison à porte cocherre située a Paris rue Macon ou pend pour enseigne l'hotel du mans', which Jaucourt had inherited from his mother. In 1740 it was valued at 20,000 livres,[85] and in 1754 the Chevalier had sold it for 21,000.[86] The deal fell through because the purchaser was unable to produce the money, even though the payments were to be spread over seven years. It may be that the Chevalier was relieved to have Le Breton take the property off his hands; at any rate he sold it to him for 18,000 livres. A letter which is attached to the contract (it is dated 5 February 1761) speaks in very rude terms

---

[82] *La Dunciade*, Vol. II, pp. 135-6.
[83] *Corr. litt.*, Vol. VII, p. 45.
[84] See the catalogue, p. 52, No. 199: 'Vente par Louis de Jaucourt d'un hôtel à André-François Le Breton, Paris, étude de Me Marchand, 11 mars 1761'.
[85] Minutier Central, I. 399.
[86] Minutier Central, XC. 379. I am indebted to Me Léonce Jarriand for permission to consult this document.

LOUIS, CHEVALIER DE JAUCOURT

(at least for Jaucourt) about Le Breton's *notaire*:

Il a épluché cette matiere avec le même soin pour vos intérets que si vous aviez à traiter pour un object d'un million avec un étranger d'Allemagne qui quitteroit Paris, et vous offriroit des terres à acheter, en vous demandant cent mille livres lors de la passation du Contrat.

Out of the sum of 18,000 livres Jaucourt received 6,000 in cash, while the remainder was to be invested with the publishers of the *Encyclopédie* at 5 per cent interest. This is confirmed by an entry in the publishers' accounts for 1761:

Ce Jour deux octobre la Compagnie a emprunté douze mille livres a M. le Ch^{er} de Jaucourt dont elle luy a fait un billet portant promesse d'en passer contrat a sa p^{ere} requisition, laquelle Somme J'ay recu cy 12000—[87]

These accounts mention two payments of 300 livres (six months' interest) in 1762, three in 1763, none in 1764 and 1765, 'deux années de sa rente' (1,200 livres) in 1766 and one payment of 600 livres in 1767, at which point they break off.[88]

At various times, from 1758 onwards, the publishers supplied Jaucourt with books to the total value of some 2,750 livres; on the last two occasions (in 1764) he received over 1,300 livres worth.[89] Apart from this, they refunded to him a few items of postage, gave his servant a gratuity of 120 livres when work on the text of the *Encyclopédie* was completed, and that was all. What Jaucourt himself thought about the matter we do not know, but, judged at any rate by modern standards, the treatment which he received from the publishers in return for writing over 17,000 articles was indefensible.

Though Jaucourt was never elected a member of any Paris academy, his reputation spread as far as Bordeaux and Stockholm, London and Berlin. In 1746, along with Voltaire among others,

---

[87] Archives Nationales, U 1051, f. 12r (under 'Recette'); cf. May, p. 108.
[88] See under 'Dépense' items 1207, 1269, 1330, 1393, 1421, 1576 and 1731. For payments after 1767 see Chap. V, pp. 142-143.
[89] See items 977, 982, 988, 1020, 1052, 1444 and 1455.

he was elected an associate member of the Bordeaux Academy.[90] No doubt his election was partly the result of the contacts which his sister-in-law, the Marquise de Jaucourt, had in that part of France; a member of the Vivens family, she was born near Tonneins and, until her death in 1775, kept up a correspondence with her kinsman, the Chevalier François de Vivens (1697-1780). After spending several years in England and Holland, the latter was elected a member of the Bordeaux Academy in 1742; he was a man of wide interests who, in addition to scientific and economic writings, published a plea for the removal of the disabilities imposed on the Huguenots entitled *Questions sur la tolérance*.[91] He was on friendly terms with his neighbour Montesquieu. The connection between Vivens and Jaucourt is brought out in a letter which the former wrote in 1758 to the secretary of the academy about the proposal to publish volumes of its proceedings. 'J'en ai fait part', he wrote, 'à un de nos confrères, M. le Chevalier de Jaucourt, afin de l'engager à vous envoyer tout ce qu'il pourra soustraire à l'Encyclopédie'.[92] There is no sign in the records of the academy of any response from Jaucourt.

The first foreign academy to seek to honour him was the Royal Swedish Academy of Sciences to which he was elected on 31 October 1755. The Librarian, Dr. A. Holmberg, who supplied this information, added the following curious detail: the minutes of the academy state that Jaucourt was 'a very literary and learned man in France, one of those who most of all have contributed to the big Dictionnaire encyclopédique, but as he never answered to the call he was excluded'. Works of reference confine themselves to recording his election.

One seeks in vain for Jaucourt's name in the index to the fourth edition of *The Record of the Royal Society for the Promotion of Natural Knowledge*,[93] but an examination of the lists of

[90] P. Barrière, *L'Académie de Bordeaux centre de culture internationale au XVIIIe siècle (1712-1792)*, Bordeaux-Paris, 1951, p. 44.
[91] Saint-Amans, *Notice biographique sur M. de Vivens*, Agen, 1829 (a copy of this rare work was lent me by Dr. Robert Shackleton).
[92] Bibliothèque de la Ville de Bordeaux, MS. 828, Vol. XX, No. 74. Information supplied by the Librarian, Monsieur L. Desgraves.
[93] London, 1940.

members elected in the middle of the eighteenth century soon leads one to discover that on 8 January 1756 a mysterious 'Jacour, Chevalier de' was elected. This was in fact Louis de Jaucourt. For his election Philip, 2nd Earl Stanhope, Charles, 3rd Duke of Marlborough, Abraham Trembley, the famous Genevan naturalist who was then living in London, and George Lewis Scott, who edited the supplement to Chamber's *Cyclopaedia* published in 1753, signed the following certificate:

We whose names are underwritten do hereby certify that we know Monsieur Le Chevalier de Jaucourt, who usually resides at Paris either personally, or by the works he has published, and that it is our opinion that he is a proper person to be admitted of the Royall Society, and likely to become a usefull member thereof.[94]

More is known about Jaucourt's election to the Berlin Academy, though the documents available are somewhat confusing. On 22 February 1764 D'Alembert wrote to Voltaire:

Je travaille . . . à donner de la considération au petit troupeau. Je viens de faire entrer dans l'académie de Berlin Helvetius & le chevalier de Jaucourt. J'ai écrit à votre ancien disciple les raisons qui me le faisoient désirer & la chose a été faite sur le champ.[95]

Sure enough, the published records of the academy show that the two men were elected on 5 January of that year.[96] On 7 February D'Alembert wrote to Frederick to convey the thanks of the two men—and his own.[97] It is puzzling therefore to learn from a note to the published records of the academy[98] that the list of new members had in fact been proposed on 2 April 1761 although the war had held up the King's approval of their election. On 7 February Jaucourt himself wrote to Formey to offer

---

[94] Information supplied by the Librarian, Mr. I. Kaye.
[95] Best. 10883.
[96] *Histoire de l'Académie royale des Sciences et des Belles-Lettres, Année 1770*, Berlin, 1772. 'Liste des membres agrégés à l'Académie depuis la présidence de M. de Maupertuis', p. 18.
[97] Frédéric le Grand, *Oeuvres*, ed. J. D. E. Preuss, Berlin, 1846-56, 31 vols., Vol. XXVII, Part III, p. 303.
[98] loc. cit.

his thanks and his quota of praise for Frederick. In reproducing this letter in his *Souvenirs d'un Citoyen*[99] Formey prefaces it with the following lines which show a very high regard for the Chevalier:

J'en ai toujours eu l'idée la plus avantageuse; & lors que M. *d'Alembert* étant ici,[1] me fit entendre qu'il n'accepteroit pas la présidence de notre académie, je lui témoignai le désir qu'elle fût conférée à M. *de Jaucourt.*

It is interesting to see Frederick himself inquiring after the Chevalier, over a dozen years later, in a letter to D'Alembert:

M. de Jaucourt, parent de l'encyclopédiste, est venu à Madgebourg voir les troupes; c'est un des aimables François que j'aie vus de longtemps . . . Je me suis informé de son parent, qui par goût a étudié la médecine chez Boerhaave; une de ses parentes a élevé ma soeur de Suède et une de mes soeurs qui est morte.[2]

D'Alembert's reply is typical:

Je ne vois plus depuis très-longtemps mon ancien confrère le chevalier de Jaucourt, l'encyclopédiste. Il vit dans la plus grande retraite, et s'occupe, dit-on, d'une nouvelle édition du Moréri; car il ne peut travailler qu'à des ouvrages en plusieurs volumes in-folio. Les petits volumes de Racine et de la Fontaine ne contiennent pas tant de mots et plus de choses.[3]

We have already seen that Jaucourt's reputation among the *philosophes* of Paris did not stand very high.

Little is known of the life of the Chevalier after he had finished his work on the *Encyclopédie*. Two letters written in 1767 and 1768 to the young Étienne Salomon Reybaz, who had recently been ordained at Geneva and was later to become one of the collaborators of Mirabeau, show him in contact with other men from the city in which he had spent his youth: the watchmaker Jean Romilly, and Théodore Tronchin. A letter of the

---

[99] Berlin, 1789, 2 vols., Vol. II, pp. 206-8.
[1] In 1763.
[2] Frédéric le Grand, *Oeuvres*, Vol. XXV, p. 77.
[3] ibid., p. 80.

former to Jean Jacques Rousseau in 1767 contains a mention of the Chevalier: 'Vous savez, je crois, que mon fils est bien placé à Londres . . . C'est par les soins du bon *Chevalier de Jaucourt* que mons fils doit sa place'.[4] Théodore Tronchin spent the last fifteen years of his life, from 1766 to 1781, in Paris as physician to the Duc d'Orléans, and his biographer mentions Jaucourt as a frequent guest at his table.[5]

Whether or not D'Alembert was correctly informed when he wrote that in 1777—at the age of 73—Jaucourt was engaged on a new edition of Moréri, there is evidence that to an advanced age he worked on various other compilations. The statement of Louis Dutens that Jaucourt was one of the contributors to the *Encyclopédie d'Yverdon*, published by De Félice between 1770 and 1780,[6] would seem to be unfounded; but he certainly contributed to the thirteen quarto volumes of the *Dictionnaire universel raisonné de justice naturelle et civile*, published at Yverdon in 1777 and 1778.[7] Moreover, he was also given a large share in another project of De Félice which never materialized—a *Dictionnaire universel raisonné de médecine*, based on the *Encyclopédie d'Yverdon* and directed by Haller. In a letter to Haller of 21 November 1775 De Félice mentions first among the other contributors to the work 'Mr. *de Jaucourt* qui me fournit tous les matériaux qu'il avoit amassés pour un pareil ouvrage et un catalogue ou nomenclature complette pour ce dictionnaire.'[8] In January 1776 while De Félice was indisposed, his secretary wrote another letter to Haller, which stresses the importance of the role which had been assigned to Jaucourt in this work:

Mr de Felice . . . a encore une autre raison pour vous en prier; c'est qu'il a trouvé un homme et le seul capable peut-être d'executer dans ce Dictionnaire une idée qu'il avoit conçue depuis

---

[4] M. Launay, 'Madame de Baugrand et Jean Romilly, horloger, intermédiaires entre Rousseau et Diderot' (*Europe*, Jan.-Feb. 1963, p. 261).
[5] H. Tronchin, *Un Médecin du XVIIIe siècle*, p. 329.
[6] 'Lettre de M. Dutens au sujet de l'*Encyclopédie d'Yverdon*' (*Journal encyclopédique*, 15 March 1772, p. 444). See Perret, p. 222.
[7] Perret, pp. 193, 399.
[8] E. Maccabez, *F. B. de Félice* (1723-1789) *et son Encyclopédie* (*Yverdon* 1770-1780), Bâle, 1903, p. 166.

longtemps (Jaucourt), c'est de faire à la fin des articles de Pratique, soit de Médecine soit de Chirurgie soit même de Pharmacie de petits Resumés avec le titre d'instruction domestique, sensés, faciles, et propres à mettre au fait tout le monde des symptômes des principales maladies et des remèdes à y appliquer. Cette personne ne saurait commencer son travail avant que d'être assurée des articles de Médecine, de Chirurgie et de Pharmacie qui devront entrer dans cet ouvrage. Or c'est votre tirage, Monsieur, qui doit le guider.[9]

Discussions between De Félice and Haller about the form to be given to the prospectus of the dictionary caused the former to speak highly of Jaucourt in another letter of 1777:

Si vous ne croyez pas devoir nommer M. *de Jaucourt* dans le titre il faudroit au moins dire dans le Prospectus que cet homme toujours zélé pour le bien de l'humanité a communiqué à M^r. de Felice tous les matériaux qu'il ramassoit depuis bien des années pour un ouvrage pareil. Au reste sans l'avoir exercée,[10] Mr de Jaucourt possede la médecine théorétique bien mieux que les trois-quarts de ceux qui l'exercent, et il est reconnu pour tel du moins en France; ainsi qu'on ne risqueroit rien à le nommer.[11]

De Félice stated publicly his indebtedness to Jaucourt when he wrote in the *Journal Helvétique*:

Avant que de finir ce prospectus, je dois rendre un témoignage public de reconnoissance à M. le chevalier de Jaucourt. Ce véritable ami de l'humanité . . . me fit parvenir généreusement par le canal de notre ami commun, M. de la Lande, six gros volumes.[12]

The Lalande in question was, of course, the astronomer, a contributor to both the *Supplément* to the *Encyclopédie* and to the *Encyclopédie d'Yverdon*, and also in these same years one of the disgruntled subscribers to the original work who joined forces with Luneau de Boisjermain.[13]

---

[9] ibid., pp. 171-2.
[10] No doubt Jaucourt never practised regularly. but he does relate in the *Encyclopédie*, in the article CHAMPIGNON, how, 'étant l'année passée dans nos terres', he had cured the cook of mushroom poisoning.
[11] Maccabez, p. 178.
[12] April 1776, p. 49 (quoted from Perret, p. 203n.).
[13] See Chap. V, p. 115.

The last months of the Chevalier's life were spent in retirement at Compiègne. He was still in Paris on 7 January 1779 for on that date he signed a receipt for the previous year's interest from a perpetual annuity upon the Duc d'Orléans,[14] and it was in Paris, on 10 April of the same year, that he made a holograph will under which his nephew, Armand Henri de Jaucourt, a naval officer, became his *légataire universel*.[15]

His death ten months later went unrecorded in the *Journal de Paris*, the *Correspondance littéraire* and Métra, but was mentioned briefly and somewhat belatedly by Bachaumont on 7 April 1780:

On a oublié de faire mention de la perte de M. le Chevalier de Jaucourt, mort le trois Février dernier. Cet homme de qualité, entraîné par son ardeur pour les sciences, avoit étudié en médecine à Leyde sous le fameux Boerhaave, & s'y étoit fait admettre au Doctorat. C'étoit un des principaux coopérateurs de l'Encyclopédie. Il possédoit plusieurs langues, surtout l'angloise, et a beaucoup aidé de ses conseils M. le Tourneur pour sa traduction des *Nuits de* Young.[16]

This date, which is wrongly given at 1779 in most works of reference, is confirmed by the burial certificate:[17]

L'an mil Sept cent Quatrevingt le Cinq fevrier le Corps de haut et puissant Seigneur Messire Louis, Chevalier de Jaucourt, décédé avant-hier âgé d'environ Soixante quatorze ans a été inhumé au Cimetiere de cette Paroisse[18] par moi Prêtre Curé Soussigné en présence de Messire Charles de Lancry, Seigneur de Rimberlieu, Lieutenant pour le Roy en Cette ville de Compiegne, de Marie Jean François Ermengard de Beauval, Major de cette Ville, et Lieutenant de la capitainerie Royale de Compiegne, et Anne Antoine de Pronnais, Conseiller du Roy, Lieutenant

---

[14] 86 AP 7(1), 47 quater.
[15] Archives Nationales, Y 5072 (5 Aug. 1780).
[16] *Mémoires secrets*, Vol. XV, p. 123. The Le Tourneur translation of Young's *Night Thoughts* appeared in 1769.
[17] I am indebted to M. Christian Gut, Directeur des Services d'Archives de l'Oise, for a photostat of this document.
[18] St. Jacques de Compiègne.

général civil et criminel au Baillage de Cette Ville, et autres qui ont Signé.

Ermengard de Beauval	Lancry de Rimberlieu
De Pronnais	De Livry
Boulanger	Perein

Thus ended the modest, industrious and unexciting career of the Chevalier de Jaucourt. The very magnitude of his contribution to the *Encyclopédie* inevitably made of him a ruthless compiler; and yet amongst the thousands of articles which he turned out there are many which show beyond a doubt that he was by no means devoid either of originality or even of a sturdy independence of judgement. But to demonstrate this would require a chapter to itself.

Before leaving the Chevalier, one ought to examine two curious stories related about him. The first is contained in the article 'Famille de Jaucourt' written by Christian Bartholmess for the *Encyclopédie des Gens du Monde* and published separately in 1841. Although a good deal of the information which he provides about Louis de Jaucourt is merely copied from the article on him in the *Biographie universelle*, Bartholmess was obviously interested in the Chevalier. In a foot-note to his article he states:

L'auteur de cet article s'occupe à réunir les ouvrages du chevalier de Jaucourt et à en publier l'ensemble, accompagné d'une notice où il lui sera permis d'entrer dans des détails que le cadre de cette Encyclopédie n'admettait pas.[19]

Nothing ever came of this plan, but in the course of his article the writer does offer us a picturesque account of the Chevalier's end (incidentally getting right his age at his death, but, like nearly all the biographical dictionaries, getting the year wrong):

Comme Voltaire avait accueilli le P. Adam, il choisit pour secrétaire un autre jésuite; c'est avec lui qu'il se retira, quelques mois avant sa fin, à Compiègne, où il espérait vivre plus tranquille; il y expira subitement le 3 février 1779, âgé de 76 ans, et l'on assure que le jésuite disparut la même nuit, important, entre autres choses, de précieux manuscrits et des livres couverts d'annotations de la main du chevalier.[20]

[19] p. 15. [20] p. 15.

Like many delightful anecdotes related about literary men of the past, the story told by Bartholmess is scarcely borne out by the documents available to us. A document found in the Archives Nationales[21] led to the discovery that a copy of the Chevalier's will[22] and the inventory of his possessions made after his death[23] were available on the premises in the Minutier Central. Thanks to the kindness of their present owner, Mᵉ Jacques Émile Delapalme, it was possible to consult them.

On 5 February 1780, on the day of the Chevalier's funeral, Pierre Charles Emmanuel Thibault, described as 'secrétaire de M. le Chevalier de Jaucourt', deposited with a *notaire* in Compiègne the holograph will made by the Chevalier in Paris on 10 April of the previous year. Under his will his nephew, Armand Henri de Jaucourt, a naval officer, was made, as we have seen, 'légataire universel des immeubles'. In addition to bequeathing 300 livres 'aux pauvres de la paroisse où je mourray' and 100 livres each to the two maids in his service, Jaucourt directed that the following legacies should be paid:

a Monsieur Nicolas Bochart Neuf mille six cens Livres
a St. Martin mon domestique Sept Mille six cens Livres
a Monsieur Jean Perein, mon Executeur testamentaire Trois mille Livres
a Monsieur L'Abbé de Schorne Mille Livres
a ma filleule Thibault Mille Livres
a Monsieur Valade Libraire huit cens Livres
a Mademoiselle Feuiltin Cinq cens Livres.

After a reference to the 'Contrat de rente du par Monsieur Le Breton Libraire' (in part-payment of the famous house which the principal publisher of the *Encyclopédie* had bought from him in 1761), the Chevalier went on:

Je donne mon mobilier, C'est a dire mes meubles meublans, glaces, Linge, argenterie, Livres, deniers Comptant, arrerages de

---

[21] 'Envoi en possession à substitution. De Jaucourt. 5 aoust 1780' (Y 5072).
[22] Minutier Central, CXVII. 891. '10 février 1780. Testament du Cher. de Jaucourt déposé'.
[23] ibid., CXVII, 892 'Inventaire de M. le Cher. de Jaucourt, 2 mars 1780'.

rentes viageres et generalement tout ce qu'on comprend sous le nom de mobilier a Monsieur et a Madame Thibault Conjointement a defaut d'un d'eux à l'autre et a defaut de tous les deux a leur fille ma filleule, voulant qu'après l'Inventaire, le tout leur soit délivré en nature.

It is clear from the will and from the legal documents drawn up after the Chevalier's death that his secretary had no need to do a moonlight flit, carrying off his master's books and manuscripts, since they had been bequeathed to him.

The inventory, which was drawn up at Compiègne between 2 and 4 March 1780, i.e. approximately a month after the Chevalier's death, lists some 2,000 volumes which were valued at a total of about 7,000 livres by a bookseller, J. B. Dessaint jr. The Chevalier's manuscripts are given a section to themselves towards the end of the inventory:

Suit l'inventaire des manuscrits faisant partie de la bibliotheque dud. deffunt S. Chevalier de Jaucourt et restés jusqu'a présent sous les scellés dud. S. Lieutenant general pour être compris au present inventaire dont la prisée a été faite par led. Me Pul de lavis dud. S. Desaint tous deux cy devant nommés qualifiés et domiciliés pour ce present.

Item deux paquets de Cinq Volumes infolio, et sept Volumes in quarto couverts en peau verte et en parchemin plus neuf cartons le tout compris sous onze numeros Commencant depuis le nombre Un Jusques et compris le nombre onze desd. Volumes Contenant des manuscrits dud. feu Seigneur Chevalier de Jaucourt prisés et estimés Le tout ensemble la somme de douze Livres cy   12^{11}

Apres lequel Inventaire le S. Perein a declaré que le S. Bochard Copiste demeurant a Paris lui a dit que feu M. le Chevalier de Jaucourt lui avoit confié et qu'il avoit en ses mains une partie d'autres manuscrits dud. feu Seigneur et a signé.

In face of such evidence the story of the nefarious exploits of the ex-Jesuit is revealed as a pure legend.

It is less easy to know what to think of a second story about the Chevalier, since, although it is even more improbable, we know so little about the details of his day-to-day existence. In 1809 it was alleged that this devoted *encyclopédiste* tried to end his days in an institution derided by the *Encyclopédie* for its pointless austerities, the monastery of La Trappe. The source of the story is the following letter, preserved in the papers of the Jaucourt family which are deposited in the Archives Nationales.[24]

a Vaubadon ce 3 Sept. 1809

Monsieur
J'ai lu ce qui suit dans vos éphémérides du n°. 18e année 1808 'Louis de Jaucourt, de la société royale de Londres, membre des académies de Berlin, de Stockholm &c, et l'un des plus infatigables collaborateurs de l'Encyclopédie, meurt a Compiègne âgé de 76 ans.' Votre note annonce que mr. de Jeaucourt mérite qu'on fasse attention a ce qui le concerne. Je vous prie d'insérer dans votre journal le fait suivant qui fait partie de sa vie, mais que je crois inconnu. Je crois devoir à la religion de le faire connoître.

L'envie de n'être pas confondu avec le commun des hommes a fait prendre a quantité de personnes le parti de l'incredulité. Ce moyen de se distinguer a paru plus aisé que celui d'une étude sérieuse. Le système de l'incredulité qui soulève la créature contre le créateur, est devenu si puissant que quantité de savans entraînés par le courant, ont cru se rendre plus célèbres en outrageant dans leurs ouvrages la religion et ses ministres. Monsieur le chevalier de Jaucourt, quoiqu'il n'eut pas besoin de ce petit moyen, est néanmoins tombé dans cette faute; mais il l'a reconnue et a voulu l'expier à la fin de ses jours.

'L'yvresse des passions ne dure pas toujours, dit Mably, la raison a ses instans pour se reconnoître, et l'idée d'un Dieu vengeur peut alors étonner et troubler salutairement le coupable. L'âge enfin survient, les passions s'affoiblissent, et les sentimens de religion font du moins réparer les maux qu'on n'a pu prévenir. On déteste ses erreurs, et on donne des exemples de vertu propres a instruire les jeunes gens de leur devoir'.[25] On va voir que M. de Jaucourt est une preuve de cette vérité et de la justesse de cette reflexion.

En 1782 je fis une visite à M. l'Abbé de la Trappe. Je crus la lui devoir comme Supérieur d'une abbaye de Bénédictins voisine de la sienne. L'austerité de vie de ses religieux ne fut pas oubliée dans notre conversation. Cette austérité, dît M. l'abbé, n'est pas approuvée des auteurs de l'Encyclopedie. 'C'est à la Trappe, disent ces auteurs, que se retirent ceux qui sont tour-

---

[24] 86 AP 7(1) 47 quinter.
[25] *Entretiens de Phocion.* 3e entretien.

mentés par des vapeurs mélancoliques et religieuses, ceux qui ont oublié Dieu, et le plus miséricordieux des pères, et qui ne voyent en lui que le plus cruel des tyrans; ceux qui réduisent a rien les souffrances, la mort, la passion de Jesus Christ. C'est de la que partent des cris, c'est la que sont pratiquées des austeritez qui abrégent la vie, et qui font injure à la divinité'.

Voici le moment, continua M. l'abbé, de vous prouver l'inconséquence du coeur humain. Croiriez-vous que M^r le Chevalier de Jaucourt auteur de cet article de l'Encyclopedie a tellement retourné sur ses pas, qu'il est venu ici me demander a être admis au nombre des penitens de cette abbaye, et qu'après que je lui eu accordé sa demande, il a suivi avec nous les exercices de la vie austère à laquelle nous nous sommes voués? Eh bien! il a fait cette demarche, il l'a soutenue pendant quelque temps, et il me dît en l'abandonnant que sa santé ne lui permettoit pas de soutenir la rigueur de notre regle. Il me demanda le secret sur cette circonstance de sa vie. Je le lui promis, et j'ai tenu ma parole pendant toute sa vie. Aujourd'hui qu'il est mort, je crois vous faire plaisir de vous le découvrir. Ce sera pour vous une nouvelle preuve, que ceux qui s'élèvent contre la religion et qui osent en decider en maîtres, finissent par reconnoître sa puissance, et se soumettre à son empire. M. l'abbé de la Trappe étoit âgé de 74 ans en 1782, et avoit, pour me servir de ses termes quarante quatre ans de Trappe. On m'a dît que son nom étoit Dom Théodore.

Je crois Monsieur que cette histoire mise dans votre journal apprendra aux fideles à mépriser les fanfaronnades de l'impie.

C'est moi M. qui vous ai demandé le supplément de Vosgien. Le Curé de Balleroi et moi nous nous sommes réunis, et nous avons votre journal a nous deux. Je vous remercie de votre envoi, ecrivez sur la marge d'une de vos feuilles ce que je vous dois. Je le verrai bien, et co^{me} la somme est petite je l'ajouterai quand nous renouvellerons l'abonnement ou en vous demandant quelque livre. J'ai l'honneur de vous saluer et de vous remercier.

Votrè très-humble et obeissant serviteur

        Le Guelinel du Routel
proche Bayeux   Desserv. de Vaubadon

The letter, which is stamped 'Rouen' and 'Septembre 10 1809', bears the following address:

  A Monsieur

    Monsieur Nicolle Libraire
    Rue de Seine. n° 12 Hotel
    de la Rochefoucault. A Paris.

Whether this letter was actually published at the time is not easy to discover. No trace of these *Ephémérides* can be found at the Bibliothèque Nationale or the Arsenal or the Mazarine. The nearest approach to such a periodical was provided by the Bibliothèque Historique de la Ville de Paris which offers the following work:

> Ephémérides politiques, littéraires et religieuses présentant pour chacun des jours de l'année un tableau des événemens remarquables qui datent de ce même jour . . . Troisième édition, revue, corrigée et considérablement augmentée. Paris chez Le Normant, Libraire, rue de Seine, no. 8/H. Nicolle, Libraire, même rue, no. 12. 1812.

Unfortunately this work contains no mention of the Chevalier.

If this obvious line of inquiry leads to nothing except for confirming that there was a bookseller named Nicolle at 12 Rue de la Seine, it cannot be said that a close examination of the contents of the letter takes one very far either. The Abbot of La Trappe from 1766 to 1783 was Théodore Chambon. It is interesting that an early nineteenth century history of the abbey specifically refers to the irritation caused to this abbot by the attacks of the *Encyclopédie*:

> Cet Abbé, qui s'amusait quelquefois à faire des vers français, avait eu le projet de publier la Vie de Rancé par dom Gervaise, avec une préface de sa composition, dans laquelle il se proposait de répondre aux articles du Dictionnaire Encyclopédique, intitulés Rancé et La Trappe; mais il fut détourné de ce projet par l'Abbé de Citeaux.[26]

It is incidentally rather curious that the writer of the letter, at one time a near neighbour of Théodore Chambon, should refer to him in such uncertain terms as 'On m'a dît que son nom étoit Dom Théodore'.

If the passage quoted in the letter from the *Entretiens de Phocion* reproduces with quite minor deviations the text of

---

[26] L. F. Du Bois, *Histoire civile, religieuse et littéraire de l'abbaye de la Trappe* (Paris, 1824), pp. 72-3.

Mably,[27] the same cannot be said of the second text put into the mouth of the Abbot—the quotation from the article TRAPPE, *abbaye de la* (*Hist. ecclés.*) from the *Encyclopédie*. How mutilated the text has become will be seen by confronting the version given in the letter with the authentic text.

> C'est-là que se retirent ceux qui ont commis quelques crimes secrets dont les remords les poursuivent; ceux qui sont tourmentés de vapeurs mélancoliques & religieuses; ceux qui ont oublié que Dieu est le plus miséricordieux des peres, & qui ne voient en lui que le plus cruel des tyrans; ceux qui réduisent à rien les souffrances, la mort, & la passion de Jésus-Christ, & qui ne voient la religion que du côté effrayant & terrible. C'est de-là que partent des cris, & là que sont pratiquées des austérités qui abregent la vie, & qui font injure à la divinité.

If one looks up the subject of La Trappe in the *Encyclopédie*, what is even more striking is to find that these words are not in the article on the abbey which bears the familiar initials 'D.J.' He was responsible only for the first of two articles on La Trappe, the one entitled TRAPPE, *moines de la* (*Géog. mod.*); the second, from which these words come, is unsigned. While it is extremely rash to attribute to Diderot all unsigned articles in the *Encyclopédie*, it is possible that the second article is an editorial addition by him, especially as we have evidence that in 1762, when he was busy with the final volumes of the *Encyclopédie*, he expressed very similar ideas about La Trappe. On 7 October he wrote to Sophie Volland about a visit which D'Holbach had paid to Caen: 'Il étoit dans le voisinage de la Trappe; il a visité et plaint ces pieux fanatiques qui voyent Dieu comme une bête féroce à laquelle ils seroient bien fâchés de ressembler'.[28]

It would be interesting to have some more information about the writer of this rather extraordinary letter. When my own researches led nowhere, M. Thilliez, Directeur des Services d'Archives of the Départment de l'Orne in which La Trappe is situated, obligingly produced for me the information that in 1782 and 1783 Robert-Jacques-François Le Guelinel was prior

[27] See the Amsterdam 1763 edition, pp. 113-14.
[28] Roth, Vol. IV, p. 188.

of the Benedictine abbey of Saint-Martin at Sées, thirty kilometres from La Trappe.[29] While this confirms one statement in his letter and the possibility that he might have discussed the Chevalier with the abbot of La Trappe, the story which he put down on paper in 1809 for publication still sounds incredible. Not only was Jaucourt one of the most important contributors to the *Encyclopédie*; he was by family tradition and upbringing (from his days in Geneva onwards) a Protestant. If in all probability his attitude to religion was less radical than that of men like Diderot and D'Holbach, he certainly seems to have recoiled from any sort of narrow religious orthodoxy. To take only one example from his signed contributions to the *Encyclopédie*, in the article SUPERSTITION we find him declaring roundly that it is 'un culte de religion faux, mal dirigé, plein de vaines terreurs, contraire à la raison & aux saines idées qu'on doit avoir de l'être suprème' and 'le plus terrible fléau de l'humanité'. He goes on:

L'athéisme même (c'est tout dire) ne détruit point cependant les sentimens naturels, ne porte aucune atteinte aux lois, ni aux moeurs du peuple; mais la *superstition* est un tyran despotique qui fait tout céder à ses chimères. Ses préjugés sont supérieurs à tous les autres préjugés. Un athée est intéressé à la tranquillité publique, par l'amour de son propre repos; mais la *superstition* fanatique, née du trouble de l'imagination, renverse les empires.

That, in the years which passed between completing his contribution to the last ten volumes of the *Encyclopédie* (published in 1765) and his death in 1780, the Chevalier should ever have had any dealings with La Trappe seems incredible. If we are relatively ill-informed about the last part of his life, his will drawn up less than a year before his death, gives no sign of adherence to Catholicism, the religion to which officially he belonged; still less does it show any interest in the monastery of La Trappe.

[29] Archives de L'Orne H 956. I am also indebted to the same source for a reference to Abbé E. Sevestre (*L'Enquête gouvernementale et l'enquête ecclésiastique sur le clergé de Normandie et du Maine*, Book I, Paris, 1918, p. 18) who publishes a list which shows that Le Guelinel was already at Vaubadon in the year IX (1800-1).

Whether Dom Théodore ever really claimed that the Chevalier lived for a time at La Trappe or whether the writer of this letter imagined the whole business are questions which cannot be answered. Perhaps one may wonder whether the chief interest of the letter does not lie in the light which it throws on the reaction of Catholic opinion in France under the Empire to the political and religious upheaval of the previous twenty years.

APPENDIX

The following is a chronological list of such fragments of the Chevalier's correspondence as it has proved possible to trace:
1. From Jaucourt to:
   J. Tronchin, 24 April 1727. BPUG: Archives Tronchin, Vol. 210, 6-7 (see *BSHPF*, 1962, pp. 51-2, where part of the letter was first published by Professor Schwab; the complete text is given above, pp. 30-31).
   J. Tronchin, 3 Jan. 1732, Archives Tronchin, Vol. 211 (see *BSHPF*, 1962, p. 70, n. 33); the complete text is given above, pp. 34-35).
   Sir Hans Sloane (jointly with T. Tronchin), 20 Nov. 1733 (in Latin). British Museum, Sloane MS. 4053, f. 86.
   T. Tronchin, 27 July 1738. Archives Tronchin, Vol. 198, 37.
   T. Tronchin, 1 Sept. 1738. Archives Tronchin, Vol. 198, 38.
   T. Tronchin, 4 Nov. 1743. Archives Tronchin, Vol. 198, 39.
   Granet, March 1746. Archives Nationales, 86 AP 6, 328.
   De Prunelé, 15 Oct. 1746. Bibliothèque Victor Cousin, MS. Vol. V, No. 23.
   T. Tronchin, 1 Jan. 1747. Archives Tronchin, Vol. 198, 40 (published, with cuts, in H. Tronchin, *Un Médecin du XVIIIe siècle*, pp. 361-3).
   Jean Louis Labat, Baron de Grandcoeur, 2 Feb. 1758. Archives Micheli, Jussy (Best. 6919).
   Le Breton, 5 Feb. 1761. Minutier Central (see the catalogue of the exhibition 'Diderot et l'Encyclopédie', Paris, 1951, No. 199).
   J. H. S. Formey, 7 Feb. 1764 (published in *Souvenirs d'un Citoyen*, Vol. II, pp. 206-8).

Reybaz, 28 Feb. 1767. BPUG, Geneva, Ms. fr. 916, 3, 4.
Jean Romilly, 28 Feb. 1767. BPUG, Ms. fr. 916, 5.
Reybaz, 28 Oct. 1768. BPUG, Ms. fr. 916, 41 (most of the text of this letter is reproduced below, Chap. V, p. 110).

2. To Jaucourt from:
Voltaire, 6 Feb. 1737. Pierpont Morgan Library (Best. 1222a: *Studies*, Vol. IV, pp. 191-2).
Voltaire, 1 March 1737. Th.B. C1058 (Best. 1233a: *Studies*, Vol. X, pp. 445-6).
Voltaire, 29 March 1737. Th.B. C1059 (Best. 1244a: *Studies*, Vol. X, pp. 447-8).
Mme de Broglie, 3 July 1743. Arch. Nat. 86 AP 6, 327.
Isabelle de Jaucourt, 1 Nov. 1743. Arch. Nat. 86 AP 6, 333.
Isaac Lawson, 2 Nov. 1745 (in English). Bibl. V. Cousin, Ms. Vol. V, No. 25.
Mme de Broglie, 3 April 1746. Bibl. V. Cousin, Ms. Vol. II, No. 82.
Caze, 13 Oct. 1747. Bibl. V. Cousin, Ms. Vol. V, No. 24.
Voltaire, 15 Oct. 1749. BN, Nouv. acq. fr. 24013, ff. 320-1 (Best. 3488).
J. B. Sénac, 8 Oct. 1750 (in Latin). Bibl. V. Cousin, Ms. Vol. V, No. 48.
Diderot, 20 Sept. 1751. Bibl. V. Cousin, Ms. Vol. V, No. 16 (Roth, Vol. I, pp. 132-3).
Louis Pierre de Jaucourt, 15 July 1752. Arch. Nat. 86 AP 7 (1), 26.
Gilly, 15 July 1752. Arch. Nat. 86 AP 6, 192.
Gilly, 28 Aug. 1753. Bibl. V. Cousin, Ms. Vol. V, No. 18.
Saint-Florentin, 15 Nov. 1764. Arch. Nat. o¹406.
Saint-Floretin, 10 Jan. 1770. Arch. Nat. o¹412.

Two letters of T. Tronchin to Jaucourt (9 Feb. and 13 July 1739) are known to exist from extracts given in nineteenth-century sale catalogues (see H. Tronchin, *Un Médecin du XVIIIe siècle*, pp. 16-17, 195).
The *Catalogue général des Manuscrits des Bibliothèques Publiques en France* offers two false trails to the inquirer. The letter in the Bibliothèque de Nancy (Vol. XLII, p. 369) which is described as being by 'de Jaucourt' is signed 'François de Jaucourt'

and is dated 22 April 1814. The entry in the catalogue of the Bibliothèque de l'Institut, 'Correspondance de Pierre-Michel Hennin (1726-1807) avec . . . le chevalier de Jaucourt' (MS. 1227) refers to a series of letters written in 1766-7 on the affairs of Geneva, but though signed 'Ch. de Jaucourt', they have no connection with Louis de Jaucourt.

III Two Unsolved Problems[1]

In the last twenty-five years or so a great deal has been added to our knowledge of the *Encyclopédie*; many problems, however, still remain unsolved. The aim of this article is to examine two of them: the value of the accounts of the whole enterprise, as published by M. Louis-Philippe May in the *Revue de Synthèse* in 1938, and the extent of the censorship exercised by the principal publisher, Le Breton, over the last ten volumes of the text, a problem on which considerable light was thrown by that fascinating volume, *The Censoring of Diderot's Encyclopédie*, published by D. H. Gordon and N. L. Torrey in 1947.

I

The full title of M. May's exciting series of articles in the *Revue de Synthèse*, which gave the world its first glimpse into the accounts of the *Encyclopédie*, is 'Documents Nouveaux sur l'Encyclopédie. L'histoire et les sources de l'Encyclopédie, d'après le registre de délibérations et de comptes des éditeurs, et un mémoire inédit.' The more closely one examines these articles, the more one is struck by the odd fashion in which the documents mentioned in the title are presented. The first sentence of the introduction has the following footnote: 'Voir le très important *Mémoire pour André-François Lebreton contre le Sieur Jean Mills, gentilhomme anglais*, 20 pages in 4° (Arch. Nat. A D VIII 8, année 1745, pièce 67), mémoire inédit d'où nous avons tiré la plupart des précisions dont nous faisons état dans cette introduction.' But clearly this so-called *mémoire inédit* was far from

[1] First published in *French Studies*, 1963, pp 121-135.

unknown in 1938; it had been duly listed in Volume III (edited by A. Corda and published in 1894 by the Bibliothèque Nationale) of the *Catalogue des Factums et d'autres documents judiciaires antérieurs à 1790*. In any case it is difficult to see how this document can be described as *inédit* since we owe our very knowledge of its contents precisely to the fact that it is not *inédit*—that it was printed and published in 1745.

That is, of course, a minor detail. What interests us, when we consult M. May's articles, is the really exciting *inédit* which he has to offer his readers—the *Livre des Délibérations* and the accounts of the four publishers of the *Encyclopédie*. Even here, however, the reader is assailed by doubts. A study of this document does not bear out the editor's claim that thanks to it, 'nous n'ignorons plus rien des conditions matérielles dans lesquelles l'*Encyclopédie* a été enterprise et poursuivie'.[2]

What in fact does the text published from document U 1051 of the Archives Nationales offer us? Pages 16-30 of the printed text reproduce the section of the volume headed 'Livre des Délibérations des Sieurs Le Breton, David l'aisné, Durand et Briasson'; this begins with the 'Copie du Traité de Société, en datte du 18ᵉ octobre 1745' and ends with an entry dated '1ᵉʳ avril 1762'. Pages 31-109 are headed 'Livre de Dépense et Recette'; the expenses (pp. 31-98) begin in 1745 and the last entry under this head occurs in 1767. The section headed 'État de la Recette actuelle' (pp. 99-109) covers the period 1745-1768.

Anyone who tries to use these accounts to investigate particular aspects of the publication of the *Encyclopédie* cannot fail to discover very quickly that they are incomplete. For one thing, the last volumes of plates did not appear until 1772, although the 'Livre des Délibérations' breaks off in April 1762, while the expenses stop in 1767 and receipts in 1768.

The fact that this volume is incomplete is made quite explicit by a sentence which occurs in the middle of p. 109—the last page of M. May's transcript of the document: 'La suite de recette est au livre nouveau.' With this we must compare the statement,

[2] p. 11.

signed by Briasson, David and Le Breton on 11 March 1768 at the end of the section dealing with expenses (p. 98): here it is agreed among the partners that a transaction with the publisher, M. M. Rey, 'est dans le cas d'être placé icy et[3] reprise sur ce livre qui est de recette et dépense journalière et non dans un compte général tel qu'il sera question de le faire en finissant l'opération . . .' What we have here then is, not the complete accounts of the *Encyclopédie*, but a 'livre de recette et dépense journalière' which breaks off several years before the whole enterprise was at last brought to a successful conclusion in 1772. In the nature of things such an incomplete document cannot, as M. May claims, tell us all we want to know about the financial side of the *Encyclopédie*. 'Cette publication', as Mme Durry bluntly puts it,[4] 'fait connaître quelques fragments des registres de comptes de l'*Encyclopédie*'.

Until the missing accounts of the *Encyclopédie* turn up (if they ever do), we must make the best use we can of this invaluable document, but our gratitude to M. May would have been greater if we felt, on comparing his transcript with the original, that he and the printer had made a better job of turning the manuscript into print. Nowhere in the article in the *Revue de Synthèse* are we offered any sort of a description of the document in the Archives Nationales. In order to discover why the published text breaks off in this arbitrary manner the curious reader is compelled to pay a visit to the Rue des Francs Bourgeois. A few minutes' inspection of the manuscript solves the mystery. At one end (ff. 1-16r°) the reader finds the 'Livre des Délibérations', and, starting at the other end of the volume, he finds (ff. 1-79r°) the 'Livre de Depense & Recette', the receipts being written on the recto of ff. 3-12, and f. 12r° ending with the words 'La suite de recette est au livre nouveau'. In other words, the 'Livre des Délibérations' comes to an end on f. 16r° (1 April 1768) when it meets the 'Livre de Depense & Recette' which, starting from the other end of the volume, had reached f. 79r° (expenses down to 11 March 1768). Moreover, the cover of the volume, at the

---
[3] The MS has *en*.
[4] *Autographes de Mariemont*, Paris, 1955-9, 4 vols., Part I, p. 599, n.2.

end where the 'Livre de Depense & Recette' begins, bears the inscription: 'Encyclopedie Journal A'; 'which would lead one to suspect that there was originally at least a 'Journal B'.[5] Why these simple facts were not explained in the introduction to M. May's article is a mystery.

Again, it might have been as well to make it clear in the introduction to the printed version of this document that it is in Briasson's handwriting; not only is this point not made clear, but at times it is obscured by the insertion of a 'M.' in front of his name. No doubt it is with good reason that the section on receipts in these accounts should be printed after the section on expenses even though in the manuscript, as we have seen, the two are mixed in together; but what is quite inexplicable is that the last words on p. 109 at the end of the section on receipts (from 'La Compagnie assemblée' down to the signatures) are completely misplaced, since they are not to be found on f. 12r° from which the rest of the page comes, but in fact occur at the end of the expenses (f. 79r°). In addition the reader might well have been informed that the section in small type on p. 98, beginning '7 avril 1760', is written on two loose scraps of paper.

Some of the methods employed in publishing the text are open to criticism. It might well be argued that the editor would have made his own task lighter and produced a much more satisfactory text if he had reproduced the document exactly as it stands. For instance, it would have been as well, in dealing with the receipts and expenses of the enterprise, to reproduce the total given at the foot of each page of the manuscript and carried forward to the top of the next page. It would have been more logical to print the abbreviations in the accounts as they stand and not expand some and leave others, just as in the case of the spelling it would have been better not to have modernized it in places and reproduced its eccentricities in others.

What is more, a higher standard of accuracy in transcribing and printing could well have been achieved. While there are whole pages which are accurately reproduced and others which

[5] For further information about the missing 'Journal B' see Chap. V, pp. 142-153.

are marred only by trivial inaccuracies, a list of significant errors of transcription in the ninety or so pages of these articles would be too lengthy to be accepted by the editor of any learned journal appearing at the present day. All that there is room for here is a few specimens. First, from the 'Livre des Délibérations':

p. 17, paragraph II. For 'profits et pertes' read 'déspenses & pertes'.

p. 20. Before the entry for 11 Oct. 1746 insert 'Ce Jour Vingt neuf Juillet mil Sept cens quarante six la Compagnie a verifié l'état de depense jusq.a ce jour qui s'est monté a Neuf mille huit Cens Cinquante quatre livres douze solz'.

p. 22. After the words '16 février 1748' insert 'Ce jour la Compagnie a verifié l'état de depense montant a trente neuf mille trois cents quatre vignt cinq livres', and begin the next paragraph with 'Plus' instead of 'Ce jour'. For 'les autres bénéfices' read 'ses autres benefices'.

p. 25 (two lines from the foot). For 'aux libraires' read 'aux Libraires de Londres'.

p. 26, first new paragraph. For 'partagés et supposés' read 'partagé et supporté'.

p. 28, paragraph II. For 'du dernier volume du *Discours de l'Encyclopédie*' read 'du dernier Vol^e. de Discours de l'Encyclopédie'.

The much longer section of the manuscript—the 'Livre de Depense & Recette'—naturally furnishes many more errors: for instance, items 284, 285 and 286 of the expenses are printed twice over, and items 279, 280 and 281 omitted. The latter read:

279. payé a M. Goussiere		12
fiacres remboursés a Mrs Diderot & David		2. 14.
280. payé a M. Landois p^r solde ce 5e aoust		354
281. fourni a M. Diderot le 7 d		15

In addition, there are all manner of curious transcriptions dotted over these pages of M. May's articles:

539. For 'diner chez le Stres' read 'diner chez le Thres [orier]' (cf. No. 542).

935. For 'Dalembert' read 'D'aubenton'. (This name is written above the line in place of 'De Buffon' which is erased).

987. Add 'H' after 'pour la lettre'. Delete 'du 8 mars' which is not in the manuscript. (In any case the correct date would have been 21 July.)
1136. For 'jar' read 'sur divers a Bisault & autres'.
1232. For 'treille' read 'traille'.
1340. For 'exemplaires' read 'pl.'.
1544. For 'le tome de fait' read 'le terms de sa r[en]te' (cf. No. 1572.
1557. For 'un voyage des caisses' read 'un Voyage a Versailles'.

There are similar errors and omissions in the transcription of the part of the volume dealing with receipts, e.g.:

p. 99. After 'Approuvé . . . donnés par Briasson' add 'lors des payements faits par les associéz pour les Contributions expliquées cydessus'.

p. 106. (20 Aug. 1751). The sum in cash paid in by Le Breton was not 863 1, but 1,863, and the total came to 2,252 1. 10s. Delete the next line, 'Autres par M. David'.

p. 108 (6 Aug. 1763). For 'rendu à M. l'abbé de Gua' read 'recu du S^r. abbé De Gua'.

A detailed study of M. May's articles thus leads one to two disagreeable conclusions: first, that they are very far from telling us all that we should like to know about the accounts of the *Encyclopédie*; and second, that any serious student of the work would do well to study the document unearthed by M. May either by going to the Archives Nationales or by means of a photostat, or both.

II

Unquestionably the most interesting work on the *Encyclopédie* which has so far appeared in the present century is Gordon and Torrey's *The Censoring of Diderot's Encyclopédie*. Although it had long been known that the last ten volumes of the *Encyclopédie* had been censored by Le Breton, until the appearance of this book in 1947 there was no means of telling what had been the nature of the cuts imposed by this self-appointed censor.

Working on an extra volume in a set of the *Encyclopédie*

which made its way from the Soviet Union to the United States in the 1930s, they discovered 318 pages of articles, rather less than 300 of which concern the last ten volumes of the work. These proofs contain a considerable number of alterations made by the publisher; indeed, the authors assure us, 'it is probable . . . that they give us the greater part of the material censored by Le Breton'. If in the past, they argue, the changes which he made had been thought to be much more drastic, that is simply because, in his blind fury at what he considered to be an unforgivable act, Diderot greatly exaggerated the amount of damage done to the work by Le Breton. Indeed, they maintain, far from being the stupid monster portrayed by Diderot in his rage at discovering what he had been up to, Le Breton was a sensible fellow who avoided a lot of unnecessary trouble with the authorities when the last ten volumes of the work appeared in 1765, and in fact showed himself a highly intelligent and competent censor.

The interpretation which Messrs. Gordon and Torrey place on the documents which they brought to light, seems to have been generally accepted by reviewers when their book appeared. Le Breton, whom Diderot in his anger had threatened with the contempt and loathing of all posterity, was now praised for his intelligence and foresight by scholars drawn from a variety of countries. The late Daniel Mornet, for instance, wrote in the *Revue d'histoire littéraire*:

Que serait-il advenu, en 1766, si Le Breton avait publié ce qu'il n'a pas voulu publier? Sans doute lui, Le Breton, et Diderot auraient été arrêtés et embastillés. Sans doute l'*Encyclopédie*, au lieu de se distribuer en fait librement, aurait été brûlée, la distribution empêchée. On peut croire que Le Breton a fait la part du feu et servi la diffusion du dictionnaire et son influence.[6]

We are thus invited to conclude that, when, in 1764, Diderot discovered Le Breton's dirty work, he was wrong to get so annoyed, and that he ought rather to have been grateful to his publisher for his prudent censoring of these volumes.

[6] 1948, p. 360.

Such an interpretation of the known facts may perhaps be valid, and yet one is left with all sorts of doubts as to whether it really coincides with these all too rare facts or even whether it can be supported by plain logic. To begin with, one cannot help wondering why neither the authors of *The Censoring of Diderot's Encyclopédie* nor reviewers see anything reprehensible in Le Breton's behaviour. After all, what modern writer or editor would not share Diderot's fury at seeing his own articles and those of his collaborators mangled by a stupid publisher and printer? Furthermore, given the constantly shifting attitudes of government, Parlement and Church in eighteenth-century France, it is not easy to guess what would have happened if the last ten volumes of the *Encyclopédie* had appeared without being expurgated by Le Breton. There is also a point which is apt to be forgotten—that Le Breton, for all his caution, landed himself in the Bastille for a week in April 1766 through his imprudence in pushing ahead with the distribution of the last ten volumes.

Above all, the theory that, despite the fuss made by Diderot, the cuts made by Le Breton were more or less insignificant, clashes with the argument—advanced almost in the same breath—that Le Breton really did Diderot a good turn by pruning his text. How can Le Breton deserve the praise lavished upon him for his prudence in preventing the last ten volumes of the text of the *Encyclopédie* being seized and the editor and chief contributors hurried off to the Bastille, if the total number of changes which he made were as insignificant as those revealed on pp. 68-107 of Gordon and Torrey?

Though the interpretation of the available facts put forward by the authors is certainly one which cannot be dismissed as untenable, in the last resort the theory that the rediscovered proofs give us the greater part of the articles tampered with by Le Breton rests on the fragile foundation of the words 'it is probable that'. According to their book[7] Messrs. Gordon and Torrey had at their disposal 284 pages of proofs of the last ten volumes of the *Encyclopédie*—i.e. 284 pages out of the 9,000 odd pages of these volumes, or approximately 3 per cent. While no

[7] p. 35.

one could claim that it is impossible that these 284 pages contain all or nearly all the alterations made by Le Breton, at the present moment we have absolutely no evidence to enable us to say what he did to getting on for 9,000 pages of these last ten volumes.

Can it be that Messrs Gordon and Torrey were looking at the whole problem through the wrong end of the telescope? Supposing we start from a different hypothesis—that these 284 pages were merely specimens of Le Breton's handiwork. Far from appearing insignificant, these alterations involve—in the space of less than 300 pages—the complete suppression of several fairly important articles (SECTES DU CHRISTIANISME; THÉOLOGIE SCHOLASTIQUE; THÉOLOGIE, *Réflexions sur la*, by Jaucourt and Morellet; and Jaucourt's TOLÉRANCE) and, leaving aside other less important changes, the removal of some very bold passages in the articles PHILOSOPHIE PYRRHONIENNE (with its praise of Bayle) and SARRASINS. If Le Breton treated the remainder of the 9,000 or so pages in anything like the same sort of fashion, we should begin to understand the rage and despair of Diderot.

We have in fact clear evidence, which is not in the least glossed over by the authors of this fascinating book, that their collection of proofs is not complete. In the letter which Diderot wrote to Le Breton in November 1764, after he had discovered what had been happening to the proofs of the *Encyclopédie*, he states: 'Vous fîtes main basse sur l'article INTENDANT, et sur quelques autres dont j'ai les épreuves.'[8] Diderot is presumably here referring to the unsigned part of the article INTENDANS & COMMISSAIRES DÉPARTIS which follows on the contribution of Boucher d'Argis; this particular article is not to be found among the collection of proofs studied by Messrs Gordon and Torrey.

According to them the principal victims of Le Breton's censoring zeal were, first, Diderot and then Jaucourt, his chief collaborator for the last ten volumes; in addition an article by Morellet was suppressed, and more or less insignificant changes made to articles by other contributors. Yet in this same letter to Le Breton, written at a moment when Diderot, still deeply involved in the

---

[8] *Corr. litt.*, Vol. IX, p. 213 (Roth, Vol. IV, p. 305).

Encyclopédie, must have had a pretty clear notion of what had gone into the last ten volumes, he twice warns him of the bitter reproaches which he must expect from a whole host of contributors: he speaks of the 'massacre' of 'le travail de vingt honnêtes gens' and mentions other contributors besides himself and Jaucourt—'Saint-Lambert, Turgot, d'Holbach . . . et autres' —as being bound to protest against the mutilation of their articles. A few pages later he again stresses the number of contributors affected: 'On serait persuadé que votre cognée ne serait tombée que sur moi, que cela suffirait pour vous nuire infiniment; mais, Dieu merci! elle n'a épargné personne.'[9] What made Diderot so furious was the thought that Le Breton had succeeded in suppressing the unorthodox ideas which he and some of the other contributors had worked into these ten volumes, for in his eyes these constituted the chief originality of the whole work. In his letter he is willing to sacrifice all the purely informative side of his encyclopaedia, including even his own articles on technology, to the passages in which he and other contributors had expressed their true thoughts on the struggle of ideas— religious, philosophical and political—which was raging in France in the 1750s and 1760s:

> Vous avez oublié que ce n'est pas aux choses courantes, sensées et communes que vous deviez vos premiers succès, qu'il n'y a peut-être pas deux hommes dans le monde qui se soient donné la peine de lire une ligne d'histoire, de géographie, de mathématiques et même d'arts, et que ce que l'on a recherché et ce qu'on y recherchera, c'est la philosophie ferme et hardie de quelques-uns de vos travailleurs. Vous l'avez châtrée, dépecée, mutilée, mise en lambeaux, sans jugement, sans ménagement et sans goût. Vous nous avez rendus insipides et plats. Vous avez banni de votre livre ce qui en a fait, ce qui en aurait fait encore l'attrait, le piquant, l'intéressant et la nouveauté.[10]

At the time Grimm too had received from Diderot the impression that the cuts imposed by Le Breton had been on a really large

---

[9] *Corr. litt.*, Vol. IX, pp. 210, 213 (Roth, Vol. IV, pp. 301, 304).
[10] *Corr. litt.*, Vol. IX, p. 212 (Roth, Vol. IV, pp. 303).

scale, since they affected, he declares, 'le plus grand nombre des meilleurs articles.'[11]

It is unfortunately difficult to interpret a piece of evidence bearing on this question which has come to light since the publication of the book under discussion. In his *Inventaire du Fonds Vandeul et inédits de Diderot*[12] Professor Dieckmann drew attention to the existence of a copy of the *Avertissement* to Volume VIII of the *Encyclopédie* which contains the unpublished footnote: [13]

Ceci regarde des corrections et suppressions qu'un des imprimeurs s'est avisé de faire à plusieurs articles après la révision des épreuves à l'insu des Editeurs et par une crainte pusillanime des Ennemis de l'Encyclopédie.

Professor Dieckmann points out that this note may have been in the original manuscript; but we simply do not know. It seems on the whole improbable, in view of Diderot's promise to the publishers not to reveal the secret of Le Breton's misdeeds. Above all, what does 'plusieurs articles' mean? Does this piece of evidence—whether or not the note was written by Diderot, it certainly emanates from his circle—support the line taken by Gordon and Torrey? No doubt it does, if *plusieurs* is understood in the modern sense of an indeterminate but fairly restricted number. On the other hand, the 1762 edition of the Dictionary of the Academy which is roughly contemporary with the *Encyclopédie*, modifies only slightly the older definition—'Beaucoup, quantité, grand nombre'—given in the 1694 edition when it defines *plusieurs* as 'beaucoup, nombre considérable, par rapport à un nombre plus grand'. What with the double uncertainty surrounding the source of this footnote and the meaning of the key-word in it, it is difficult to draw any clear conclusions from this new piece of evidence.

No doubt, if Messrs Gordon and Torrey are correct in their

---

[11] *Corr. litt.*, Vol. IX, p. 208.
[12] Geneva-Lille, 1951, p. 58. See BN, Nouvelles acquisitions françaises 13753, f. 175 verso.
[13] It refers to the following words in the text: ' . . . nous consentons que tous les défauts de cette édition nous soient imputez sans reserve'.

conclusion that this extra volume of a set of the *Encyclopédie* contains all or virtually all of the changes made by Le Breton, then Diderot was wrong to kick up such a fuss. But can one ignore all the evidence that he was quite shattered by his discovery of what Le Breton had been up to? According to Grimm, when Diderot found out the truth in November 1764, 'cette découverte le mit dans un état de frénésie et de désespoir que je n'oublierai jamais'.[14] In her *Mémoires sur Diderot* Mme de Vandeul describes how, down to the very end of his life, her father never got over this discovery:

> Mon père pensa en tomber malade; il cria, s'emporta, il voulait abandonner l'ouvrage; mais le temps, la bêtise, les ridicules excuses de ce libraire, qui craignait la Bastille plus que la foudre, parvinrent à le calmer, mais non à le consoler. Jamais je ne l'ai entendu parler froidement à ce sujet: il était convaincu que le public savait comme lui ce qui manquait à chaque article, et l'impossibilité de réparer ce dommage lui donnait encore de l'humeur vingt ans après.[15]

Another person who was close to Diderot in the last part of his life, Naigeon, speaks of 'ce cruel abus de confiance' and goes on:

> Il en témoigna à Le Breton, dans les termes les plus énergiques, toute son indignation; il ne se rappeloit jamais cette circonstance, une des plus critiques de sa vie, sans frémir des excès auxquels un ressentiment, d'ailleurs très-juste, peut quelquefois porter l'homme le plus honnête, et du caractère le plus doux.[16]

Then we have, of course, Diderot's own direct reactions as reflected in his letters of this period. In the long letter of reproaches which he wrote to Le Breton in November 1764, he speaks of 'une atrocité dont il n'y a pas d'exemple depuis l'origine de la librairie'. 'En effet', he goes on, 'a-t-on jamais ouï parler de dix volumes in-folio clandestinement mutilés, tronqués, hachés,

---

[14] *Corr. litt.*, Vol. IX, p. 208.
[15] AT, Vol. I, p. XLV.
[16] Diderot, *Oeuvres*, ed. J. A. Naigeon, Paris, 1798, 15 vols., Vol. I, p. xxvii n. Naigeon does not mention this episode in his *Mémoires historiques et philosophiques sur la vie et les ouvrages de D. Diderot*, published posthumously in 1821.

déshonorés par un imprimeur?'[17] There is an unfortunate gap in his letters to Sophie Volland between November 1762 and February 1765, so that we cannot learn from this source what were his immediate reactions to his discovery of Le Breton's dirty work in November 1764. But nine months after the event his indignation boils over again in a letter to his mistress:

> L'homme le plus intéressé au succès de l'enterprise nous fait lui seul plus de mal que nous n'en avons souffert des efforts de tous nos ennemis réunis; n'est-ce pas une aventure à rendre fou? Il s'est complu pendant quatre ans de suite dans son infamie. Il se levoit pendant la nuit pour mettre le feu à ses magasins; et cela lui paroissoit plaisant.[18]

Le Breton had by no means heard the last of the affair. In a letter of March 1769 which has only recently come to light,[19] Diderot hurled fresh reproaches at his publisher:

> Vous appellez ma première lettre un libelle. Je ne scais si c'en est un : mais ce que je n'ignore pas et ce que votre conscience doit vous dire, c'est que personne depuis qu'on imprime, n'ayant de sa propre autorité, aussi injustement, aussi sourdement, aussi cruellement lesé un auteur que je l'ai eté par vous, il n'y a sorte de discours, sorte de procedé que je ne pusse avoir, tenir, sans que vous fussiez en droit de vous en plaindre. J'étois fort le maître de quitter l'entreprise; en ce cas j'étois autorisé, obligé d'en dire publiquement le motif. Je vous ruinois; je vous deshonorois. Vos associés le sentoient bien. Je n'en ai rien fait. Je me suis tu. J'ai souffert la plus cruelle peine que j'aye ressenti de ma vie; et j'ai achevé votre ouvrage; et j'ai eu la condescendance d'aller l'achever chez vous. Pour bien appretier cette action, il faut quitter la place d'imprimeur, et se mettre a celle d'un auteur estropié, demembré, mutilé, et cela pendant deux ou trois ans, et la durée de sept volumes in folio.[20]

Later in the same year a letter to an unknown correspondent on his relations with Le Breton shows that he still had the incident very much on his mind:

---

[17] *Corr. litt.*, Vol. IX, p. 211 (Roth, Vol. IV, p. 302).
[18] Roth, Vol. V, p. 92.
[19] *Autographes de Mariemont*, Part I, pp. 593-8 (Roth, Vol. IX, pp. 28-35).
[20] *Autographes de Mariemont*, Part I, p. 593 (Roth, Vol. IX, pp. 28-29).

Ma conduite ne s'est jamais démentie, et j'ai toujours rendu à Mr. Le Breton le bien pour le mal.
Mr. Le Breton massacra clandestinement dix volumes in-fol. Indignité qui n'eut et n'aura jamais d'exemple. Un mot indiscret de ma part le ruinoit.
Je me suis tû.[21]

During his stay at the court of Catherine the Great, in 1773-4, Diderot put before the Empress a plan for a new edition of the *Encyclopédie*; in recounting the troubles which the work had brought on him, he does not fail to mention Le Breton: '. . . Pour comble de disgrâce, un infâme imprimeur, qui dépeçait mon ouvrage à mon insu pendant la nuit, a mutilé dix volumes et brûlé les manuscrits qu'il ne jugeait pas à propos d'employer.'[22]

Indeed, so great was Diderot's indignation at his treatment by Le Breton that in 1770 he rashly told Luneau de Boisjermain, then involved in lawsuits against *libraires* in general and the publishers of the *Encyclopédie* in particular, what had been done to the last volumes of the *Encyclopédie*. It is true that he at once repented of this step and wrote to Luneau to ask him not to make use of this information:

J'ai une bien autre grace à vous demander, que vous ne me refuserez certainement pas; c'est de ne point faire mention dans vos Mémoires DES SEPT DERNIERS VOLUMES DE L'ENCYCLOPEDIE CHARPENTÉS. Ce fait ne peut être sçu que par moi. Il est étranger à votre affaire. Je puis encore avoir des démêlés d'intérêt avec les associés. Cela pourroit les irriter & m'embarrasser. Ainsi j'attends de vous cette marque d'estime que je sçaurai bien vous rendre dans l'occasion.

We only know of this letter because it was printed by Luneau de Boisjermain in one of the innumerable publications to which his lawsuit against the publishers of the *Encyclopédie* gave rise.[23]

---

[21] Roth, Vol. IX, p. 242.
[22] *Memoires pour Catherine II*, ed. P. Vernière, Paris, 1966, p. 262.
[23] *Lettre de M. Luneau de Boisjermain à M. Diderot et Réponses à la Lettre adressée aux Srs Briasson & Le Breton par M. Diderot* (1 December 1771), p. 3. (See Roth, Vol. X, p. 20.)

Grimm's claim in the *Correspondence Littéraire* of 1 January 1771 that the whole affair was 'absolument ignoré du public'[24] could not have been made less than twelve months later since, in addition to publishing this letter of Diderot, Luneau proceeded to give to the world his version of what the latter had so indiscreetly told him:

Je n'ai point parlé dans mon Mémoire du fait que vous vouliez ensevelir dans l'oubli. Si le sieur Le Breton a eu *l'indignité de charpenter,* c'est-à-dire d'elaguer, raccourcir & supprimer tout-à-fait les articles qui étoient de votre composition dans les volumes VIII, IX, X, XI, XII, XIII & XIV de l'Encyclopédie, ce n'est point par moi que l'on a sçu comment vous vous en êtes apperçu. Vous me dîtes qu'on vous pria de travailler aux explications des planches. *'Vous demandâtes bonnement les volumes de discours où se trouvoient les articles dont ces planches devoient dépendre. Le Breton sentit que, s'il vous les fournissoit, il vous feroit toucher au doigt les mutilations qu'avoient souffert vos productions. Il craignit que vous ne renonçassiez tout-à-fait à cet ouvrage, si vous veniez à vous appercevoir de l'outrage qu'on vous avoit fait. Il éloigna, il éloigna tant qu'il put la remise des volumes charpentés.'* Le temps plus fort que son intérêt & le vôtre, augmenta son embarras. Les volumes charpentés furent enfin portés chez vous. Vous vîtes de *vos propres yeux* l'opération douloureuse qu'on avoit faite à vos chef-d'œuvres. Un silence morne s'empara de vous; vous recueillîtes vos esprits; vous jurâtes de ne plus travailler au grand œuvre. A la vérité, vous avez oublié, depuis, ce serment; mais vous jurâtes de ne plus parler à cet Imprimeur. Tout le monde sçait que vous avez manqué à cette autre promesse. Je n'ai point contribué à divulguer ce mystère. Il a sans doute percé tout seul; car je ne puis croire que ni vous ni les Libraires vous ayez contribué à le pousser dans le monde, quoiqu'on prétende qu'un secret a bien de la peine à se taire auprès d'eux & de vous.[25]

---

[24] Vol. IX, p. 206.
[25] *Lettre,* p. 3 (Roth, Vol. X, pp. 1-2). The same work contains (pp. 10, 12, 19, 20) other allusions to Le Breton's handiwork as well as (p. 16) the more detailed statement: 'Vous vous êtes plaint à tous les Gens de Lettres, qu'il avoit châtré tous les articles qui étoient de vous. Vous avez été si fâché de ne les pas trouver dans l'Encyclopédie que vous ne vouliez plus le voir'. (It will be noticed that Luneau aways speaks as if only Diderot's articles had been censored. For further details concerning his revelations of Le Breton's activities see Chap. V, pp. 128-131.)

If we leave aside for a moment the question of the extent of Le Breton's operations on the last volumes of the *Encyclopédie*, we can see how all these varied and at times contradictory statements—all of which come directly or indirectly from Diderot alone—pose all manner of problems which are not altogether solved by the account given by Gordon and Torrey of what happened to the volumes which appeared after the *Arrêt du Conseil* of March 1759. Their version of how Diderot came to make his discovery is by no means wholly convincing:

The years 1762-1764 marked the height of his enthusiasm. The ten final volumes of text were coming steadily from the presses. He reviewed each page and wrote his customary 'correct and print' at the bottom of each group of page proofs, strongly suspecting, but not knowing for certain, that Le Breton and his compositor were busy with their secret censoring. At one point, however, Diderot needed the printed sheets in the preparation of the volume of plates and Le Breton let him have them. The chances were small that the philosopher would notice anything amiss. But Diderot had a sentimental attachment for his article on the Saracens, of which, five years earlier, he had inserted extensive paragraphs into a letter to Sophie Volland. His discovery of Le Breton's deletions wounded him to the quick. He looked at other spots where he remembered having been unusually bold and found additional evidence of the trick that had been played upon him.[26]

This account of the matter scarcely squares with Grimm's version (quoted at length by the authors) of what happened. He speaks of Diderot finding out the truth when he consulted 'un des grands articles de philosophie de la lettre S', but nowhere mentions specifically the article SARRASINS.[27] Far from suggesting that Diderot had any previous suspicions of what Le Breton was up to, Grimm gives the impression that Diderot discovered the truth all of a sudden. On the other hand there is some evidence that he already had his suspicions, particularly the marginal note—heavily erased by Le Breton—to the proof of the article

[26] pp. 22-3.
[27] Elsewhere in the book the authors take it for granted that this is the article in question, but without offering the slightest proof.

MENACE (Vol. X), though we do not, of course, know at what precise date this note was written.

When he spoke in general terms of Le Breton's actions, Diderot, as we have seen, used the round figure of 'dix volumes' having been thus affected; but on two occasions he is more precise in referring to 'sept volumes'. In his letter to Le Breton of 4 March 1769 he speaks of the censorship as having gone on 'pendant deux ou trois ans, et la durée de sept volumes in folio'. Here he fails to specify *which* seven volumes were treated in this way; but in his letter of 1770 to Luneau de Boisjermain he is more precise when he speaks of the 'sept derniers volumes'—i.e. Vols. XI-XVII. On the other hand, Luneau de Boisjermain interpreted this as meaning that the volumes affected were VIII to XIV (down to SEMYDA). In the postscript to his letter of November 1764 to Le Breton[28] Diderot speaks as if, even at that late date, the setting up of the type of the last volumes of the text of the *Encyclopédie* were not complete, since he writes: '. . . Je vais rendre la parole à ceux à qui j'avais demandé et qui m'avaient promis des secours, et restituer à d'autres les articles qu'ils m'avaient déjà fournis, et que je ne veux pas livrer à votre despotisme.'[29] We can only infer from this that Le Breton had not yet received the complete manuscript of the work. Indeed the composition of the text was still not completed nine months later, in August 1765. On 25 July Diderot wrote to Sophie Volland: 'Il ne nous reste plus que quatorze cahiers à imprimer: c'est l'ouvrage de huit ou dix jours'; but on 18 August the work was still not finished. 'Notre ouvrage seroit fini', he wrote to Sophie on that date, 'sans une nouvelle bêtise de l'imprimeur qui avoit oublié dans un coin une portion du manuscrit. J'en ai, je crois, pour le reste de la semaine.'[30]

However, in actual practice the last three volumes (from SEN to ZZUÉNÉ) do not seem to have escaped Le Breton's censorship, if we may judge from the proofs brought to light by Gordon and

---

[28] The postscript is omitted by Gordon & Torrey in their translation of the relevant passage from Grimm. pp. 28-34.
[29] *Corr. litt.*. Vol. IX, p. 214 (Roth, Vol. IV, p. 306).
[30] Roth, Vol. V, pp. 64, 91.

Torrey. If these reveal only three minor cuts for Volume XVII of the *Encyclopédie*, we know that there were substantial cuts in Volume XVI (TEANUM—VÉNERIE), while Volume XV (SEN—TCHUPRIKI) contains bitter marginal notes by Diderot at the head of his own article, SOCRATIQUE, PHILOSOPHIE, and of Jaucourt's article, SOUVERAINETÉ, protesting against the censorship which was being exercised on these articles.[31] On the other hand, as Gordon and Torrey point out,[32] in his angry letter of November 1764 Diderot had told Le Breton that he did not care now if what remained of the work was censored too: 'Au demeurant, disposez du peu qui vous reste à exécuter comme il vous plaira: cela m'est de la dernière indifférence.'[33] In that case it is odd that Luneau de Boisjermain should make Diderot speak as if Vols. XV, XVI and XVII had not been censored. Luneau de Boisjermain may have interpreted 'les sept derniers volumes' wrongly, but if Diderot meant Vols. XI-XVII, the fact remains that the article INTENDANTS is in Vol. VIII, and, as we have seen, he complained to Le Breton about the way in which it had been mangled. The known facts cannot well be interpreted in quite so neat a fashion as that suggested by Gordon and Torrey.

Another puzzle is the fact that, whereas, assuming that Le Breton had made larger cuts than those suggested by Gordon and Torrey, one might expect to find abundant traces of these last-minute changes in such matters as faulty pagination and an abnormally small number of lines on a page, in practice these are difficult to find. In dealing with the cuts made in the pages of proofs which they were studying, the authors several times draw attention to minor technical points of this kind; but an examination of all the last ten volumes of the work does not add much to the details which they mention. One finds only one example of faulty pagination which goes beyond the mere wrong numbering of pages. In Vol. XI, in the middle of the article PAPE, while the text continues quite smoothly, the pages follow the order 835, 836, 829, 830, 832, etc. No comment

---

[31] Gordon & Torrey, pp. 83-4.
[32] p. 63.
[33] *Corr. litt.*, Vol. IX, p. 211 (Roth, Vol. IV, p. 302).

TWO UNSOLVED PROBLEMS

is offered on this point by Gordon and Torrey, but it is puzzling. At moments, it must be confessed, the absence of any serious disorder in the set-up of the last ten volumes weighs heavily against the hypothesis that the cuts made by Le Breton which are actually known to us could be merely specimens of his handiwork; but we simply do not know the answer to this problem.

One last point which this excellent work does not face up to is this: while we now know what sort of cuts Le Breton was capable of making in the work of the contributors to the *Encyclopédie*, the fact remains that, whether the extent of his cuts was large or small, what Diderot called the 'petit comité gothique' undoubtedly let pass phrases, sentences, paragraphs and even whole articles at least as dangerously subversive as those we now definitely know to have been removed. One could give dozens of examples from the volumes covering the letters H to Z, but the fact is too well known to require such a list. It is certainly odd and difficult to account for. Perhaps Le Breton was not, after all, such an efficient censor as has lately been made out.

No doubt one should not look a gift horse in the mouth; yet our gratitude for the book should not blind us to the fact that *The Censoring of Diderot's Encyclopédie* does not by any means solve the problem of the last ten volumes of the *Encyclopédie* as neatly and as completely as the authors and reviewers of the book seem to have imagined.

IV Mme Geoffrin and the *Encyclopédie*[1]

Mme Geoffrin has apparently acquired an undisputed place in the history of the *Encyclopédie*. In the exhibition held at the Bibliothèque Nationale in 1932, she was represented by four items in the section 'Les Protecteurs. Les Salons Encyclopédistes'.[2] In the exhibition held at the same place in 1951, she figured even more prominently. She comes first, ahead even of Mme de Pompadour and Malesherbes, in the section of the catalogue entitled 'Défenseurs et Adversaires'; no fewer than five portraits are listed among the twelve items under her name.[3] Ten years later, in May 1961, appeared a number of *La Documentation Photographique* devoted to the *Encyclopédie*. If a portrait of Mme Geoffrin is not to be found among the illustrations, she appears prominently in the introduction. Indeed in the table of those associated with the work she figures, in a rectangular box all on her own, among the very 'top people':

> MADAME GEOFFRIN
> *Appui financier*

Although apparently a government publication, *La Documentation Photographique* is produced to appeal to a fairly wide

---

[1] First published in the *Modern Language Review*, 1963, pp. 219-222.
[2] *L'Encyclopédie et les Encyclopédistes, Exposition organisée par le Centre International de Synthèse* (Bibliothèque Nationale, 1932), nos. 246-9.
[3] Nos. 345-54.

audience and its views on the role of Mme Geoffrin as patron of the *Encyclopédie* are of no great concern to students of the work. What is more impressive is the fact that the catalogue of the 1951 exhibition at the Bibliothèque Nationale, a publication which has been of immense help to scholars, should reproduce in its commentary on Nattier's portrait of the youthful Mme Geoffrin,[4] a sentence from Le Gras's *Diderot et l'Encyclopédie*:[5] 'Mme de la Ferté-Imbault, fille de Mme Geoffrin, reprochait à sa mère d'avoir dépensé plus de cent mille écus pour l'*Encyclopédie*.' If we turn to Le Gras, we find these words in a footnote to a sentence in the text which reads: 'D'autres enfin ouvrent leur bourse. C'est ainsi que la généreuse Mme Geoffrin avancera des sommes importantes et renouvellera ces avances chaque fois que l'*Encyclopédie* se trouvera en mauvaise posture financière, c'est à-dire fort souvent.'

The curious reader will find no trace of Mme Geoffrin's financial assistance to the *Encyclopédie* in that part of its accounts which M. Louis-Philippe May brought to light in 1938. On the other hand, if he looks up the topic in the standard work on Mme Geoffrin, the Marquis de Ségur's *Le Royaume de la Rue Saint-Honoré, Madame Geoffrin et sa fille*,[6] he will find a colourful paragraph describing how she came to the rescue of Diderot in the crisis which overtook the *Encyclopédie* in March 1759:

> Le plus grand service qu'elle lui ait rendu remonte au jour où un arrêt du Conseil du Roi révoqua le privilège de l'Encyclopédie. La publication, à moitié achevée, en reçut un coup terrible. Plusieurs des plus célèbres rédacteurs, d'Alembert entre autres, prirent peur, et firent mine de se retirer de l'affaire; et, bien que l'intervention de M. de Malesherbes eût en partie raccommodé les choses, la timidité de l'imprimeur, et le manque des fonds nécessaires pour relever son courage, faillirent amener l'avortement de cette vaste entreprise. Pour Diderot, c'était la ruine complète, la ruine de ses biens comme de ses espérances. Ce fut madame Geoffrin qui le sauva. Elle s'engagea auprès de l'éditeur pour une somme considérable, que madame de la Ferté-Imbault, en revoy-

---
[4] No. 345.
[5] Amiens, 1928, p. 45.
[6] Paris, 1897, pp. 318-19.

ant plus tard les comptes de sa mère, n'évaluait pas à moins de cent mille écus; et cette intervention généreuse, dont elle voulut garder l'anonyme, permit la continuation de l'ouvrage.

It will be noticed that neither Legras nor, earlier, Ségur offered any source for this story. What is more, neither the fragments of the accounts of the *Encyclopédie* which have come down to us nor the information about the finances of the whole undertaking brought to light by the campaign carried on against Le Breton and his partners by Luneau de Boisjermain between 1769 and 1778 gives one the impression that the publishers were on the verge of ruin in 1759. What was threatened was, not their whole financial position, but their profits. Since, if true, the story of Mme Geoffrin's intervention is obviously important, I was driven some years ago to test its truth by putting in several days' work at the Minutier Central. If Mme Geoffrin had furnished Le Breton and his partners with such substantial sums of money, then the transaction must have been recorded by the *notaire* whom one or the other normally employed in financial and legal matters.

Without knowing in which *étude* to begin one's search, one cannot get anywhere at the Minutier Central; but on my arrival Mme Jurgens promptly produced for me two most promising documents. The first concerned the joint annuity of 1,200 *livres* which Mme Geoffrin bought for the benefit of Abbé Morellet;[7] the second was the inventory of Le Breton's possessions and papers drawn up after his death in 1779.[8] Yet another trail had been suggested by the catalogue of the exhibition 'Diderot et l'Encyclopédie'; among its other riches, this brought into the light of day the legal document which showed that, as Grimm had maintained, the Chevalier de Jaucourt did sell a house to the publisher, Le Breton.[9] With the papers of these three *études*— XXVII, C and CXVII—to explore, the next step was to turn over

---

[7] Cf. Morellet, *Mémoires*, Paris 1821, 2 vols., Vol. 1, p. 250. (Minutier Central, CXVII, 856—'Constitution â Morellet et à Mme Geoffrin'.)

[8] Minutier Central, XXVII, 406 (11 October 1779).

[9] No. 199 (*Étude* C at the Minutier Central).

the pages of the heavy ledgers, known as *répertoires*, in which the notarial documents are listed. Several days' work covering 1759 and the years before and after that date produced a number of documents concerning both Le Breton and Mme Geoffrin, but nothing with the slightest bearing on the financial assistance which Mme Geoffrin is alleged to have given to the *Encyclopédie*. Researches in the Minutier Central are only too apt to lead to disappointment. Even if each individual always kept to the same *notaire*, the papers of that particular étude may have gaps.[10] In practice, most people employed the services of more than one *notaire*, and documents concerning them could in theory be found in the papers of well over a hundred different *études*. Thus, while it is all very well if one is fortunate enough to light upon a document which does provide some positive information, failure to discover the kind of document which was being sought on this occasion proved precisely nothing. Eventually the search was called off.

The sad thing is that, looking back, one feels it ought never to have been begun. It is essential for any student of the *Encyclopédie* to peruse with the utmost care the pages of Grimm's *Correspondance littéraire*, since during the years in which Diderot was most actively engaged on the work, Grimm was probably his closest friend; and many interesting things he has to tell us in the *Correspondance littéraire* about the inside story of the whole enterprise. But not one word has he to say about Mme Geoffrin's rescue operation.

It is, however, in this very work that the passage on which the whole story is based is to be found; but the passage in question belongs to the period after Grimm had handed over his editorial duties to Meister. Before considering the key passage, it might be as well to see how the term 'l'*Encyclopédie*' is used by Meister in the *Correspondance littéraire* on two other occasions when he is describing the last illness of Mme Geoffrin who died on 6 October

[10] For instance, the holograph will of Baron d'Holbach, potentially a most interesting document, is duly listed as deposited on 21 January 1789 in *étude* XCIX, and the inventory of his possessions is registered on 9 February. Unfortunately all the documents belonging to this particular *étude* for the first ten months of 1789 are missing.

1777. In the October number of the previous year he noted how her daughter, Mme de la Ferté-Imbault,

> a fait fermer durement sa porte à MM. d'Alembert, Marmontel et autres, tous anciens amis de sa mère, qu'elle n'avait jamais pu souffrir à cause qu'ils étaient Encyclopédistes.... La conduite de Mme de la Ferté-Imbault a révolté contre elle tout le parti philosophie; l'ordre des *Lanturelus* et des *Lampons* (plaisanterie établie chez Mme de la Ferté-Imbault, pour se moquer des académies et de l'esprit de parti) s'est trouvé sérieusement aux prises avec toute l'Encyclopédie.[11]

In December of the same year he gave up space to the reproduction of what he described as 'deux vieilles chansons que les tracasseries de Mme de la Ferté-Imbault avec l'*Encyclopédie* ont fait revivre'.[12] It will be seen that both in these two passages and in the crucial one which follows (it is taken from the January 1777 number) Meister is using the term 'l'*Encyclopédie*' not in its literal sense, but to stand for those writers on whom Mme Geoffrin lavished her generosity. The passage from which the legend of her financial support for the *Encyclopédie* obviously derives, begins with a mention of her gifts to two writers, Suard and Thomas, who, so far as can be established, were not even contributors to the work:

> J'ignore si c'est à cette occasion [Meister continues] que Mme de La Ferté-Imbault, en revoyant les comptes de sa mère, a trouvé qu'elle avait dépensé plus de cent mille écus pour soutenir l'*Encyclopédie* et ses dépendances. J'ignore si le compte est juste; mais il est sûr que Mme Geoffrin a fait infiniment de bien, il est sûr aussi que Mme de La Ferté-Imbault, sans oser blâmer les dispositions de sa mère, n'a pu s'empêcher de témoigner quelques regrets de voir une somme si forte prodiguée à un parti qu'elle n'a jamais cru aussi nécessaire à la gloire de Dieu et de l'État que l'ordre dont elle est la grande maîtresse, le sublime ordre des Lampons et des Lanturelus. A cela que peut-on trouver à redire?[13]

Taken together and in their context, all these passages make it

[11] *Corr. litt.*, Vol. XI, p. 366.
[12] Ibid. p. 394.
[13] Ibid., Vol. XI, p. 408.

MME GEOFFRIN AND THE *ENCYCLOPÉDIE*

quite clear that Meister was not suggesting that Mme Geoffrin's money was handed over, as is commonly assumed, to the publishers of the *Encyclopédie* to save their tottering enterprise. It went to the support of writers. It is true that these were the writers of a party—what Meister calls 'le parti philosophe'—but Mme Geoffrin's gifts were lavished, not only on the two editors of the *Encyclopédie*, on Diderot and D'Alembert, and on other lesser contributors like Marmontel and Morellet, but also on many other men who stood aside from the whole enterprise. By no stretch of the imagination can one twist these words of Meister into meaning that Mme Geoffrin came to the assistance of Le Breton and his partners in the crisis of 1759.

V Luneau de Boisjermain *v*. the Publishers of the *Encyclopédie*[1]

The lawsuit between the publishers of the *Encyclopédie* and Luneau de Boisjermain—a somewhat belated subscriber who did not buy his way into the club until 1767[2]—lasted from 1769 to 1772 and, then with a break of four years during which the Parlement Maupeou had given way to the restored Parlement, from 1776 to 1778. Some day no doubt a specialist in the legal system of eighteenth-century France will give us a full account of the long battle; and very interesting it will certainly be. The aim of this chapter is more limited; it is to extract from the voluminous literature to which this lawsuit gave rise the information which is of interest to the historian of the *Encyclopédie*.

It would be absurd to claim to have 'discovered' this collection of documents since for decades scholars have made reference to them and reproduced parts of them. Yet nowhere is there in print a detailed and systematic study of these documents from this particular angle; indeed even a list of them does not seem to be in existence. The first prerequisite for any serious study of the problem was obviously to establish such a list; this is reproduced at the end of the chapter.

When one examines the documents themselves, the information which they can be made to yield is seen to vary not only in interest but also in degree of reliability. These writings are full of repetitions, contradictions, half-truths, downright lies, ex-

[1] First published in *Studies on Voltaire and the Eighteenth Century*, Vol. XXIII, 1963. pp. 115-177.

[2] No. 11, p. 130 (the numbers quoted in this chapter are those used in the bibliographical appendix, pp. 153-158).

LUNEAU DE BOISJERMAIN V. THE PUBLISHERS

aggerations, under-statements and all manner of distortions of the facts. Sometimes it is possible to check the information which they furnish; sometimes it is not. In what follows an attempt will continually be made to separate out what is 'hard' information from what is in varying degrees less certain. Yet, even when all allowances have been made, it will be seen that, taken as a whole, these polemical documents do furnish a welcome amount of useful information to historians of the *Encyclopédie*.

One thing which gives a certain value to some of Luneau's disclosures about the inner history of the *Encyclopédie* is that, at the beginning of his struggle with the publishing world, Diderot was on his side and provided him, so he alleged, with some useful information. This Diderot was later to deny; he was certainly entitled to draw a clear distinction between Luneau's first lawsuit, that against the powerful corporation of the Paris *Libraires*, and his second, that against the four publishers of the *Encyclopédie* or their heirs.[3] In this pamphlet, *Au Public et aux Magistrats*, a work written with superb force and logic,[4] he put the point beyond all doubt:

> Dans une première affaire, les *Libraires en corps* formèrent contre M. Luneau des prétentions révoltantes pour tout homme de lettres. Je le dis, je l'écrivis. Je le dirois, je l'écrirois encore.
> Dans l'affaire actuelle, qui n'est liée avec la précédente que par le ressentiment de M. Luneau, il forme contre les Libraires associés à l'Encyclopédie des prétentions qui me semblent d'une injustice et d'une absurdité palpables. Je le dis et je le démontre.[5]

Brilliantly as Diderot performs this task in the pages of this *factum*, he was obviously embarrassed by the fact that, in his dealings with Luneau over the first of his two lawsuits, he had opened his mouth too wide about his own grievances against

---

[3] David l'aîné had died in 1763. Durand died in 1770 and Briasson in 1775, before the lawsuit was finally disposed of (No. 38, folding sheet facing p. 12). Le Breton survived until 1779, by which date the case had finally been decided against Luneau.
[4] See the five letters of Gerbier to Diderot on the subject (Roth, Vol. XI, pp. 130, 155-6, 190-2, 253-4).
[5] No. 18 (Roth, Vol. XI, p. 100).

the publishers of the *Encyclopédie*. In the second of his two replies to Diderot's letter of 31 August 1771[6] to Le Breton and Briasson in support of their case, Luneau could write triumphantly:

> J'ai retrouvé dans mes papiers une Lettre de ce Sçavant que je ne dois plus tenir secrette. On y verra que M. Diderot m'ayant instruit des faits qui ne pouvoient être sçus que par lui, n'a pas dû me laisser ignorer ceux qui étoient plus connus de tous ses coopérateurs. Ainsi j'ai eu raison de dire que c'étoit de lui que je tenois la connoissance de toutes les manoeuvres secrettes des Libraires associés dans l'impression de l'Encyclopédie.[7]

He then reproduced a letter of Diderot in which the latter had begged him 'de ne point faire mention dans vos Mémoires des sept derniers volumes de l'Encyclopédie charpentés. *Ce fait ne peut être sçu que par moi*'.[8] After this he proceeded to rub in Diderot's indiscretions:

> Pour vous justifier, vous dites que je ne vous suis pas connu. Mais à qui le persuaderez-vous? De qui puis-je tenir ce que je sçais sur l'impression de l'Encyclopédie? Est-ce de M. d'Alembert? Il n'a jamais rien connu aux détails de l'Imprimerie: il n'y a pris aucune part. Je ne lui ai jamais parlé . . . On ne croira donc pas qu'il m'ait rien appris sur l'Encyclopédie. Tout le monde au contraire sçaura, Monsieur, que c'est vous qui m'avez remis tous les avis des Srs Briasson & Le Breton. C'est vous qui m'avez ouvert le secret de leurs opérations; c'est de vous que je tiens toutes les anecdotes dont mon Mémoire est rempli; c'est à vous que je dois la connoissance secrette de tout ce qui s'est passé entre vous & le sieur Le Breton. Je n'ai rien appris que de vous. Vous le niez. Le Public en devinera bien la raison.[9]

Diderot's defence of his position in *Au Public et aux Magistrats* is somewhat embarrassing, when one remembers the terms of the letter reproduced by Luneau:

> M. Luneau prétend que tout ce qu'il sait de l'Encyclopédie, il le tient de moi; il est sûr que conduit chez moi par un homme

---

[6] No. 12 (Roth, Vol. XI, pp. 145-153).
[7] No. 17, p. 1 (Roth, Vol, XI, p. 228).
[8] No. 17, p. 3 (Roth, Vol. XI, p. 230).
[9] No. 17, pp. 4-5.

de lettres, dont la présence me garantissoit la probité de M. Luneau, je ne lui célai rien des détails littéraires. Quant à l'affaire de commerce, je lui dis: 'Monsieur Luneau, je n'y entends rien; je ne lirai point vos calculs, que je crois très fautifs. Je ne suis pas payé pour défendre les libraires; ils sont durs, mais vous ne me persuaderez jamais que ce soient des fripons'; et sur ce propos il remporta son énorme cahier de chiffres, sans avoir pu me résoudre à le regarder. M. Luneau ne niera point ce fait, parce qu'il mentirait inutilement.[10]

No doubt if Diderot tried to play down his indiscretion in his dealings with Luneau, the latter exaggerated his debt to the editor of the *Encyclopédie*. Yet, apart from technical details concerning the publication of the work, Diderot—as the letter written to Luneau shows—undoubtedly confided in him such secrets as the censoring of the last ten volumes of the *Encyclopédie* by Le Breton.[11]

It is difficult to unravel from this mass of material those strands which throw new light on the history of the *Encyclopédie*. For the sake of clarity the points of interest may be arranged, without too much overlapping, under the following heads:

I. THE STATE OF THE MS. IN 1750

The central point of the whole dispute between Luneau and the publishers of the *Encyclopédie* was that a work announced in the prospectus of 1750 as containing eight volumes of text and two of plates, costing 280 livres, came in the end to have seventeen volumes of text and eleven of plates, costing in all 980 livres. Again and again reference is made in the course of the controversy to the opening words of the Prospectus: '*L'Ouvrage que nous annonçons, n'est plus un Ouvrage à faire. Le Manuscrit & les Desseins en sont complets.*'

To the modern reader who in Diderot's letters to Sophie Volland catches glimpses of the editor and his faithful adjutant, Jaucourt, toiling away at the last ten volumes of text a whole

[10] No. 18, ff. 376-7 (Roth, Vol. XI, pp. 115-16).
[11] See below, pp. 128-131.

decade later,[12] the first sentence of the prospectus seems a trifle odd. While it is true that in the 'Conditions proposées aux Souscripteurs' at the end of the prospectus the publishers had taken the precaution of saying that there might be one extra volume, it is clear that if the manuscript and plates had been complete in 1750, they could not have miscalculated so wildly as to produce twenty-eight volumes instead of ten.

What the publishers and Diderot have to say on this question in the course of the controversy with Luneau throws some light on the way in which the work was composed. Luneau seized upon the statement of the publishers[13] that, after distributing seven volumes between 1751 and 1757, 'il n'y en eut point en 1758 à cause de la retraite d'un des principaux Auteurs' (D'Alembert), alleging that this proved that at that date 'il y avoit encore dix volumes à faire'—clean contrary to the different *privilèges* of the work which required that the complete manuscript should be approved before printing started.[14] To this charge the publishers replied, not very truthfully: 'En disant que le manuscrit & les dessins étoient complets, les Editeurs disoient vrai, en ce qui les regardoit: leur composition personnelle étoit finie, & l'Encyclopédie auroit été donnée en l'état où elle étoit alors, que ç'eût été encore un ouvrage vraiment estimable.'[15]

A more convincing explanation of the contrast between the statement of 1750 and the final result of twenty-eight volumes was furnished by Stoupe in his defence of the publishers:[16]

> Lorsqu'en 1750 ils annoncerent l'Encyclopédie en dix Volumes *in-folio,* dont deux de Planches, ils avoient en manuscrit & en dessins de quoi former à-peu-près ce nombre . . . [In announcing the subscription] ils promirent ce qu'ils avoient, du manuscrit pour huit ou neuf Volumes de Discours & des Dessins pour deux

---

[12] See Roth, Vol. III, p. 265 (25 November 1760) and p. 300 (12 September 1761). A certain number of articles must have been written even later than this. For instance, ZENDA VESTA is said to have been taken from the *Annual Register . . . of the year 1762.*

[13] No. 6, p. 4.
[14] No. 10, p. 2.
[15] No. 12, p. 14.
[16] No. 16, p. 3.

LUNEAU DE BOISJERMAIN V. THE PUBLISHERS

Volumes; & ils n'en attendoient pas davantage. Mais à peine les premiers Volumes de cet Ouvrage eurent-ils été publiés, qu'il leur vint de toutes les contrées de l'Europe des richesses littéraires envoyées par ce qu'il y avoit de plus éclairé dans tous les genres. Que falloit-il qu'ils fissent alors? Ils devoient ou refuser cette augmentation ou l'annoncer aux Souscripteurs pour savoir si elle leur convenoit: ils prirent ce dernier parti.

The same explanation, with the same stress on the unexpected amount of aid furnished by a wide variety of writers outside the original circle of editors and contributors, is furnished by Diderot:

Lorsqu'on mit sous presse le prospectus de l'Encyclopédie, nous annonçâmes dix[17] volumes de discours et environ six cents planches; c'étoit en effet tout ce que nous possédions alors. Si j'assure que la nation entière s'intéressa à la perfection de l'ouvrage, et qu'il nous vint des secours des contrées les plus éloignées, c'est un fait connu et démontré par les noms des surnuméraires et la multitude de leurs articles. Nous nous trouvâmes en un instant associés à ce qu'il y avait de gens habiles en histoire naturelle, en physique, en mathématiques, en théologie, en philosophie, en littérature, en arts libéraux et mécaniques. Que falloit-il faire des matériaux de M. de Voltaire, du président de Montesquieu, de M. Turgot l'intendant, de M. le président de Brosses, de M. de Saint-Lambert, de M. de Marmontel, de M. le chevalier de Jaucourt et d'une infinité d'autres? M. Luneau les auroit peut-être brûlés. Moi, je supprimai souvent mon travail et le remplaçai par celui de ces auxiliaires. C'est ainsi que, pour la première fois peut-être, on a vu un ouvrage souscrit se perfectionner d'un volume à un autre.[18]

It is, of course, obvious that, while this does explain how outside contributions helped to swell the promised eight or nine volumes of text into seventeen, the claim made in the prospectus that the work was already complete was simply untrue.

II. THE CONTRIBUTORS

Two points of interest emerge here from the documents in

---
[17] This should surely read *huit*.
[18] No. 18, p. 367. (Roth, Vol. XI, pp. 105-6).

question. The first arises from a footnote to Luneau's *Mémoire* of 1771:

> Un des auteurs de l'Encyclopédie, M. l'abbé *** écrivit au sieur le Breton, de Hollande, où il étoit, une lettre, dans laquelle il le prioit de lui completter l'exemplaire de cet ouvrage, dont il lui avoit fourni les deux premiers volumes comme co-opérateur: il lui rappelloit en même temps qu'il n'avoit pas achevé de payer ce qui lui étoit dû pour les articles qu'il avoit composés. Le sieur le Breton, qui avoit envie d'éluder le paiement qu'on lui demandoit, répondit verbalement au commissionnaire envoyé par l'Auteur, qu'il n'avoit pas fait usage des articles dont il réclamoit le paiement. L'Auteur ne pouvoit s'assurer dans le pays où il étoit de la vérité d'une pareille réponse; il cessa ses poursuites, il ne parla plus ni de paiement, ni des volumes qui devoient completter son exemplaire. Le hazard a voulu qu'à son retour en cette ville, un de ses amis l'a prié de parcourir un manuscrit de sa composition, dans lequel il a trouvé des morceaux tirés de l'Encyclopédie, qu'il a reconnu être de lui. Cette découverte lui a fait naître l'envie de compulser les 17 volumes de cet ouvrage; il y a trouvé tous les articles qu'il avoit composés, à l'exception de quelques-uns auxquels on en a substitué d'autres. Il a écrit au sieur le Breton pour lui en demander le paiement, & les 22 volumes de l'Encyclopédie: le sieur le Breton a rendu au commissionaire la lettre, en disant que sa réponse étoit contenue dans sa lettre, & M. l'abbé *** n'y en trouva aucune. On se dispense de faire des réflexions sur une pareille conduite: il n'est personne qui ne sente combien elle est indécente de la part d'un Imprimeur à l'égard d'un homme de lettres d'un mérite bien supérieur à sa réputation.[19]

If it is possible that Luneau embroidered upon this anecdote, it certainly fits in splendidly with what Professor Venturi has to say on the collaboration of Abbé Yvon in the *Encyclopédie* in his invaluable *Origini dell'Enciclopedia*.[20]

After the scandal of the Abbé de Prades Yvon was compelled to remove himself to Holland, with the result that it is only in the first two volumes of the *Encyclopédie* that his signature appears at the end of the articles which he composed. 'M. l'abbé Yvon qui avoit la lettre X', the editors stated very tactfully at

---

[19] No. 11, p. 22.
[20] Florence, 1946, pp. 40-8, and the important notes (pp. 136-40).

the end of Vol. III, 'est absent'. In fact, Yvon's articles continued to appear in this and the later volumes, but they were unsigned, with the result, as Professor Venturi has pointed out, that acting on the dangerous principle that unsigned articles in the *Encyclopédie* are by Diderot, the editors of the Assézat-Tourneux edition, followed by many modern scholars, attributed to Diderot a considerable number of articles which, in some cases certainly, in others probably, ought to be restored to Yvon.

So far as payments to contributors to the *Encyclopédie* were concerned, there was an unbridgeable gulf between the claim of Luneau that payments to Diderot, D'Alembert and the other contributors came to the modest total of 150,000 livres (some £6,000 *in English money of the time*) and the publishers' statement that they were 'en état de justifier par quittances que la copie a coûté près de 400,000 livres'.[21] It must be said that the publishers' claim seems ill-founded, especially as they add that in 1759 'la copie entiere étoit payée'.[22] Even though the accounts of the whole enterprise have come down to us only in a very incomplete form,[23] we do know that payments were made to contributors, especially Diderot, well after that date.

Le Breton and his partners continued to cling to their story that the manuscript of the *Encyclopédie* had cost them 400,000 livres,[24] but when their opponents were able to do their sums on the accounts which the publishers had been compelled to deposit with the Parlement,[25] they declared that this figure was preposterous:

> Dans le Journal du sieur Briasson on trouve que les Libraires n'ont payé aux Editeurs ou Auteurs que 149,061 liv. 6 s. 6 den.; à divers travailleurs, dont le travail n'est pas déterminé dans le Journal, & à d'autres personnes désignées sous le nom de Copistes 9029 liv. 16 sols; en tout 158,091 liv. 2 sols 6 den. M. Diderot n'a eu pour sa part suivant le livre, que 79996 liv. 13 s. 6 den. Les autres Auteurs ont été payés de la maniere la plus mesquine.[26]

[21] No. 20, p. 2.
[22] ibid., p. 7.
[23] See May, and Chap. III, pp. 71-76 above.
[24] No. 30, *Tableau analytique* facing p. 38.
[25] See below, pp. 142-153.
[26] No. 31, p. 7.

A footnote to the sentence concerning Diderot adds: 'On ne comprend point dans cette somme les 19342 liv. 11 sols payées à M. Diderot pour les intérêts de 30000 l. qui ont resté entre les mains des libraires depuis 1760 ou 1761.'

It is not altogether easy to check these figures as we lack the part of the accounts covering money expended after March 1768; these must contain a few payments to contributors and especially to Diderot as editor of the plates, as well as entries on payments to Diderot and Jaucourt of the interest on the money which they had invested with the publishers.[27]

There are even complications of various kinds in calculating, from the part of the accounts which we do possess, the total amount paid down to March 1768 both to all contributors and to Diderot himself. If one tries to redo the sums of the disgruntled subscribers, one encounters all manner of difficulties in deciding exactly who was a contributor, whether certain sums paid out were merely to cover expenses, and what weight (if any) one should give to presents to contributors, especially of books (Diderot in particular received a quite expensive collection of books from the publishers). One is in fact astonished at the intrepidity with which the litigants in question professed to state down to the last *sou* and *denier* exactly how much the publishers paid the contributors to the *Encyclopédie*. On the other hand, so far as one can make out with only incomplete accounts before one, it would seem that the answers provided in this document are approximately correct. There is in fact no doubt whatever that the publishers grossly exaggerated the amount of money which they paid to Diderot and his colleagues.

---

[27] There is a reference to the repayment of the capital of these two sums on p. 4 of the same document; apparently the repayment to Diderot was noted under the number 2230 of the expenses and that to Jaucourt under number 2193. There are references to Diderot's 30,000 livres in the part of the accounts which has come down to us under the items 1037 and 1059 for the year 1760 and under the items 1101, 1117 and especially 1140 (8 August) for the following year. Cf. also in the receipts for 1761 the entry for 8 August: 'Recu de M. Diderot pr parfaire les 30000[11] de l'acte a luy souscrit ce jour 925.' There are, of course, innumerable entries concerning interest payments to both men in MS. U1051.

III. THE SUBSCRIBERS

It is fairly easy to establish, from the documents published by M. May, the size of the printings of the successive volumes of the *Encyclopédie*.[28] Originally fixed at 1,625 copies,[29] this number had been raised by July 1751 to 2,075. In February 1754, after 3,125 copies of Volume III had been printed and a reprint of 1,100 copies of Volumes I and II made, it was agreed to reprint another 1,100 copies of Volumes I-III and to print 4,225 copies of Volume IV and the succeeding volumes.[30] What is not clear, owing to the fragmentary nature of these accounts, is how many of these 4,225 copies went to subscribers or were otherwise sold.

In the course of the controversy all sorts of figures about the size of the printing were bandied about—more or less informed guesses on the part of Luneau and his associates, evasions on the part of the publishers. Luneau began by declaring that at first 2,125 copies were printed, and that the same number of copies of Volumes I and II then had to be reprinted, so that it was decided to print 4,250 copies of later volumes. His calculations of the publishers' profits were therefore based on this figure, minus an allowance for 50 copies being imperfect and 100 given away to contributors and 'aux Seigneurs qui ont honoré cette entreprise de leur protection'—i.e. a net total available for sale of 4,100.[31] Challenged to deny this figure, the publishers had no difficulty in replying through their mouthpiece, Stoupe, that 'il est de la plus exacte vérité que cet Ouvrage n'a été imprimé ni à *4100* ni à *4250 exemplaires*'.[32] However, in 1777 an inspection

---

[28] May, pp. 17, 25, 27.
[29] This is the figure given in the earliest agreement on the printings of the work (p. 17), but that of 1,500 is mentioned on 3 July 1751 (p. 25).
[30] 4,000 copies of the plates were printed (see the agreement of 16 December 1768, Archives d'Etat, Geneva, Notaires Dunant et Mercier, VIII. p. 1305, reproduced in *Essays*, p. 59).
[31] No. 11, p. 35n.
[32] No. 16, p. 22.

of the accounts of the *Encyclopédie* finally put the other litigious subscribers on the right track and they were able to state that 4,225 copies of the work were printed from Volume IV onwards and that Volumes I-III were reprinted to bring the number of copies of them up to the same number.[33] This made Le Breton appear rather foolish as he had claimed—perhaps mentally deducting imperfect and presentation copies—that only 4,050 copies had been printed.[34]

So far as the number of subscribers was concerned, Luneau began with the claim that there were at least 4,100, and that 'au 29 Avril 1751, le sieur Briasson seul avoit déjà distribué 1002 souscriptions, valant un peu plus de 60120 livres',[35] the latter statement being apparently based on the fact that Luneau had seen a copy of a dead subscriber's receipt, signed by Briasson and dated April 1751, 'numérotée 1000 et plus'. This sum was easily challenged by Stoupe:

> Pourquoi dire *un peu plus*, quand on est sûr soi-même que c'est *beaucoup moins*? Les 1002 souscriptions à 60 liv. valent juste 60120 liv. Mais M. Luneau, qui nous assure qu'aucun homme de Lettres ne connoît la Librairie comme lui, devoit-il oublier d'avouer que tous les Libraires font à leurs Confreres une diminution sur ce qu'ils leur vendent? Cette diminution a été, sur la seule souscription de l'Encyclopédie, de 12 livres pour les Libraires de Paris, de 24 livres pour ceux de Province, & de 36 livres pour l'Etranger: on la cede même souvent à certains particuliers. M. Luneau devoit d'autant moins se permettre cette réticence, que sa propre souscription est dans ce cas-la; elle porte le n°. 1339 *a.s.* a été prise par M. Viard le 25 Juin 1751, & n'a été payée que 48 liv. Une remise proportionnée a été faite sur chaque Volume de Planches par les Libraires associés, & sur les dix derniers Volumes de Discours par le Libraire étranger qui les a vendus. Les Libraires, Colporteurs, Commissionnaires ou autres à qui on a fait cette diminution, consomment ordinairement les trois quarts des Editions. Cet objet seul diminue la recette de l'Encyclopédie de 150,000 liv.[36]

The publishers' own statements on the subject varied some-

[33] No. 31, p. 9.
[34] No. 30, *Tableau analytique* facing 38.
[35] No. 11, p. 10.
[36] No. 16. pp. 21-2.

what. In discussing their dealings with the public over the plates, they speak of 'deux ou trois mille souscripteurs'.[37] In *Au Public et aux Magistrats*,[38] Diderot is rather more forthcoming when he speaks of 'entre trois à quatre mille'; but gradually the publishers fixed on the figure of 'près de quatre mille Souscripteurs' and stuck to it.[39]

The aggrieved subscribers who joined Luneau in 1777 started off on the wrong foot with a claim that there were '4500 souscriptions';[40] but they soon had at their disposal a document which is not available to modern scholars—'une espece de registre de souscriptions[41] dans lequel on ne trouve, ni la date, ni les paiements qui ont été faits, ni les personnes qui ont souscrit. On voit par ce Journal qu'il a été délivré 3931 Souscriptions'.[42]

This confirms Grimm's statement—generally accepted by scholars—that by the time of the appearance of the seventh volume in 1757 the number of subscriptions had risen to 'près de quatre mille'.[43] Allowing for the fact that there were purchasers who were not technically subscribers, in addition to the 3,931 who were, on paper the publishers can have had little difficulty in disposing of all the copies available for sale out of the 4,225 printed. Does not Diderot himself tell us in his *Au Public et aux Magistrats* that the public freely accepted the extra volumes of text and plates? 'Tel a été son empressement', he exclaims, 'qu'il n'est pas resté un exemplaire complet dans le magasin du libraire'.[44]

---

[37] No. 12, p. 35.
[38] No. 18, p. 365 (Roth, Vol. XI, p. 104).
[39] No. 20, p. 17; No. 30. pp. 2, 7; No. 34, pp. 1-2.
[40] No. 29, p. 24.
[41] Luneau states (No. 32, p. 6): 'Mon nom se lit à la lettre L, dans la copie au net de leur livre de souscription qui est produit'. He later speaks of 'les registres des Souscriptions produits au Procès, qu'on ne peut déchiffrer, tant ils sont barbouillés' (No. 41, p. 9).
[42] No. 31, p. 9.
[43] *Corr. litt.*, Vol. III, p. 457. It is, however, disconcerting to find that, in discussing the position of the publishers after the two *Arrêts du Conseil* of 1759, both Malesherbes and an anonymous spokesman for the publishers reckon the total number of subscribers at that date as only 2,600 (BN, Nouv. acq. fr. 3345, ff. 180-192).
[44] No. 18, p. 368 (Roth, Vol. XI, p. 106).

In actual practice, owing to the long period of over twenty years which it took to complete the whole work, things do not seem to have worked out as smoothly as all that for Le Breton and his partners. One should, of course, treat with scepticism publishers' hard luck stories, particularly when they are engaged in an awkward lawsuit in the course of which they have told a certain number of downright lies as well as an even larger number of half-truths. By the second half of the 1760s complete sets (or sets complete except for the volumes of plates still to appear) may well have been at a premium; but this is not incompatible with the publishers' experiencing some difficulty in getting rid of copies of the last ten volumes of text and especially of the very expensive volumes of plates which cost 654 livres out of the 980 to be paid for a complete set.[45] In 1772 the publishers retorted to Luneau's figures about their vast profits:

> Il suppose que tous les exemplaires ont été retirés; cependant il est de fait qu'il reste encore 4 à 500 exemplaires des dix derniers Volumes, & une bien plus grande quantité d'exemplaires de tous les Volumes de Planches. De ce grand nombre de Souscripteurs les uns sont morts, & les héritiers ne se sont point encore présentés; d'autres ont été hors d'état de fournir à une dépense si considérable; plusieurs ont entrepris des voyages de long cours, dont ils ne sont point encore revenus; il y en a enfin qui attendent les deux derniers Volumes de Planches pour prendre en même tems les dix derniers Volumes de Discours & tous ceux des Planches.[46]

To their opponents' calculations of their profits, based on the assumption that all one needed to do to work out their receipts was to multiply the number of copies printed by the cost of a subscription, they retorted again in 1777 that, in addition to allowing for presentation copies, discounts to booksellers, bankruptcies and damage from a fire, one must also count in what

---

[45] No. 38, p. 5. The first seven volumes of text cost 18 livres each and the last ten 20 livres, a total of 326 livres; the eleven volumes of plates cost 654 livres, making 980 livres altogether.
[46] No. 20, p. 3.

are listed as 'Objets de reprise dont la rentrée est éloignée et incertaine':

> Cinq cent exemplaires des dix derniers volumes à 200 livres
> Cinq cent corps complets des onze volumes de figures à 540 livres
> Environ cinq mille volumes séparés & imparfaits, estimés 60,000 livres.[47]

No doubt, Le Breton and his partners are not to be believed unless there is some corroboration of their claims, but, as we shall later see,[48] there is some evidence that the volumes of the *Encyclopédie* were taken up only slowly in the years from 1765 onwards.

On the other hand, it does seem a fact that by the second half of the 1760s secondhand sets of the whole work (or rather of all the volumes so far published) were at a premium. When Luneau and other litigious subscribers kept on complaining that the whole work cost them 980 livres instead of 280, the publishers could retort that, if the malcontents sold their copies, they would have no difficulty in getting back more than they had paid for them, and that the folio reprints being carried out abroad where labour was cheaper than in Paris and, of course, without any payments to the contributors, were pretty expensive too.

Quite a lot of figures were quoted in the course of the controversy about the prices reached in book sales by sets of the *Encyclopédie*. To interpret these correctly one has to bear in mind that the price of 980 livres which a subscriber paid for his set of the *Encyclopédie* did not include binding. On the cost of this the publishers offer us in 1771 some valuable information:

> Le prix de la reliure a varié suivant les tems, & la cherté des peaux. En 1751, la reliure ordinaire de l'*in-folio* ne coutoit que 4 liv. ou 4 liv. 10 sols; elle a ensuite augmenté, elle a valu 5 liv. & elle vaut actuellement 6 liv. La reliure des Planches a toujours couté un peu plus que l'autre; depuis environ cinq à six ans, elle se paye 7 livres.[49]

---

[47] No. 30, *Tableau analytique* facing p. 38; cf. No. 39, p. 13.
[48] See below, pp. 116-117, and also *Essays*, pp. 60-61.
[49] No. 12, p. 30.

Allowing an average of 5 livres each for the seventeen volumes of text (i.e. 85 livres) and 7 livres each for the eleven volumes of plates (i.e. 77 livres), we find that the subscriber would have had to pay some 160 livres for binding, making the total cost of his set some 1,140 livres. We have some evidence outside this controversy for the relatively high cost of a set of the *Encyclopédie* by the latter part of the 1760s. The prospectus for the Panckoucke-Cramer reprint of the *Encyclopédie*[50] speaks of the first edition as being 'entierement épuisée' and of the price of a set (presumably bound . . .) as being 'de 13 à 14 cens livres, quand on peut la trouver'.[51] However, one must bear in mind that Panckoucke was here trying to make out that the 840 livres which he was asking for his edition of the work, 'entierement & exactement conforme à la premiere', was quite a modest price. More disinterested testimony on the point is to be found in a letter of Jaucourt to Reybaz, written in 1768:

Si vous avez eû, Monsieur, le bonheur de trouver hier une bonne place à la Comédie, j'ai eû de mon côté celui de vous trouver un bon exemplaire de l'Encyclopédie, complete,[52] bon exemplaire pour le papier, les planches, la reliure, tout y est réussi, et en même tems à un prix favorable dans cette conjoncture à 1150 Livres. Je vous conseille de ne pas manquer l'occasion de l'acquérir de peur qu'elle ne vous échape. Outre que le prix de cet ouvrage augmente sous les jours, et augmentera dans la suite, ou du moins se soustiendra en cas de contrefaction même bien exécutée, je crains que le Roi de Danemarck, et quelques-uns des Seigneurs qui sont à sa suite n'enlevent à tout prix le petit nombre d'exemplaires qu'ils pourront trouver dans Paris. Si vous pensez de même que moi, vous pourriez Lundi prochain vous procurer l'exemplaire dont je parle et l'emporter chez vous.[53]

The publishers were certainly entitled to retort to Luneau that

---

[50] See *Essays*, p. 62.
[51] BN, Ms. Fr. 22069, ff. 170-171. The text is reproduced in No. 11, *Pièces justificatives*, pp. 42-4.
[52] As Volume VI of the plates did not appear until 1768, this set must have lacked at least five volumes of the complete work.
[53] BPUG, Ms. Fr. 916, 41.

he had no reason to be dissatisfied with the bargain he had made
in 1767 in acquiring a set of the *Encyclopédie*:

> Si le Souscripteur n'a reçu de vous que le prix de la souscription, vous avez fait un excellent marché, puisque l'Encyclopédie, qui revient actuellement aux Souscripteurs à 737 liv.[54] se vend couramment 1100 liv. & si vous en voulez ce prix, vous le trouverez facilement. Nous vous adresserons volontiers ceux qui viennent tous les jours nous en demander à ce prix.[55]

Diderot joined in with the same observation in his *Au Public et aux Magistrats*:

> Aujourd'hui, l'ouvrage exposé dans une vente, monte à deux cents cinquante, trois cents, quatre cents livres même, au-delà du prix de la souscription. Et voilà comment le libraire ou moi, nous avons trompé notre souscripteur.[56]

In 1772, at a moment when the work was shortly to be completed by the publication of the last two volumes of plates, the publishers pointed out that so far Luneau's twenty-six volumes had cost him 850 livres:

> Les vingt-six Volumes se vendent dans les ventes publiques 11 & même 1200 liv. . . . Quel est donc l'intérêt qui agite si fort le sieur Luneau? C'est d'avoir pour 280 liv. un Ouvrage dont le prix est de 11 à 1200 liv. dans le commerce, & qui sera de 13 à 1400 livres, dés que les deux derniers Volumes de Planches auront été livrés.[57]

Finally, in 1777, five years after the publication of the last two volumes of plates, the publishers could claim that the lowest price fetched by any of the sixteen sets of the *Encyclopédie* which had passed at book-sales since 1770 was 1,125 livres, 'toutes les autres ayant été portées à 12, 13, 1400 & tant de livres'. Specially fine sets had fetched very considerably more: 'Il est même notoire que celui en grand papier du feu sieur Randon de Boisset, avec deux volumes du Supplément, a été adjugé pour 3220 liv., &

---

[54] At this point (1771) 4 volumes of plates had still to appear.
[55] No. 12, pp. 18-19.
[56] No. 18, p. 368. (Roth, Vol. XI, p. 106).
[57] No. 20, pp. 4-5.

que le sieur Debure l'aîné en a vendu un pareil, relié en maroquin, 3600 livres.'[58]

To return from the folio volumes of the *Encyclopédie* to its subscribers. One of the most interesting problems for a study of the influence which the work exercised in France between 1751 and the Revolution, is to know roughly how many copies of the first edition found a home inside the frontiers of France and how many were exported. Unfortunately on this crucial point the documents before us are of little use, simply because the figures quoted by the publishers are produced in support of somewhat specious arguments.

Diderot, in his *Au Public et aux Magistrats*, first uses the argument that Luneau is highly unpatriotic in urging his fellow subscribers, abroad as well as at home, to insist on getting most of their money back. To Luneau's specific complaint that the number of plates had been increased far beyond what was originally offered, Diderot retorts: 'Le compatriote a été satisfait; l'argent de l'étranger nous est venu, et M. Luneau s'imagine que cet argent lui sera renvoyé par le magistrat, contre l'intention du ministère, qui a bien montré par son indulgence combien il lui aurait déplu que l'ouvrage, suspendu ici, s'achevât au loin.'[59]

It is in the context of this charge of lack of patriotism which was hurled at Luneau that we must view the precise figure for foreign subscribers given by the publishers:

Il n'y a eu qu'environ douze cens souscriptions prises en France, tout le reste a été enlevé par l'Etranger. Ce sera donc l'Etranger qui profiteroit d'environ les trois quarts de cette somme immense; c'est ainsi que le sieur Luneau est Citoyen; c'est ainsi qu'il a à coeur les intérêts de sa patrie.[60]

Although this figure for foreign subscribers is repeated in the most categorical terms on the following page—'Les quatre mille souscripteurs étoient repandus dans toute l'Europe; il n'y en avoit qu'environ douze cens en France.'—it is obviously impossible

---

[58] No. 38, p. 7.
[59] No. 18, p. 370. (Roth, Vol. XI, pp. 108-9).
[60] No. 20, p. 6.

to accept it. It becomes even more impossible when one sees the exaggeration carried still further in a document signed by the great *avocat*, Gerbier. 'Et pour récompense . . .', he concludes his defence of the publishers, with a fine rhetorical flourish, 'on appelle de tous les pays de l'Europe trois mille Etrangers, pour exercer contre eux des répétitions qui, en les ruinant, appauvriront la nation!' A marginal note informs us that 'Près des trois quarts des souscriptions ont été prises pour l'Etranger'.[61]

One's scepticism is in fact justified by other figures supplied by the publishers themselves. These wild statements omit an important element in between the publishers (together with their colleagues in the Paris book trade), and the booksellers of foreign countries—namely French provincial booksellers and the subscribers behind them. We are told elsewhere that it was 'Les Libraires de Province & les Libraires étrangers, qui avoient pris le plus grand nombre des souscriptions.'[62] On another occasion we learn that, the partnership between Le Breton and Briasson having been dissolved on 21 April 1772, the latter's heirs were now in sole charge of the whole undertaking of the *Encyclopédie* and had in their possession 'les quittances & décharges les plus pleines & les plus absolues de plus de deux mille quatre cens Souscripteurs, tant de Paris que de Province'.[63] The importance of the rôle played by provincial booksellers in the distribution of the *Encyclopédie* is underlined by the same document when it states that 'les trois quarts des Souscriptions ont été prises par les Libraires de province & des pays étrangers'.[64]

It is amusing to see how in this lawsuit even the most improbable and absurd figures were swallowed by the publishers' opponents if they happened to fit in with the point they were trying to establish. In arguing that very few of the subscribers could have had an opportunity to examine the samples of the typography of the *Encyclopédie* displayed in a Paris bookshop, they plunge into the most absurd juggling with figures:

De 4500 souscriptions,[65] les Libraires nous apprennent qu'il n'y

---

[61] No. 25, p. 10.
[62] No. 21, p. 3.
[63] No. 27, p. 26.
[64] No. 27, p. 31.
[65] This figure is, of course, much too high (see above, p. 107).

en a eu que 1200 pour la France, & que tout le reste a été enlevé pour l'étranger. Des 1200 prises en France, les deux tiers, au moins, ont été dispersées dans les Provinces. N'est-il pas risible d'entendre les Libraires soutenir que les Souscripteurs ont approuvé les innovations typographiques, sur l'exposition faite, dans une boutique de la rue de la Harpe, de quelques feuilles d'impression, que personne n'a peut-être vues, & que les onze douzièmes des Souscripteurs ont été certainement dans l'impossibilité d'y voir?'[66]

One must regretfully conclude that one problem which these documents do not solve is the number of sets of the first edition of the *Encyclopédie* which were sold abroad.

They do, however, throw some light on another problem: who were the people—abroad, but especially in France—who actually subscribed to this expensive work? One finds scattered through the hundreds of pages of this collection of documents quite a substantial amount of information which is worth examining, because here we find a certain number of names of subscribers— illustrious or otherwise—and some indication as to their social status or occupation. Occasionally we also obtain information about which libraries purchased the work.

In 1776 the publishers produced certificates, signed by certain illustrious subscribers, stating that they were entirely satisfied with their bargain. The names of the signatories which are actually quoted in the document in question[67] are those of 'M. le Maréchal Duc de Noailles, M. le Maréchal de Mouchy, M. le Duc de la Valliere, M. le Marquis de Paulmy, M. le Marquis de Noailles.' A very different subscriber is mentioned by the publishers' opponents in the next document[68]—'M. le F. de Pom. Premier Président de la Cour des Aides de Montauban', whose name is spelt out in full as 'Le Franc de Pompignan' in a later *mémoire*.[69]

This last document produces on its very first page quite a harvest of names as it was put out on behalf of a group of subscribers who are described as 'Intervenants & Demandeurs en

[66] No. 29, p. 24.
[67] No. 27, p. 26.
[68] No. 28, p. 6.
[69] No. 29, p. 42.

restitution' in the lawsuit between Luneau and the publishers of the *Encyclopédie*:

le Marquis de Camille Massimo,
le Marquis de la Saone,
le Marquis de Lansegue, *Conseiller au Parlement de Toulouse*,
le Sieur de Jossan, *Résident en France du Prince de Hohen-Lohe*,
le Sieur de la Lande, *de l'Académie des Sciences, &c.*
le Sieur Bachelier, *Directeur des Ecoles gratuites de Dessein*,
le Sieur Pechin, *Conseiller au Présidial de Langres*,
le Sieur Grenaud, *Gouverneur de la Ville de Nantes*,
et les Sieurs Boitel de Richeville, de la Court,[70] Hillou, & autres . . .

Interesting as this list is (it contains one famous name, that of the astronomer, Lalande, a contributor to both the *Supplément* to the *Encyclopédie* and to the *Encyclopédie d'Yverdon*),[71] it is far from clear that all the persons named here were actually subscribers. The publishers, who claimed (one would think rightly) that the original subscription had been annulled by the *Arrêts du Conseil* of 1759, followed up their victory over Luneau in 1777 by publishing what they claimed to be the facts about their relations with the *Intervenants*.[72]

Two more names appear in this document—those of a certain Duval de Lepinois and of 'le sieur Leguay,[73] se disant représenter les sieur & dame Hurbain'. The publishers alleged that, like Luneau, Duval de Lepinois and de Lacourt had taken all the volumes except the last four of plates, signing a receipt and *décharge*. Lalande, they declared, was 'dans un cas plus défavorable', as he had received all 28 volumes. The Marquis de Lansegue and the Marquis de Camille Massimo, like Daudet de Jossan, had also received the whole work all but four volumes of plates. On the other hand, Pechin, they declared, had never been a subscriber, but merely had an arrangement with a bookseller at Langres; he could be presumed to have all 28 volumes. Grenaud

---

[70] Described as 'Chantre & Chanoine d'Amiens' in No. 36, p. 2.
[71] Perret, pp. 222n., 237-8.
[72] No. 36, pp. 1-7.
[73] No doubt the chief of the *Intervenants* in 1772 (cf. no. 19).

(or Grenot), the Governor of Nantes, was said to have received 24 volumes, but Bachelier, Leguay and Boitel de Richeville[74] claimed to have still in their possession the subscription coupon for Volumes VIII, IX and X—i e. they had not taken any volumes since number VII, published in 1757. Whereas under the terms of the *Arrêt du Conseil* of 21 July 1759 they were entitled merely to a refund of 72 livres in lieu of Volumes VIII-X, they were now claiming the last ten volumes of text and all eleven volumes of plates for a further payment of 40 livres! Finally the publishers stated that the Marquis de la Saone appeared only to have received Volumes I-V of the text; they declared their willingness to give him Volumes VI and VII and to offer him the choice between receiving 72 livres or paying the usual price for the remaining volumes of text and plates.

Clearly there was considerable confusion as to who exactly was a subscriber and there were often long delays in the distribution of the successive volumes of text and plates, since some people were years behind in claiming them. The difficulty of tracing subscribers was stressed in one of the last documents of the case to emanate from the publishers:

> La difficulté est insurmontable, surtout par rapport à ceux qui s'annoncent pour subrogés aux droits de souscripteurs domiciliés dans les provinces. Let titres étoient envoyés à des Libraires enregistrés à Paris, pour autant de souscriptions qu'ils en demandoient; à mesure des livraisons, ils remettoient les volumes aux souscripteurs qui de leur côté, rendoient le titre; il repassoit aux Libraires de Paris, adressé par ceux de province, & dans la plus considérable partie de ces titres, n'avoient pas été employés les noms des souscripteurs; ils étoient demeurés dans leurs mains, comme un billet au porteur, dont les Libraires de province étoient responsables envers eux.[75]

Various documents put out by the publishers contain from time to time references to the names of other individual subscribers. Thus we learn of a certain Moreau, described as

---

[74] There is a further note on his position as on that of Lalande in No. 39 (p. 2).

[75] No. 39, p. 3.

LUNEAU DE BOISJERMAIN V. THE PUBLISHERS 117

'Procurer du Roi du Châtelet', who took only volumes I-VII of the *Encyclopédie*;[76] of a certain Sully de Bellegarde,[77] a letter by whom had been quoted—anonymously—by Luneau;[78] and—in connection with the distribution of the last ten volumes of text in 1766—Starhemberg, the Imperial ambassador in Paris, and the Infante Don Philippe of Parma.[79] However, of all these documents the most important as a source for names of subscribers is Luneau's last *mémoire*.[80] This contains letters of support from the following subscribers:

M. de la Colonge, Lieutenant-Général de la Sénéchaussée de Villefranche en Beaujollais.
M. de Préménil, Château de la Brientaye par S. Malo.[81]
M. la Londe de Sainte-Croix, Lieutenant Général au Bailliage & Siège Présidial de Bayeux.[82]
M. Heubens, Gand.
M. Morel de Villiers, Trésorier de France, Châtillon-sur-Seine, Bourgogne.[83]

---

[76] No. 34, p. 12.
[77] No. 38, p. 6.
[78] No. 32, p. 14n.
[79] No. 39, pp. 6-7. On p. 7 it is stated that Le Breton also received government permission to deliver seven sets of the last ten volumes to a bookseller for transmission to London.
[80] No. 41, *Pièces justificatives*, pp. 2-13.
[81] 'Il convient, Monsieur, que vous soyez prévenu du peu de Souscripteurs qu'il y a ici, & par conséqent du nombre très médiocre des Exemplaires existants aujourd'hui de cet Ouvrage. Il est cependant l'arsenal où se fournissent quelques petits Salmonées qui jappent contre les choses sacrées, mais qui au fond apprécient assez leurs opinions empruntées pour n'en pas donner plus qu'elles ne valent, lorsqu'ils s'arrangent pour qu'elles ne leur coûtent rien'. He admits that he gave up taking the *Encyclopédie* after Volume VII.
[82] It is not easy to see why the next letter—from M. Paterelle of Gournay-en-Bray—should be printed here since it begins: 'Monsieur, je n'ai point souscrit pour le Dictionnaire Encyclopédique'.
[83] 'Je suis le seul des trois de ma ville qui avoient souscrit pour cet ouvrage, qui ai reçu les 17 volumes de discours, & les 11 volumes de planches. L'un des trois est mort, & ce qu'il avoit de ce livre a passé à son héritier, qui est Président à la Chambre des Comptes de Dijon. L'autre a seulement tiré les 17 volumes de discours, & la premiere livraison des planches qui a été faite, n'ayant pas voulu les suivantes, à cause du prix excessif que l'on en a voulu avoir & de l'augmentation.'

M. d'Olimpies, Olimpies.
M. Marel, Secrétaire perpétuel de l'Académie, Dijon.[84]
M. de Titelouze de Gournay, S. Omer.
M. Royer, Chanoine du Chapitre de Notre-Dame d'Amboise.[85]
M. Gillaboz, Conseiller-pensionnaire de Cambray, & Subdélégué de l'Intendance du Hainault.
Mlle Clisson, Chartres.[86]
feu M. de la Condamine[87]

Yet more names of subscribers are provided in the same *factum*[88] in a list of those who had signed a document in support of Luneau's claims. The following is the list in the form given by him (it will be noticed that a few of the names given above are repeated here):

A Soissons le 12 Juin 1777. M. le Duc de Tournelle Trésorier de France, Receveur des décimes; Desevelinge Seigneur d'Espagin de l'Académie de Soissons; Maréchal, ancien Capitaine de Cavalerie; Brayer, Avocat en Parlement; Madame Veuve Quinquet; M. Lemaire, ancien Directeur des Domaines; Madame Veuve Branche-Godart de Ruixet; MM. Laurès, Procureur de l'Abbaye de S. Jean de Vignes; Petit, Docteur en Médecine.

A Amboise le 12 Juin 1777 M. Royer aîné, Chanoine du Chapitre noble d'Amboise.

A Paris le 18 Mai 1777. MM. Maignan de Savigny, ancien Avocat, Conseiller à la Table de marbre, & Censeur Royal; Adams ci-devant chargé des affaires du Roi à Venise tant pour lui que pour défunt M. Pierre Frazé, dont il est exécuteur Testamentaire.

A. S. Omer le 15 Juin 1777. MM. Titelouze de Gourney, Gaillon Avocat, Duval.

A Chatillon sur Seine le 15 Juin 1777. M. Lambert, Procureur du Roi à la Maréchaussée, ayant souscrit lui seul pour 2 Exemplaires.

A Tournai le 5 Juillet 1777. M. J. T. de Flinne, Libraire.

[84] 'J'avois souscrit à Paris en 1752, pour un de mes oncles' (now dead).
[85] 'Je suis le seul Souscripteur de cette ville'.
[86] She states that she has paid 588 livres, without counting in the cost of binding, for the *Encyclopédie*, having given up when the plates reached the letter H because she was disgusted with the mounting cost of the work.
[87] A letter from him, dated 2 June 1774, is reproduced. In this he refers to Luneau's struggle with the publishers: 'Où en est votre procès avec eux au sujet de l'Encyclopédie? Je ne vois point de souscripteur qui ne pense comme vous; mais on vous laisse attacher le grelot; ainsi va la monde.'
[88] No. 41, *Pièces justificatives*, pp. 14-15.

LUNEAU DE BOISJERMAIN V. THE PUBLISHERS

A Bourges le 13 Juin. M. Baraton de Dame, Subdélégué de l'Intendance de Berry; & le 14 Juin 1777: M. Lemonnier, Docteur en Médecine.
A Abbeville le 17 Juin 1777 M. Landais.
A Carcassonne, le 10 Septembre 1777. MM. Rondel de Beriac, de l'Acamémie de Cortone, Receveur des Tailles; Malluet, Ingénieur; Simand, Négociant.
A Etampes le 15 Juin 1777. M. Closier, Correspondant de l'Académie des Sciences.
A Sainte Menehoult le 12 Juin 1777. M. Nicolas-Remy Lesure, Conseiller du Roi, Président, Lieutenant-général du Bailliage de Sainte Menehoult, Légataire universel de défunt M. Jean le Sure, Avocat en Parlement, Souscripteur de l'Encyclopédie.
A S. Quentin le 6 Mai 1777. MM. Neret, Receveur général des Finances: Cottin de Fontaine, Fromagil.
A Arras le 27 Juin 1777, par M. Cornuet, ancien Avocat en Parlement, & au Conseil d'Artois, Echevin de la ville & cité d'Arras; Michel, négociant; Dom Nicolas Hebert, Religieux Bénédictin de l'Abbaye Royale de S. Waast.
A Hesdin, par J. P. Tholiez, Abbé de Dampmartin.
Les mêmes faits sont consignés dans un certificat signé à Avignon par le Comte de Bourk le 17 Juillet 1777.

The last pages of the same document[89] yield the names of other subscribers: the Baron de Heiss, mentioned in a letter to a bookseller of Colmar—Madame la veuve Fontaine; le père Richard, Dominicain, acting as librarian of his convent; and, finally, from letters written by Sartine in 1767, giving permission for subscribers to obtain the last ten volumes of text come the following names:

M. de Maudave qui doit les emporter dans l'Inde . . .
M. le Curé de Saint-Eustache.
M. l'Allemant de Beze.
M. Riballier, Syndic de Sorbonne.[90]
Le Prince d'Esterhazy.[91]

Putting all these together, we have the names of something

---
[89] No. 41, Pièces justificatives, pp. 16-18.
[90] He was also to receive one copy for the Sorbonne library and one for the library of the Collège Mazarin.
[91] Two copies.

like two per cent of the subscribers to the *Encyclopédie*. It is inevitably a somewhat random sample, in which foreign subscribers are obviously under-represented and in which—since most of them are names of supporters of Luneau[92]—those who wanted 'something for nothing' (or next to nothing) are over-represented. Yet this list of names does help to give us some idea of what sort of people put their money into this investment. It cannot be said that, given what we know both of the relatively high cost of the work and of the society of eighteenth-century France, it contains any surprises.[93] The names are those of *grands seigneurs* of the court and of some country gentlemen; representatives of the secular and regular clergy (and their libraries); a great number of lawyers—judges and *avocats* particularly; quite a number of relatively high officials; one or two doctors; some merchants, and so on. We also learn something about the diffusion of the *Encyclopédie* in the provinces of France. It is perhaps surprising, for instance that Châtillon-sur-Seine should have boasted three subscribers, even if only one of them stayed the course, while Amboise and Saint-Malo had only one; but our sample is really too small to base many deductions on it.

IV. THE CRISIS OF 1759

On 23 January 1759, after the *réquisitoire* of Omer Joly de Fleury, the Parlement decided to order an examination of the first seven volumes of the *Encyclopédie*, and on 6 February it appointed nine persons 'pour donner leur avis sur lesdits sept Volumes', in the meantime forbidding 'Durand, Briasson, David, le Breton, & . . . tous autres Imprimeurs ou Libraires, & . . .

[92] We must remember too that he was not very scrupulous in establishing that his supporters were in fact subscribers.
[93] Cf. Daniel Mornet, 'Les Enseignements des bibliothèques privées (1750-1780)' (*RHL*, 1910, p. 469): 'L'*Encyclopédie* se rencontre dans les bibliothèques de 5 avocats, 6 membres de la noblesse, 14 fonctionnaires, 3 parlementaires, 3 ecclésiastiques, 2 abbés, Choiseul archevêque de Cambrai, 2 apothicaires, 2 médecins, 1 académicien (académie des Sciences), La Popelinière, Lamoignon, Hénault.'

toutes personnes de vendre & débiter aucun Exemplaire desdits sept Volumes, sous telles peines qu'il appartiendra, jusqu'à ce qu'autrement par la Cour en ait été ordonné . . .' On 8 March the government intervened with an *Arrêt du Conseil* which revoked the *privilège* of the *Encyclopédie*.

Two interesting comments on this *Arrêt du Conseil* are to be found in the documents of the Luneau case. The *Encyclopédie* was published by virtue of a *privilège* granted on 30 April 1748, but as Luneau and his supporters pointed out for their own purposes,[94] the *Arrêt du Conseil of* 8 March 1759 revoked, not this *privilège*, but an earlier one—that of 21 January 1746. What deduction did Luneau and his associates draw from this undoubted fact? Their aim was to show that the subscriptions to the *Encyclopédie* were not cancelled by this *Arrêt du Conseil* as the publishers claimed; but in advancing this argument, they touch on a second and more interesting question—the reasons behind the government's intervention. If, in practice, the printing of the remaining volumes of text as well as of the volumes of plates went ahead from 1759 onwards,

> Cette exécution de la souscription, cette impression de l'Ouvrage est une preuve que le Gouvernement n'a jamais entendu révoquer le privilège, & que ce n'est point par erreur que l'Arrêt du Conseil a révoqué un vieux privilège au lieu de celui de 1748, en vertu duquel on avoit souscrit. En effet, comme les Libraires le disent eux mêmes, (page 51 de leur Précis)[95] . . . *Le Gouvernement a nécessairement été instruit de cette impression*; il ne l'a point empêchée; donc le Gouvernement a été persuadé que le privilège n'étoit point révoqué. L'Arrêt du Conseil n'a été rendu, suivant les apparences, que pour arrêter les poursuites du Parlement, dont l'attention se tournoit sur cet Ouvrage, & pour donner aux Editeurs la liberté de faire les corrections que le Gouvernement avoit jugées nécessaires, en laissant croire au Parlement que le privilège étoit révoqué.[96]

The exact aim of the government in revoking the *privilège* of

[94] No. 33, p. 5; No. 35, p. 10; the publishers answered this point in No. 34, p. 11.
[95] No. 27.
[96] No. 33, p. 5.

the *Encyclopédie* in March 1759 still remains far from clear. It must be remembered that the clash between government and Parlement over the *Encyclopédie*, when the latter encroached upon the prerogatives of the Chancellor who was responsible for the censoring and licensing of books, was part of a much wider conflict between the Crown and the *cours souveraines* which had raged since the beginning of the 1750s. Several contemporaries—Barbier, Grimm and Voltaire, for instance[97]—insinuate more or less clearly that the *Arrêt du Conseil* of 8 March was an attempt to put the Parlement in its place. Unfortunately Malesherbes's *Mémoires sur la Librairie*, although composed at the very moment of the conflict and full of references to the Parlement's attack on both *De l'Esprit* and the *Encyclopédie*,[98] do not provide a clear answer to the problem; nor does his *Mémoire sur la liberté de la presse*.[99] As his biographer points out,[1] Malesherbes may well have thought that the best way to get the *Encyclopédie* completed was to have the last volumes of text printed clandestinely, without a *privilège*, but nowhere apparently does he reveal what his attitude or that of the government really was.

A second *Arrêt du Conseil* on the subject of the *Encyclopédie* followed in the same year. On 21 July the government decreed that the publishers should refund to the subscribers, in lieu of the 114 livres which they had paid for volumes that they had not received, the sum of 72 livres. 'Aucun Souscripteur', the publishers proclaimed in the very first of their *mémoires* in the lawsuit,[2] 'ne se présenta pour recevoir le remboursement de 72 liv. Le Public desiroit & espéroit la continuation de l'Encyclopédie'. This statement has been repeated parrot-like in modern works on

[97] Barbier,*Chronique de la Régence et du règne de Louis XV* (Paris, 1866), Vol. VII, p. 141; Grimm, *Corr. Litt.*, Vol. IV, p. 96; Voltaire, *Œuvres complètes* (ed. L. Moland), Vol. I, p. 58. Grimm and Voltaire argue, of course, that the Chancellor ought to have quashed the Parlement's *arrêt*.
[98] *Mémoires sur la Librairie et sur la liberté de la presse*, Paris, 1809. See especially pp. 7-11, 15-29, 40-4.
[99] ibid., see especially pp. 351-2.
[1] P. Grosclaude, *Malesherbes témoin et interprète de son temps*, Paris, 1961, pp. 137-8.
[2] No. 6, p. 5.

the *Encyclopédie*³ and also, alas, in modern lectures. Unfortunately it is untrue. It is known that Malesherbes did his best to help the publishers by keeping the news of this government decree out of the *Gazette*,⁴ so that they could go ahead with their plans for publishing the volumes of plates of the *Encyclopédie* which they intended to offer the original subscribers, counting the 72 livres—or rather the full sum of 114 livres—as a contribution towards their cost, i.e. avoiding making any sort of a refund.

Luneau had a right to complain that Le Breton and his partners ought to have offered publicly to repay the sum in question: 'Les Libraires', he maintained, 'auroient dû offrir publiquement dans les Journaux le remboursement des 72 livres. Ils auroient dû prévenir les Souscripteurs de cet Arrêt qui a été inconnu à la plus grande partie d'entr'eux, au moins aux Souscripteurs étrangers.'⁵ There seems absolutely no doubt, however, that quite a number of subscribers did hear of this second *Arrêt du Conseil* and did ask for their 72 livres; but they got a rude reception from the publishers. Perhaps Luneau exaggerates slightly in his account of what followed, but it is not uncorroborated:

> Les Libraires refuserent d'abord de les payer: ils dirent que le Roi *étoit bien le maître d'ordonner ce remboursement; mais qu'il n'avoit qu'à leur faire donner de l'argent pour le faire*: ce sont les paroles de feu David, Libraire, à feu M. le Maréchal de L***, en présence de M.*** actuellement vivant. Pendant ce temps ils solliciterent un privilège pour imprimer le premier volume de planches de l'Encyclopédie. Dès qu'ils l'eurent obtenu, ils répondirent à tous les Souscripteurs qui se présenterent pour être remboursés, qu'ils les rembourseroient en planches.⁶

First Luneau himself,⁷ then the *Intervenants* mentioned a letter to Lefranc de Pompignan, Premier Président of the Cour des Aides at Montauban, refusing to refund the 72 livres. This

---

³ E.g. J. Le Gras, *Diderot et l'Encyclopédie*, Amiens, 1928, p. 133.
⁴ Grosclaude, Malesherbes, p. 135 (see *Essays*, p. 360).
⁵ No. 11, p. 142.
⁶ No. 11, p. 143n.
⁷ No. 28, p. 6 (cf. No. 29, p. 42).

is how the *Intervenants* describe the publishers' behaviour:

> Ils disoient à ceux qui se présentoient pour retirer les 114 livres d'avance. L'Arrêt que voici nous autorise à vous rembourser 72 l. au lieu de 114 liv. Un privilège nous permet de publier un recueil de mille planches. On montroit quelques planches gravées ou des dessins de la forme de l'Encyclopédie. Si vous voulez les prendre, on vous tiendra compte des 114 liv. & vous ne perdrez rien. Si vous ne les prenez pas, vous attendrez que le Roi nous ait fait donner l'argent nécessaire pour vous remplir. Cette réponse est l'extrait de la lettre écrite à M. Lefranc de Pompignan, dont le port est compris sous le n°. 1011 de leurs livres.[8]

What is more, in his last *mémoire* Luneau reproduced a letter from the Père Richard, the librarian of a Dominican convent, dated 22 April 1777, in which he relates how he was snubbed by the publishers when he asked for the refund of his 72 livres:

> Vous souhaitez savoir, Monsieur, si j'ai été remboursé en 1759, de 72 liv. portées dans l'Arrêt du Conseil, qui permettoit aux Libraires de ne rembourser que cette somme sur les 114 liv. que j'avois avancées lors de la livraison des sept premiers volumes. La vérité m'oblige de vous répondre, Monsieur, que m'étant présenté en qualité de Bibliothécaire de notre maison pour être remboursé de ces 72 livres, M. Briasson refusa de faire ce remboursement; & qu'au lieu de me rembourser, il me rebuta avec mépris, & me dit qu'il y auroit bien d'autres comptes à faire. Je fus obligé par-là d'en passer forcément par tout ce que ce Libraire voulut . . .[9]

In contradicting the publishers' famous statement that in 1759 nobody asked for their money back, Luneau even goes so far as to declare that some subscribers did actually succeed in extracting the 72 livres from them: 'Une preuve qu'il s'est présenté des Souscripteurs pour être remboursés, c'est qu'ils ont remboursé feu M. l'Abbé***, Conseiller au Parlement, & quelques autres personnes qu'il est inutile de nommer ici.'[10] The reader,

---

[8] No. 32, p. 4. (For the reference to the publishers' accounts see May, p. 72).
[9] No. 41, *Pièces justificatives*, p. 17.   [10] No. 11, p. 142.

who is accustomed to the exaggerations and crack-brained notions of Luneau, is tempted to regard this story as a mere invention. But his scepticism is chastened when he reads an admission by the publishers themselves that *one* subscriber at any rate did get his money back:

> De près de 4,000 Souscripteurs, il ne s'en présenta qu'un seul, M. Moreau, Procureur du Roi du Châtelet, qui le 31 du même mois de Juillet 1759, reçut & donna quittance des 72 livres au pied de *la reconnoissance de souscription & promesse* des Libraires.[11]

If even one subscriber got his money back, how many more tried to do so, but failed to make the publishers disgorge? I, for one, will never repeat again, either in a lecture or in print, their original claim that 'aucun Souscripteur ne se présenta pour recevoir le remboursement de 72 liv.'

V. THE PLATES

No sooner had the publishers acquired their *privilège* for the separate publication of the plates of the *Encyclopédie* than they were accused in the *Année littéraire*[12] of plagiarizing the work of Réaumur in this field. As might have been expected, Luneau renewed the charge in his very first *mémoire* of 1770[13] and developed it further in a later document.[14] In this he penned a peculiarly vivid passage on the behaviour of the publishers after the committee of the Académie des Sciences had investigated the accusation of plagiarism:

> Les sieurs le Breton & Briasson formerent dès-lors le projet de dissimuler tellement l'emprunt qu'ils avoient fait à M. de Réaumur, qu'on ne les soupçonnoit pas d'en avoir fait le moindre usage. Le moyen qu'ils prirent pour y réussir, fut de mêler les

[11] No. 34, p. 12.
[12] 1759, Vol. VII, pp. 340-51; 1760, Vol. I, pp. 246-57 (the publishers' reply to these allegations is to be found in 1760, Vol. II,, pp. 45-8).
[13] No. 8, p. 7.
[14] No. 11, pp. 48-9, 81, and *Pièces justificatives*, pp. 34-42.

planches de ce sçavant écrivain avec d'autres planches gravées, qu'ils ramasserent de tous côtés. Le sieur ***, le plus grand Bouquiniste en estampes qu'il y ait dans Paris, se chargea de former cette collection. Le temps acheva bientôt la réunion de tous les chiffons qu'il destinoit aux Libraires. Ces gens-là, disoit-il, prendront tout ce que je leur donnerai, pourvu que cela ait l'air d'une planche gravée.[15]

Naturally the publishers defended themselves on this point,[16] and Diderot joined in the controversy with his letter of 31 August 1771.[17] This in turn provoked rejoinders from Luneau.[18]

Whether all this adds much that is new to recent discussions of the question of the originality of the plates of the *Encyclopédie*,[19] it is not easy to say. These documents do, however, throw light on the meaning of a recently published letter of Diderot—the bitter epistle which he wrote to Le Breton on 4 March 1769.[20] It contains an apparently obscure passage about Diderot's relations with Daubenton, which Mme Durry explains as follows:

L'objet du nouveau litige est simple. Le Breton ne veut rien savoir pour exécuter le contrat passé avec Daubenton, qui a rédigé et fait rédiger pour l'Encyclopédie les articles d'histoire naturelle, sauf l'article *Nature* dû à Buffon[21]—contrat évidemment analogue à un autre, qui est connu, lui, et qui avait été passé avec d'Alembert.[22]

---

[15] No. 11, p. 49.
[16] No. 12, pp. 22-5.
[17] No. 12, p. 72 (Roth, Vol. XI, p. 150).
[18] No. 13, pp. 13, 23, 26: No. 15, pp. 50-2; No. 17, pp. 24, 27.
[19] G. Huard, 'Les planches de l'*Encyclopédie* et celles de la *Description des Arts et Métiers*' in *L'Encyclopédie et le progrès des sciences et des techniques* (Paris, 1952), pp. 35-46; J. Proust, 'La documentation technique de Diderot dans l'Encyclopédie' (*RHL*, 1957, pp. 334-52) and J. P. Seguin, 'Courte histoire des planches de l'*Encyclopédie*' in *L'Univers de l'Encyclopédie*, Paris, 1964, pp. 23-35.
[20] *Autographes de Mariemont*, ed, M. J. Durry, Paris, 1955-9, Part I, Vol. II, pp. 593-601 (Roth, Vol. IX, pp. 28-35).
[21] Although it was announced in the preface to Vol. II that Buffon had promised to write the article NATURE, the articles NATURE (*Philos.*) and NATURE, *lois de la* were taken straight from Chambers, even if D'Alembert's signature appears after the second of them (see *Essays*, p. 232).
[22] *Autographes de Mariemont*, p. 599.

This commentary is not convincing; it is difficult to see why in 1769 Diderot should have been haggling with his publisher over payment for work which the famous naturalist, Louis-Jean-Marie Daubenton, had done years earlier for the seventeen volumes of text. The elements of a correct interpretation are to be found in the documents of the lawsuit. Luneau having accused the publishers of charging extortionate prices for the volumes of plates, Stoupe replied on their behalf that the extra amount charged for the volume of plates on Natural History (Volume VI) was due to the fact that 'les 104 premiers Dessins de cette partie ont coûté 6000 livres, & un exemplaire complet de l'ouvrage'.[23]

A full explanation of the matter is offered by Diderot in *Au Public et aux Magistrats*:

> Avant que d'envoyer aux graveurs nos dessins d'histoire naturelle, il me vint en pensée de les soumettre à l'examen du plus célèbre naturaliste de l'Europe, M. Bernard de Jussieu, qui les proscrivit tous. Je ne balançai point à les déchirer; et, sans consulter aucun des associés, en mon nom, de mon autorité privée, je traitai pour cette partie avec un homme dont le mérite est bien décidé dans ce genre: M. Daubenton le jeune.[24]
>
> Au bout de trois années consacrées à ce travail surérogatoire, j'assemblai les libraires et je leur produisis l'ouvrage et le traité. Je ne dirai point que mon precédé leur fot agréable; mais la proposition de publier ce volume à mes frais et dépens arrêta sur le champ leurs plaintes. J'exigeai, en leur cédant mon traité, que cette partie seroit exécutée comme je le désirerois, et il leur fallut encore souscrire à cette condition.
>
> En conséquence, 2,000 écus stipulés dans le traité avec M. Daubenton furent payés.
>
> Au lieu d'imprimer sur du papier à seize francs, on imprima sur du papier à vingt-quatre.
>
> Le prix du tirage fut augmenté d'un quart en sus, et je touchai trois ans de mes honoraires.
>
> Le libraire a-t-il été libre de suivre le prix courant de ses planches?—On voit que non.[25]

---

[23] No. 16, p. 11n.
[24] Diderot describes him as a cousin of Louis-Jean-Marie in the preface to Vol. VI of the plates (see *Essays*, pp. 116-117).
[25] No. 18, p. 375. (Roth, Vol. XI, pp. 113-14).

It is obvious that this passage from *Au Public et aux Magistrats* fits in perfectly with Diderot's letter to Le Breton of 4 March 1769, since it concerns Volume VI of the plates which had appeared the previous year and in particular the undertaking to supply Daubenton le jeune with a complete set of the work. Not only is the account of Daubenton's work for Volume VI of the plates confirmed in another document put out by the publishers which contains a 'Déclaration de M. Benard, Graveur, qui a été le plus employé & qui a dirigé toute l'enterprise',[26] but this same document also throws some light on another point in the letter to Le Breton. This is the reference to D'Holbach's part in the preparation of what Diderot calls 'toute la partie minéralogique'.[27] The engraver's certificate also includes a statement—on the subject of the extra expenses which the publishers had been compelled to incur in connection with their volumes of plates—'qu'il y a eu plus de 60 dessins payés à raison de 30 livres chaque, au moins les doubles comptés pour deux, lesquels composent la partie du regne végétal & minéral, dont M. le Baron d'Holbac est l'auteur'.[28]

VII. LE BRETON'S CENSORING OF THE LAST TEN VOLUMES OF TEXT

It was on 1 January 1771 that Grimm first revealed to the select circle of foreign subscribers to the *Correspondance littéraire*[29] the gruesome story of Le Breton's activities. Before the year was out, Luneau was to broadcast the story, since, moved no doubt by the sort of persistent anger towards Le Breton which is shown in his letter of March 1769 published in the *Autographes de Mariemont,* Diderot had indiscreetly revealed the secret to him. The first allusion to the affair occurs in Luneau's *Mémoire* which is analyzed in Bachaumont in August of this same year. In a footnote[30] he lets the cat out of the bag:

[26] No. 30, p. 41.
[27] p. 595.
[28] No. 30, p. 41 (See *Essays*, pp. 116-117).
[29] Vol. IX, pp. 206-14.
[30] No. 11, p. 53n.

LUNEAU DE BOISJERMAIN V. THE PUBLISHERS

L'inattention avec laquelle l'Encyclopédie a été imprimée est si grande, qu'il y a un très-grand nombre d'articles auxquels on a renvoyé dans l'Encyclopédie, qui ne s'y trouvent pas. Cela est sans doute arrivé par l'effet de la liberté qu'a pris le sieur le Breton de châtrer lui-même un très-grand nombre d'articles.

Worse was soon to follow. Stung by the intervention of Diderot on the side of the publishers in his letter of 31 August 1771,[31] Luneau issued two replies which are full of references—particularly the second—to the editor's articles having had 'le malheur d'être charpentés'.[32]

A typical passage occurs in both of Luneau's replies:[33] 'Dans le choix que vous avez fait des *matériaux* de l'Encyclopédie, il y a bien des articles qu'on auroit pu jetter au feu sans regret. M. le Breton s'en est apperçu comme moi. Vous vous êtes plaint à tous les Gens de Lettres, qu'il avoit châtré tous les articles qui étoient de vous. Vous avez été si fâché de ne les pas trouver dans l'Encyclopédie, que vous ne vouliez plus le voir.' Another reference to Le Bretons activities as censor is the following: 'Vous m'avez appris que jamais il n'avoit voulu consentir à laisser dans l'Encyclopédie vos articles tels que vous les avez faits. Vous m'avez écrit qu'il les avoit *charpentés*.'[34]

Luneau's aim in making these revelations was obviously not to provide material for historians of the *Encyclopédie*, but to avenge himself on Diderot by causing the maximum amount of damage to his reputation with the public[35] and possibly also to embroil him with the authorities, as for instance, when he wrote: 'Allons; dites-nous votre secret. Si l'on n'avoit rien mis dans l'Encyclopédie de contraire aux principes de la Religion & de notre Législation, n'est-il pas vrai que l'Encyclopédie n'auroit pas été interrompue? Il y a plus; n'est-il pas vrai que,

---

[31] No. 12, pp. 68-74 (Roth, Vol. XI, pp. 145-153).
[32] No. 17, p. 10.
[33] No. 13, p. 20 and No. 17, p. 16.
[34] No. 13, p. 21 and No. 17, p. 19 (the last sentence is in no. 17 only).
[35] He certainly seems to have succeeded in doing so with Bachaumont, which offers a whole series of comments hostile to Diderot in 1771 and 1772 (Vol. V, pp. 311, 312, 321; Vol. VI, pp. 64, 151-2, 154).

si l'on ôtoit de cet ouvrage tout ce qui y est répréhensible, il n'y resteroit rien du vôtre?'[36]

It can well be imagined that these revelations of Luneau did not pass unnoticed in 1771; they are commented on, for instance, in Bachaumont.[37] The publishers preserved a discreet silence on the question, unless one takes their claim that the *Encyclopédie*—particularly in its last ten volumes—makes edifying reading as an indirect allusion to Le Breton's handiwork: 'Depuis que ces dix derniers Volumes sont dans le Public, aucune voix ne s'est élevée contr'eux; cette partie de la Métaphysique qui peut égarer, en a été bannie, la Religion, l'autorité publique y sont respectées, tout est dans les bornes de la sagesse; & l'on s'y est uniquement livré aux Sciences & aux Arts dont la discussion n'est jamais à craindre ni pour l'Etat, ni pour le Religion.'[38]

Although, after his exploits as censor of the last ten volumes, Le Breton may well have believed this, it is one of the puzzling features of the whole problem that modern scholars find it difficult to distinguish between the degree of subversiveness to be detected in the first seven volumes of the *Encyclopédie* and the last ten.

In their later publications Luneau and his allies did not let the matter drop entirely. In 1776 he returned to the point: 'Tout Paris a entendu le sieur Diderot se plaindre du sieur le Breton qui a CHARPENTÉ à son insçu, un très-grand nombre de ses articles sur les épreuves qu'il avoit corrigées & sur lesquelles il avoit mis *son bon à tirer*.'[39] In another *factum*, published a few days later he expanded what he had to say in trying to establish that the last ten volumes of text were printed, not in Neuchâtel, but in Paris:

> Le sieur Diderot a corrigé les épreuves de ces volumes dans l'Imprimerie du sieur le Breton. Ce Philosophe a dit que cet Imprimeur avoit eu l'indignité de CHARPENTER les feuilles que M. Diderot avoit corrigées, sur lesquelles ce vertueux Compilateur avoit mis BON A TIRER. Ce CHARPENTAGE est vrai. M. Diderot en

[36] No. 13, pp. 21-2, and No. 17, p. 20.
[37] 20 December 1771 (Vol. VI, p. 64).
[38] No. 20, p. 34.
[39] No. 26, pp. 23-4.

parle dans une de ses lettres qu'il m'a écrites. Le sieur le Breton n'auroit pas CHARPENTÉ les dix volumes de l'Encyclopédie s'ils avoient été imprimés en Suisse. Il est donc certain qu'ils ont été imprimés à Paris.[40]

The *Intervenants* had this to say on the subject, in 1777, when speaking of the effect on the *Encyclopédie* of the *Arrêt du Conseil* of March 1759:

C'en étoit fait pour toujours de cette grande entreprise, si les Editeurs ne s'étoient empressés d'épurer le reste de l'Ouvrage, des traits répréhensibles qui avoient attiré la proscription du commencement. Leur docilité conserva aux lettres & aux sciences ce monument précieux & respectable malgré toutes ses imperfections. Une censure sévère présida à la révision du manuscrit. Le sieur le Breton lui-même, le scalpel à la main, se mit à la tête des Censeurs; il élagua, coupa, charpenta l'Ouvrage de M. Diderot. On a entendu les cris qu'ont arrachés à ce célebre Editeur les mutilations faites à son travail, par l'impitoyable Imprimeur.[41]

While these later references do not add anything to our knowledge of this incident, they do show that Le Breton's censoring of the last ten volumes of the *Encyclopédie* was far from being completely unknown among Diderot's contemporaries in France.

VII. THE DISTRIBUTION OF THE LAST TEN VOLUMES OF TEXT

This question is somewhat befogged in the documents which we are studying because, at any rate so long as Louis XV was alive, the publishers had to keep up the fiction that the last ten volumes of text had been printed at Neuchâtel by Samuel Fauche, a statement which Luneau sought by every means in his power to prove wrong. Yet in the midst of this rather pointless controversy we do encounter from time to time some interesting details about the attitude of the government to the distribution of the last ten volumes of text and about the stages by which it was carried out.

In their first *mémoire* the publishers reproduced the text of the notice issued in January 1766 by Samuel Fauche inviting

[40] No. 28, p. 2.   [41] No. 29, pp. 6-7.

subscribers to collect their volumes,[42] and then made a discreet reference to Le Breton's sojourn in the Bastille in April of that year:

> Le Libraire étranger étoit seul publiquement connu pour auteur de l'impression des dix Volumes; on ne pourroit pas même exciper de ce qu'un des Libraires de Paris avoit facilité la distribution de quelques exemplaires de ces dix Volumes, parce que le Roi a pris connoissance de la part que peut y avoir eu ce Libraire, qu'il lui a fait subir la peine que sa justice & sa prudence ont cru convenable; & qu'il y auroit aujourd'hui plus que de l'indiscrétion à vouloir examiner ce point de fait.[43]

Although embarrassed in his reply ('Je ne veux point lever un voile que la sagesse du Government laisse baissé', Luneau declares), he poured scorn on the whole story of what he refers to contemptuously as 'ce fantôme de Neufchâtel'.[44]

The publishers, however, stuck to their story. In another of the earlier documents in the case they explain that the last ten volumes of text 'avoient paru dès la fin de 1765, & la grande distribution s'en étoit faite en 1766'.[45] In his *Au Public et aux Magistrats*, in answering Luneau's complaint that the last ten volumes, at 20 francs apiece, cost two francs more than the price of the volumes of text as announced in the original prospectus, Diderot throws a little light on the government's whole attitude to the publication of the last part of the text and on the complications which faced both publishers and would-be purchasers. He is here supporting the publishers' argument that the *Arrêt du Conseil* of July 1759 put an end to the whole subscription: 'Si la suite de l'ouvrage paroît à l'ombre d'une tolérance tacite, inspirée par l'intérêt national, le commerçant et l'acquéreur sont par rapport aux dix derniers volumes, proscrits avant que d'être nés, comme si l'un demandoit à l'autre un Bayle, ou quelque ouvrage de cette nature.'

He goes on to produce an imaginary dialogue between subscriber and publisher:

[42] No. 6, p. 16.
[43] No. 6, pp. 26-7.
[44] No. 8, p. 9.
[45] No. 12, p. 18.

L'ACQUÉREUR. J'ai les sept premiers volumes de votre ouvrage, et je voudrois en avoir la suite.
LE LIBRAIRE. Je ne me mêle plus de cette entreprise. Je vous dois des planches, et je vous en fournirai quand il en paroîtra; mais pour toute ma fortune je ne vous délivrerois pas ici ce que vous me demandez.
L'ACQUÉREUR. Comment ferai-je donc?
LE LIBRAIRE. Si vous m'indiquiez quelqu'endroit au loin, on pourroit se charger de vous compléter: à vos risques et fortunes, s'entend.[46]

In 1772 the publishers still continued to maintain that the last ten volumes of the *Encyclopédie* were printed by Fauche. Indeed they were able to produce a letter, sent to them by Fauche, in which the Comte de Saint-Florentin accepted the latter's offer of a copy of the last ten volumes of the work:

A Fontainebleau le 10 Decembre 1765.

J'ai reçu, Monsieur, votre lettre du 27 Octobre dernier. Je suis fâché d'avoir tant tardé à vous répondre; mais la quantité d'affaires que j'ai eues me l'avoient fait perdre de vue. Il est vrai que j'ai les premiers Volumes de l'Encyclopédie, que les Imprimeurs de Paris m'ont donnés dans le tems; & comme je serois fort aise d'avoir la suite, je vous remercie de l'offre que vous me faites de me l'envoyer, & je recevrai les dix derniers Volumes de cet Ouvrage avec plaisir. Je suis véritablement, Monsieur, entierement à vous.

Signé, SAINT-FLORENTIN.

M. S. Fauche, Libraire à Neuchâtel.[47]

It is interesting to see how the French government participated in this comedy over the publication of the last ten volumes of the *Encyclopédie*. Yet on the very same page of this document we find the publishers arguing that, since ten folio volumes could not have been printed in Paris without the fact becoming known, 'il en résulte que ces dix Volumes n'auroient pas pu être imprimés à l'insçu des Officiers de la Chambre Syndicale & desdits Inspecteurs; une seconde conséquence seroit que le Gouvernement

---

[46] No. 18, pp. 377-8. (Roth, Vol. XI, pp. 116-17).
[47] No. 20, p. 39.

auroit été instruit de cette impression; & la derniere conséquence, que ne l'ayant point empêchée, le Gouvernement auroit tacitement permis, ou, si l'on veut, toléré cette impression . . .' This is, of course, precisely what did happen.

Le Breton also stresses here the direct interest which Louis XV took in the publication of the last ten volumes: 'Personne n'ignore que Le Roi a pris personnellement connoissance de la distribution des dix Volumes'[48]—a fact which is confirmed by the correspondence of Saint-Florentin with Sartine in this period. The publishers develop this point further in another document of 1776:

Que l'on ne croye pas que les Libraires hasardent trop, en avançant que le feu Roi a pris personnellement connoissance de la distribution de ces dix volumes faits au nom de Fauche, & que le Gouvernement savoit tout ce qui se passoit: les Libraires seroient en état da le prouver jusqu'à l'évidence.[49] Par plusieurs lettres de M. de Sartine, alors Lieutenant général de Police, aujourd'hui Ministre, au sieur Le Breton, commissionnaire de Fauche, ils en ont produit quelques unes au procès, deux entre autres des 15 Avril & 3 May 1766, par lesquelles ce Ministre marque *au nom du Roi au sieur Le Breton, de remettre, lui-même à des Ministres étrangers la suite de l'Encyclopédie.* On voit même que le sieur Le Breton a remis le 28 Décembre 1768 les trois exemplaires d'usage à la Bibliothèque du Roi, & personne n'a ignoré dans Paris qu'il en a remis également, toujours au nom du sieur Fauche & suivant l'usage, dans les Bibliothèques particulieres du Roi, & par suite à ceux qui avoient reçu en présent les sept premiers volumes les exemplaires des dix derniers; c'est-à-dire aux premiers Magistrats & aux Ministres.

Il est donc démontré que le Gouvernement a parfaitment sçu tout ce qui se passoit, & que le surplus est devenu le mystere du Gouvernement.[50]

One of the controversial points which kept the attitude of the government to the distribution of the last ten volumes of the *Encyclopédie* in the foreground of the case and thus gradually

---

[48] No. 20, p. 40.
[49] It is obvious that the sentence should end two lines lower (after 'commissionnaire de Fauche').
[50] No. 27, p. 4.

produced some interesting material about this period in the history of the work, was the charge made by the publishers for the *port et emballage* of these volumes. When this was denounced by Luneau as a typical example of the publishers' extortions, Gerbier replied on their behalf that, as the distribution of the work was banned in Paris, copies for subscribers living there had to be sent into the provinces:

> Fauche ayant fait parvenir à Paris des exemplaires des dix derniers Volumes, plusieurs possesseurs des sept premiers voulurent se les procurer, à quelque prix que ce fût. Comme ils savoient que la distribution en étoit défendue à Paris, ils demanderent qu'on les leur adressât en Province, à des distances plus ou moins éloignées. Il a fallu les emballer, pour faire ces envois; & rien n'a été plus juste que de faire payer les frais de ces emballages à ceux qui ont exigé ces envois. Il faut observer qu'il n'y a pas la huitieme partie des acquéreurs qui ait supporté cette dépense.[51]

If this figure could be taken literally—and of that there is considerable doubt—this would mean that less than 500 out of 4,000 or so subscribers were domiciled in Paris and thus had to have their copies sent out into the provinces so long as the ban on their distribution in the capital continued.

It is noticeable that in the second phase of the lawsuit, the period 1776-8, the passage of time and the replacement of Louis XV by Louis XVI enabled the contending parties to speak rather more freely of the conditions under which the last ten volumes were published. In answering once again the charge of extortionate manœuvres over the *emballage et port* of these volumes, the publishers offered an interesting account of the attitude of the government to the resumption of work on the *Encyclopédie* after the crisis of 1759:

> L'Encyclopédie de plus en plus, mémorable par les orages qui l'assaillirent en 1759, conserva des protecteurs également zélés & puissans; la plupart des personnes qui inclinoient à l'extérieur, pour sa proscription publique, faisoient les voeux les plus ardens

[51] No. 25, p. 8.

pour qu'elle fût continuée dans l'ombre du silence. L'autorité supérieure s'y prêta, mais sous des modifications[52] séveres qui se soutinrent pendant long-tems, avec une fermeté extrême. Elle ne se relâcha que pour des cas rares de faveur & de prédilection, qui en devenant une exception à la loi générale, confirment avec éclat, l'intérêt sensible qu'elle prenoit à la voir exécuter.

A partir du rétablissement tacite de l'Encyclopédie, opéré après la tempête de 1759, quiconque voulut se procurer, sous les nouvelles conditions proposées, la continuation de l'ouvrage, se trouva obligé d'en recevoir livraison en province, à l'adresse qu'il donna aux Libraires constitués dans l'interdit absolu d'en faire aucune à Paris, sous les peines les plus graves. Il fallut alors nécessairement faire emballer & transporter les volumes . . . Telle est le source de ces frais d'*emballage* & *de port*, crayonnés avec tant de noirceur par le sieur Luneau . . .[53]

The publishers then proceed to offer documentary proof of the ban on the distribution of the last ten volumes of the *Encyclopédie* in Paris. This consists of letters from Sartine, the *Lieutenant de Police*, to Le Breton allowing a very limited number of exceptions to this ban:

Le magistrat chargé de la police, écrivoit au sieur le Breton, le 15 Avril 1766: M. le Comte de . . . (ministre & secrétaire d'Etat)[54] me mande que le Roi a bien voulu consentir qu'il soit délivré à M. de Stharemberg, ambassadeur de l'Empire, *la suite de l'Encyclopédie* . . . faites, je vous prie, porter à son hôtel, *cette suite, par une personne sûre, afin qu'on n'abuse point de cette facilité*; & par un *post-scriptum* tracé de la propre main du magistrat: je desire que vous preniez la peine d'aller vous-même chez M. l'ambassadeur.

The publishers also refer to a letter of 3 May 1766 from Sartine giving permission to deliver to the 'Ministre plénipotentiaire de

---

[52] Presumably in the sense indicated by the 1762 edition of the *Dictionnaire de l'Académie Française*: 'Modération, restriction, adoucissement d'une proposition, d'une convention. (Il faut apporter quelque modification à ces articles-là.)'
[53] No. 39, p. 5.
[54] i.e. Saint-Florentin.

Parme' a set of the last ten volumes for the Infante Don Philippe.[55]

The ban continued into the year 1767, for the publishers also mention a third letter from Sartine, dated 15 April of that year, allowing seven sets of the last ten volumes to be delivered to a bookseller for dispatch to London—'*en prenant cependant,* dit le Magistrat, *des précautions pour qu'on ne les voye pas sortir de chez vous.*'[56] After mentioning five more letters of the year 1767 allowing sets to be sent to 'des personnes en place', but with the same precautions, the publishers continue:

> S'il n'a fallu rien moins que ces titres respectables pour sortir les Libraires de la défense générale qui leur avoit été intimée, il s'ensuit de nécessité, qu'ils n'ont pas dû délivrer à Paris, d'autres exemplaires que ceux énoncés en ces lettres, ou dans des permissions tacites accordées pendant le tems de la prohibition.
> Aussi est-il vrai de dire, qu'ils s'y sont religieusement conformés. Ceux des anciens souscripteurs domiciliés à Paris, ou ailleurs, qui ont désiré dans le cours de la défense, *la suite* des volumes de discours, n'en sont devenus possesseurs qu'après que les volumes ont été *emballés & chargés* sur les voitures publiques, par les Libraires, aux adresses qu'on leur donnoit pour la Province.

Further light on this question is furnished by the last of Luneau's *mémoires*. Repulsed in his accusations about the publishers' extortions for *port et emballage*, he now used the letters of Sartine to Le Breton to prove that the subscription to the *Encyclopédie* had not been annulled by the *Arrêt du Conseil* of 1759, since, as he put it, 'les lettres que M. de Sartine a écrites & que le sieur le Breton a produites au procès, prouvent que les Ministres du Roi ne permettoient à ce Libraire de délivrer les dix derniers volumes de Discours qu'aux personnes qui avoient

---

[55] No. 39, p. 6. The Archives Nationales (o¹408) possess file copies of a letter of Saint-Florentin to Sartine (15 April 1766) (p. 269) giving the King's permission for the volumes to be delivered to the Austrian ambassador 'qui est sur son départ' and another (21 April) (p. 286) giving permission for a set to be delivered to D'Argental for the Infante Don Philippe on condition that they be dispatched at once to Parma.

[56] No. 39, p. 7.

souscrit'. He then obligingly goes on to provide us with more details about some of the letters mentioned by the publishers. He reproduces the letter of Sartine of 15 April 1767, concerning the seven sets to be sent to London by the bookseller, Hochereau, and four other letters of the same year, dated respectively 7 May, 27 May, 2 June and 1 November.[57] These last letters gave instructions to provide sets for the following persons: M. de Maudave 'qui doit les emporter dans l'Inde'; the *curé* of Saint-Eustache; M. M. l'Allemant de Bèze; Voltaire's old friend Riballier, the *syndic* of the Faculty of Theology (who was also to receive a copy for the Bibliothèque de Sorbonne and another for that of the Collège Mazarin); and the Prince d'Esterhazy (who received two copies).

The sticky attitude adopted by the government over the distribution of copies of the last ten volumes of the *Encyclopédie* in the Paris region is well-known. This partly tied up with the meeting of the Assemblée du Clergé, as Bachaumont pointed out on 24 April 1766: 'Le Clergé a trouvé très-mauvois qu'on eût choisi le moment où il venoit de proscrire authentiquement l'Encyclopédie, & celui où il alloit se rassembler, pour publier la continuation complette de cet ouvrage, au nombre de dix volumes. Il a tant crié que M. de St. Florentin s'est fait donner les noms de tous ceux qui en avoient retiré les exemplaires, & leur a donné un ordre du Roi de les rapporter au Lieutenant de Police.'[58]

If the news item which follows on the next page—'Les Libraires, Auteurs & Co-opérateurs des travaux de cette Edition, sont mis à la Bastille'—was grossly exaggerated since only Le Breton was imprisoned there, the *Mémoires secrets* were correct in stating that those subscribers who had received their copies were told to return them. On 21 April Saint-Florentin wrote to Sartine:

Le Roy ayant fait faire des deffenses aux Libraires, qui ont entrepris l'Edition de l'encyclopédie, a été informé qu'il en avoit été envoyé un grand nombre d'exemplaires à Versailles, Sa Majesté m'a donné ses ordres pour faire retirer les dix derniers volumes de cet ouvrage, ce qui est deja executé icy; mais l'inten

[57] No. 41, pp.17-18. [58] Vol. III, p. 23.

LUNEAU DE BOISJERMAIN V. THE PUBLISHERS

tion de sa Majesté est que vous vous informiés de tous ceux auxquels on en a delivré à Paris, et que vous vous les fassiés raporter, en avertissant qu'on en fera rendre le prix de la souscription. Vous aurés agreable de me metre en etat de rendre Compte à sa majesté de ceux qui vous auront fait raporter leurs Exemplaires, et de ceux qui après l'avis que vous leur auréz donné, difereroient de se conformer aux intentions de sa Majesté et attendu que le sieur le Breton est reprehensible d'avoir commencé cette distribution, malgré la deffense qui luy en a été faite, je joins icy l'ordre du Roy pour le faire conduire à la Bastille.[59]

It would be interesting to discover how long the severe restrictions on the distribution of these last ten volumes persisted. We know from the letters of Sartine quoted above that it certainly lasted until November 1767; but neither the publishers nor Luneau state when the restrictions came to an end. All that the publishers have to tell us on the subject is contained in the not very helpful sentence: 'Ces obstacles momentanés n'ont pas plutôt cessé, que les frais d'*embellage & de port* ont péri avec eux.'[60]

VIII. DIDEROT'S CRITICISMS OF THE ENCYCLOPÉDIE

This well-known document (reproduced in the Assézat-Tourneux edition)[61] is one of the most interesting among those preserved for posterity by the lawsuit between Luneau and the publishers. In the printed documents which we are examining the first reference to it occurs in the *Précis pour les Libraires associés à l'Encyclopédie, contre le sieur Luneau de Boisjermain & contre sept Intervenans* which appeared in June 1772:

Quatrieme Point. Les imperfections de l'Encyclopédie. On a mis dans la bouche des Intervenans la critique la plus amere de

---

[59] Archives Nationales, o¹ 408, p. 287. This letter is reproduced, somewhat inaccurately, in *Les Archives de la Bastille*, ed. F. Ravaisson, Paris 1866-1904, 19 vols., Vol XII, p. 476, which offers further details on Le Breton's imprisonment both there and in Vol. XIX, pp. 12, 267n. and 269.
[60] No. 39, p. 8.
[61] Vol. XX, pp. 129-33.

cet Ouvrage; on a lu un Mémoire présenté pour obtenir le Privilege pour une nouvelle Edition; on rapporte dans ce Mémoire tous les défauts, tous les vices de l'Ouvrage, remarqués, dit-on, par le principal Editeur de l'Encyclopédie; & les Intervenans n'ont pas craint de donner aux Libraires quelque part aux témérités qui ont attiré la condamnation de l'Ouvrage.[62]

To this Luneau retorted:

On a mis dans la bouche des Intervenans la critique le plus amere de cet ouvrage. Comment peut-on accuser les Intervenans d'avoir critiqué l'Encyclopédie? Il est vrai qu'ils ont fait lire à l'audience un Mémoire dans lequel *on rapporte tous les défauts, tous les vices de cet ouvrage, remarqués, dit-on, par le principal éditeur.* Ils n'ont eu d'autre objet que de montrer qu'on avoit eu tort de se prévaloir de sa perfection, pour prouver qu'on n'avoit (*sic*) eu raison de la leur faire payer 850 livres. Si cette critique est amere ce n'est pas aux intervenans qu'on doit s'en prendre: ils n'y ont rien mis du leur: la voici telle qu'elle a été rapportée à l'audience. Deux Libraires vouloient donner une nouvelle édition de l'Encyclopédie;[63] ils rendent compte de ce que le sieur Diderot leur a dit à ce sujet.[64]

He then went on to quote the passage beginning 'L'imperfection de l'Encyclopédie' . . . and the rest of the opinions expressed by Diderot as given in the version which appears in the Assézat-Tourneux edition.[65] In this first version the names of the contributors to the *Encyclopédie* are, of course, omitted. Luneau added after this long passage an extremely pertinent comment on the fact that Panckoucke should have abandoned his original project for a revised edition of the *Encyclopédie* in favour of a straightforward reprint of the original work: 'Ce qui doit paroître bien étonnant, c'est qu'après la connoissance que le Libraire Panckoucke avoit des défauts de l'Encyclopédie, il s'est engagé à la faire imprimer ligne pour ligne, mot pour mot . . .'[66]

Naturally the publication of this frank account of the shortcomings of the work created something of a stir, as we see for

---

[62] No. 20, p. 31.
[63] See *Essays*, p. 58.
[64] No. 22, p. 10.
[65] i.e. Vol. XX, pp. 130-3.
[66] No. 22, p. 13.

instance from the comments on this part of Luneau's *mémoire* in Bachaumont, both when the work first appeared and especially a few days later.[67] On the second occasion Bachaumont explains the origins of this document as follows:

> C'est à l'occasion d'une nouvelle Edition que le Sr. Panckoucke vouloit donner de l'Encyclopédie, qu'il avoit présenté à M. de Sartines, comme Lieutenant de police & chef de la Librairie, un Mémoire rédigé par M. Diderot, où celui-ci, sous prétexte de montrer à ce Magistrat les raisons du travail qu'on proposoit, prouvoit combien le premier ouvrage étoit informe & méritoit une refonte. Cette critique, dans laquelle les auteurs étoient nommés, & qui a été rendue publique dans la réponse signifiée à[68] M. Luneau, avoit été lue publiquement à l'audience par Me. Bellot, l'un des Avocats plaidans pour les souscripteurs.

After relating how Gerbier, who appeared for the publishers, had tried to interrupt the reading to demand an explanation of the source of the document in question, the *Mémoires Secrets* continue: 'Au surplus, le Mémoire est authentique, & sort des Bureaux de la Police, dont M. de Sartines a bien voulu le laisser enlever. Mais l'anecdote fait un vacarme du diable parmi tous les auteurs critiqués, & attire au Sr. Diderot une multitude d'ennemis sur les bras.'

Not content with publishing this document in 1772, Luneau reproduced it again in 1776 amongst the *pièces justificatives* of yet another *mémoire*, with a title—'Extrait d'un Mémoire présenté en 1768 à Monsieur le Chancelier par MM.**, Libraires de Paris, pour obtenir la permission de faire une nouvelle Edition de l'Encyclopédie en France' and with a longer introduction.[69] Once again, the names of the criticized contributors are replaced by asterisks.

While it is possible to identify most of them fairly easily, there are some doubtful cases, and the identifications suggested in the Assézat-Tourneux edition are not always satisfactory. It would

---

[67] Vol. VI, pp. 151-2 (23 June 1772) and pp. 154-5 (29 June 1772).
[68] This should read *de* (see the title of No. 22).
[69] No. 26, pp. 37-9. This is the version reproduced in AT, Vol. XX, pp. 129-33.

be extremely interesting to have the full text of the original *mémoire*, but so far all efforts to trace it have failed.[70]

A typical example of the sort of difficulty presented by the absence of names in this document is found in the case of the last contributor referred to in it: 'J'oubliois de dire qu'il y a en tout genre au moins quatre volumes in-folio du ***, dont il y a très-peu de choses à conserver. Il n'en peut rester que la nomenclature.' The Assézat-Tourneux edition suggests that the missing name is that of Chambers, but there is every reason to accept the suggestion put forward by M. Jean Mayer that we should here insert the name of the unfortunate Chevalier de Jaucourt.[71] It would certainly be interesting to have the original text of the *mémoire*.

IX THE PUBLISHERS' ACCOUNTS

These were made available to scholars, although in an incomplete form, by M. Louis Philippe May's series of articles published in the *Revue de Synthèse* in 1938.[72] The precious volume which M. May discovered in the Archives Nationales[73] is incomplete since the 'Livre des Délibérations' breaks off in April 1762, while the expenses stop in 1767 and the receipts in 1768, although the last volumes of plates did not appear until 1772. Moreover the cover of the volume, at the end where the 'Livre de Depense & Recette' begins, bears the inscription: *Encyclopedie Journal A*, which leads one to the conclusion that there must have been at least a *Journal B*.

In publishing *Journal A* M. May pointed out[74] that it had

[70] It will be noticed that whereas, according to Bachaumont, the *mémoire* was addressed to Sartine, Luneau gives it out (No. 26, p. 37) as being addressed to the Chancellor. Cf. Gerbier to Diderot (Roth, Vol. XI, p. 254): 'Qu'est-ce que cette critique de l'Encyclopédie, que M. Pankouke a citée comme de vous dans un mémoire à M. de Sartine. On en a fait un grand étalage'. Panckoucke himself quoted some of Diderot's remarks from this *mémoire* in the prospectus of the *Encyclopédie méthodique* (n.p., 1782), pp. 5-6.
[71] *Diderot homme de science* (Rennes, 1959), p. 37n. (See Chap. II, pp. 49-50).
[72] See Chap. III, pp. 71-76.   [73] U1051.
[74] In a note entitled 'Histoire du Document' on an unnumbered page which follows p. 109.

been deposited with the Paris Parlement on 4 February 1777,[75] along with other papers of the publishers, and that while the rest of these documents were returned in February of the following year, this one must have been mislaid, which would explain its presence among the archives of the Paris Parlement.

A great deal of light is thrown on the nature and contents of the documents deposited by the publishers in 1777 by one of the most interesting of the forty odd publications to which Luneau's lawsuit gave rise—the *Supplément au Mémoire des Souscripteurs Intervenants* which appeared in March 1777.[76] The publishers' opponents, who managed to obtain access to these documents, describe them as consisting of the following items:

Le sieur Le Breton appelle *livres de dépense de l'Encyclopédie*, le journal sur lequel le sieur Briasson, chargé de la caisse de la société, rendoit compte à lui-même & à ses Associés de l'argent que la distribution de l'Encyclopédie a fait passer par ses mains. Ce journal forme deux volumes; il renferme une partie de la recette des Libraires associés, & quelques-unes de leurs délibérations.

Deux mille trois cents trente-trois articles rangés par ordre de numéros,[77] comprennent dans ces deux volumes tout ce qui a été payé par le sieur Briasson aux personnes employées à la confection de l'Encyclopédie, ou aux Libraires ses associés. Le premier volume de ce journal commence au premier Décembre 1745; la dépense continue dans le second volume, & finit en 1775.[78]

As for the other documents deposited by the publishers, the *Supplément* makes the following statement: 'Le sieur le Breton ne nous a pas procuré sur sa recette les mêmes secours d'instruction que sur ses dépenses. Ses Journaux de recette n'ont pas été

---

[75] At the top of the first page at the end of the volume which contains the expenses and receipts there is the inscription (reproduced by M. May on p. 31n): 'Premiere [pièce] m[ise] au greffe le 4 fevrier 1777'.
[76] No. 31. See also No. 32, pp. 4-6, No. 35, p. 11, No. 41, pp. 6-7, 9, and (this contains the publishers' indignant protest against these documents being communicated to their opponents) No. 38, pp. 9-10.
[77] *Journal A* contains only 1,763 items under this head.
[78] No. 31, p. 3. In this document the two volumes in question are frequently referred to as *Journal A* and *Journal B*.

produits.[79] Il s'est contenté de mettre au jour une espece de registre de souscriptions dans lequel on ne trouve, ni la date, ni les paiements qui ont été faits, ni les personnes qui ont souscrit.'[80] The documents deposited with the court consisted then of three: *Journal A*, *Journal B* and the register of subscriptions, of which only the first has so far been discovered.

In thinking of such a large undertaking as the *Encyclopédie*, one tends to imagine that by the time the work was completed the accounts must have filled rows and rows of large ledgers. One must, however, reckon with the possibility that the publishers' book-keeping was of a very rudimentary character—perhaps deliberately so. They may well have preferred to keep accounts down to a minimum, both to save time and to avoid difficulties with the tax-collector. It is quite possible that a large number of their transactions were never neatly entered in any ledger. After all, we must remember that tax-evasion, while apparently of long standing on both sides of the Channel, is reputed to flourish even more to the south than to the north of it. It is at least possible that, unsatisfactory as these documents may have been, both to the publishers' opponents and to the historian of the *Encyclopédie*, they were all that the publishers had kept in the way of books.

It is also obvious that when they published extracts from the publishers' accounts, the litigants were not concerned to fill in the gaps in our knowledge of the history of the *Encyclopédie* produced by the disappearance of *Journal B*. What they were out to do was to prove that the publishers had made enormous profits by charging the subscribers an extortionate price for the work. Far from transcribing the whole of the missing volume for the benefit of posterity, they merely selected a small number of items which, they thought, supported their case. What is more,

---

[79] This is misleading. Starting at the end of *Journal A* which contains the 'Livre de Depense & Recette', we find the receipts, down to 1768, written in on the recto of ff. 3-12, and f. 12r⁰ ends with the words 'La suite de recette est au livre nouveau' (cf. May, pp. 99-109). This might lead one to suppose that *Journal B* also contained information about the receipts.

[80] No. 31, p. 9. For a discussion of the light which this document throws on the number of subscribers see above, p. 106.

where we can check their methods of transcription by reference to *Journal A*, they do not appear to be anything like one hundred per cent accurate.

To take some examples. In the *Supplément* the subscribers state: 'On lit sous les Nº. 183 et suivants; *payé à M. Goussier 6 liv. pour un dessein; 12 liv. pour deux desseins*, & ainsi de suite; sous le Nº. 1073: *24 liv. à M. Goussier, pour trois desseins, y compris un voyage.*'[81] The second of these references is correct; the first, perhaps owing to a printer's error, is wrong. In his next publication[82] Luneau states perfectly correctly that 'une délibération écrite dans les Livres journaux des Libraires, avoit autorisé le sieur Briasson à retirer ce coupon le plus qu'il pourroit'.[83] He then adds: 'On voit sur les Livres des Libraires qu'avant cette délibération, les Libraires de Londres avoient payé les volumes de planches 18 liv. On y lit que les Libraires de Province ne devoient les payer que 25 liv., tant qu'il y en auroit, & les Souscripteurs 28 liv.'

This gives a false impression of what we actually find in *Journal A*:

Elle est convenue en outre qu'il sera fait aux libraires de province trois livres de rabbais sur chacun des Volumes des planches ..., en sorte qu'au lieu de 28^{11} que payent les Souscripteurs, Ils ne payeront chacun de ces Vol^{es} que 25^{11} en feuilles, pour autant de Volumes qu'il en pourra paroitre; mais comme les Srs Vaillant & Nourse lib^{res} a Londres, ont refusé pour les exemple^{res} qu'ils ont tirés, les premieres avances que les Souscripteurs ont fait: et qu'ils ont exigé les Vol^{es} au prix seulement de 18^{11}, La Compagnie a decidé qu'ils payeroient chacun des Vol^{es} de planches a raison de cinquante livres piece, au lieu de Cent livres a quoy ils sont fixés pour ceux qui n'ont pas souscrit, leur abandonnant les 50^{11} restant pour leur proffit.[84]

---

[81] No. 31, p. 7.
[82] No. 32, p. 3.
[83] May, p. 29 (26 February 1762). The actual words of the MS are: 'Elle autorise le d^t Briasson a retirer le plus qu'il pourra les souscriptions en donnant a la place un billet conçu en ces termes ...'
[84] Cf. May, p. 30.

It is a somewhat partial interpretation of this text to pretend that the London booksellers in question actually *paid* 18 livres a volume, carefully suppressing the rest of the sentence which gives the price as 50 livres.

Luneau then proceeds to give a lurid account of the manœuvres employed by the publishers to secure the issue of the *Arrêt du Conseil* of 21 July 1759: 'On trouve sur leurs livres les dépenses qu'ils ont faites en voyages, diners, festoiements, carrosses pour cet objet. On lit expressément au n°. 987, *course chez M. de ******, au sujet de l'arrêt qui ordonne la restitution de 72 liv. 9 liv. 12 sols.* Autres chez M. *** qui l'a signé.'[85] This is not a particularly accurate transcription of item 987 in *Journal A*; it reads:

Deux Courses chez M. De Malesherbes au Sujet de l'arrest
qui ordonne[86] le remboursem^t de 72^{11} 3. 10
seconde Course chez le meme et chez Mgr le Chancelier
Mr de Bombarde & ailleurs   4. 12
Course de M^{rs} le Breton & David chez plus^{rs} Magistrats 3.   [87]

What we are in fact offered is a very garbled version of this particular part of *Journal A*. The figure of '9 l. 12s.' is taken from item 991—'remboursé a M. Le Breton p^r courses 9. 12.'; there were two visits to Malesherbes, and not one, under the first item quoted above; the *Arrêt du Conseil* in question was signed 'Phelypeaux' and his name does not appear in the publishers' accounts. In this part of *Journal A* there is mention of quite a number of visits to various official personages, but the only suggestion of any sort of *diners* or *festoiements* at this period in the history of the *Encyclopédie* occurs under the item 971 (at least nominally in 1758):[88] 'Diners & Voitures p^r les Editeurs 50. 14'.

[85] No. 32, p. 5.
[86] Luneau reproduces the word as *ordonne* in the above passage, but later (No. 35, p. 11) he gave it as *ordonnera*, adding in a marginal note: 'Il y a une rature dans le Livre. La syllabe RA est effacée.' On the MS there seems to be nothing but a blot between *ordonne* and *le*.
[87] Cf. May, p. 71.
[88] The page covering items 959 to 984 is headed '1758', but the last item on it—600 livres paid to Patte—was paid on 9 June 1759 according to a receipt produced by the publishers (*Année littéraire*, 1760, Vol II, p. 48).

In other words, the corrupt methods which, Luneau was trying to insinuate, were used to secure the *Arrêt du Conseil* of 21 July 1759, were merely a figment of his imagination.

One last example of the inaccuracy with which the publishers' opponents transcribed the accounts contained in *Journal A* is the following:

L'arrêté de la dépense des Libraires, d'après leurs
livres, monte, au 2 Avril 1760 à .... 380,219 liv. 12s. 2d
Celui du 28 Décembre 1757 monte à ...... 270,585 liv. 15s.

Dans l'intervalle de ces deux époques,
les Libraires n'ont rien délivré aux
Souscripteurs, & ils ont dépensé pour
la continuation de l'Encyclopédie .... 109,633 liv. 17s. 2d[89]

Compare these figures with those contained in *Journal A*: the sum of 270,585 liv. 15s. was roughly the total expended down to 28 December 1754, and that of 380,219 liv. 12s. 2d. the amount expended down to 2 April 1757.[90]

Such errors, whether careless or deliberate, do not inspire confidence in the correct transcription of the items selected from the missing volume of accounts, *Journal B*. Yet, as beggars cannot be choosers, we must content ourselves with such items from this second volume as the litigants cared to extract. Some of these are not without interest. *Journal A* breaks off at the point where, on 11 March 1768, the expenses had reached, with item 1763, a total of 1,039,642. 1. 7s. 3d. *Journal B* carried the number of items down to 2333 and the total expenses came to 2,205,839 1. 4s.[91] The total receipts of the enterprise, according to the publishers' *requête* of 4 February 1777, came to 'quatre millions, sauf les reprises'.[92] This last term meant in practice the sum of 430,000 livres which represented the value of unsold volumes of text and plates.

In endeavouring to make mincemeat of the publishers' denial

---

[89] No. 32, p. 5.
[90] Cf. May, pp. 67, 69. The exact amount disbursed down to 28 December 1754 was 270,886 l. 15s.
[91] No. 31, p. 3.
[92] No. 36, p. 2.

that they had made immense profits out of the *Encyclopédie*, the litigious subscribers brought to light a certain amount of information from the missing volume of accounts. Claiming that the expenses included 'le paiement d'un grand nombre d'objets, tout-à-fait étrangers à leur entreprise', they began by pointing out that among these were sums amounting to 822,000 livres which Le Breton and his partners paid out to themselves. If 516,000 livres of this sum are covered by *Journal A*,[93] we learn here that there was an extra disbursement of 306,000 livres in April 1769.[94] They also quote from *Journal A*[95] purchases of *Récipissés des Fermes* costing, including expenses, 40,003 l. 4s. and then go on to exclaim: 'Ainsi pour convaincre le sieur Luneau d'erreur, de mensonge & de mauvaise foi, le sieur le Breton présente comme une dépense faite pour l'exécution de l'Encyclopédie, 862,000 l. levées sur les Souscripteurs, à titre de bénéfice . . . Et c'est avec un journal de dépense, ainsi disposé, que le sieur le Breton prétend établir *la fausseté des assertions du sieur Luneau & de ses adhérens.*'[96] They point out quite correctly that 'Le Caissier Briasson n'a porté ces 862,000 l. à la dépense de l'Encyclopédie, que pour rendre compte à sa caisse de l'argent qui en sortoit'.

Not content with claiming that this substantial sum should be removed from the expenses of the *Encyclopédie*, the publishers' opponents proposed a great many more deductions, starting with the repayment of a loan of 16,000 livres, plus interest.[97] The next deduction suggested concerns the interest on sums of 30,000 livres and 12,000 livres which Diderot and Jaucourt received respectively from the publishers from 1761 onwards;[98] basing themselves on *Journal B,* they declare that the total interest paid to the two men came to some 26,000 livres.[99]

---

[93] 36,000 livres in July 1751 (items 701, 703, 707, 708, 711); 30,000 livres in February 1752 (items 748-751); and 450,000 livres on 16 March 1768 (the last item in *Journal A*) (see May, p. 109).
[94] *Journal B*, items 1788, 1789, 1790 and 1889.
[95] Items 1663 and 1666 (end of 1766 and beginning of 1767).
[96] No. 31, p. 4.
[97] Items 10 and 105.
[98] Cf. May, p. 108.
[99] *Journal A* contains numerous references to these interest payments.

In addition the subscribers would have liked to deduct from the expenses listed in the accounts—not always justly, one would imagine—what they describe as '24,0000 liv. environ provenant du remboursement fait au sieur le Breton de dépenses etrangeres à l'Encyclopédie; des frais d'escompte; du rabais fait à divers Libraires sur des numéros de souscriptions, ou pour surhaussement à leur prix qu'il a fallu restituer; des paiements fait[s] pour des volumes de l'Encyclopédie, rachetés à la Chambre; pour transport de ceux qu'on a envoyés par commission; pour leur relieure; pour l'acquisition de l'Imprimerie de Trévoux; pour les livres achetés & rendus aux Libraires, &c. &c. &c.'[1] This is followed by an attack on the publishers' expense-accounts; it is suggested that '1,200 liv. environ dépensées en voitures, courses, diners, parties de plaisirs pour entretenir la joyeuseté des Libraires associés, en gratifications à des domestiques &c. &c.'[2] should also be struck out.

Then come two items from *Journal B* which are not without interest: first, 'l'argent payé sous le n°. 1969, pour intercepter à Lyon les Mémoires que le sieur Luneau envoyoit à ses connoissances';[3] and then an amusing item which casts a little new new light on the relations of Le Breton and his partners with the Neuchâtel publisher under whose imprint the last ten volumes of the *Encyclopédie* appeared—'*834 liv. 10 sols données à Samuel Fauche pour le bénéfice de son nom*. Comment les Libraires osent-ils présenter, dans un état de dépense destiné à faire disparoître l'idée du bénéfice injuste qu'ils ont fait, une somme payée pour accréditer une IMPOSTURE qui a servi à tromper les Souscripteurs[?]'.[4]

---

[1] No. 31, pp. 4-5.
[2] No. 31, p. 5.
[3] Luneau was very grieved by the fate of copies of his *mémoires*; cf. No. 32, p. 11: 'Ceux que j'envoyai en Province furent interceptés. On trouve sur les livres des Libraires associés, sous le n°. 1969, la dépense faite à Lyon pour cet objet'.
[4] No. 31, p. 5. There is further reference in the *Supplément* (pp. 10-11) to this payment to Samuel Fauche from which we learn that this item of expenditure bore the number 1796, which occurred just too late for inclusion in *Journal A*; this means that he did not get the money until after March 1768.

The next deduction which the subscribers propose is a rather farcical one—'Les 6 liv. employées sur le n°. 1007, pour l'incendie de la rue de la Harpe'.[5] The actual wording of this item in *Journal A* is 'remboursé au Commissaire lors du feu rue de la harpe 6.' The subscribers draw the most sinister deductions from this item: 'Dans le tableau analytique du sieur le Breton,[6] les pertes occasionnées par ce désastre, sont portées à 20,000 liv. Le journal véridique du sieur Briasson répare à bien peu de frais cette calamité.' The modern reader, however, is not by any means convinced that this one item in the accounts necessarily rules out extensive damage by fire to the publishers' stock.

When they had finished this list of items which, they claimed, should be deducted from the total of the expenses, the whole amount was raised from the sum of 862,000 livres to 936,219 liv. 14 sols 2d.[7] When this sum was taken away from the total expenses listed in *Journal A* and *Journal B* (2,205,839 l. 4s.), these were reduced to 1,269,619 l. 9s. 10d. The subscribers further argued that the publishers had wasted money by buying paper on credit and that, since they had been amply compensated by the interest earned for them by the subscribers' money, another deduction—'les 85,216 liv. payées inutilement aux Marchands de papier'—should be made from the total expenses, thus reducing them to 1,184,403 l. 9s. 10d.[8]

The subscribers next turned their attention to what the accounts reveal about the payments made to the editor of the *Encyclopédie*, to the authors who contributed to it, and to those who drew and engraved the plates. We have already dealt with the payments to Diderot and his colleagues.[9] By referring to the accounts, the subscribers had no difficulty in disproving completely Le Breton's claim that each drawing made for the plates had cost 30 livres,[10] and Goussier's certificate stating that some of his drawing had been paid for at the rate of 18 livres and others at 24, 'non compris ses frais de voyages dans différentes

[5] No. 31, p. 5.
[6] No. 30, facing p. 38.
[7] No. 31, p. 5.
[10] No. 30, *Tableau analytique* facing p. 38.
[8] No. 31, p. 6.
[9] See above, pp. 103-104.

Provinces'.[11] After referring to some early payments to Goussier in *Journal A*, the subscribers proceed to quote item 1073 (under the date of 1760): '24 liv. à M. Goussier, pour trois desseins, y compris un voyage', and then go on to give the following analysis of the work which he did for the *Encyclopédie* down to the end of his connection with it:

Ce voyage est le seul du sieur Goussier dont il soit fait mention dans les livres des Libraires. Si l'on en croit le Certificat de ce dessinateur, il a couru toutes les Manufactures de la France.

Trente-cinq dessins seulement ont été payés au sieur Goussier 18 l. & 24; mais cette grace ne lui a été faite qu'en 1771. Pendant 24 ans M. Groussier a trouvé que ses dessins étoient très-bien payés à 6 liv.

Les Libraires ont fait un tel cas des talents de M. Goussier, qu'ils ont récompensé 28 années de son travail par une gratification de 600 liv.

Pour mettre le comble à leurs bons procédés à son égard, ils se sont déterminés en 1771 à payer son loyer. Cette faveur est ainsi consignée: N°. 2124, *payé à Goussier pour son loyer, par extraordinaire, 60 liv.*

Les autres Dessinateurs ont été payés avec la même générosité que le sieur Goussier.[12]

According to their calculations the total sum which the publisher had spent on drawings came to 27,831 livres, which, for a total of 2,891 plates, meant an average cost of 9 l. 8s. 3d.—and not the 30 livres claimed by Le Breton. As for Le Breton's claim that the average cost of the engraving of the plates was 72 livres, they made out that the total paid for engraving was 164,229 l. 10s. i.e. an average cost of 56 l. 5s. 4d. They conceded, it is true, that another 17,464 livres had been paid to the engravers for such things as corrections, but they claimed that this came under the heading of 'faux frais'; this would have added another 6 livres or so to the average cost.[13]

Turning now to the receipts of the enterprise, the subscribers established from the publishers' books that there had been 3,931

---

[11] No. 30, p. 42.
[12] No. 31, p. 7.
[13] No. 31, p. 8.

subscribers and that 4,225 copies of the work had been printed.[14] Unfortunately the sums which they proceeded to do in order to establish the total receipts for the *Encyclopédie* are partly fantasy. Having ascertained from the list of subscribers that the first 1,367 paid the minimum amount before the subscription price was raised—i.e. 980 livres—and that the remaining 2,564 subscribers paid an extra 24 livres, i.e. 1004 livres, they then go on to produce a quite fantastic calculation:

Les 3931 souscriptions remplies, il restoit entre les mains des Libraires 294 exemplaires vendus à des personnes qui n'avoient point souscrit, à raison de 1525 liv. par exemplaire, conformément aux conditions de leur Prospectus,[15] la vente de ces 294 exemplaires a produit.

448,350 l.[16]

The notion that every one of the 4,225 copies printed had actually been sold—let alone that the last 294 sets had fetched this extraordinarily high price—was surely nonsensical. Obviously a considerable number of copies had been given away—partly to contributors, but also to highly placed persons such as Saint-Florentin and to libraries.[17] Moreover, it is quite clear that the publishers never received from all the 3,931 subscribers the total sum of 980 or 1,004 livres to which they were nominally entitled. There was a commission to be offered to other booksellers and to *colporteurs* and there were bad debts, as well as unsold copies of the last ten volumes of text and of the volumes of plates.[18]

Considerable as the publishers' profits no doubt were, they cannot conceivably have been as great as the disgruntled subscribers maintained when, deducting from total receipts of

[14] No. 31, p. 9.
[15] The original prospectus had, of course, laid it down that non-subscribers would pay more per volume than subscribers.
[16] No. 31, p. 9.
[17] Le Breton put the number of presentation copies at 170 (no. 30, *Tableau analytique* facing p. 38). See the passage quoted above, p. 134.
[18] The commission was stated by Le Breton to be 44 livres; the bad debts were put at 50,000 livres and the value of the unsold copies at 430,000 livres (No. 30, Tableau analytique facing p. 38). For the number of copies unsold in 1768 see the document quoted in *Essays*, pp. 60-61.

4,362,266 livres total expenses of 1,187,201 l. 11s., they claimed that a profit of 3,175,064 l. 9s. had been made.[19] Nor was this, they alleged, the full extent of the publishers' gains: 'Si l'on joint à ce bénéfice les 408,037 l. 10 sols d'intérêts que les Libraires ont retiré, de l'argent des Souscripteurs, depuis les époques où ils en ont fait le partage; le produit des récépissés sur les Fermes; les 230 mille livres que le sieur Panckoucke a payées pour les cuivres des planches de l'Encyclopédie, & pour la cession du droit de faire imprimer cet Ouvrage;[20] le bénéfice que les Libraires ont fait sur les Transactions philosophiques, imprimées avec l'argent de l'Encyclopédie, on verra que, tous frais déduits, ils ont gagné sur l'Encyclopédie, plus quatre millions, dont le sieur le Breton, comme principal intéressé, a reçu plus des deux tiers.'

After this the *Supplément* sinks back into a dreary repetition of the more absurd claims of this group of subscribers. Yet, although it was no doubt far from their thoughts to do so, in the first ten pages of their *factum* they provided historians of the *Encyclopédie* with some interesting data drawn from the vanished *Journal B* and the list of subscribers.

BIBLIOGRAPHICAL APPENDIX

The following list of contemporary documents bearing on the case is in approximate chronological order, based on remarks in the documents themselves, on dates written in by hand and on comments in Bachaumont and Hardy. .

*=not in A. Corda, *Catalogue des Factums et d'autres documents judiciares antérieurs à 1790*. Paris, 1890-1905, 7 vols. The class-marks given below are those of the Département des Imprimés of the Bibliothèque Nationale, Paris, or, where the documents are not listed in Corda, those of the Département des Manuscrits. Sometimes two or more copies of these documents are

---

[19] No. 31, p. 9.
[20] In reality Panchoucke and his partners agreed to pay a total of 200,000 livres (see *Essays*, p. 59).

available in this library, but only the one actually used has been listed. All the documents for the years 1776-8 (nos. 26-41) are also available at the library of the Cercle de la Librairie, Boulevard Saint-Germain, except for no. 33.

Bach. = Bachaumont, *Mémoires secrets*.

Hardy = S. P. Hardy, *Mes Loisirs*, ed. M. Tourneux and M. Vitrac, Paris, 1912, Vol. I.

1. Mémoire signifié pour le Sieur Luneau de Boisjermain, Défendeur contre les Syndic & Adjoints des Libraires & Imprimeurs de Paris, Demandeurs. (Paris, 1768). pp. 16, 4° Fm. 19941.

2. Précis signifié pour les Syndic & Adjoints des Libraires & Imprimeurs de Paris, Demandeurs, contre le Sieur Luneau de Boisjermain, Défendeur. (Paris, 1769). pp. 16. 4° Fm. 25056.

3. Réponse signifiée pour le Sieur Lunean de Boisjermain au *Précis signifié par les Syndic & Adjoints des Libraires de Paris.* (Paris, 1769). pp. 54. 4° Fm. 19942.

*4. Réplique et Consultation signifiées pour les Syndic & Adjoints des Libraires & Imprimeurs de Paris contre le Sieur Luneau de Boisjermain. (Paris, 1769). pp. 23. Ms. fr. 22069, ff. 59-70.[21]

5. Dernière Réponse signifiée & Consultation pour le Sieur Luneau de Boisjermain contre les Syndic & Adjoints des Libraires de Paris (Paris, 1769). pp. 37. 4° Fm. 19943 (Bach. Vol. V, p. 36: 29 Dec. 1769).

6. Mémoire à consulter pour les Libraires associés à l'Encyclopédie. (Paris, 1770). pp. 30. 4° Fm. 34420(1). (Bach. Vol. V, pp. 59-60: 1 Feb. 1770).

7. Jugement rendu par M. de Sartine, . . . Lieutenant Général de Police . . . , entre le Sieur Luneau de Boisjermain et les Syndic & Adjoints de la Librairie & Imprimerie de Paris. (Paris, 1770). pp. 7. 4° Fm.34420(2). (Bach. Vol. V, p. 65: 14 Feb. 1770).

8. Mémoire et Consultation pour M. Luneau de Boisjermain, Souscripteur de l'Encyclopédie, contre le Sieur Briasson, Libraire, Syndic des Libraires & Imprimeurs, Ancien Adjoint de sa Com-

[21] It was a remark on p. 17 of this *Réplique* which sparked off the controversy about the *Encyclopédie*; Luneau replied to it in no. 5 (pp. 27 f.).

munauté, et le Sieur Le Breton, ancien Syndic & Adjoint de la même Communauté, associé avec le sieur Briasson pour l'impression de l'Encyclopédie. (Paris, 1770). pp 14. 4° Fm. 34420(3). (Bach. Vol. V, pp. 77-80: 10, 13 March 1770).

9. Précis pour le Sieur Le Breton, premier Imprimeur ordinaire du Roi, Juge en la Jurisdiction Consulaire de Paris, & l'un des Libraires associés à l'Encyclopédie. (Paris, 1770). pp. 8. 4° Fm. 34420(4). (Bach. Vol. V, p. 85: 24 March 1770).

10. A Nosseigneurs de Parlement en la Tournelle Criminelle ('Supplie humblement Pierre-Joseph-François Luneau de Boisjermain . . .'). (Paris, 1771). pp. 20. 4° Fm. 19945.

11. Mémoire pour Pierre-Joseph-François Luneau de Boisjermain, Souscripteur de l'Encyclopédie . . . , Paris, 1771. pp. viii +152+50 (=*Pièces justificatives*). 4° Fm. 34420(5). (Bach. Vol. V, pp. 298-302: 23, 24 Aug. 1771; Hardy, pp. 280-1: 21 Aug. 1771).

12. Mémoire pour les Libraires associés à l'Encyclopédie contre le sieur Luneau de Boisjermain. (Paris, 1771). pp. 74 (pp. 68-74. Lettre de M. Diderot à Messieurs Briasson & Le Breton, Libraires associés à l'Encyclopédie, dated 31 Aug. 1771). 4° Fm. 34420(8). (Bach. Vol. V, p. 311: 6 Sept. 1771; Hardy, pp. 284-5: 4 Sept. 1771). (For Diderot's letter see Roth, Vol. XI, pp. 145-53).

13. Précis pour le Sieur Luneau de Boisjermain, servant de réponse au Mémoire distribué contre lui sous le nom des Libraires associés à l'Encyclopédie, et aux Piéces y jointes. (Paris, 1771). pp. 28. 4° Fm. 34420(6). (Bach. Vol. V, p. 312: 7 Sept. 1771) (See Roth, Vol. XI, pp. 158-78, 186-9).

14. Addition au Précis du Sr Luneau de Boisjermain. (Paris, 1771). pp. 4. 4° Fm. 34420(7).

15. Réponse de M. Luneau de Boisjermain au Mémoire des Libraires associés à l'Encyclopédie, distribué au mois d'août 1771. (Paris, 1771). pp. iv+84. 4° Fm. 34420(9).

16. (Stoupe,) Réflexions d'un Souscripteur de l'Encyclopédie sur le procès intenté aux Libraires associés à cet ouvrage par M. Luneau de Boisjermain. (Paris, 1771). pp. 24. 4° Fm. 34420(34). (Bach. Vol. VI, pp. 52, 55: 5, 9 Dec. 1771).

17. Lettre de M. Luneau de Boisjermain à M. Diderot, et Réponses à la lettre adressée aux Srs Briasson & Le Breton par M. Diderot. (Paris, 1771). pp. 32. 4° Fm. 34420(12). (Bach. Vol.

VI, p. 63: 20 Dec. 1771) (Roth, Vol. XI, pp. 228-48).
*18. Diderot, Au Public et aux Magistrats. Copy of printed text in Diderot MSS in Leningrad (Vol. XVIII); MS copy of work in Fonds Vandeul (Bibliothèque Nationale, Nouv. acq. fr. 13753); reprinted by M. Tourneux in 'Un Factum inconnu de Diderot' (*Bulletin du Bibliophile*, 1901, pp. 349-85) and in Roth, Vol. XI, pp. 99-124.

19. A Nosseigneurs de Parlement ('Supplient humblement N. Leguay & Consorts, Souscripteurs du Livre intitulé *Encyclopédie*, Intervenants en la cause pendante en la Grand' Chambre entre P. J. F. Luneau de Boisjermain . . . & les Sieurs Briasson & Le Breton . . .') (Paris, 1772). pp. 8. 4° Fm. 34420(10).

20. Précis pour les Libraires associés à l'Encyclopédie contre le sieur Luneau de Boisjermain & contre sept Intervenans. (Paris, 1772). pp. 42. 4° Fm. 34420(13). (Bach. Vol. VI, p. 151: 23 June 1772; Hardy, p. 350: 22 June 1772).

*21. Exposition de la Diffamation dont les Libraires associés à l'Encyclopédie demandent une Réparation authentique. (Paris, 1772). pp. 7. Ms. Fr. 22086, ff. 248-251 (Hardy, p. 350: 22 June 1772).

22. Réponse signifiée de M. Luneau de Boisjermain au Précis des Libraires associés à l'impression de l'Encyclopédie, distribuée le 15 Juin 1772. (Paris, 1772). pp. 20. 4° Fm. 34420(14). (Bach. Vol. VI, p. 151: 23 June 1772).

23. Précis sur délibéré, prononcé le 22 Juin 1772, entre Pierre-Joseph-François Luneau de Boisjermain, & les sieurs Le Breton & Briasson, & les héritiers des feus sieurs David & Durand, Libraires Associés à l'impression de l'Encyclopédie. (Paris, 1772). pp. 16. 4° Fm. 34420(15). (Bach. Vol. VI, p. 155: 1 July 1772).

*24. Dernier Memoire pour le Sieur Briasson, ancien Syndic de la Librairie & Imprimerie de Paris, ancien Juge-Consul, et le sieur Le Breton, premier Imprimeur ordinaire du Roi, ancien Syndic de la Librairie & Imprimerie de Paris, ancien Juge-Consul, Libraires associés au Privilège de l'Encyclopédie, contre le sieur Luneau de Boisjermain. Paris, 1772. pp. 105. Ms. fr. 22086, ff. 258-311.

25. Sommaire sur délibéré pour les Libraires associés à l'Encyclopédie, contre le sieur Luneau & sept Intervenans. (Paris, 1772). pp. 10. 4° Fm. 34420(16).

26. Mémoire pour le sieur Luneau de Boisjermain, Souscrip-

LUNEAU DE BOISJERMAIN *V*. THE PUBLISHERS 157

teur de l'Encyclopédie, contre le sieur Le Breton, Imprimeur de cet ouvrage, & les héritiers des feus sieurs Briasson, David & Durand, Libraires associés à cette entreprise. (Paris, 1776). pp. 42. 4° Fm. 34420(19). (Bach. Vol. IX, p. 178: 2 Aug. 1776).

27. Précis pour la Dame veuve Briasson, Libraire, & le Sieur Le Breton, premier imprimeur ordinaire du Roi, ci-devant associé au Livre intitulé *Encyclopédie*, contre le sieur Luneau & contre les Intervenans. (Paris, 1776). pp. 54. 4° Fm. 34420(17). (Bach. Vol. IX, p. 190: 16 Aug. 1776).

28. Réponse signifiée du sieur Luneau de Boisjermain au Précis de la Dame Briasson, Libraire, et du sieur Le Breton, premier Imprimeur du Roi, distribué le 24 Juillet 1776. (Paris, 1776). pp. 40. 4° Fm. 34420(18). (Bach. Vol. IX, pp. 190-1: 16 Aug. 1776).

29. Mémoire pour le Marquis de Camille Massimo, le Marquis de la Saone, le Marquis de Lansegue . . . & autres . . . (Paris, 1777). pp. 47. 4° Fm. 34420(20). (Bach. Vol. X, pp. 25-7, 45: 31 Jan., 1 & 21 Feb. 1777).

30. Réponse pour les Libraires associés à l'Encyclopédie au Mémoire du Marquis de la Saone & Consors, Intervenans, et contre le sieur Luneau de Boisjermain. (Paris, 1777). pp. 42. 4° Fm. 34420(21). (Bach. Vol. X, pp. 41-2: 18 Feb. 1777).

31. Supplément au Mémoire des Souscripteurs Intervenants, contre le Sieur Le Breton, Imprimeur de l'Encyclopédie, & ses Associés à la vente de cet Ouvrage. (Paris, 1777). pp. 21+2. 4° Fm. 34420(23). (Bach. Vol. X, pp. 66-7: 14 March 1777).

32. Précis pour le Sieur Luneau de Boisjermain, Souscripteur de l'Encyclopédie, contre le Sieur Le Breton & les Libraires associés à l'Impression de l'Encyclopédie. (Paris, 1777). pp. 15. 4° Fm. 34420(25). (Bach. Vol. X, pp. 89-91: 6 April 1777).

33. Observations pour les Souscripteurs de l'Encyclopédie contre les Libraires associés. (Paris, 1777). pp. 7. 4° Fm. 34420(22).

34. Observations sommaires pour les Libraires associés à l'Encyclopédie contre le Sieur Luneau de Boisjermain, sur partage d'opinions à la Grand'Chambre. (Paris, 1777). pp. 18. 4° Fm. 34420(26).

35. Récapitulation de faits physiquement démontrés par pièces produites, au procès que le Sieur Le Breton & ses Associés à l'impression de l'Encyclopédie ont intenté au Sieur Luneau de Boisjermain, au sujet de la connoissance qu'il a donnée, au mois de Décembre 1769, des surprises faites au Public dans la

souscription ouverte pour cet ouvrage. (Paris, 1777). pp. 20. 4°
Fm. 34420(24). (Bach. Vol. X, p. 130: 11 May 1777).

36. Analyse succincte des Prétentions de chaque Intervenant, d'après ce qui a été décidé, sur partage d'Opinions, en faveur des Libraires associés à l'Encyclopédie, contre le sieur Luneau de Boisjermain. (Paris, 1777). pp. 10. 4° Fm. 34420(27).

37. Copie de deux Pièces nouvellement fabriquées par le sieur Luneau de Boisjermain, étant en original, dans la possession des Libraires associés à l'Encyclopédie. (Paris, 1777). pp. 8. 4° Fm. 34420(28).

38. Résumé pour les Libraires associées à l'Encyclopédie, contre le Sieur Luneau de Boisjermain & les Intervenans. (Paris, 1777). pp. 12. 4° Fm. 34420(29).

39. Réflexions ultérieures, servant de complément à la justification des Libraires associés à l'Encyclopédie contre les Intervenans, en présence du Sieur Luneau de Boisjermain. (Paris, 1777). pp. 16. 4° Fm. 34420(30).

40. Dernier état des chefs à juger en l'instance, pour les Libraires associés à l'Encyclopédie, contre le sieur Luneau de Boisjermain & les Intervenans, ses prête-noms. (Paris, 1778). pp. 28. 4° Fm. 34420(31). (Bach. Vol. XII, pp. 70-2: 15 Aug. 1778).

41. Mémoire pour P. J. Fr. Luneau de Boisjermain, servant de réponse à un Mémoire du Sieur Le Breton & de ses Associés, Intitulé: *Dernier état des choses à juger*. (Paris, 1778). pp. 12 + 18 (=*Pièces justificatives*). 4° Fm. 34420(32). (Bach. Vol. XII, p. 72: 16 Aug. 1778).

VI The Problem of the Unsigned Articles[1]

The question of the authorship of the unsigned articles in the *Encyclopédie*, with which it is convenient to associate that of the articles bearing Diderot's editorial asterisk, has been taken up seriously only in recent years.[2]

It is true that, in Chapter VI of *Diderot as a Disciple of English Thought*,[3] the problem was touched on by R. Loyalty Cru who offered some information on the debt of Diderot to Chambers's *Cyclopedia*. He has, for instance, some interesting comments to make on the use of articles from Chambers in *Encyclopédie* articles which bear the editorial asterisk. *ANAGRAMME reproduces ANAGRAM with quite minor cuts and additions, and *AVALER (apart from some curiously careless mistranslations) is simply taken over wholesale from SWALLOWING, except for the addition of a reference to the memoirs of the Académie de Chirurgie. *BEURRE, he rightly points out, is an article for which the Assézat-Tourneux edition reproduces the passages taken straight from Chambers, BUTTER, and leaves out the original part on the technique of butter-making. However, he sometimes exaggerates, as we shall later see, Diderot's debt to Chambers. It is, for instance, misleading to speak of CERTITUDE as 'being borrowed from Chambers and much enlarged'. It is true that the starting-point of the

---
[1] First published in *Studies on Voltaire and the Eighteenth Century*, Vol. XXXII, 1965, pp. 327-390.
[2] Chap. III of *Essays*—on D'Holbach's contribution to the *Encyclopédie*—offers further material on the problem of the unsigned articles.
[3] New York, 1913.
[4] pp. 260-263.

introduction to CERTITUDE (it bears the editorial asterisk) is Chambers's CERTITUDE, but even it is considerably expanded. One change, though small, is interesting: a cross-reference to PROBABILITÉ replaces Chambers's reference to TRADITION. Then follows the main part of the article by Abbé de Prades,[5] and after that the concluding editorial remarks. Even 'much enlarged' seems a decided understatement.

Shortly after this book there appeared an interesting article by Pierre Hermand,[6] which showed that certain of the articles attributed to Diderot came wholly or largely from earlier works; this attack on the problem was carried slightly further in a posthumous work by the same writer, *Les Idées morales de Diderot*[7]—especially in Chap. VIII. Yet, valuable as their contributions have been to subsequent students of Diderot and the *Encyclopédie*, neither of these scholars went beyond the search for Diderot's sources to the fundamental question: are the unsigned articles from the *Encyclopédie* reprinted by Assézat and Tourneux to be accepted as coming from his pen?

It is really only since 1945 that scholars have brought this question out into the open. First in the field came Franco Venturi who in *Le Origini dell'Enciclopedia*[8] pointed out that four lengthy articles reprinted in the standard edition of Diderot's works—IMMATÉRIALISME, LIBERTÉ, MANICHÉISME and POLYTHÉISME —were almost certainly written by Abbé Yvon. Close on this followed a series of publications by Herbert Dieckmann which had an important bearing on the problem of Diderot's part in the unsigned articles in the *Encyclopédie*. In *Le Philosophe. Texts and Interpretation*[9] he showed that the article PHILOSOPHE must be removed from the canon of Diderot's writings, and three years later, in addition to publishing his *Inventaire du Fonds Vandeul* which is obviously of considerable importance for a study of the

---

[5] Abbé Yvon later claimed to have had a hand in this part of the article (see F. Venturi, *Le Origini dell'Enciclopedia*, Florence, 1946, p. 139).

[6] 'Sur le texte de Diderot et sur les sources de quelques passages de ses Œuvres' (*RHL*, 1915, pp. 361-70).

[7] Paris, 1923.

[8] pp. 138-40.

[9] Saint Louis, 1948.

whole question, he also published two articles which deal directly with it. 'L'*Encyclopédie* et le Fonds Vandeul'[10] was the first detailed discussion of the whole problem of Diderot's contribution, as editor and author, to the *Encyclopédie*; while he showed that the Fonds Vandeul threw disappointingly little light on the question, he produced a document which compels us to transfer from Diderot to Baron d'Holbach the authorship of three very important articles—PRETRES, REPRÉSENTANTS and THÉOCRATIE. In the same year, in an article with the somewhat uncommunicative title of 'The Sixth Volume of Saint-Lambert's Works'[11] he showed that we must assign to Saint-Lambert thirteen unsigned articles in the Encyclopédie, nine of which—among them the important articles GÉNIE, INTÉRÊT (*Morale*), LÉGISLATEUR and LUXE—were reprinted by Assézat and Tourneux and which, even a decade after Professor Dieckmann's article, still continue to be attributed to Diderot.

Two recent theses on Diderot throw yet more light on this problem—one of them (Jean Mayer, *Diderot homme de science*,[12]) only incidentally and yet in ways which repay careful study, the other (Jacques Proust, *Diderot et l'Encyclopédie*[13]) offering the most thorough and systematic examination of the whole baffling question which has yet been attempted. Professor Proust's contribution to this particular aspect of Diderot's part in the production of the *Encyclopédie* is obviously outstanding for both its thoroughness and its lucidity, and yet—as he is the first to point out—he cannot claim to have exhausted the problem. This chapter is written in the belief that, while no dramatic solution of the whole problem can be achieved, the material at our disposal allows us to move a little further in the direction of a solution.

Leaving aside one or two points of detail, there are two major questions on which one may differ from Professor Proust. First, while he gives us a fairly complete list of the articles which were wrongly included by Assézat and Tourneux, he does not provide

[10] *RHL*, 1951, pp. 318-32.
[11] *Romanic Review*, pp. 109-21.
[12] Rennes, 1959.
[13] Paris, 1962 (second edition, 1967).

an equivalent list of those articles, either unsigned or with the editorial asterisk, which they omitted from their edition even though we can confidently assign them to Diderot.[14] And second, while the caution with which he repeatedly declines to attribute to Diderot any article in the *Encyclopédie* for which positive proof of his authority is not available, perhaps deserves the epithet of 'scholarly', it involves carrying scepticism to lengths which appear at times excessive. Diderot did write works of his own—long and short—before, during and after the period of nearly twenty years in which he edited and wrote for the seventeen volumes of text of the *Encyclopédie*; it may well be that with certain unsigned articles for the authorship of which we have no external evidence, we can be guided by their relationship to earlier, contemporary and later writings of Diderot to attribute them to him.

As Professor Proust points out,[15] the information given us in the preliminary matter of successive volumes of the *Encyclopédie* about the authorship of articles bearing the editorial asterisk and those which are unsigned, is distinctly confusing. The *Prospectus*, written by Diderot, has this to say about the use of the asterisk:

> Le seule partie de notre travail, qui suppose quelqu'intelligence, c'est de remplir les vuides qui séparent deux Sciences ou deux Arts, & de renouer la chaîne dans les occasions où nos Collegues se sont reposés les uns sur les autres de certains articles qui, paroissant appartenir également à plusieurs d'entre eux, n'ont été faits par aucun. Mais afin que la personne chargée d'une partie, ne soit point comptable des fautes qui pourroient se glisser dans des morceaux surajoutés, nous aurons l'attention de distinguer ces morceaux par une étoile.[16]

The relationship between articles or parts of articles marked with an asterisk and those which are left unsigned is defined as follows in the preliminary matter of the first volume:

---

[14] The account which he gives of Naigeon's handling of Diderot's articles (pp. 138-9) is, as we shall see, incomplete and at times inaccurate. FETICHISME, for instance, is ascribed by Naigeon to De Brosses, not Diderot.
[15] pp. 131-8.
[16] AT, Vol. XIII, p. 135.

Les Articles qui n'ont point de lettres à la fin, ou qui ont une étoile au commencement, sont de M. Diderot; Les premiers sont ceux qui lui appartiennent comme étant un des *Auteurs* de l'Encyclopédie; les seconds sont ceux qu'il a suppléés comme *Editeur*.[17]

Although oddly enough it is also used by Robinet, the editor of the *Supplément*,[18] not only is this distinction between Diderot's functions as author and editor by no means easy to grasp; it has also been at the root of a ghastly misunderstanding—the belief of nineteenth century editors of Diderot's works, from Belin to Assézat and Tourneux, that unsigned articles in the *Encyclopédie* must automatically be attributed to Diderot.

At the end of the second volume,[19] in addition to the words '* au commencement de l'article, M. Diderot', there is one sentence which explodes this whole notion:

'Les articles dont l'Auteur n'est ni nommé, ni désigné, sont de M. DIDEROT, ou de plusieurs Auteurs qui en ont fourni les matériaux, ou de différentes personnes qui n'ont pas voulu être connues, ou qui sont nommées dans le Discours Préliminaire.

The third volume of the *Encyclopédie*, which repeats under the heading 'Marque des Auteurs' '* M. Diderot', renews this warning about the authorship of unsigned articles:

Entre les articles sans marque des Auteurs, il y en a plusieurs qui ont été faits par des Personnes qui n'ont point voulu être connues.[20]

A hint of a further complication is contained in the tactful reference to the departure abroad of Abbé Yvon after the row over the thesis of Abbé de Prades—'M. l'abbé Yvon qui avoit la lettre X est absent': there is every reason to think that his contributions continued to be made use of, but without any signature.[21]

[17] p. xlvi.
[18] Vol. I, p. lv.
[19] p. 871.
[20] p. 905.
[21] See Venturi, *Le Origini dell'Enciclopedia*, pp. 138-40; Proust, pp. 156-9; and Chap. V, pp. 102-103.

Neither Vol. IV nor Vol. V contains any information about regular contributors and their *marques*, and all that Vols. VI and VII tell us about Diderot's contributions is to repeat '* M. Diderot'. In the *Avertissement des Editeurs* to Vol. VI there is, however, another warning about a number of unsigned articles which came from contributors who wished to remain anonymous. In addition to several contributions sent in by 'une Femme que nous n'avons pas l'honneur de connoître', there is mention of four sets of unsigned articles: 'Quatre Personnes que nous regrettons fort de ne pouvoir nommer, mais qui ont exigé de nous cette condition, nous ont donné différens articles'.[22] The *Avertissement des Editeurs* of Vol. VII also refers to 'cinq Personnes qui ne veulent pas être connues'.[23]

When the last ten volumes appeared all together after a break in publication of eight years, they offered only one hint about the authorship of unsigned articles. After gliding over the awkward point of the defections which had taken place among regular contributors in the crisis years 1757-9, the *Avertissement* of Vol. VIII speaks of certain new contributors—vaguely described as 'des hommes de lettres & des gens du monde'—who had come to the editor's aid, and then adds, as a preliminary to a eulogy of Jaucourt: 'Que ne nous est-il permis de désigner à la reconnoissance publique tous ces habiles & courageux auxiliaires!'[24] Here we have yet another warning that the original statement that unsigned articles were by Diderot no longer applied.

To add to the confusion, the use of the editorial asterisk gradually fades out. It still continues to appear with normal regularity in Vol. VIII (H-Itzehoa), the first of the post-1757 volumes, becomes much rarer in Vol. IX (Ju-Mamira) and fades out entirely after *MARBREUR *de papier*, the only article bearing an asterisk in the whole of Vol. X.[25]

[22] p. vi. The identity of one of these (Abbé Morellet) is revealed in the *Avertissement* of Vol. VII (p. xiii); the other three were Turgot, Quesnay and Saint-Lambert.
[23] p. xiv. Among them were Turgot and Saint-Lambert.
[24] AT, Vol. XIII, p. 172.
[25] Cf. Proust, p. 135; as we arrived independently at the same conclusion, it may presumably be taken to be established.

The reasons for the gradual disappearance of the editorial asterisk in the last ten volumes are not altogether clear. There is perhaps an explanation of its continued presence in Vol. VIII. Contemporary evidence would suggest that by the time of the Parlement's onslaught on the *Encyclopédie* in 1759 the printing of this volume was already far advanced. On 15 February 1759 Grimm stated that 'le huitième [volume] s'imprime actuellement';[26] and in the same month in two successive entries in Barbier's journal[27] we find the statements; 'On met actuellement sous presse le huitième volume de l'*Encyclopédie* qu'on commence à imprimer', and 'Le huitième est actuellement sous presse'. If true, this could explain why the distribution of asterisks in this volume is very much the same as in the first seven.[28] The only contemporary reference to the absence of asterisks in the remaining nine volumes appears to be the following, which is to be found in a letter of D'Holbach to Servan, written on 27 April 1765. In speaking of the imminent appearance of the last ten volumes he states that 'les signes distinctifs disparoîtront'.[29] At first sight this remark about the absence of the contributors' signs does not seem to make sense, as a considerable number of articles, right to the end of Vol. XVII continue to bear either the contributor's name or else one of the symbols indicated in the first seven volumes. '(—)'—D'Holbach's own sign—continues to appear frequently. Yet some of the more outspoken of his articles, including PRETRES, REPRÉSENTANTS and THÉOCRATIE, as we see from the list supplied by his son,[30] appeared without signature, and at some stage in the clandestine production of the last ten volumes it seems to have been decided to dispense with certain symbols, including the editorial asterisk, though clearly this was

[26] *Corr. litt.*, Vol. IV, p. 81.
[27] *Chronique de la Régence et du règne de Louis XV (1718-63)*, Vol. VII, pp. 126-7. Professor Proust (p. 54) refers to a letter from Diderot to Grimm of 1 May 1759 (Roth, Vol. II, p. 121), but this has no bearing on the printing of the *Encyclopédie*.
[28] On the other hand there is the awkward point that Diderot wrote to Sophie Volland on 26 September 1762: 'Le huitième volume de discours tire à sa fin' (Roth, Vol. IV, p. 172).
[29] *Autographes de Mariemont*, Paris, 1955-9, 4 vols., Part I, p. 558.
[30] *RHL*, 1951, p. 332.

not done in a systematic or coherent fashion.

As Professor Proust points out, it is not easy to see how a clear line of demarcation can be drawn between those articles of Diderot which bear the editorial asterisk and those which were left unsigned. However, it is a fact that the articles which are preceded by an asterisk do carry a guarantee that in some degree Diderot mixed his labour with them. As they are in quite a different category from the unsigned articles, it is regrettable that —with one exception which modesty forbids me to specify— nineteenth- and twentieth-century editors of the works of Diderot or of selections of articles from the *Encyclopédie* have omitted to place the editorial asterisk in front of such articles when they chose to reproduce them.

Assézat made it clear right from the beginning that he had no intention of attempting to reproduce in the *Œuvres complètes* all the articles in the *Encyclopédie* marked with Diderot's asterisk, since the total, especially in the opening volumes, was staggeringly large and since in any case many of his contributions were mere compilation. It is obvious that even a twentieth-century editor of the complete works of Diderot, however much he might look down his nose at Assézat and Tourneux, could not undertake to reproduce all of these articles. However, it may justly be held against Assézat that his selection from the articles bearing Diderot's editorial asterisk was not a very good one, that he included articles of little interest and left out quite a number which are of much greater significance. Obviously there are dangers—as Professor Proust points out[31]—in any editor deciding what is or is not 'significant'; but it is better to draw attention to such articles since they are otherwise lost in the fifteen thousand or so folio pages of the *Encyclopédie* than to ignore them as Assézat did or to do virtually nothing to 'rescue' them, like Professor Proust in his *Diderot et l'Encyclopédie*, where he tells us in most useful detail what articles in Assézat and Tourneux are *not* by Diderot, but offers practically no guidance as to which of his articles are omitted in Vols. XIII-XVII of the *Œuvres Complètes*.

[31] p. 124.

What is especially puzzling in *Diderot et l'Encyclopédie*[32] is the restricted use made by Professor Proust of the testimony of Naigeon. Working mainly on the other side of the Channel and for a long period in complete ignorance of the parallel researches of Professor Proust, I had arrived independently at the same conclusions regarding the capital importance of the evidence furnished by Naigeon as to Diderot's contribution to the *Encyclopédie* in three works composed in the period following his master's death—the volumes on ancient and modern philosophy in the *Encyclopédie Méthodique*,[33] his edition of Diderot's works (1798) and the *Mémoires historiques et philosophiques sur la vie et les ouvrages de D. Diderot* which appeared posthumously in 1821.

Given the importance which he rightly attaches to this testimony, it is strange that Professor Proust should have made such limited use of it. In the extremely useful appendix in which he lists the articles contained in Vols. XIII-XVII of the Assézat-Tourneux edition he gives the following thirty-one articles marked with an asterisk as being guaranteed to be by Diderot in one or more of Naigeon's three works:

[32] pp. 136-49.
[33] It is incorrect to describe them as 'publiés en 1791' as Professor Proust does (p. 138). Vol. I is dated 1791, but an 8-paged pamphlet, bound in with the Edinburgh University Library copy and dated 'Lundi 21 Mai 1792', announces that the forty-ninth *livraison* of this encyclopaedia consists, among other volumes, 'du tome premier, deuxième Partie de la Philosophie Ancienne & Moderne, par M. Naigeon', and states that 'si le premier volume de son Ouvrage n'a point paru plutôt', this is due to the enormous labour in which the editor is involved. Vol. II bears the date 1792; when it appeared in these troubled years is uncertain. Vol. III bears on the title-page the date 'L'An deuxième de la République française une et indivisible' (i.e. between 22 September 1793 and 21 September 1794), but an 8-paged pamphlet bound in with the Edinburgh University Library copy and dated 'le 16 brumaire, an sixième. . . . (Le lundi 6 novembre 1797, vieux style)' states that the seventy-third *livraison* consists, among other volumes, of 'la seconde partie du troisième & dernier volume de *la Philosophie ancienne & moderne*, par le citoyen Naigeon'. The long period over which both the composition and the publication of these three volumes was spread, combined with the new situation brought about by the Revolution, perhaps explains why Naigeon gradually felt freer to reveal more and more about the part played by Diderot in the composition of the *Encyclopédie*.

*ACOUSMATIQUES, *ASCHARIENS, *AZARECAH, *BACCHIONITES, *BASSESSE, *BELBUCH, *BOIS DE VIE,[34] *BRACHMANES, *BRAMINES, *CHAVARIGTES, *CHINOIS, *COTERIE, *CYNIQUES, *CYRENAIQUE, *DRANSES, *ECLAIRÉ, *ECLECTISME, *EGYPTIENS, *ELEATIQUE, *ENCYCLOPEDIE, *EPICUREISME, *ETHIOPIENS, *FORDICIDIES, *GRECS, *HAMBELIENS, *HERACLITISME, *HOBBISME, *IONIQUE, *JAPONAIS, *JOQUES, *JUIFS.

Yet, if one looks closely at Naigeon's writings, one discovers other articles bearing the editorial asterisk and reproduced by Assézat and Tourneux, which he also attributes to Diderot.

Information about these additional articles is to be found in the second and third volumes of Naigeon's history of ancient and modern philosophy in the *Encyclopédie méthodique*. In the second volume, in the course of his article on Diderot, he reproduces sixty-four passages from the latter's writings under the heading *Réflexions Philosophiques sur divers sujets*. The majority of these are taken from one or sometimes more articles in the *Encyclopédie*.[35] In addition, in the third volume he reproduces a certain number of articles written by Diderot from the *Encyclopédie*, but under a different head-word, as Professor Proust duly noted in the case of one article, *DRANSES, which he labels NAISSANCE.

1

An examination of these two volumes of the *Encyclopédie*

[34] A slip for *BOIS SACRÉS which is the article reproduced by Naigeon (*Mémoires*, pp. 59-60).
[35] pp. 197-217. I have been unable to trace the following passages either in the *Encyclopédie* or in Diderot's works: p. 201, *Sur la mort*; p. 209, *Sur une observation de Lucrèce*; p. 213, *Sur l'instinct & le tact*; pp. 214-15, *Sur quelques effets d'un mauvais gouvernement*; p. 215, *Sur la brièveté de la vie*; pp. 216-17, *Sur les inconvéniens de la méthode dans l'étude de l'histoire naturelle*. Five of the passages do not come from the *Encyclopédie*: pp. 204-5, *Sur les duels*—AT, Vol. VI, pp. 390-2; pp. 205-6, *Sur l'origine du mal*—AT, Vol. II, p. 85; pp. 213-14, *Sur l'infaillibilité des sens lorsqu'ils ne sont pas contredits par la raison*—AT, Vol. II, p. 87; p. 214, *Sur les passions*—AT, Vol. II, p. 88; and ibid., *Sur la justice*—AT, Vol. I, pp. 86, 98.

UNSIGNED ARTICLES

Méthodique yields the following additional articles of Diderot, bearing an asterisk and reproduced by Assézat and Tourneux:

*AFFECTION (*Physiol.*): *PAM*, Vol. II, p. 212 (*Sur ce sentiment vif de plaisir ou d'aversion que les objets, quels qu'ils soient, occasionnent en nous*).
*AIGLE: *PAM*, Vol. II, p. 212—(*Sur le penchant de l'homme à la superstition,* first 13 lines of extract).
*AIR: ibid. (last 7 lines of extract).
*ALECTO: *PAM*, Vol. III, p. 625—under THEOLOGIE EMBLEMATIQUE.
*AMENTHÈS: *PAM*, Vol. II, p. 203 (*Sur un dogme de la théologie des grecs.*)
*BETE, ANIMAL, BRUTE: *PAM*, Vol. II. pp. 212-13 (*Sur l'ame des bêtes*).
*CHANGEMENT, VARIATION, VARIETÉ: *PAM*, Vol. III, p. 758—under VARIATION, VARIETÉ, CHANGEMENT.
*CHARIDOTES: *PAM*, Vol. II, p. 201 (*Effets des histoires scandaleuses que les payens attribuoient à leurs dieux*).
*CONJECTURE: *PAM*, Vol. III, p. 759—under VRAISEMBLANCE.
*CONSERVATION: *PAM*, Vol. II, p. 204. (*Sur le suicide*).
*CONTINENCE: *PAM*, Vol. II, p. 216 (*Sur cette vertu morale par laquelle nous résistons aux impulsions de la chair.*)
*COQ (*Mythol.*): *PAM*, Vol. III, pp. 758-9—under VIGILANCE.
*FACE: *PAM*, Vol. II, p. 206 (*Sur la folie de l'astrologie judiciaire.*)
*FANTOME: *PAM*, Vol. II, p. 217 (*Sur les fantômes.*)[36]
*HARMONIE: *PAM*, Vol. II, pp. 203-4 (*Sur les causes finales—* second paragraph).
*HESITATION: *PAM*, Vol. II, p. 210 (*Sur la co-existence necessaire de plusieurs sensations, soit pour comparer, soit pour juger, &c.*).
*HIERACITES: *PAM*, Vol. II, p. 210 (*Sur les effets d'une opinion répandue parmi les premiers chrétiens.*)
*IMAGINAIRE: *PAM*, Vol. II, p. 201 (*Sur ce qu'il faut entendre par un plaisir ou une peine qui n'est que dans l'imagination.*)
*IMPARFAIT: *PAM*, Vol. II, p. 210 (*Sur les monstres*—last 16 lines).
*IMPARTIAL: *PAM*, Vol. II, pp. 210-11 (*Sur certaines qualités morales très-rares dans tous les hommes.*)
*IMPERCEPTIBLE: *PAM*, Vol. II, p. 206 (*Sur les animaux que leur petitesse dérobe à notre vue.*)
*IMPERISSABLE: *PAM*, Vol. II, p. 212 (*Sur le principe d'Aristote,* corruptio unius, generatio alterius—first 9 lines).

[36] * FORDICIDIES (*PAM*, Vol. III. p. 596) under SUPERSTITION is also given in part in the *Mémoires* and is therefore listed by Professor Proust.

*INCOMPRÉHENSIBLE: *PAM*, Vol. II, p. 207 (*Sur une conséquence très-importante de l'ancien axiôme*, nihil est in intellectu quod non prius fuerit in sensu.)
*INCONSEQUENCE, INCONSEQUENT: *PAM*, Vol. II, p. 625—under TENEBRES.
*INCROYABLE: *PAM*, Vol. II, p. 207 (*Sur les caractères d'un bon examen en matière de faits qui ne paroissent pas dignes de foi.*)
*INDECENT: *PAM*, Vol. II, p. 207 (*Sur le jugement plus ou moins sévère qu'on doit porter des mêmes fautes, selon les différentes causes auxquelles on peut les attribuer & l'instant où on les commet.*)
*INDECIS: *PAM*, Vol. II, p. 207 (*Sur cet acte de l'entendement que les philosophes appellent* délibération.)
*INDISTINCT: *PAM*, Vol. III, pp. 371-2—under NOTIONS INDISTINCTES.
*INNÉ: *PAM*, Vol. II, p. 198 (*Sur l'absurdité du principe des idées innées*).
*INSEPARABLE: *PAM*, Vol. II, p. 207 (*Sur quelques erreurs très-communes dans les écrits des théologiens & même des philosophes.*)
*IRASCIBLE: *PAM*, Vol. III, pp. 599-600—under SYSTEME DE L'AME.
*IRRELIGIEUX: *PAM*, Vol. III, pp. 512-13—under RELIGIEUX, IRRELIGIEUX.
*ISOLÉ, ISOLER: *PAM*, Vol. III, p. 561—under SOLITAIRE, ISOLÉ (paragraphs 2—5).[37]
*JOURNEE DE LA SAINT-BARTHÉLEMY: *PAM*, Vol. II, p. 208 (*Sur le massacre de la Saint-Barthèlemy*).

2

The volumes of the *Philosophie ancienne et moderne* yield, by contrast, very few Diderot articles bearing the editorial asterisk, which are not to be found in the Assézat-Tourneux edition:

*AMER: *PAM*, Vol. II, p. 217 (*Sur les saveurs en général*).
*ARITHMETIQUE (*Machine*) *PAM*, Vol. I, p. vii n., Vol. III, p. 862n.
*BARAICUS: *PAM*, Vol. III, pp. 373-4—under ORACLE D'HERCULE.
*ESCULAPE: *PAM*, Vol. III, pp. 465-6—under PRODIGE.

[37] The first paragraph reads 'Interrogez votre coeur, & il vous dira que l'homme de bien est dans la société, & qu'il n'y a que le méchant qui soit seul' (from *Le Fils Naturel*, iv. 3—see AT, Vol. VII, p. 66).

*IMBIBER: *PAM*, Vol. II, p. 201 (*Sur la manière physique dont se fait l'imbibition*).
*INTEMPÉRIE: *PAM*, Vol. III, p. 350—under NATURE, INTEMPERIE DE LA.

However, nowhere did Naigeon claim that he was seeking either to reproduce or to refer to all the articles, with or without asterisks, which Diderot had contributed to the *Encyclopédie*. In his edition of the *Œuvres*, all he set out to offer in Vols. V, VI and VII, entitled 'Opinions des anciens philosophes', was what he called Diderot's 'Essai d'une histoire critique de la philosophie ancienne et moderne'.[38] Indeed, he makes it perfectly plain that he did *not* intend to include a whole host of other Diderot articles from the *Encyclopédie*: 'Les articles de Diderot sur les arts mécaniques, la grammaire, la politique, la morale et la philosophie, réunis sous le titre général de *Mélanges*, formeroient seuls plus de trois volumes *in-4°*; et j'ajoute qu'il y auroit peu de lecture plus variée, plus agréable et plus instructive.' In a sense we could dispense with his testimony that the articles marked with an asterisk are by Diderot; where it is of particular value is, as we shall see, with the unsigned articles.

3

Before dealing with these, however, it might be useful to provide a list of significant articles marked with an asterisk in the *Encyclopédie*, but omitted in the Assézat-Tourneux edition and not vouched for by Naigeon. No doubt not everyone will agree as to what is 'significant' in this context;[39] but at least it could be claimed that the articles which appear in the following list are more characteristic of the outlook and interests of Diderot than many articles of this type which Assézat and Tourneux reproduced in their edition.[40]

[38] Vol. I, p. xxiv.
[39] Jean Mayer, as will be seen from the following list, also considers a good number of these articles worthy of comment.
[40] '*. . .' indicates that the article is by another contributor, but that Diderot made an addition to it which is marked with an asterisk.

*ABAREMO-TEMO, s.f. arbre qui croît, dit-on, dans les montagnes du Brésil . . . (account of its wonderful medicinal qualities). . . . Il ne reste plus qu'à s'assurer de l'existence de l'arbre & de ses propriétés. Voilà toujours son nom (cf. J. Mayer, *Diderot homme de science*, p. 109).
*ABARNAHAS: cf. J. Mayer, op. cit., p. 163.
*. . . ABSENT: (the article is by D'Alembert): . . . En attendant que nous exposions à l'*article* PROBABILITÉ cette théorie nouvelle (i.e. of probability) qui est de M. de Buffon, nous allons mettre le lecteur en état de se satisfaire lui-même sur la question présente des *absens réputés pour morts* . . . (cf. J. Mayer, op. cit., p. 71).
*AGUAPA, subst. m. (*Hist. nat. bot.*) arbre qui croît aux Indes occidentales, dont on dit que l'ombre fait mourir ceux qui s'y endorment nuds, & qu'elle fait enfler les autres d'une maniere prodigieuse. Si les habitans du pays ne le connoissent pas mieux qu'il ne nous est désigné par cette description, ils sont en grand danger.
*ALLEMAGNE
*ALSACE: chiefly information about mines, based on a *mémoire* by Comte d'Hérouville de Claye.
*ALUN: cf. J. Mayer, op. cit., p. 163.
*. . . AME: (the article is by Abbé Yvon). Aux quatre questions précédentes sur l'origine, la nature, la destinée de l'*ame*, & sur les êtres en qui elle réside, les Physiciens & les Anatomistes en ont ajouté une cinquieme, qui sembloit plus être de leur ressort que de la Métaphysique; c'est de fixer le siége de l'ame dans les êtres qui en ont. Ceux d'entre les Physiciens qui croyent pouvoir admettre la spiritualité de l'*ame*, & lui accorder en même tems de l'étendue, qualité qu'ils ne peuvent plus regarder comme la différence spécifique de la matiere, ne lui fixent aucun siége particulier: ils disent qu'elle est dans toutes les parties du corps; & comme ils ajoûtent qu'elle existe toute entiere sous chaque partie de son étendue, la perte de certains membres ne doit rien ôter à ses facultés, ni à son activité, ni à ses fonctions. Ce sentiment résout des difficultés: mais il fait naître d'autres, tant sur cette maniere particuliere & incompréhensible d'exister des esprits, que sur la destruction de la substance spirituelle & de la substance corporelle: aussi n'est-il guere suivi. Les autres philosophes pensent qu'elle n'est point étendue, & pourtant il y a un lieu particulier où elle réside, & d'où elle exerce son empire. (Discusses theories of Descartes, Vieussens, Lancisi and La Peyronie).
*ANGLETERRE
*ANIMAL, s.m. Reproduces copious extracts from Buffon, *His-*

UNSIGNED ARTICLES

toire naturelle, Vol. II, but interspersed with Diderot's comments and questions (cf. J. Mayer, op. cit., pp. 56, 214-15).

*... ARISTOCRATIE. Quant aux lois relatives à l'aristocratie on peut consulter l'excellent ouvrage de M. de Montesquieu. Voici les principales (23 numbered paragraphs taken from *Esprit des Lois*).

*ARITHMETIQUE POLITIQUE: cf. J. Mayer, op. cit. p. 426 (not to be confused with the unsigned article POLITIQUE ARITHMETIQUE, which comes straight from Chambers, POLITICAL ARITHMETIC, see below, p. 188; *ARITHMETIQUE POLITIQUE is a considerably expanded version of the article in Chambers.)

*ASSAZOÉ, subst. f. (*Hist. nat. bot.*) plante de l'Abyssinie, qui passe pour un préservatif admirable contre les serpents; son ombre seule les engourdit: ils tombent morts s'ils en sont touchés . . . Une observation que nous ferons sur l'*assazoé* & sur beaucoup d'autres substances naturelles, auxquelles on attribue des propriétés merveilleuses, c'est que plus ces propriétés sont merveilleuses & en grand nombre, plus les descriptions qu'on fait des substances sont mauvaises; ce qui doit donner de grands soupçons contre l'existence réelle des substances, ou celle des propriétés qu'on leur attribue (cf. J. Mayer, op. cit., p. 109).

*AZUR FACTICE: cf. J. Mayer, op. cit., p. 163.

*BARBARIE

*BATRACHITE: s.f. (*Hist. Nat.*) pierre qui se trouve, dit-on, dans la grenouille. On lui attribue de grandes vertus contre les venins: mais l'existence de la pierre n'est pas encore constatée (cf. J. Mayer, op. cit., p. 110).

*CERF: often attacked by hostile critics.

*CHEF-D'ŒUVRE: (*Arts & Mét.*): an attack on the guilds (see *Selected Articles*, pp. 20-1).

*CHEVEUX: cf. J. Mayer, op. cit., pp. 134n., 149; based on Chambers, HAIR, but much expanded.

*COACTIF, adj. (*Théol. & Jurispr.*) qui peut légitimement contraindre & se faire obéir par la force. Les souverains ont seuls le pouvoir *coactif*: il y a cette différence entre les lois de l'Eglise, & les lois de l'état, que celles de l'Eglise, en qualité simple de lois de l'Eglise, n'ont que force directive, au lieu que les lois de l'état ont par elles-mêmes force *coactive*. Les lois de l'Eglise n'ont force coactive que quand elles sont devenues lois de l'état.

*COACTION, s.f. (*Théol.*) action sur la volonté, qui en ôte ou diminue le libre exercice, d'où il s'ensuit que la *coaction*, si elle avoit lieu, excuseroit entierement ou en partie la créature du crime, & lui ôteroit le mérite de la bonne action: car le mérite & le démérite diminuent & disparoissent aussitôt que la nécessité

de vouloir ou de ne pas vouloir commence. *Voyez* LIBERTÉ, GRACE.
*CRAPAUD *(Mat. med.)* on doute de la qualité venéneuse de notre *crapaud*. Je vais en raconter ce que j'en sai par expérience; on conclura ce que l'on jugera à propos. J'étois à la campagne vers le tems de la Quasimodo; j'apperçus sur un bassin, à l'extrémité d'un parc, une masse de *crapauds* collés les uns contre les autres: cette masse flottoit & étoit suivie d'une foule d'autres *crapauds*; je l'attirai au bord du bassin avec une canne, puis je l'enlevai de l'eau avec une branche fourchue, & je me mis à séparer ces animaux, au centre desquels j'apperçus une femelle, apparemment étouffée. Tandis que j'étois occupé à mon observation, je me sentis prendre au nez d'une vapeur très-subtile, qui me passa de la gorge dans l'estomac, & de-là dans les intestins; j'eus des douleurs de ventre, & je fus incommodé d'un crachement assez abondant qui dura trois ou quatre heures, au bout desquelles ces accidens cesserent avec l'inquiétude qu'ils me donnoient & à la personne avec laquelle je me trouvois: c'étoit M. l'abbé Mallet, maintenant professeur royal en Théologie, alors curé de Pesqueux, village voisin de Vernouillet, lieu de la scene que je viens de raconter[41] (followed by an ironical account of three *fables* concerning toads). (cf. J. Mayer, op.cit., pp. 134n., 363-4).
*DYDIME, s.m. *(Géog. mod. & Divination)* lieu célebre dans l'île de Milet, par un oracle d'Apollon que Licinius consulta, dit-on, sur le succès de la guerre qu'il se proposoit de recommencer contre Constantin, & qui lui répondit en deux vers d'Homere; *Malheureux, ne t'attaque point à de jeunes gens, toi que les forces ont abandonné, & qui es accablé par le faix des années.* On ajoute que l'empereur Julien, qui n'étoit pas un petit génie, fit ce qu'il put pour remettre cet oracle en honneur, & qu'il prit lui-même le titre de prophete de l'oracle de *Dydime.* Mais il ne faut pas donner dans les contes d'oracles. Quelle que soit l'autorité qui les appuie, elle ne supplée jamais entierement à la vraisemblance qui leur manque par leur nature. Il faut s'en tenir fermement à l'expérience, qui leur est contraire dix mille fois, pour une seule où elle ne les autorise ni les conduit. Il faut bien se garder surtout de confondre ces faits avec les faits naturels & historiques. Ceux-ci acquierent de plus en plus de certitude avec le tems; les autres en perdent de plus en plus. Le témoignage de la tradition & de l'histoire est par rapport aux uns & aux autres, comme le témoignage d'un homme que nous surprendrions en mensonge sur un certain nombre de faits, toutes les fois que nous serions

---

[41] According to D'Alembert in his *Éloge de l'Abbé Mallet (Encyclopédie,* Vol. VI, p. iv) Mallet was appointed to his chair in Paris in 1751.

à portée de les vérifier, & qui nous diroit constamment la vérité, sur un autre genre de faits. N'y auroit-il pas beaucoup d'apparence que cet homme auroit menti, même dans les occasions où nous n'aurions pû nous en assurer; & cette seule réflexion ne suffit-elle pas pour renverser toutes les inductions que les esprits forts ont prétendu tirer des oracles & des autres miracles du paganisme? *Voy.* ORACLES.

*EGAGROPILES, s.f. pl. (*Mat. med.*) elles n'ont aucune propriété médicinale. Cependant combien ne leur en a-t-on pas attribué? Avant qu'on en connût la nature, elles étoient bonnes pour le flux de sang, pour les hémorrhagies; elles avoient la vertu de toutes les plantes dont on les croyoit composées; elles guérissoient du vertige & des étourdissemens. Quand la nature en a été connue, elles n'ont plus été bonnes à rien. Il est donc de la derniere importance de ne rien assûrer sur la formation & les élémens des choses qu'après un grand nombre d'expériences. Quand on a obtenu de l'expérience tout ce qu'on pouvoit en attendre, sur la nature des choses, il en faut faire de nouvelles sur leurs propriétés, si l'on ne veut pas prendre les substances pour ce qu'elles ne sont pas, ordonner des masses de poil & d'herbes pour des spécifiques & tomber dans le ridicule de Velschius qui a composé un livre des propriétés de l'*égagropile* (cf. J. Mayer, op. cit., p. 110).

*ENTREPRISE, s.f. (*Gramm.*) c'est en général ou le dessein d'exécuter quelque chose, ou l'exécution même de ce dessein. On dit d'un homme, *qu'il ne voit pas tous les dangers de son entreprise; que son entreprise lui a réussi; qu'il y a gagné cent mille écus. Entreprise,* dans un autre sens, est synonyme à *usurpation,* comme dans ces phrases: *la puissance civile peut former des entreprises sur la puissance ecclésiastique; la puissance ecclésiastique peut former des entreprises sur la puissance souveraine.* Le même terme a lieu, selon la même signification, dans les Arts & Métiers. Si les maîtres de quelque communauté s'immisçoient de faire des ouvrages qui fussent du ressort d'une autre communauté, comme si les Orfévres vouloient débiter des pincettes de fer, ce qui appartient aux Serruriers, ces sortes d'*entreprises* occasionneroient infailliblement de grandes contestations.

*EPÉES (*Hist. mod.*) l'ordre des deux *épées* de J.C. ou les chevaliers du Christ des deux *épées,* ordre militaire de Livonie & de Pologne en 1193. Dans ces tems où l'on croyoit suivre l'esprit de l'Evangile & se sanctifier, en forçant les hommes d'embrasser le Christianisme, Bertold, second évêque de Riga, engagea quelques gentilshommes qui revenoient de la croisade, de passer en Livonie & d'employer leurs armes à l'avancement de la religion; mais ce projet ne fut exécuté que par Albert son frere, chanoine de Reims, & son successeur. La troupe de nos soldats convertisseurs fut érigée en ordre militaire. Vinnus en fut le premier grand-maître en 1203. Ils portoient dans leurs bannieres deux *épées* en sautoir. Ils s'opposerent avec succès aux entreprises des idolatres.

*EXHUMER, v. act. (*Gramm.*) c'est tirer un cadavre de la terre, ce qui se fait quelquefois licitement, comme lorsque les lois l'ordonnent.

On lit dans Brantôme & dans le dictionnaire de Trévoux, qu'après la mort de Charles Quint, il fut arrêté à l'inquisition en présence du roi Philippe II son fils, que son corps seroit *exhumé* & brûlé comme hérétique, parce que ce prince avoit tenu quelques propos légers sur la foi. Ces peuples sont bien revenus de cette barbarie, comme il le paroît par les propositions avantageuses qu'ils ont faites récemment à M. Linnaeus.

*FAMILISTES, s.m. pl. (*Hist. ecclés.*) hérétiques qui eurent pour chef David-Georges Delft. Cette secte s'appelle *la famille d'amour* ou *de charité*, & leur doctrine eut pour base deux principes qu'on ne peut trop recommander aux hommes en général; c'est de s'aimer réciproquement, quelque différence qu'il puisse y avoir entre leurs sentimens sur la religion, & d'obéir à toutes les puissances temporelles, quelque tyranniques qu'elles soient. Delft se croyoit venu pour rétablir le royaume d'Israël; il faisoit assez peu de cas de Moyse, des Prophetes, & de Jesus-Christ: il prétendoit que le culte qu'ils avoient prêché sur la terre, étoit incapable de conduire les hommes à la béatitude; que ce privilége étoit réservé à sa morale; qu'il étoit le vrai Messie; & qu'il ne mourroit point, ou qu'il ressusciteroit: il eut des disciples qui ajoûterent à son système d'autres opinions de cette nature: ils soûtinrent que toutes les actions de l'impie sont nécessairement autant de péchés, & que les fautes sont remises à celui qui a recouvré l'amour de Dieu.

*FEU (*Pompe à*) Hydraul. & Arts méchaniques: la premiere a été construite en Angleterre; plusiers auteurs se sont occupés successivement à la perfectionner & à la simplifier. On en peut regarder Papin comme l'inventeur: car que fait celui qui construit une *pompe à feu*? il adapte un corps de pompe ordinaire à la machine de Papin. *Voyez son ouvrage,*[42] *l'article* DIGESTEUR,[43] & sur-tout *l'article précédent*.[44]

---

[42] *Nouvelle manière pour lever l'eau par la force du feu* (Cassel, 1707).
[43] This article has at the end 'Chambers (d)' (=D'Aumont).
[44] FEU (*Physiq.*) by D'Alembert.

Tout ce que nous allons dire de cette pompe est tiré d'un mémoire qui nous a été communiqué avec les figures qui y sont relatives, par M. P . . .[45] homme d'un mérite distingué, qui a bien voulu s'intéresser à la perfection de notre ouvrage. (The article runs from p. 603a to p. 609a; it ends with a general reflection which contrasts with the severely technical tone of the main part of the article and which may well be an editorial addition). Le jeu ce cette machine est très-extraordinaire, & s'il falloit ajouter foi au système de Descartes, qui regarde les machines comme des animaux, il faudroit convenir que l'homme auroit imité de fort près le Créateur, dans la construction de la *pompe à feu,* qui doit être aux yeux de tout Cartésien conséquent une espece d'animal vivant, aspirant, se mouvant de lui-même par le moyen de l'air, & tant qu'il y a de la chaleur.

*FIGER (SE): cf. J. Mayer, op. cit., p. 186.
*GEOMETRIE SOUTERREINE: cf. J. Mayer, op. cit., pp. 71, 80
*GIROVAGUE, s.m. (*Hist. ecclés.*) espece de moines, la quatrieme dont S. Benoît fasse mention dans sa regle; ces *girovagues* ne s'attachoient à aucune maison; ils erroient de monastere en monastere, genre de vie que l'indépendance leur faisoit préférer à celui de Cénobites. S. Benoît n'aimoit pas ces couvens-là. Mais le meme nom de *girovagues* ne conviendroit-il pas également à ces moines qui n'habitent leur cloître que le moins qu'ils peuvent, qui sont plongés dans les embarras du monde & les dissipations, qui intriguent, qui cabalent, & qu'on rencontre dans tous les quartiers, dans toutes les maisons de la ville? Si S. Benoît pouvoit élever sa voix de dessous sa tombe, ne leur crieroit-il pas: '*Girovagues,* vous êtes pires que les Sarabaïtes'.

*GOG & MAGOG (*Théol.*) c'est par ces noms que l'Ecriture a désigné des nations ennemies de Dieux. Ceux qui se sont mêlés d'interpreter cet endroit de l'Ecriture, ont donné libre carriere à leur imagination; ils ont vu dans *gog* & *magog* tout ce qu'ils ont voulu; les uns des peuples futurs, d'autres des peuples subsistans, les Scythes, les Tartares, les Turcs, &c.

*HUMAINE ESPECE (*Hist. Nat.*) . . . *Voyez l'Histoire naturelle de Mrs. de Buffon & D'Aubenton* (summary of the section *Variétés dans l'espece humaine.* Vol. III, pp. 371-530).

*INCULTE, adj. (*Gramm.*) qui n'est pas cultivé. Des terres *incultes.* Il est démontré qu'en tout pays où il reste des terres *incultes,* il n'y a pas assez d'hommes, ou qu'ils y sont mal employes.

---

[45] Perronnet, according to J. Mayer, op. cit., p. 201.

Inculte se dit aussi au figuré; les hommes de cette province ont de l'esprit, mais *inculte*.

Il y a peu de terres *incultes* en France, mais elles y sont mal cultivées.

*INDISPOSÉ: cf. J. Mayer, op. cit., p. 385.

*INFUS, INFUSE, adj. (*Gram.*) On dit science *infuse*, grace *infuse*, sagesse *infuse*, c'est-à-dire qu'on n'a point acquise par ses soins, mais qu'il a plû à Dieu de verser dans quelques ames privilégiées.

On a agité & l'on agite encore dans les écoles sur toutes ces qualité *infuses*, beaucoup de questions frivoles que la saine philosophie n'a point encore décriées.

C'est bien peu de chose que ce qu'on a par *infusion*.

*INTERMINABLE, adj. (*Gram.*) qui ne peut être terminé. On dit un bruit *interminable*. Sans une autorité infaillible, les disputes de religion sont *interminables*. Le mépris seroit un moyen bien aussi sûr que l'autorité. Les Théologiens ne disputent guere quand on ne les écoute pas.

*IRRÉGULARITÉ, s.f. (*Gram.*) défaut contre les regles; par-tout où il y a un système de regles qu'il importe de suivre, il peut y avoir écart de ces regles & par conséquent *irrégularité*.

On peut meme quelquefois en accuser les ouvrages de la nature; mais alors il y a deux motifs qui doivent nous rendre très-circonspects; la nécessité absolue de ses lois & le peu de connoissance de la variété de ses opérations.

*JOUER (*Gramm.*): the article in itself is not particularly important, but it is interesting to note that the next article, *JOUER (*Gram. Mathémat. pures*), is reproduced in AT not only under the wrong label—(*Morale et Mathém.*)—but also in a truncated version which omits over six columns devoted by Diderot to the application of the theory of probability to gaming (cf. J. Mayer, op. cit., pp. 71, 80-6, and J. Proust, op. cit., p. 125).

4

If we turn now to the problem of the unsigned articles properly speaking, we must begin by excluding a large number of those which are wrongly included in the Assézat-Tourneux edition. The list which follows incorporates the articles rejected by Professor Proust, but will be found to be even longer:

ACRIDOPHAGES: cf. Loyalty Cru, op. cit., p. 282n.; straight from Chambers, ACRIDOPHAGI.⁴⁶

ADORATION (*Théol.*) ⎫ Adapted from Chambers, ADORATIO
ADORATION (*Hist. mod.*) ⎬ but without any sign of Diderot
                                     ⎭ hand.

ADORER (*Théol.*): not from Chambers, but no sign of Diderot's hand in it.

AEDES: not Chambers, AEDES, but no sign of Diderot's hand in it.

AFFINITÉ (*Jurisprud.*): the next article, AFFINS, *terme de Droit*, is signed '(H)' (=Toussaint).⁴⁷

ALMAGESTE: expanded from Chambers, ALMAGEST, but no sign of Diderot's hand in it.

ARCHONTES: the next article, ARCHONTIQUES (*Théol.*) is signed '(G)' (=Mallet).

BENIN: certainly not by Diderot as it comes not from the *Encyclopédie*, but from the *Supplément* (Vol. I, p. 875).⁴⁸

BIBLIOMANE: largely from La Bruyère (*Caractères*, XIII, 2).

CATHÉDRALE (*Hist. ecclés.*): the next article, CATHÉDRATIQUE (*Hist. ecclés.*) is signed '(G)' (=Mallet).

CENTON: straight from Chambers, CENTO.

CHRISTIANISME: although much attacked at the time, this article bears no signs of being by Diderot himself.

DISTINCTION: not from Chambers, but no sign of Diderot's hand in it.

FANTAISIE (*Morale*): the *Encyclopédie* (Vol. VII, p. xiv) attributes to an anonymous writer 'les mots FANTAISIE, FRAGILITÉ (*Morale*), FRIVOLITÉ, & GENIE (*Littér*)'; attributed to Saint-Lambert by Grimm, *Corr. Litt.*, Vol. III, p. 222, and reproduced in Vol. VI of his *Œuvres Philosophiques* (pp. 1-2).

⁴⁶ The problem of Diderot's use of articles from Chambers is complicated. Diderot himself was apparently not responsible for the translation which had been made of the *Cyclopaedia*. Where an article in the *Encyclopédie* is merely a translation of one from Chambers, we may safely remove it from the list of Diderot's writings. Where the article is adapted—whether it is abridged or enlarged—in some way which can be held to reflect Diderot's interests or style, it seems reasonable to attribute it to him. Where an article which is not a mere translation of an article from Chambers, fails to reflect Diderot's manner, it has been rejected in the above list.

⁴⁷ Cf. *Encyclopédie*, Vol. I, p. xlvi: 'N.B. Lorque plusieurs articles appartenant à la même matière, & par conséquent faits ou revûs par la même personne, sont immédiatement consécutifs, on s'est contenté quelquefois de mettre la lettre distinctive à la fin du dernier de ces articles.'

⁴⁸ The article is accidentally marked with an asterisk in Professor Proust's list (p. 532).

FASTE (*Morale*): attributed to Saint-Lambert by Grimm (ibid.) and although not in his *Œuvres philosophique*, the *Encyclopédie* (Vol. VI, p. vi) attributes to an anonymous writer 'les mots FASTE, FAMILIARTÉ, FRIVOLITÉ, FERMETÉ, FLATTERIE, & quelques autres'.

FERMETÉ:[49] attributed to Saint-Lambert by Grimm *Corr. Litt.*, Vol. III, f. 222; see FASTE.

FONDATION (*Politique & Droit naturel*): see Turgot, *Œuvres*, ed. G. Schelle, Vol. I, pp. 584-93.

FORTUNE: from 'Articles omis' of Vol. XVII; the second and third paragraphs come from Chambers, FORTUNE; there is no evidence that Diderot had any hand in it.[50]

FRAGILITÉ (*Morale*) see FANTAISIE: attributed to Saint-Lambert by Grimm, *Corr. litt.*, Vol. III, p. 458; reproduced in Saint-Lambert, *Œuvres philosophiques*, Vol. VI, pp. 5-7.

FRIVOLITÉ (*Morale*): see FANTAISIE and FASTE: reproduced in Saint-Lambert, *Œuvres philosophiques*, Vol. VI, pp. 7-8

GÉNIE (*Philosophie & Littér.*): see FANTAISIE: attributed to Saint-Lambert by Grimm, *Corr. litt.*, Vol. IV, p. 457. and reproduced in his *Œuvres philosophiques*, Vol. VI, pp. 8-20 (it is pretty clear that Diderot 'edited' this article fairly heavily, as there are some notable differences between the text of the *Encyclopédie* article and that of Saint-Lambert's works).

GLORIEUX, GRAVE, GRAVITÉ, GRONDEUR: all from the 'Articles omis' of Vol. XVII of the *Encyclopédie*, and very dubious Diderot.

HAMMON (*Belles Lettres*): in the *Encyclopédie* the two paragraphs reproduced in AT are followed by the words '*Corne d'Hammon, terme d'histoire naturelle. Voyez* CORNE. (G)'. The article is presumably by Mallet.

IDENTITÉ: this article is alleged by Loyalty Cru (p. 266) to be taken from Chambers, IDENTITY, but this is not the case; there is no reason to attribute it to Diderot.

ILIADE: the beginning—down to the paragraph concerning 'M. Barus' (= Barnes!)—is from Chambers, ILIAD; as M. Trousson points out in a note to p. 204 of 'Diderot et Homère' (*Diderot Studies VIII*), the next four paragraphs are taken from Voltaire's *Essai sur la poésie épique,* which leaves only two paragraphs unaccounted for, and these do not bear the stamp of Diderot.

IMMATERIALISME: almost certainly by Yvon (see Venturi, *Le Origini* . . . , p. 140).

---

[49] FERMETÉ is by Voltaire, which leaves only FERMETÉ & CONSTANCE unsigned.

[50] Professor Proust (p. 118n.) points out that the article FORTUNE in Vol. VI, which is signed by Jaucourt, follows in some respects the article on the same subject which did not appear until Vol. XVII.

INDUCTION: ??
INTÉRÊT (*Morale*): Reprinted in Saint-Lambert, *Œuvres philosophiques*, Vol. VI, pp. 45-34 (*sic*).
JAKUTES: by D'Holbach? (see *Essays*, pp. 123-124).
JUSTE, INJUSTE: taken mainly from F. H. Strube de Piermont, *Ébauche des loix naturelles et du droit primitif* (Amsterdam, 1744); cf. L. Thielemann, *Diderot Studies IV*, pp. 261-83.
KING (*Hist. moderne, Philos.*): by D'Holbach? (see *Essays*, pp. 186-87).
LABOURAGE OU AGRICULTURE (*Hist. anc.*): although unsigned, AGRICULTURE is certainly by Diderot (*Encyclopédie*, Vol. I, p. xliii); the words 'Voyez AGRICULTURE' at the end of the article in AT are not in the *Encyclopédie*, and there seems no reason to attribute it to him.
LAO-KIUN: by D'Holbach? (see *Essays*, pp. 187-88).
LÉGISLATEUR (*Politiq.*): reprinted in Saint-Lambert, *Œuvres philosophiques*, Vol. VI, pp. 34-87.
LIAISON (*Métaphysique*): a piece of pure compilation?
LIBERTÉ (*Morale*): see Naigeon, *PAM*, Vol. I, pp. 89n. and 96n.; he claims for himself 'les quatre premières colonnes' and attributes the rest to Abbé Mallet. Venturi (*Le Origini* . . . , pp. 139-40) shows that the article must have been by Yvon, in whose *Histoire de la religion* (Vol. II, pp. 28-68) the second part of the article is reproduced.
LIBERTÉ NATURELLE (*Droit naturel*): compiled from Burlamaqui, *Principes du Droit politique*, presumably by Jaucourt whose signature follows the next article but one, LIBERTÉ POLITIQUE.
LIBERTÉ CIVILE (*Droit des nations*): compiled from Burlamaqui and Montesquieu, presumably by Jaucourt whose signature follows the next article, LIBERTÉ POLITIQUE.
LIGATURE: paragraphs I, V-IX and XI are taken from Chambers, LIGATURE: paragraphs XIII and XIV consist of a long quotation from Montaigne; there is no reason to attribute the final paragraph and paragraphs II-IV and X to Diderot. See the note to MALÉFICE.
LOGIQUE: compiled from a variety of sources, including Fontenelle and Buffier (see Hermand, *RHL*, 1915, pp. 364-6 and *Idées morales*, pp. 232, 243).
LOI NATURELLE (*Morale*): this cannot very well have been compiled by Jaucourt, as he was responsible for another article, NATURELLE, *loi*; but it seems very dubious Diderot.
LOUANGE (*Morale*): reprinted in Saint-Lambert, *Œuvres philosophiques*, Vol. VI, p. 87.
LUXE: attributed to Saint-Lambert by Grimm, *Corr. litt.*, Vol.

V, p. 465, printed anonymously as *Essai sur le luxe* (s.l., 1764) and reprinted in *Œuvres philosophiques*, Vol. VI, pp. 88-134.

MALÉFICE: this article which has a cross-reference to LIGATURE is taken straight from Chambers, WITCHCRAFT; the only differences lie in the introductory definition and in the addition of a few lines in the middle of paragraph IX, the last sentence of paragraph X and the whole of paragraph XI. There is nothing to connect these additions with Diderot.

MANES (*Mythologie*): by Polier de Bottens (cf. R. Naves, *Voltaire et l'Encyclopédie*, p. 32).

MANICHEISME: almost certainly by Yvon (see Venturi, *Le Origini* . . . , p. 140).

MANIERES (*Gram. Pol. Moral.*) reprinted in Saint-Lambert, *Œuvres philosophiques*, Vol. VI, pp. 135-47.

MANSTUPRATION: by Ménuret de Chambaud. Jean Mayer (*Diderot homme de science*, p. 343 n.) points out that the author refers to a medical thesis which he had sustained at Montpellier. However, the article was not written, as he suggests, by Hugues Maret, but by Ménuret de Chambaud, who in MARIAGE which bears his symbol—'(m)'—mentions that this article is by him (see J. Roger, *Les Sciences de la vie dans la pensée française du XVIIIe siècle*, p. 631 n.).

MARABOUS: by D'Holbach? (see *Essays*, 219-20).

MONT-FAUCON: perhaps by Jaucourt who at this point in the *Encyclopédie* was responsible for a whole series of geographical articles, the last of which is signed 'D.J.'.

NÉCESSITÉ (*Métaphysiq.*) reproduced by Naigeon in *PAM*, Vol. III, p. 365, but not attributed to Diderot; described as '*Anonyme*'.

NGOMBOS: by D'Holbach, according to his son (*RHL*, 1951, p. 332); reproduced *PAM*, Vol. III, p. 370 but without signature.

ODIN: by D'Holbach? (see *Essays*, p. 140).

ODYSSÉE: paragraphs I-VI and the last part of paragraph IX are taken straight from Chambers, ODYSSEY; paragraph VIII is also secondhand, and there is really nothing to connect the article with Diderot (see R. Trousson, '*Diderot et Homère*', p. 204).

OFAVAI: by D'Holbach? (see *Essays*, p. 177). The reference to SIAKA (not in AT) is to another unsigned article.

PAIN CONJURÉ: straight from Chambers, CORSNED BREAD.

PARÉAS: by D'Holbach? (see *Essays*, p. 198).

PASSIONS: the first part of the article (as is acknowledged in a parenthesis—AT. Vol. XVI, p. 213) comes from Levesque de Pouilly, *La Théorie des sentiments agréables*. While the source of the rest has not been identified, there seems no reason to

attribute the article to Diderot.
PATIENCE: from Toussaint and Fontenelle (see P. Hermand, *RHL*, 1915, pp. 364, 366, and *Idées morales* . . . , pp. 233, 243).
PERFECTION: ??
PHILOSOPHE: cf. Naigeon, *PAM*, Vol. III, p. 203, 'Un anonyme a tiré de cette dissertation (as published in the *Nouvelles libertés de penser*, 1743) la matière d'un article qu'on trouve dans l'ancienne Encyclopédie au mot PHILOSOPHE; mais cet extrait est trés-infidéle & trés-mal fait' (see Dieckmann, *Le Philosophe. Texts and Interpretation*).
PHILOSOPHIE: as Hermand (*RHL*, 1915, p. 365, and *Idées morales*, pp. 237, 243) pointed out, contains borrowings from Malebranche and Fontenelle; the fact that Naigeon does not attribute it to Diderot would seem to exclude it from his collected works.
PIACHES: by D'Holbach? (see *Essays*, pp. 157-58).
PLAISIR: see Hermand, *RHL*, 1915, p. 364, and *Idées morales*, p. 232, and also Levesque de Pouilly, *Théorie des sentimens agréables*, Paris, 1774, 5th edition, p. xi: '. . . . Les Auteurs de l'Encyclopédie . . . ont pris la peine de fondre entièrement cet ouvrage dans un des articles de leur Dictionnaire; ils en ont même copié mot à mot une foule de phrases, qui véritablement ne déparent point leur travail. (Note. Voyez Dictionn. Encyclop. au mot *Plaisir*).'
PLASTIQUE: not reproduced by Naigeon in his *PAM*, where he prints another article under the same heading.
POLI, CIVIL: at this stage in the *Encyclopédie*'s history Jaucourt had taken over articles on synonyms. Although unsigned, this article which is from Girard with only minor changes is followed by a 5-lined article signed 'D.J.'.
POLITIQUE: cf. Proust, p. 553n.
POLITIQUE, GRACE: this is presumably the article by an anonymous contributor which is mentioned in the introduction to Vol. VII of the *Encyclopédie* (p. xiv): 'D'autres personnes nous avoient aussi fourni des secours que nous n'avons pu employer, quelquefois parce qu'ils sont arrivés trop tard; de ce nombre est l'article GRACE (*Politiq.*).'
POLYTHÉISME: almost certainly by Yvon (see Venturi, *Le Origini* . . . , p. 140); not reproduced by Naigeon in *PAM* where he prints a different article under the same heading. Yvon's article ATHEES ends with the cross-reference: 'Lisez l'article du POLYTHEISME, où l'on examine quelques difficultiés de cet auteur' [i.e. Bayle].
POSSIBLE: not attributed to Diderot by Naigeon.

PRASSAT: by D'Holbach? (see *Essays*, p. 202).

PRÉDESTINATIENS: straight from Chambers, PRÉDESTINARIAN, except for the last paragraph; there is nothing to connect the article with Diderot.

PRÉMOTION PHYSIQUE: a summary of L. F. Boursier, *De la prémotion physique* (Lille, 1713); not attributed to Diderot by Naigeon. Note the final cross-reference to CONCOURS (unsigned) which in turn refers to PRÉMOTION.

PRÉOCCUPATION: borrowings from Malebranche (see Hermand, *RHL*, 1915, p. 365, and *Idées morales*, p. 238).

PRESCIENCE: ??

PRÉSOMPTION: it is the following article, PRÉSOMPTUEUX, which bears the mark of Diderot.

PRETRES: according to his son, by D'Holbach (*RHL*, 1951, p. 332).

PRINCIPES, PREMIERS: borrowings from Buffier, *Traité des premières vérités*. AT omits '*Voyez* AXIOMES' in the first paragraph and in the second '*Voyez* AXIOMES où nous prouvons combien ils ont peu d'influence pour étendre nos connoissances'. AXIOMES is by Yvon. There are also cross-references to SENTIMENT INTIME and SENS COMMUN.

PRIVILEGE: this interesting, but dully written article surely never came from Diderot's pen. It is worth noting that AT cuts out the last words of the article—'Sur quoi il faut aussi observer de n'en pas charger un pays par les raisons qui sont exposées *article* FORGE'—i.e. FORGES (GROSSES) by Bouchu?

PROBITÉ: can the sentiments expressed in this article possibly be attributed to Diderot?

PROMESSE: ??

PROPHÈTE, PROPHETIE: the *Encyclopédie* has a second article, PROPHETIE (also 4 columns in length, but not reproduced in AT). This second article, as Loyalty Cru (op. cit., p. 264) points out, is based fairly closely on Chambers, PROPHECY, but is less bold; indeed at one point it refutes Chambers comments on Surrenhuisis's *Sepher Hamechave* (. . . 'qu'il faut n'avoir pas lu pour dire, comme fait M. Chambers, que ces regles sont forcées & peu naturelles. *Voyez* ce que nous avons dit *au mot* CITATIONS.') CITATION (*Théolog.*) which discusses Surrenhuisis's work is signed '(G)'—i.e. Mallet). PROPHÈTE, PROPHÉTIE has no connection with Chambers, PROPHET, nor, as far as one can see, with Diderot.

PROPRIÉTÉ (*Métaphysique*): from Buffier, *Traité des premières vérités*, in *Cours de Sciences*, col. 627-9.

PROVIDENCE: the article ends with a cross-reference to MANICHEISME, which is probably by Yvon (see above).

PRUDENCE: source untraced, but can it be by Diderot?

PSYCHOLOGIE: the very form of this article (more notes than text) suggests a different author from Diderot.

PUISSANCE: this article is followed by PUISSANCE LÉGISLATIVE, EXÉCUTRICE & DE JUGER which is signed 'D.J.' who could well have been responsible for both.

RAISONNEMENT: a compilation from Malebranche (see Hermand *RHL*, 1915, pp. 364-5, and *Idées morales*, pp. 232, 238), Buffier, *Principes du raisonnement* in *Cours de Sciences*, col. 855-8, and Condillac.

REPRÉSENTANTS: according to his son, by D'Holbach (*RHL*, 1951, p. 332).

SEMI-PÉLAGIENS: expanded from Chambers, SEMI-PELAGIANS, but with no trace of Diderot's hand.

SENSATIONS: concludes with a passage from Malebranche (see Hermand, *RHL*, 1915, p. 365 and *Idées morales*, p. 238); nothing in the article suggests Diderot.

SENTIMENT INTIME: from Buffier, *Traité des premières vérités* in *Cours de Sciences*, col. 557-61; there is a cross-reference from the article PRINCIPES, PREMIERS.

SOCIÉTÉ: a large part of the article consists of borrowings from Buffier's *Traité de la société civile* (see Hermand), but it has other sources too and contains a strong attack on Ultramontanism. There is a cross-reference (omitted in AT, Vol. XVII, p. 144) to ATHÉES, which is by Yvon. It is a curious fact that the *Extrait d'une lettre écrite à l'éditeur sur la vie et les ouvrages de Mr. Boulanger* which introduces the postumous *Antiquité dévoilée* ends with the sentence (not reproduced in AT, Vol. VI, pp. 339-46): 'Il a fourni à l'Encyclopédie les articles *Déluge, Corvée & Société*' (Amsterdam, 1766, 4°, p. vi).

SPINOSA: reproduced by Naigeon, *PAM,* Vol. III, pp. 566-8, but described as '(ANONYME)'.

SUICIDE: in view of the long account given here of Donne's *Biathanatos*, one is tempted to seek the source in Chambers, but the word is not given there or in the Supplement. Is there anything to make one attribute the article to Diderot?

THÉOCRATIE: according to his son by D'Holbach (*RHL*, 1951, p. 332).

TORTURE: straight from Chambers, TORTURE.

TYRAN: the three articles which follow—TYRANS, LES TRENTE; TYRANNICIDE; and TYRANNIE—are by Jaucourt, but the approach of the last of these is different from that of TYRAN; neither Diderot nor Jaucourt would seem to be responsible for the first article in the series.

ULEMA: by D'Holbach? (see *Essays*, p. 223).
VÉRITÉ: from Buffier, *Principes du raisonnement*, in *Cours de Sciences*, col. 787-93 (see Hermand, *RHL*, 1915, p. 364)
VRAISEMBLANCE: from Buffier, *Traité des premières vérités* in *Cours de Sciences*, col. 606-15.

5

The aim of a historian of the *Encyclopédie* is not confined to establishing what Diderot did or did not write for it; he is concerned with all the contributors and would like, as far as possible, to see their property restored to them. Hence before turning to consider what, after this purge, is left of Diderot's contribution to the *Encyclopédie*, it might be useful to examine briefly which other unsigned articles can be assigned to these contributors even if their articles have not had the honour of being reprinted by Assézat and Tourneux. Despite the lamentable gaps in our knowledge there are certain well established facts, which, conveniently summarized, might help to prevent in future the unfortunate mistakes in attribution which continue to occur.

ACCOUCHEMENT: 'On a oublié (Y) (i.e. Louis) à la fin de l'article ACCOUCHEMENT' (*Encyclopédie*, Vol. I, p. xlvi).
ACTE: 'On a oublié (G) (i.e. Mallet) à la fin d'ACTE' (*Encyclopédie*, Vol. I, p. xlvi).[51]
AIGU: 'On a oublié (E) (i.e. Abbé de la Chapelle) à la fin de l'article AIGU' (*Encyclopédie*, Vol. I, p. xlvi).[52]

[51] ACTION, ADULTÈRE, AGIR, AMITIÉ, AMOUR: in Vol. III (p. iv) of the *Encyclopédie* the reader is informed: 'N.B. Un mal entendu, qui n'aura pas lieu dans ce volume & dans les suivans, est cause que dans le premier volume la lettre de M. l'abbé Yvon se trouve aux articles AGIR, AMITIÉ, AMOUR, ADULTÈRE, ACTION, qui ont été fournis par une autre personne.' This statement, as Venturi points out (*Le Origini* . . . , p. 139), is untrue; it was simply a rather weak retort to the criticisms directed by the *Journal de Trévoux* against the plagiarisms which Yvon had perpetrated in the composition of these articles.
[52] AIGUILLE, ANATOMIE and ARDOISE (not reproduced in AT) are specifically attributed to Diderot in the *Encyclopédie* (Vol. I, p. xliii). It might be convenient to recall here that, according to Grimm (*Corr. Litt.*, Vol. VIII, p. 224), in the article VINGTIEME (not unsigned, but published by Damilaville under the name of Boulanger) 'ce qu'il y a de bon . . . y a été fourré par M. Diderot.'

ALCORAN: 'On a oublié (G) (i.e. Mallet) à la fin d'ALCORAN' (*Encyclopédie*, Vol. I, p. xlvi).

CONTINGENCE: 'A la fin de l'article CONTINGENCE . . . mettez un (O)' (i.e. D'Alembert) (*Encyclopédie*, Vol. IV, p. iv).

ÉTYMOLOGIE ⎫ The *Avertissement des Editeurs* of Vol. VI of
EXISTENCE ⎬ the *Encyclopédie* (p. vi) speaks of four
EXPANSIBILITÉ ⎭ persons who wished their articles to remain anonymous: 'Nous devons à la première les mots ÉTYMOLOGIE, EXISTENCE & EXPANSIBILITE'. See Turgot, *Œuvres*, ed. Schelle, Vol. I, pp. 473-576.

EVIDENCE: See the same *Avertissement*: 'Nous devons . . . à la seconde les mots EVIDENCE & FONCTIONS DE L'AME'. See J. Hecht, 'La vie de François Quesnay' in *François Quesnay et la Physiocratie*, Vol. I, pp. 252-3 (the article FONCTIONS DE L'AME was not published in the *Encyclopédie*).

FAMILIARITÉ: See the same *Avertissement*: 'Nous devons . . . à la quatrième . . . FAMILIARITÉ . . .'; attributed to Saint-Lambert by Grimm, *Corr. litt.*, Vol. III, p. 222, and reprinted in his *Œuvres philosophiques*, Vol. VI, pp. 2-4.[53]

FLATTERIE: See the same *Avertissement*: 'Nous devons . . . à la quatrième . . . FLATTERIE . . .' Attributed to Saint-Lambert by Grimm, *Corr. litt.*, Vol. III, p. 222, but not reprinted in his *Œuvres philosophiques*.

FOIRE: 'Cinq personnes qui ne veulent pas etre connues, nous ont donné . . . la troisième, les articles FOIRE & FONDATION' (*Encyclopédie*, Vol. VII, p. xiv). See Turgot, *Œuvres*, ed. Schelle, Vol. I, pp. 577-83 for the text of FOIRE (FONDATION is reproduced in AT: see above, p. 180).

HAWAMAAL: According to his son, by D'Holbach (*RHL*, 1951, p. 332).

HONNETE (*Morale*): reprinted in Saint-Lambert, *Œuvres philosophiques*, Vol. VI, pp. 20-8.

HONNEUR (*Morale*): reprinted in Saint-Lambert, *Œuvres philosophiques*, Vol. VI, pp. 28-44.

INSTINCT: reprinted in *Lettres philosophiques sur la perfectibilité et l'intelligence des animaux* of Charles Georges Leroy (see AT, Vol. XV, p. 226n.) PIÉGE which bears Leroy's signature has a cross-reference to INSTINCT.

KIJUN: by Polier de Bottens (see R. Naves, *Voltaire et*

[53] FINESSE: 'de M. de Voltaire et de M. de Saint-Lambert' according to Grimm, *Corr. litt.*, Vol. III, p. 222, but not mentioned in the *Avertissement des Editeurs* to Vol. VI of the *Encyclopédie* and not reprinted in the *Œuvres philosophiques* of Saint-Lambert: the two articles are in fact signed by Voltaire and Marmontel.

l'Encyclopédie, pp. 32-3).
LITURGIE: } by Polier de Bottens (ibid.)
LOGOMACHIE: }
MADRÉPORES: according to his son, by D'Holbach (*RHL*, 1951, p. 332).
MAGICIENS: }
MAGIE: }
MALACHBELUS: } by Polier de Bottens (Naves, pp. 32-3).
MAOSIM: }
MESSIE: }
OMBIASSES: according to his son, by D'Holbach (*RHL*, 1951, p. 332).
OVISSA: } according to his son, by D'Holbach (*RHL*,
PAVÉ DES GÉANTS: } 1951, p. 332).
POLITIQUE ARITHMÉTIQUE: straight from Chambers, POLITICAL ARITHMETIC (*ARITHMETIQUE POLITIQUE is an adaptation, not a straight translation, of the very same article).
SAMBA-PONGO: according to his son, by D'Holbach (*RHL*, 1951, p. 332).
SENSORIUM: straight from Chambers, SENSORY.
TOPILZIN: according to his son, by D'Holbach (*RHL*, 1951, p. 332); reproduced by Naigeon, *PAM*, Vol. III, pp. 725-6, where it is attributed to D'Holbach.
TRANSFUGE (*Art milit.*) in 'Articles omis' (Vol. XVII); reprinted anonymously as *De la Désertion* (Hambourg, 1766); attributed to Saint-Lambert by Grimm, *Corr. litt.*, Vol. VII, p. 128, and reprinted in his *Œuvres philosophiques*, Vol. VI, pp. 147-83.

6

It may perhaps be convenient for reference if we now put together under *authors* the unsigned articles contained in lists IV and V for which a contributor can be named:

Alembert, D': CONTINGENCE
Chambers: ACRIDOPHAGES; CENTON; PAIN CONJURÉ; POLITIQUE ARITHMETIQUE; SENSORIUM; TORTURE
Holbach, D': HAWAMAAL; MADRÉPORES; NGOMBOS; OMBIASSES; OVISSA; PAVÉ DES GÉANTS; PRETRES; REPRÉSENTANTS; SAMBA-PONGO; THEOCRATIE; TOPZILIN[54]

[54] And probably also JAKUTES, KING, LAO-KIUN, MARABOUS, ODIN, OFAVAI, PAREAS, PIACHES, PRASSAT and ULEMA (see *Essays*, Chap. III).

UNSIGNED ARTICLES

Jaucourt: LIBERTÉ NATURELLE; LIBERTÉ CIVILE
La Chapelle: AIGU
Louis: ACCOUCHEMENT
Leroy: INSTINCT
Mallet: ACTE; ALCORAN; ARCHONTES; CATHÉDRALE; HAMMON
Ménuret de Chambaud: MANSTUPRATION
Naigeon: LIBERTÉ (*Morale*) (first 4 columns).
Polier de Bottens: KIJUN; LITURGIE; LOGOMACHIE; MAGICIENS; MAGIE; MALACHBELUS; MANES; MAOSIM; MESSIE
Quesnay: EVIDENCE[55]
Saint-Lambert: FAMILIARITÉ; FANTAISIE; FASTE; FERMETÉ; FLATTERIE; FRAGILITÉ; FRIVOLITÉ; GÉNIE; HONNETETE; HONNEUR; INTÉRET (*Morale*); LEGISLATEUR; LOUANGE; LUXE; MANIERES; TRANSFUGE
Toussaint: AFFINITÉ
Turgot: ÉTYMOLOGIE; EXISTENCE; EXPANSIBILITÉ; FOIRE; FONDATION
Yvon: IMMATÉRIALISME; LIBERTÉ (*Morale*) (except for the first 4 columns); MANICHEISME; POLYTHÉISME

7

If so far this article has been largely devoted to removing from the canon of Diderot's writings articles from the *Encyclopédie* which belong to other contributors, that is by no means the end of the story. If Assézat and Tourneux reprinted many unsigned articles which are not by him, they also—as with those bearing the editorial asterisk—left out many that undoubtedly are.

Professor Proust lists as being by Diderot the following forty-eight unsigned articles from the *Encyclopédie* reproduced by Assézat and Tourneux:

AGRICULTURE,[56] ANTÉDILUVIENNE, ARABES, ART,[57] ASIATIQUES,

---

[55] François Quesnay's other two articles—FERMIERS (*Economic Politique*) and GRAINS (*Economie politique*)—are signed 'M. Quesnay le fils'.
[56] *Encyclopédie*, Vol. 1, p. xliii. (Where no note is supplied here for the different articles in Professor Proust's list, it is because he relies on Naigeon's authority in attributing them to Diderot).
[57] See the postscript to the *Lettre au R. P. Berthier, Jésuite* (AT, Vol. XIII, p. 168): 'Je joins à cette lettre un article du Dictionnaire. J'ai choisi, pour cette fois, l'article ART. Il est de moi.'

ENCYCLOPÉDIE

AUTORITÉ POLITIQUE,[58] CHALDEENS, IMPORTANCE, INDIENS, INTOLERANCE,[59] JÉSUITE, JÉSUS-CHRIST, JORDANUS BRUNUS, JOUISSANCE, LEIBNITZIANISME, LOCKE, LOISIR, MACARIENS, MACHIAVÉLISME, MALABARES, MALEBRANCHISME, MÉGARIQUE, MOSAÏQUE, NATAL, NATURALISTE, NEANT, ORIENTALE, PARMÉNIDEENNE, PERIPATETICIENNE, PERSES, PHÉNICIENS, PLATONISME, POPLICAIN, PRODUCTION, PUÉRILITÉ, PYRRHONIENNE, PYTHAGORISME, RESURRECTION,[60] ROMAINS, SARRASINS, SCEPTICISME, SCHOLASTIQUES, SCYTHES, SOCRATIQUE, STOÏCISME, THEOSOPHES, THOMASIUS, ZEND-AVESTA.

Yet in the Assézat-Tourneux edition there are a considerable number of other unsigned articles which are specifically attributed to Diderot by Naigeon, although they are not on Professor Proust's list:

IMMOBILE: *PAM*, Vol. II, DIDEROT, *Réflexions philosophiques sur divers sujets*, p. 211: *Sur un des caractères de la philosophie stoïcienne*.

IMMORTALITÉ: ibid., p. 211: *Sur l'amour de la gloire & le respect de la postérité*.[61]

INVISIBLE: ibid., p. 207: *Sur les aveugles*.

INVOLONTAIRE: ibid, p. 203; first 23 lines of column a.[62]

LAIDEUR: ibid., p. 208: *Sur les causes finales* (first paragraph.)

LÉGISLATION: ibid., p. 208: *Sur l'art de donner des loix aux peuples*.[63]

---

[58] Although Professor Proust does not provide a note ascribing this article to Diderot, in discussing the article in the text of the book he does attribute it to him. On the problem of its authorship see *Essays*, pp. 424-429.

[59] There is, of course, even stronger evidence for Diderot's authorship in letters to his brother of 29 Dec. 1760 (Roth, Vol. III, pp. 283-8) and 13 November 1772 (Roth, Vol. XII, p. 171).

[60] The article which Naigeon quotes from in *PAM* (Vol. III, p. 513) is in fact RESSUSCITER.

[61] IMPORTANCE, which, as Professor Proust notes, is partially reproduced in Naigeon's *Mémoires* (p. 65), is also drawn upon in *PAM*, Vol. II, p. 206, under the title: *Sur le mépris que le gouvernement doit témoigner pour toutes les querelles théologiques*.

[62] This passage is also quoted by Naigeon, though the author is described simply as 'un philosophe célèbre', in a note to his article FRÉRET (*PAM*, Vol. II, pp. 520-1).

[63] MACHIAVÉLISME, as Professor Proust point out, is reproduced under that heading in *PAM*, Vol. III, pp. 156-7. However, only the first 3 paragraphs are reprinted there; the rest is to be found in the article DIDEROT under the heading *Sur le but que Machiavel s'est proposé en écrivant son traité* du Prince. (*PAM*, Vol. II, p. 208.) The article was tampered with by Le Breton (Gordon & Torrey, p. 69.)

MALFAISANT: ibid., p. 208: *Sur la nécessité de changer certaines dénominations peu exactes dont on fait un grand usage dans la morale* (first 14 lines only).
MENACE: ibid, p. 216: *Sur différentes acceptions métaphoriques données au même mot dans une même langue;* (cf. Gordon & Torrey, p. 70).
MODIFICATION: ibid, p. 208: the last 8 lines of the section of which MALFAISANT forms the first part.
MULTITUDE: ibid., p. 198: *Sur le peu de confiance que meritent les jugemens de la multitude.*
NAITRE: ibid., pp. 197-8: *Sur les termes de vie & de mort.*
OINDRE: ibid., pp. 208-9: *Sur l'ancien usage de consacrer par l'onction certains êtres animés ou inanimés*; Chambers, UNCTION, much adapted.
PERFECTIONNER: ibid., p. 209; *Sur les obstacles que la nature oppose quelquefois aux efforts que nous faisons pour nous rendre moins imparfaits.*
PRODUIRE: ibid., p. 210; *Sur les Monstres* (Naigeon reproduces only 'La nature ne produit des monstres que par la comparaison d'un être à un autre; mais tout naît également de ses loix, & la masse de chair informe, & l'être le mieux organisé')[64]

8

What is even more interesting, however, is to see the number of unsigned articles from the *Encyclopédie*, among those *not* reprinted by Assézat and Tourneux, which are assigned to Diderot by Naigeon.

BAS (*métier à*): *PAM.* Vol. I, p. viin.
IMPIE, adj. (*Gram.*) (*PAM*, Vol. II DIDEROT, *Réflexions philosophiques sur divers sujets*, p. 206: *Sur l'inutilité des censures de la Sorbonne & des arrêts du parlement contre l'auteur d'un livre hétérodoxe*). Un homme a ses doutes; il les propose au public. Il me semble qu'au lieu de brûler son livre, il vaudroit beaucoup mieux l'envoyer en sorbonne, pour qu'on en preparât une édition,

[64] PRODUCTION is listed by Professor Proust as it appears under that heading in *PAM*, Vol. III, pp. 466-7; there one finds a cross-reference to the article DIDEROT (Vol. II, p. 210) which is to an extract from the article PRODUIRE listed above. The second half of PRODUCTION is, however, also reproduced in the article DIDEROT (Vol. II, p. 212) in the section entitled *Sur le principe d'Aristote*, 'corruptio unius, generatio alterius'.

où l'on verroit, d'un côté les objections de l'auteur, de l'autre les réponses des docteurs. Que nous apprennent une censure qui proscrit, un arrêt qui condamne au feu? rien. Ne seroit-ce pas le comble de la témérité, que de douter que nos habiles théologiens dispersassent comme la poussiere toutes les misérables subtilités du mécréant. Il en seroit ramené dans le sein de l'Eglise, & tous les fidèles édifies s'en fortifieroient encore dans leur foi. Un homme de goût avoit proposé à l'académie françoise une occupation bien digne d'elle, c'étoit de publier de nos meilleurs auteurs, des éditions où ils remarqueroient toutes les fautes de langue qui leur auroient échappé. J'oserois proposer à la sorbonne un projet bien digne d'elle, & d'une toute autre importance; ce seroit de nous donner des éditions de nos hétérodoxes les plus célebres, avec une réfutation, page à page.

INCORORPEL: adj. (*Gram & Métaphys*) (*PAM*, Vol. III, p. 349, under MOUVEMENT) . . . Les idées indépendantes du corps ne peuvent ni être corporelles, ni être reçues dans un sujet corporel. Elles nous découvrent la nature de notre ame, qui reçoit ce qui est *incorporel*, & qui le reçoit au-dedans de soi d'une maniere *incorporelle*, excepté le mouvement que mon ame reçoit tout-à-fait à la maniere des corps. Voilà donc une modification divisible dans un sujet indivisible.[65]

INTERMEDIAIRE: *PAM*, Vol. III, p. 726, under TRANSMISSION.

METAPHYSIQUE, s.f. (*PAM*, Vol. II, DIDEROT, *Réflexions philosophiques*, p. 198: *Sur l'utilité de la métaphysique*) c'est la science des raisons des choses. Tout a sa *métaphysique* & sa pratique; la pratique, sans la raison de la pratique, & la raison sans l'exercice, ne forment qu'une science imparfaite. Interrogez un peintre, un poëte, un musicien, un geometre, & vous le forcerez à rendre compte de ses opérations, c'est-à-dire à en venir à la *métaphysique* de son art. Quand on borne l'objet de la métaphysique à des considérations vuides & abstraites sur le tems, l'espace, la matiere, l'esprit, c'est une science méprisable; mais quand on la considere sous son vrai point de vue, c'est autre chose. Il n'y a guère que ceux qui n'ont pas assez de pénétration qui en disent du mal.

OPÉRATION, s.f. (*PAM*, Vol. III. p. 373: the opening lines of the article as given there are supplied by Naigeon) en *Logique*, se dit des actes de l'esprit. On en compte quatre: savoir *l'appréhension* ou *perception*, le *jugement*, le *raisonnement* & la *méthode*, *voyez-les chacun à son article*. Toutes les *opérations* de notre ame s'engendrent d'une premiere: voici l'ordre de leur génération.

[65] Naigeon adds in brackets: 'Diderot auroit pû écrire au bas de cet article, SAPIENTI SAT.'

Nous commençons par éprouver des perceptions dont nous avons conscience. Nous formons-nous ensuite une conscience plus vive de quelques perceptions: cette conscience devient attention. Dès-lors les idées se lient, nous reconnoissons en conséquence les perceptions que nous avons eues, & nous nous reconnoissons pour le même être qui les a eues; ce qui constitue la réminiscence. L'ame réveille-t-elle ses perceptions; c'est imagination. Les conserve-t-elle; c'est contemplation. En rappelle-t-elle seulement les signes; c'est mémoire. Dispose-t-elle de son attention; c'est réflexion; & c'est d'elle enfin que naissent toutes les autres. C'est proprement la réflexion qui distingue, compare, compose, décompose & analyse; puisque ce ne sont là que différentes manieres de conduire son attention. De-là se forment, par une suite naturelle, le jugement, le raisonnement, la conception.

PRESSENTIMENT: *PAM*, Vol. III, p. 465.

RECOMPENSE, s.f. (*PAM*, Vol. II, DIDEROT, *Réflexions philosophiques*, p. 209: end of article from 'Quelle bizarrerie dans nos lois . . .'; ibid. Vol. III, p. 512: only the beginning—down to 'ainsi que tous les autres animaux'—corresponds to the text given in the *Encyclopédie*) prix accordé pour quelque action qu'on juge bonne & utile. Dans la croiance[66] des Chrétiens, & même des Déistes, il y a des châtimens & des *recompenses* à venir. Il y a des philosophes qui nient l'immortalité de l'ame & la vie future, admettant l'existence de Dieu, parce que la vertu selon eux, est suffisamment *recompensée* par elle-même, & le vice suffisamment puni dès ce monde-ci. Ils croyent que la loi qui anéantit les êtres sans retour, est universelle, & s'exécute sur l'homme, ainsi que sur tous les autres animaux. Rien ne dégoute plus de bien faire, que les *recompenses* mal placées. Quelle bizarrerie dans nos lois! Tous les crimes ont leur punition; aucune vertu n'a sa récompense; comme si les citoyens n'avoient pas autant de besoin d'être encouragés à la vertu, qu'effrayés du vice. En cela les Chinois sont plus sages que nous. *Pourquoi vous recompenser? vous avez fait votre devoir.* Mais ne m'a-t-il rien coûté pour faire ce devoir? (cf. Diderot to Sophie Volland, 19 Aug. 1762—Roth, Vol. IV, p. 110).

RÉFUGIÉS; (*PAM*, Vol. II, DIDEROT, *Réflexions Philosophiques*, p. 199; *Sur les effets funestes du zèle aveugle & inconsidéré de Louis XIV pour la religion*): an attack on the persecution of the Huguenots by Louis XIV.

REMORDS, s.m. (*Gram*.) (ibid., p. 199: *Sur les reproches secrets*

---

[66] Before being censored by Le Breton, this read 'le système' (Gordon & Torrey, p. 78).

de la conscience) il est impossible de l'éteindre lorsqu'on l'a mérité, parce que nous ne pouvons nous en imposer au point de prendre le faux pour la vrai, le laid pour le beau, le mauvais pour le bon. On n'étouffe point à discrétion la lumiere de la raison, ni par conséquent la voix de la conscience. Si l'homme étoit naturellement mauvais, il semble qu'il auroit le *remords* de la vertu, & non le *remords* du crime. Celui qui est tourmenté de *remords*, ne peut vivre avec lui-même; il faut qu'il se fuie. C'est-là peut-être la raison pour laquelle les méchans sont rarement sédentaires; ils ne restent en place que quand ils méditent le mal, ils errent après l'avoir commis. Que les brigands sont à plaindre! poursuivis par les lois, ils sont obligés de s'enfoncer dans le fond des forêts, où ils habitent avec le crime, la terreur & le *remords*.

RESSENTIMENT, s.m. (*Gram.*) (ibid. pp. 199-200 : *Sur une des premières & des plus fortes passions de l'homme*) c'est ce mouvement d'indignation & de colere qui s'éleve en nous, qui y dure & qui nous porte à nous venger ou sur le champ ou dans le suite d'une injustice qu'on a commise à notre égard. Le *ressentiment* est une passion que la nature a placée dans les êtres pour leur conservation. Notre conscience nous avertit qu'il est dans les autres comme en nous, & que l'injure ne les offense pas moins que nous. C'est un des caracteres les plus évidens de la distinction que nous faisons naturellement du juste & de l'injuste. La loi qui se charge de ma vengeance a pris la place du *ressentiment*, la seule loi dans l'état de nature. Plus les êtres sont foibles, plus le *ressentiment* est vif & moins il est durable; il faut qu'il soit vif dans la guêpe pour inspirer la crainte de l'irriter; il faut qu'il soit passager en elle, pour qu'il ne la conduise pas à sa perte.

RESSUSCITER, v. act. (*Gramm.*) (*PAM*, Vol. III, p. 513, under RÉSURRECTION) revenir à la vie. Jésus-Christ a *ressuscité* le Lazare. Lui-même est *ressuscité*. Il y a des *résurrections* dans toutes les religions du monde; mais il n'y a que celles du christianisme qui soient vraies; toutes les autres. sans exception, sont fausses . . . *Voyez* RÉSURRECTION.

REVE, s.m. (*Métaphysique*) (*PAM*, Vol. II, *Réflexions philosophiques*, p. 200: *Sur la cause des rêves*: first 17 lines) songe qu'on fait en dormant. *Voyez* SONGE.

L'histoire des rêves est encore assez peu connue, elle est cependant importante, non-seulement en médecine, mais en métaphysique, à cause des objections des idéalistes; nous avons en rêvant un sentiment interne de nous-mêmes, & en même-tems un assez grand délire pour voir plusieurs choses hors de nous; nous agissons nous-mêmes voulant ou ne voulant pas, & enfin tous les objets des *rêves* sont visiblement des jeux de l'imagination.

Les choses qui nous ont le plus frappé pendant le jour, apparoissent à notre ame lorsqu'elle est en repos; cela est assez communément vrai, même dans les brutes, car les chiens rêvent comme l'homme, la cause des rêves est donc toute impression quelconque, forte, fréquente & dominante.

REVENANT, adj. (*Gram.*) (*PAM*, Vol. III, p. 513) qui revient; c'est ainsi qu'on appelle les personnes qu'on dit reparoître après leur mort: on sent toute la petitesse de ce préjugé. Marcher, voir, entendre, parler, se mouvoir, quand on n'a plus ni piés, ni mains, ni yeux, ni oreilles, ni organes actifs! Ceux qui sont morts le sont bien, & pour long-tems.

REVER, v.n. (*Gram.*) (*PAM*, Vol. II, DIDEROT, *Réflexions philosophiques*, p. 200: *Sur la cause des rêves*—last sentence) c'est avoir l'esprit occupé pendant le sommeil. Il est certain qu'on *rêve*, mais il n'est rien moins que certain qu'on *rêve* toujours, & que l'ame n'ait pas son repos comme le corps . . .

RIGORISME, s.m. (*Gram.*) (ibid., p. 200, *Sur les vues étroites de ceux qui ont inventé les différentes religions de la terre*). profession de la morale chrétienne, ou de la morale en général dans toute sa rigueur. La plupart des fondateurs de religion, de sociétés, de sectes de monasteres, ont destiné leurs institutions à un grand nombre d'hommes, quelquefois à toute la terre, tandis qu'elles ne pouvoient convenir qu'au petit nombre de ceux qui leur ressembloient. D'où il est arrivé à la longue qu'elles sont devenues impraticables pour ceux-si; & il s'en est suivi la division en deux bandes, l'une de rigoristes & l'autre de relâchés. Il n'y a guere qu'une morale ordinaire & commune qui puisse être pratiquée & suivie constamment par la multitude. Il y a & il y aura dans tout établissement, dans toute profession théologique, monastique, politique, philosophique & morale, du jansénisme & du molinisme; cela est nécessaire.

SACCAGER: Naigeon, *Mémoires*, p. 65.

SCHOOUBIAK, s.m. (*Hist. mod.*) (*PAM*, Vol. III, p.551, and *Œuvres*, 1798) secte qui s'est élevée parmi les Musulmans: ceux qui la professent, disent qu'il ne faut faire aucune acception des orthodoxes aux hétérodoxes; qu'il faut en user également bien avec tous, & qu'il n'appartient qu'à Dieu de scruter les reins & les esprits. Ainsi l'on voit que si la folie est de tout pays, la raison est aussi de tout pays. Voilà des hommes autant & plus entetés de leur religion qu'aucun peuple de la terre, prêchant la tolérance à leurs semblables; on les accuse, comme de raison, d'incrédulité, d'indifférence & d'athéisme; ils sont obligés de se cacher de leur doctrine; on les persécute; & cela parce que les prêtres étant les mêmes partout, il faut que la tolérance soit détestée par-tout.

SPÉCULATION, s.f. (*Gram.*) (*PAM*, Vol. III, p. 566) examen profond & réfléchi de la nature & des qualités d'une chose. Ce mot s'oppose à *pratique*. La *spéculation* recherche ce que c'est que l'objet; la pratique agit. Ainsi l'on peut dire que la philosophie, la vertu, la morale, ne sont pas des sciences de pure *spéculation*. Celui qui n'en a que la *spéculation*, n'est que le fantôme d'un philosophe, d'un homme vertueux, religieux, moraliste. La physique a ses *spéculations* qu'il faut mettre à l'épreuve de l'expérience: que seroit-ce que les mathématiques sans les problèms d'utilité auxquelles (*sic*) on arrive par la démonstration de ses propositions spéculatives? Les théorèmes sont la partie de spéculation. Les problèmes sont la partie de pratique.

SPINOSISTE, s.m. (*Gram.*) (*PAM*, Vol. III, p. 581, and *Œuvres*, 1798) sectateur de la philosophie de Spinosa. Il ne faut pas confondre les *Spinosistes* anciens avec les *Spinosistes* modernes. Le principe général de ceux-ci, c'est que la matiere est sensible, ce qu'ils demontrent par le développement de l'oeuf, corps inerte, qui par le seul instrument de la chaleur graduée passe à l'état d'être sentant & vivant, & par l'accroissement de tout animal qui dans son principe n'est qu'un point, & qui par l'assimilation nutritive des plantes, en un mot de toutes les substances qui servent à la nutrition, devient un grand corps sentant & vivant dans un grand espace.[67] De là ils concluent qu'il n'y a que de la matiere & qu'elle suffit pour tout expliquer; du reste ils suivent l'ancien spinosisme dans toutes ses conséquences.

SPONTANÉITÉ: (*PAM*, Vol. III, p. 581).

SUBIT, adj. (*Gram.*) (Naigeon, *Mémoires*, p. 68) qui s'exécute tout-à-coup; il y a des coups *subits*, des échecs *subits*, des bonheurs *subits*, des fortunes, des élévations *subites*. C'est alors qu'on considere les hommes élevés si subitement, & qu'on se demande comment cela s'est fait, sans pouvoir se répondre. On se rappelle seulement un endroit où Lucien introduit Jupiter fatigué des clameurs qui s'élevoient de la terre, mettant la tête à sa trape, & disant de la grêle en Scythie, un volcan dans les Gaules, la peste ici, la famine là; refermant sa trape, achevant de s'enyvrer, s'endormant entre les bras de Ganymede ou de Junon & appellant cela gouverner le monde.[68]

SUCCÈS, s.m. (*Gram.*) (*PAM*, Vol. III, p. 595) fin ou issue bonne ou mauvaise d'une affaire. Le *succès* d'une entreprise ne dépend

---

[67] Cf. the *Entretien entre d'Alembert et Diderot* and Diderot's letter to Duclos (10 October 1765: Roth, Vol. V, p. 141).

[68] Cf. *Salon de 1765* (AT, Vol. X, p. 312) and *Réfutation d'Helvétius* (AT, Vol. II, pp. 449-50).

pas toujours de la prudence. Cette vertu nous console seulement lorsqu'il ne répond pas à notre attente. Quel que soit le *succès* d'une chose, il vient de Dieu. Il n'arrive jamais, que ce qui doit arriver. Si le *succès* étoit autre, il faudroit que l'ordre universel changeât. Lorsque l'Etre tout-puissant gratifie une créature d'un bon succès, il fait un miracle aussi grand que quand il créa l'univers. Il faut la même puissance pour changer l'enchaînement universel des causes, que pour l'instituer. Si Dieu écoutoit nos souhaits & qu'il nous accordât des succès tels que nous les desirons, il feroit marcher l'univers à notre fantaisie, & souvent il nous châtieroit séverement. Qui est ce qui sait, si le *succès* qu'il demande, est celui qui convient vraiment au bon sens? Reconnoissons donc la vanité & l'indiscrétion de nos voeux, & soumettons-nous aux événemens.

SURPRISE: *PAM*, Vol. II, DIDEROT, *Réflextions philosophiques*, pp. 198-9: *Sur les mouvemens de l'ame occasionnés par quelque phénomène étranger.*

SYNCRETISTES, HENOTIQUES *ou* CONCILIATEURS: *PAM*, Vol. III, pp. 596-9, and *Œuvres*, 1798. It is odd that this important article which has obvious links with THÉOSOPHES should have been omitted in AT: it is reprinted in the Belin and Brière editions.

VEILLE, s.f. (*Physiolog.*) (*PAM*, Vol. III, p. 758) dans l'économie animale l'état du corps humain dans lequel les actions des sens internes & externes, & des muscles peuvent se faire facilement, sans trouver aucune résistance. Je suis sûr que je veille lorsque mes yeux ouverts apperçoivent les corps que m'environnent; car mes yeux voyent confusément quand j'ai envie de dormir, & je ne vois plus rien quand je dors. Je veille si j'entens les sons qui sont à la portée de mon oreille; je dors si je ne les entends pas. Je veille lorsque je parle ou je marche à volonté; je veille lorsque mon cerveau est dans cette disposition physique, au moyen de laquelle les impressions externes appliquées à mes organes excitent certaines pensées. Je veille enfin lorsque le principe moteur des muscles, au moindre changement du principe pensant, est prêt à être déterminé vers les muscles. quoique souvent il n'y coule point actuellement.

VELOURS: (*PAM*, Vol. I, p. viin.)

. . . VICE, s.m. (*Droit naturet, Morale, &c.*) (*PAM*, Vol. II, DIDEROT *Réflexions philosophiques*, p. 199: *Sur la fausseté de quelques distinctions établies par l'usage entre certains mots de la langue*, and Naigeon, *Mémoires*, pp. 69-70: an addtion to an article by Jaucourt.) L'usage a mis de la différence entre un *défaut* & un *vice*; tout *vice* est *défaut*, mais tout *défaut* n'est pas *vice*, On suppose à l'homme qui a un *vice*, une liberté qui le rend coupable à nos yeux; le défaut tombe communément sur le compte de la nature; on excuse l'homme, on accuse la nature. Lorsque la philosophie discute ces distinctions avec une exactitude bien scrupuleuse, elle les trouve souvent vuides de sens. Un homme est-il plus maître d'être pusillanime, voluptueux, colère en un mot, que louche, bossu ou boiteux? Plus on accorde à l'organisation, à l'éducation, aux moeurs nationales, au climat, aux circonstances qui ont disposé de notre vie, depuis l'instant où nous sommes tombés du sein de la nature, jusqu'à celui où nous existons, moins on est vain des bonnes qualités qu'on possede, qu'on se doit si peu à soi-même, plus on est indulgent pour les défauts & les *vices* des autres, plus on est circonspect dans l'emploi des mots vicieux & vertueux, qu'on ne prononce jamais sans amour ou sans haine, plus on a de penchant à leur substituer ceux de malheureusement & d'heureusement nés, qu'un sentiment de commisération accompagne toujours. Vous avez pitié d'un aveugle; & qu'est-ce qu'un méchant sinon un homme qui a la vue courte, & qui ne voit pas au-delà du moment où il agit?

VINDICATIF, adj. (*Gram.*) (*PAM*, Vol. II, DIDEROT *Réflexions philosophiques*, pp. 200-1: *Sur ce qui constitue l'esprit de vengeance.*) celui qui est enclin à la vengéance. Je ne voudrois pas appeller *vindicatif* celui qui se rappelle facilement l'injure qu'il a reçue; car il y a des hommes qui se souviennent très-bien, qui n'oublient même jamais les torts qu'on a avec eux, & qui ne s'en vengent point, qui ne sont point tourmentés par la rancune & le ressentiment, c'est une affaire purement de mémoire. Ils ont l'insulte qui leur est propre, présente à l'esprit à-peu-près comme celle qu'on a faite à un autre, & dont ils sont témoins. Il y a donc dans l'esprit de vengeance quelque chose de plus que la mémoire de l'injure. Je pense qu'au moment de l'injure le ressentiment naît plus ou moins vif; dans cet état du ressentiment, les organes intérieurs sont affectés d'une certaine maniere, nous le sentons au mouvement qui s'y produit. Si cette affection dure, tient longtems; si elle passe, mais qu'elle reprenne facilement; si elle reprend avec plus de force qu'auparavant; voilà ce qui constituera le *vindicatif*. *Mutatis mutandis,* appliquez les mêmes idées à toutes les autres passions, & vous aurez ce qu'on appelle le *caractere dominant*. C'est un tic des organes intérieurs, vice qu'il est très-dangereux de prendre, qu'on peut contracter de cent manieres différentes, auquel la nature dispose & qu'elle donne même quelquefois. Lorsqu'elle le donne, il est impossible de s'en défaire; c'est une affection des organes intérieurs, qu'il n'est pas plus possible de changer que celle des organes extérieurs; on ne refait pas plus son coeur, sa poitrine, ses intestins, son estomac, les fibres passionnées, que son front, ses yeux ou son nez. Celui qui est colere par ce vice de conformation, restera colere; celui qui est humain, tendre, compatissant, restera tendre, humain, compatissant; celui qui est cruel & sanguinaire, trouvera du plaisir à plonger le poignard dans le sein de son semblable, aimera à voir couler le sang, se complaira dans les transes du moribond, & repaîtra ses yeux des convulsions de son agonie. Si l'on a vu des hommes prendre des caracteres tout opposés à ceux qu'ils avoient ou paroissoient avoir naturellement, c'est que le premier qu'ils ont montré n'étoit que simulé, ou que peut-être il est possible que les organes aient d'abord la conformation qui donne telle passion dominante, tel fond de caractere; qu'en s'étendant, qu'en croissant avec l'âge, ils prennent cette conformation habituelle qui rend le caractere différent, ou même qui donne un caractere opposé. Il en est ainsi des organes extérieurs; tel enfant dans ses premieres années est beau, & devient laid; tel autre est laid, & devient beau.

VOLONTÉ, s.f. (*Gram. & Philosophie morale*) (*PAM*, Vol. II, DIDEROT, *Réflexions philosophiques*, pp. 202-3; Naigeon quotes the same passage in a footnote to his article FRERET, ibid., p. 520, but merely refers to the author as 'un philosophe célèbre') c'est l'effet de l'impression d'un objet présent à nos sens ou à notre réflexion, en consequence de laquelle nous sommes portés tout entiers vers cet objet comme vers un bien dont nous avons la connoissance, & qui excite notre appétit, ou nous en sommes éloignés comme d'un mal que nous connoissons aussi, & qui excite notre crainte & notre aversion. Aussi il y a toujours un objet dans l'action de la *volonté*; car quand on veut, on veut quelque chose; de l'attention à cet objet, une crainte ou un désir excité. De-là vient que nous prenons à tout moment la *volonté* pour la liberté. Si l'on pouvoit supposer cent mille hommes tous absolument conditionnés de même, & qu'on leur présentât un même objet de désir ou d'aversion, ils le désireroient tous & tous de la même maniere, ou le rejetteroient tous & tous de la même maniere. Il n'y a nulle différence entre la *volonté* des fous & des hommes dans leur bon sens, de l'homme qui veille & de l'homme qui rêve, du malade qui a la fievre chaude & de l'homme qui jouit de la plus parfaite santé, de l'homme tranquille & de l'homme passionné, de celui qu'on traîne au supplice ou de celui qui y marche intrépidement. Ils sont tous également emportés tout entiers par l'impression d'un objet qui les attire ou qui les repousse. S'ils veulent subitement le contraire de ce qu'ils vouloient, c'est qu'il est tombé un atome sur le bras de la balance, qui l'a fait pencher du côté opposé. On ne sait ce qu'on veut lorsque les deux bras sont à-peu-près également chargés Si l'on pese bien ces considérations, on sentira combien il est difficile de se faire une notion quelconque de la liberté, sur-tout dans un enchaînement de[s] causes & des effets, tels que celui dont nous faisons partie.

VOLUPTUEUX, adj. (*Gram.*), (*PAM*, Vol. II, DIDEROT, *Réflexions philosophiques*, pp. 215-16: *Sur l'usage innocent des plaisirs sensuels*) qui aime les plaisirs sensuels: en ce sens tout homme est plus ou moins *voluptueux*. Ceux qui enseignent[69] je ne sais quelle doctrine austere qui nous affligeroit sur la sensibilité d'organes que nous avons reçue de la nature qui vouloit que la conservation de l'espece & la nôtre fussent encore un objet de plaisirs; & sur cette foule d'objets qui nous entourent & qui sont destinés à émouvoir cette sensibilité en cent manieres agréables, sont des atrabilaires à enfermer aux petites-maisons. Ils remercieroient volontiers l'être tout-puissant d'avoir fait des ronces, des épines, des venins, des tigres, des serpens, en un mot tout ce qu'il y a de nuisible & de malfaisant; & ils sont tout prêts à lui reprocher l'ombre, les eaux fraîches, les fruits exquis, les vins délicieux, en un mot les marques de bonté & de bienfaisance qu'il a semées entre les choses que nous appelons *mauvaises* & *nuisibles*. A leur gré, la peine, la douleur ne se rencontrent pas assez souvent sur notre route. Ils voudroient que la souffrance précédât, accompagnât & suivît toujours le besoin; ils croient honorer Dieu par la privation des choses qu'il a créées. Ils ne s'apperçoivent pas que s'ils font bien de s'en priver, il a mal fait de les créer; qu'ils sont plus sages que lui; & qu'ils ont reconnu & évité le piege qu'il leur a tendu.[70]

VULNERABLE; Naigeon, *Mémoires*, p. 62 (under the heading INVULNERABLE).

It will be noticed that a considerable number of the articles attributed to Diderot by Naigeon are short, or relatively short, grammatical articles. In his *Philosophie ancienne et moderne* he has several important remarks to make on the interest which Diderot showed in questions of language and on his contributions to the *Encyclopédie* in this field. In the article DIDEROT, for instance, he states:

[69] Le Breton replaced 'nous prêchent' by 'enseignent' (Gordon & Torrey, p. 107).
[70] Le Breton cut out the words 'aussi bêtement que méchamment' which came before *tendu* (ibid.)

Diderot avoit conçu de bonne heure le plan d'un ouvrage qu'il n'a jamais perdu de vue, & dont le projet avoit même pris plus d'importance dans sa tête, à mesure que l'expérience, produit trop tardif du tems, étoit venue confirmer ce que la réflexion lui avoit appris. Il vouloit faire ce qu'il appelloit le *dictionnaire universel & philosophique de la langue*: il a même dispersé dans l'Encyclopédie un grand nombre de matériaux qui devroient servir un jour à la composition de ce vocabulaire par lequel il avoit résolu de terminer sa carrière littéraire.[71]

After explaining that this project was not realized because Diderot never recovered from the after-effects of his journey to Russia, Naigeon continues: 'On peut voir dans la première édition de l'Encyclopédie quelques fragmens épars du travail particulier de *Diderot* sur l'objet en question. C'est à lui qu'on doit presqu'entièrement cette partie de la grammaire qui exige le plus de goût, de finesse & de philosophie, celle des synonimes'.[72]

This last remark is misleading. As Professor Proust points out in an excellent appendix to his *Diderot et l'Encyclopédie*,[73] even in the early volumes Diderot did not monopolize the treatment of synonyms in the *Encyclopédie*. In the later volumes the task seems to have been taken over by the grammarians, Douchet and Beauzée, and especially by Jaucourt. It is noticeable that none of the short unsigned articles attributed to Diderot by Naigeon deals with synonyms.[74]

It is only in the last volume of his *Philosophie ancienne et moderne*, in introducing the article PRODUCTION, that Naigeon gives a satisfactory account of the grammatical articles which Diderot contributed in such abundance to the later volumes of the *Encyclopédie*, and shows their importance for the student of his ideas:

[71] Vol. II, p. 219.
[72] p. 220.
[73] pp. 555-63.
[74] There is a curious lapse here on Naigeon's part; he reproduces in a footnote a passage on the difference between *abjection* and *bassesse*, which, he claims, comes from notes written by Diderot on a copy of the enlarged edition of Abbé Girard's *Synonymes françois*, published by Beauzée in 1769. In fact it is simply the article *BASSESSE, ABJECTION, which appeared in Vol. II of the *Encyclopédie*.

.... Par une suite nécessaire de la tyrannie & de tous les vices du gouvernement sous lequel il vivoit, par l'effet de cette terreur que lui inspiroient les actes arbitraires des ministres, l'intolérance des prêtres & le fanatisme sanguinaire du parlement, la plupart des matériaux qu'il avoit recueillis dans le silence de l'étude & de la méditation, & qui, employés avec discernement par d'aussi habiles mains, auroient été si utiles pour perfectionner l'entendement humain, & pour mettre dans la langue philosophique cette exactitude & cette précision sans lesquelles on n'éclaircit rien, se trouvent épars, isolés, perdus dans des articles où personne jusqu'à présent ne les a découverts, où personne même ne les suppose, ne les cherche & où Diderot semble même les avoir déposés, moins comme des vérités positives, déjà constatées par l'expérience, & pour ainsi dire, jugées & senties, que comme des espèces de germes qui attendent leur développement & leur fécondation du progrès des lumières & de l'irradiation des esprits.[75] From this point onwards he proposes to give various examples of this type of article:

C'est là qu'on peut observer que par le seul choix des exemples, Diderot, en travaillant au dictionnaire universel de la langue qu'il regardoit avec raison comme l'instrument le plus propre à déraciner tous les préjugés religieux & politiques, a eu l'art d'insinuer, d'établir *tout doucement,* pour parler comme Bayle, & en gardant toujours le caractère peu suspect de grammairien, les principes d'une philosophie, qui, pour n'être communément ni reçue ni connue, n'en est pas moins la seule raisonnable, la seule admissible & la seule vraie.[76]

Obviously Naigeon reproduced some of the more characteristic unsigned articles of this type, which Diderot contributed to the *Encyclopédie,* but not, as we shall see, by any means all.

9

Naigeon's testimony adds quite a number of interesting articles to the canon of Diderot's writings. But are we compelled to stop at the point where it and a few other scraps of contemporary

---

[75] Vol. III, p. 466.
[76] For further comments by Naigeon on the same subject see *PAM,* Vol. III, p. 512.

evidence as to the authorship of the unsigned articles in the *Encyclopédie* are no longer there to guide us? The safest thing is no doubt to go no further.[77] And yet, rash as it may be to venture beyond this point, there are solid reasons for doing so. We know that Naigeon never claimed to reprint or even mention *all* the articles which Diderot had contributed to the *Encyclopédie*; we have his guidance to take us part of the way. But that is not all. Occasionally some help may be obtained from cross-references from one article to another; sometimes comparisons with the text of Chambers's articles reveal significant additions and other changes. Above all, we have a basis of comparison in our own knowledge of Diderot's other writings—produced before, during and after the years of his labours on the *Encyclopédie*. No doubt the authorship of a considerable number of unsigned articles will always remain a mystery; yet, even without Naigeon's help, we might conceivably have worked out for ourselves that such articles as MALFAISANT, MODIFICATION, SPINOSISTE, VICE, VOLONTÉ and VOLUPTUEUX were, indeed must be, by Diderot.

In the two lists which follow—the first consisting of unsigned articles reproduced by Assézat and Tourneux, and the second of articles *not* reproduced in their edition—an attempt has been made to distinguish between those which may, with reasonable certainty, be attributed to Diderot, and those about which there is a certain amount of doubt. Those in the second category are preceded by a question-mark. It goes without saying that the range of certainty and uncertainty is much broader than is indicated by this division into two categories; but it would require about a dozen different symbols to indicate everything from absolute, provable certainty (derived, for instance, from parallel passages in Diderot's other writings) to a fair degree of doubt. The result would become fantastically complicated. In the following lists such evidence of authorship as was available, has been

[77] I ought perhaps to make it clear that further research has long since led me to effect a withdrawal from the exposed position represented by the sentence in the introduction to the original edition of *Selected Articles* (p. xv): 'Where the prefaces of the different volumes fail to give information about the authorship of unsigned articles, we must continue to attribute them to Diderot except when . . . other information is available to us'.

produced; and in the second list, which is devoted to articles buried in the *Encyclopédie*, extracts from a number of the more characteristic articles have been given. The preponderance of short, grammatical articles in this second list is in line with Naigeon's observations on Diderot's interest in these questions.

First, the list of unsigned articles reprinted by Assézat and Tourneux which may reasonably be attributed to Diderot despite the absence of Naigeon's guarantee:

ARTISAN
ARTISTE
ASSAISONNEMENT
ASSEZ, SUFFISAMMENT
ASSURER, AFFIRMER, CONFIRMER
ASSURÉ, SUR, CERTAIN
ATTACHER, LIER
ATTÉNUER, BROYER, PULVÉRISER
AUSTERE, SÉVERE, RUDE
AUTORITÉ POLITIQUE; see *Essays*, pp. 424-429.
AUTORITÉ *dans les discours & dans les écrits.*
BATTE
BIBLIOTHÈQUE: not from the short Chambers article, LIBRARY, except for the passage on the Bodleian Library (p. 449).
BOURREAU
BROCHURE
BUT, VUE, DESSEIN
CALICUT
CARAÏBES
CEILAN
CONSOLATION: only the definition is taken from Chambers, CONSOLATION.
CORDELIER: although Diderot does not admit his responsibility for this article in discussing cross-references in the article *ENCYCLOPÉDIE (AT, Vol. XIV, p. 465), can one doubt that the author of *CAPUCHON was also that of CORDELIER?
DIEUX: freely adapted from the second part of Chambers, GOD.[78]
FOIBLE: Chambers, FOIBLE is at most the the starting-point of this article.
GALANTERIE (*Morale*)
HABITUDE: note 'heureusement né' and 'malheureusement né' (AT, Vol. XV, p. 71).

[78] In Professor Proust's list (p. 533) the article ÉPREUVE, ESSAI, EXPÉRIENCE lacks the asterisk which it has in the *Encyclopédie*.

HÉLAS
HÉROÏSME
HOTEL-DIEU: there is a cross-reference to this article and to *CHARITÉ at the end of *HOPITAL.
HUMANITÉ
HUMBLE: cf. Diderot to Sophie Volland, 18 Aug. 1759 (Roth, Vol. II, p. 236): 'Je me souviens seulement d'avoir lu une fois sur la table d'un docteur de Sorbonne ces deux mots: *Humilité*, pauvre vertu; *hypocrisie*, vice dont il ne seroit pas difficile de faire l'apologie.'
HUMILITÉ
?HYLOPATHIANISME: followed by the words '*Hist. de la Philologie*' in AT (the *Encyclopédie* has *Phylologie*); the fact that it was neither reprinted nor mentioned by Naigeon seems to remove it from the Diderot canon, but in content and style it seems to belong to his series of contributions to the *Histoire de la Philosophie*.
HYPOCRITE
IGNORANCE (*Métaphys.*): adapted from Chambers, IGNORANCE: the article is rounded off with exactly the same sentence as *Pensées Philosophiques*, xxviii.
?IGNORANCE (*Morale*): not from Chambers.
ILLIMITÉ
ILLUSION
IMAGINATION (POUVOIR DE L')
IMMONDE
IMPRESSION
IMPURETÉ
INCOGNITI
INCOMMODE
?INDÉPENDANCE
INDOLENCE
INDULGENCE
INFIDÉLITÉ: a significant cut was made in the article by Le Breton (Gordon & Torrey, p. 68).
INGÉNUITÉ
INJURE, TORT: quite different from the article in Girard, *Synonymes françois*.
INQUIÉTUDE
INSENSÉ
INSENSIBILITÉ: contains a cross-reference (AT, Vol. XV, p. 223) to Diderot's STOÏCISME.
INSERTION DE LA PETITE VÉROLE
INTERMEDE

... INTOLÉRANT: an addition to an article by Jaucourt.
INTRÉPIDITÉ
INTRIGUE
INVINCIBLE
INVIOLABLE
IRRÉSOLUTION
JANSÉNISTE (*Mode*)
... JEU: an addition to JEU (*Droit naturel & Morale*) by Jaucourt.
?JUDAÏSME: the first six paragraphs come from Chambers, JUDAISM, the last two are added (there is a cross-reference to *JUIFS).
LABEUR
LABORIEUX
LABOUREUR
LANGRES
LANGUEUR
LAQUAIS
LEÇON
LÉGÈRETÉ
LESTE
LIBERTINAGE
LIBRAIRIE: text altered by Le Breton (Gordon & Torrey, p. 69).
LICENCE
LOUER
LUBRIQUE, LUBRICITÉ
MACÉRATION: censored by Le Breton (Gordon & Torrey, p. 69).
MACHER
MACHIAVÉLISTE
MACHINAL: cf. the 'cent mille hommes' of VOLONTÉ, attributed to Diderot by Naigeon; it is interesting that Naigeon made use of the same example of 'cent mille femmes' in his part of the article LIBERTÉ (AT, Vol. XV, p. 481).
MAGISTRAT: Professor Proust (p. 135) points out that this article is followed by MAGISTRAT (*Jurisprud.*) which is signed '(A)' (= Boucher d'Argis), and could therefore be by the same author; but 1. MAGISTRATURE ends with the words '*Voyez l'article* MAGISTRAT' and 2. as we shall see, Diderot shows a distinct interest in the Parlements in his 'grammatical' articles.
MAGISTRATURE
MAGNANIME
MAGNIFIQUE
MAINTIEN
MALADROIT, MALADRESSE

MALE
MALÉDICTION (*Gram.*)
MALÉDICTION (*Jurispr.*): expanded from Chambers, MALEDIC-
TION, by the addition of the last fifteen words.
MALICE
MALIGNITÉ
MALINTENTIONNÉ
MALVEILLANCE et MALVEILLANT
MANIERES, FAÇONS: quite different from the comparable article in Girard, *Synonymes françois*.
MASSACRE: cf. *JOURNÉE DE LA SAINT-BARTHÉLEMY and, for a similar attack on the Abbé de Caveirac, INTOLERANCE (AT, Vol. XV, p. 239) and PACIFIQUE (Vol. XVI, p. 184).
MÉCONNAISSABLE
MÉCONTENT
?MEDISANCE: some debt to Toussaint, *Les Moeurs* (see Hermand, *RHL*, 1915, p. 364).
MÉDITATION: the starting-point of the article is Chambers, MEDITATION.
MÉFIANCE
MÉLANCOLIE: cf. *Salons* (ed. Seznec & Adhémar), Vol. II, p. 99n. for another reference to Feti's picture.
MENÉE
MENSONGE OFFICIEUX: a rural tale from Sadi; cf. SARRASINS (AT, Vol. XVII, pp. 76-84), *Réfutation d'Helvétius* (AT, Vol. II, p. 408) and *Le Gulistan* (AT, Vol. IV, p. 487).
MENTION
MÉPRIS
MERCENAIRE
?MÉTEMPSYCOSE: not from Chambers, METEMPSYCHOSIS.
MISÉRABLE
MISÈRE
MODICITÉ, MODIQUE
MOEURS
MOMERIE
MOTIF
MUNIFICENCE

NATIF
NATUREL
?NÉCESSAIRE
NÉCESSITANT
NIAIS
NIGRO-MANTIE

NOCTAMBULE
NOMMER: the idea contained in this article ('Quand on veut exclure un rival d'une place, et lui ôter le suffrage de la cour, on le fait *nommer* par la ville . . .') was a favourite one with Diderot; see, for instance, *Mémoires pour Catherine II*, ed. P. Vernière, p. 37.
NONCHALANCE
NOURRICE
NU
NUIRE
?OBÉISSANCE: as Hermand points out (*Idées morales*, p. 206) the source of the story of the Vicomte d'Orte is Agrippa d'Aubigné's *Histoire universelle*, no doubt via *Esprit des lois*, iv. 2.
OBJECTER: censored by Le Breton (Gordon & Torrey, p. 71)
OBSCÈNE
OBSCUR
OBSCURITÉ
OBSTINATION
OBTENIR
OBVIER
OCCASION
OCCURRENCE
ODIEUX
OFFENSE: the image 'introduire un rayon de soleil dans un nid de hiboux' had already been used in . . . *AIGLE.
OFFICIEUX
OH
?OLIGARCHIE
OMPHALOMANCIE
ONOMANCIE: from Chambers, ONOMANCY (see Loyalty Cru., p. 262), but with some additions.
?ONTOLOGIE
?OPHIOMANCIE
OPPOSER
OPPRESSEUR
OPPRESSION: censored by Le Breton (Gordon & Torrey, p. 71)
OPPROBRE
OPULENCE
ORDONNER
?ORIGÉNISTES: Chambers, ORIGENIANS and ORIGENISTS, expanded.
ORIGINAIRE
ORIGINAUX

ORIGINAL
ORIGINALITÉ
ORIGINE
ORNEMENT
OSÉE
OUBLI
OUBLIER
PACIFICATION: greatly expanded from the six lines of Chambers, PACIFICATION.
PACIFIQUE: cf. INTOLÉRANCE and MASSACRE for the attack on Abbé de Caveirac.
PAIN BÉNI
?PAIX: cf. Proust (p. 537n.) on Diderot's mention of this article in a letter to Damilaville (Roth, Vol. III, p. 358).
PALE
PALINODIE: from Chambers, PALINODY, greatly expanded.
?PAMILLIES
PAN
PAPEGAI
PARAITRE
PARCOURIR
PARDONNER
PARLER
PAROLE
PAROLE ENFANTINE
PARTICULIER
PARTIR
PARTISAN
PARVENIR
PASQUIN: the first four paragraphs come from Chambers, PASQUIN; the last is added.
PASQUINADES: not from Chambers, PASQUINADES.
PASSAGER: on the attractions of cloisters for adolescents cf. Diderot to Sophie Volland, 20 Sept. 1760 (Roth, Vol. III, p. 77), 21 Nov. 1765 (ibid., Vol. V, p. 191) and *Jacques le Fataliste* (AT, Vol. VI, p. 182).
PASSANT
PASSE-DROIT
PASSIONNER
PÉCUNE
PÉDALIENS
PEINE
PÉNÉTRATION
PÉNÉTRER

PÉNIBLE
PERDRE
PERFIDE
PÉRIR: last sentence cut by Le Breton (Gordon & Torrey, p. 71).
PERPÉTUER
PERPLEXE
PERSÉCUTER
PERSISTER
PERSONNAGE
PERSUASION
PERVERS
PESER les malades: appears to come from Chambers, but under what heading? The last paragraph, relating to France, must have been added.
PETIT
PETIT-MAITRE
PETITESSE
PHYSIONOMIE
PINDARIQUE: from Chambers, PINDARIC (see Loyalty Cru, p. 264), but considerably expanded.
PIQUANT
PIRE
PITOYABLE
?POLITESSE
?POLYANDRIE
POMPE
POPULAIRE
POSTÉRITÉ
?POUVOIR
PRATIQUER
PRÉADAMITE: the first five paragraphs come from Chambers, PREADAMITE, but the great bulk of the article is added.
PRÉCAUTION
PRÉCIEUX
PRÉDILECTION
PRÉSOMPTUEUX
PRESSENTIR
PRÉVALOIR
PROIE
PROMETTRE
PROMISSION
PROPAGATION DE L'ÉVANGILE: as Loyalty Cru points out (p. 265), the first short paragraph is from Chambers, SOCIETY *for propagating the gospel in foreign parts*; but the longish paragraph which

UNSIGNED ARTICLES

follows does not come from this source.
PROPOSITION (*poésie*): based on Chambers, PROPOSITION *in poetry*, but much expanded.
?PROPRIÉTÉ (*droit naturel et politique*)
PROSTITUER
PROTATIQUE: the definition only comes from Chambers, PROTATICUS.
?PROTECTION
PROVENIR
PRUDE
PUBLICAINS: much expanded from Chambers, PUBLICAN.
?PURITAINS: not from Chambers which has only a very brief article.

QUOTIDIEN, JOURNALIER: not in the index of Girard, *Synonymes françois*.

?RAISON
REGARDER
?RÉSURRECTION: as Loyalty Cru (pp. 265-6) points out, based on Chambers, RESURRECTION, but much expanded.[79]
ROMANCE

SCANDALEUX
?SOUVERAINS
SUBVENIR
TENIR

VOLAGE

The following is a list of unsigned articles which are not to be found in the Assézat-Tourneux edition, but which, despite Naigeon's silence, may fairly be attributed to Diderot:[80]

Vol. I.
ARCANE, s.m. (*Chimie*): an attack on charlatans and a defence of medicine. . . . On ne doit avancer que la Médecine est

---

[79] Professor Proust (p. 538 wrongly gives RÉSURRECTION as being reproduced in *PAM* (see above p. 190).
[80] '. . .' before the heading of an article indicates that the article is signed by another contributor, but followed by an unsigned addition.

conjecturale, que parce qu'on peut dire que toutes les connoissances humaines le sont: mais si l'on veut examiner sincerement la chose, & juger sans préjugé, on trouvera la Médecine plus certaine que la plûpart des autres sciences . . .
Il est du devoir d'un citoyen de faire tous ses efforts pour arracher les hommes à une prévention qui expose souvent leur vie, tant en les écartant des vrais secours que la science & le travail pourront leur donner, qu'en les jettant entre les mains des prétendus possesseurs de secrets, qui achevent de leur ôter ce qui leur reste de santé. Combien d'homme ont été dans tous les tems, & sont encore tous les jours, les victimes de cette conduite! . . .
(The four lines of Chambers, ARCANUM, are expanded to over a column: cf. J. Mayer, *Diderot homme de science*, pp. 163, 363).

Vol. II
698 CARPOCRATIENS (*Hist. ecclés.*): from Chambers, CARPOCRATIANS, expanded.

Vol. III
19 CHALCÉDOINE (*Géog. anc. & mod.*)
338 CHINE (LA) (*Géog.*: cross-reference to *CHINOIS (PHILOSOPHIE DES).

Vol. IV
743-4 DÉFICIENT (*Arithmétique*): cf. J. Mayer, pp. 71, 80.

Vol. VI
48 . . . ETERNITÉ (*Métaphys.*) (by Jaucourt and Formey). Nous rapportons ces objections des Thomistes & des Scotistes, 1° parce qu'elles appartiennent à la Philosophie, qui est l'objet de notre ouvrage: 2° parce qu'elles servent à montrer dans quel labyrinthe on se jette, quand on veut raisonner sur ce qu'on ne conçoit pas.

Vol. VII
535 GAZETIER, s.m. (*Hist. mod.*) celui qui écrit une *gazette*; un bon *gazetier* doit être promptement instruit, véridique, impartial, simple & correct dans son style; cela signifie que les bonnes *gazettes* sont rares.

Vol. VIII
143 . . . HERALDIQUE (*Art*): (by Jaucourt, who attacks 'la science vaine & ridicule des armoiries', quoting La Fontaine, *Fables*, x.16.) Cependant comme le tems n'est pas encore venu parmi nous, où *l'art héraldique* sera réduit à sa juste valeur, *voyez*

volume II. de nos Planches & de leurs explications, les principes généraux du Blason, avec des figures relatives à chacun des termes qui lui sont propres.

440 JAMAIS, adv. de tems (*Gramm.*) Il se dit par négation de tous les périodes de la durée, du passé, du présent, de l'avenir. Il est impossible que l'ordre de la nature soit *jamais* suspendu. De quelque phénomene que les tems passés ayent été témoins, & quelque phénomene qui frappe les yeux des hommes à venir, il a la raison de son existence, de sa durée, & de toutes ses circonstances dans l'enchaînement universel des causes qui comprend l'homme, ainsi que tous les autres êtres sensibles, ou non.

598 IMPLORER (*Gramm.*)
604 IMPOT *en faveur du Théâtre*
656 INCORRIGIBLE (*Gram.*)
809-10 ? . . . INTENDANS & COMMISSAIRES: an unsigned addition to an article by Boucher d'Argis; cf. Diderot to Le Breton, 12 Nov. 1764: '. . . . Vous fîtes main-basse sur l'article *Intendant* et sur quelques autres dont j'ai les épreuves'. (Roth, Vol. IV, p. 305), but this does not tell us whether he himself wrote the addition to the article.
830 INTERLOCUTEUR (*Gram.*)
847 INVECTIVE, s.f. (*Gramm. & Morale*) . . . Tous nos écrivains modernes *invectivent* contre le luxe; tous nos prédicateurs, contre les progrès de l'incrédulité; mais on les laisse dire: on n'en est pas moins fastueux, ni plus croyant.
869 INVÉTÉRÉ (*Gramm.*)

Vol. IX
3 JUDAÏSER (*Gram. Théolog.*)
601-11 LIVRE (*Littér.*): Loyalty Cru (pp. 267-9) points out that the article is derived from Chambers, BOOK; Diderot's hand is visible in only one or two places of this long article, e.g., in the second paragraph in the example 'l'histoire de Grece de *Temple Stanyan* est un fort bon *livre,* divisé en trois *volumes*'.
627 LOCUTIUS (*Mythol.*): cross-reference to *AIUS LOCUTIUS.
717 LUL (*bot. exot.*)
771 LUXURE (*Morale*): the sting in the article was removed by Le Breton (Gordon & Torrey, p. 69).
861-2 MAGOT (*Gramm.*)

Vol. X
188 MATÉRIALISTES, s.m. (*Théol.*): the first two paragraphs are taken straight from Chambers, MATERIALISTS; the third paragraph reads: 'On donne encore aujourd'hui le nom de *matérialistes* à

ceux qui soutiennent ou que l'ame de l'homme est matiere, ou que la matiere est éternelle, & qu'elle est Dieu; ou que Dieu n'est qu'une ame universelle répandue dans la matiere, qui la meut & la dispose, soit pour produire les êtres, soit pour former les divers arrangemens que nous voyons dans l'univers. *Voyez* SPINOSISTES'.

This passage is reproduced faithfully (down to the cross-reference) as the first paragraph of the anonymous article MATÉRIALISTES in *PAM* (Vol. III, p. 208), but it is not attributed to Diderot.

311 MÉLANGE, s.m. (*Gram.*) . . . Le *mélange* des animaux produit des monstres & des mulets. On ne s'est pas assez occupé du *mélange* des especes.

313 MELER (*Gram.*)

330 MÉNAGERIE, s.f. (*Gram.*) . . . Il faut détruire les *ménageries*, lorsque les peuples manquent de pain; il seroit honteux de nourrir des bêtes à grands frais, lorsqu'on a autour de soi des hommes qui meurent de faim.

458-60 MÉTHODE, *divison méthodique des différentes productions de la nature*: cf. RUDIMENT, 'J'ai déjà dit au mot MÉTHODE...'

521 MINCE, adj. (*Gramm.*) . . . Il y a des gens d'un mérite assez *mince*, à qui l'on a accordé des places très-importantes, soit dans la robe, soit dans l'église, soit dans le gouvernement, soit dans le militaire.

712 MORGUE, s.f. (*Gramm.*) Si vous joignez la dureté & la fierté à la gravité & à la sottise, vous aurez la *morgue*. Elle est de tous les états; mais on en accuse particulièrement la robe, & la raison en est simple. Il y a dans la robe, tout autant de gens sots & fiers que dans l'église & le militaire, ni plus ni moins; mais la gravité est particulièrement attachée à la magistrature; dépositaire des lois qu'elle fait parler ou taire à son gré, c'est une tentation bien naturelle que d'en promener partout avec soi la menace. Les gens de lettres ont aussi leur *morgue*, mais elle ne se montrera dans aucun plus fortement que dans le poëte satyrique.

713 MORIGENER, v.act. (*Gramm.*) . . . Il est difficile qu'un enfant qui n'a point été *morigené*, soit assez heureusement né pour n'en avoir pas eu de besoin.

860 MULTLIPICITÉ

910 MUTUEL, adj. (*Gramm.*) terme qui marque le retour, la réciprocité . . . Toute obligation est *mutuelle* sans excepter celle des rois envers leurs sujets. Les rois sont obligés de rendre heureux leurs sujets, les sujets d'obéir à leur rois; mais si l'un manque à son devoir, les autres n'en sont pas moins obligés de persévérer dans le leur.

Vol. XI
254 NOVATEUR (*Gram.*)
302 OBLAT (*Hist. ecclés.*): adapted from Chambers, OBLATI.
332 OCCULTE: adapted from Chambers, OCCULT.
631 ORIX (*Gramm. & Hist. nat.*)
719 OUTRAGE, OUTRAGEANT, OUTRAGER (*Gramm.*)
OUTRANCE
OUTRÉ (*Gramm.*)
719-20 OUTRER: v. act. . . . qui est-ce qui a donné au public mêlé de tout état & de toute condition ce tact délicat, qui dans la représentation d'une piece lui fait discerner un sentiment juste d'un sentiment *outré*, une expression vraie d'une expression fausse? Il le fait souvent à étonner les hommes du goût le plus délicat; & qu'on vienne après cela me dire que l'homme ne se connoît pas, qu'il s'en impose à lui-même, qu'il se trompe, qu'il a la conscience hébétée, &c . . . il n'en est rien. On peut s'envelopper pour les autres, mais non pour soi. Quand on cherche à détourner de soi son regard, on s'est vu, on s'est jugé.
727 OUVRIR (*Gramm.*)
782-3 PALIBOTRE, s.m. (*Hist. anc.*) nom que les rois de Perse ont long-tems porté dans l'antiquité; ce nom venoit d'un roi persan très-révéré, dont il étoit le nom propre. Un souverain est bien vain d'oser prendre le nom d'un prédécesseur illustre; conçoit-il la tâche qu'il s'impose? La comparaison continuelle qu'on fera de lui avec celui dont il porte le nom? Mais ce n'est pas la vanité des rois qui leur fait prendre un titre si incommode, & qui leur prescrit leur devoir chaque fois qu'on leur prononce (*sic*), ou qu'on leur reproche d'y manquer; c'est la bassesse des peuples qui le leur donne; ou si ce n'est pas leur bassesse, mais une invitation honnête faite au prince de leur restituer l'homme chéri, le bon maître qu'ils ont perdu; je les loue de ce moyen, quoiqu'il leur réussisse assez mal . . . Les rois de Perse s'appelloient *palibotres*, comme les rois d'Egypte *Pharaon*, comme les rois de France aujourd'hui *Louis*.
940 PARFAIRE
PARFAIT, adj. . . . Il n'y a rien d'imparfait dans la nature; tout ce qui est nécessaire dans toutes ses parties est *parfait* (cf. *IMPARFAIT).

Vol. XII
69 PARLEMENTAIRE, s.m. (*Gram. & Hist.*) c'est dans les troubles de l'état celui qui est attaché au parti du parlement, contre celui de la cour. Alors il s'agit des intérêts de la nation que le parlement & le roi veulent, mais qu'ils entendent mal l'un ou l'autre. Pour

l'ordinaire, lorsqu'il y a deux factions, la faction des *parlementaires* & la faction des royalistes, les premiers pourroient prendre pour devise *pour le roi contre le roi.*

396 PERQUISITION, s.f. (*Gramm.*) recherches ordonnées par un supérieur, & occasionnées par un délit sur lequel on n'a pas les connoissances nécessaires. La publication de ce livre donna lieu aux *perquisitions* les plus rigoureuses. Avec toutes ces *perquisitions*, on ne trouva rien.[81]

430 PERSONNALISER (*Grammaire*)

440 PERTURBATEUR, s.m. (*Gram.*), homme turbulent, inquiet, séditieux, qui émeut les esprits des citoyens & cause du désordre dans la société. Après cette définition, ou une autre peu différente, on ajoute dans le *dictionnaire de Trév.* que les Théologiens sont ordinairement *perturbateurs* de l'état.[82]

Vol. XIII

300 PRÉPOSÉ, PRÉPOSER, v. act. (*Gram.*) c'est charger de la conduite d'une chose. Le roi l'a *préposé* à l'entretien des grands chemins du royaume. Les *intendans* sont *préposés* par la cour pour exercer l'autorité du roi sur les provinces; mais l'autorité consiste à réprimer le mal & faire le bien.

359 PRIEZ-DIEU, s.m. *terme d'Eglise* . . . Ce luxe peu sensé qui s'est établi dans les églises catholiques, consacrées à l'humiliation devant l'être suprême, a peut-être même en bonne politique, plus d'inconvéniens que d'avantage (*sic*) . . .

360 PRIER (*Gram.*)

389 PRIVILEGE, s.m. (*Gramm.*) avantage accordé à un homme sur un autre. Les seuls *privileges* légitimes, ce sont ceux que la nature accorde. Tous les autres peuvent être regardés comme injustices faites à tous les hommes en faveur d'un seul. La naissance a ses *privileges*. Il n'y a aucune dignité qui n'ait les siennes; tout a le *privilege* de son espece & de sa nature.

393 PROBABILISTE (*Gram. Théol.*)

393-400 ?PROBABILITÉ cf. *. . . ABSENT (p. 172 above), CERTITUDE (p. 159-160) and J. Mayer, pp. 71, 85-6.

523 PROVINCIAL, adj. & subst.

533 . . . PRUSSE: addition to an article by Jaucourt, on Frederick the Great's poetic gifts, ending with the words 'il n'a manqué à cette flûte admirable qu'une embouchure un peu plus nette' (cf. R. Mortier, *Diderot en Allemagne*, p. 166) and AT, Vol. VI, pp. 322-323).

[81] An allusion to the events of February 1752 after the suppression of the first two volumes of the *Encyclopédie*.

[82] The quotation is accurate.

UNSIGNED ARTICLES

727-8 QUODLIBÉTAIRE ou QUODLIBÉTIQUE; expanded from Chambers, QUODLIBETICAL *question.*
- 751 RACONTER (*Gramm.*)
- 755 RAFFINEMENT (*Gram.*)
- 776 RAISONNABLE (*Gramm.*)
- 779 RALENTIR (*Gram.*)
- 779-80 RALLUMER (*Gram.*)
- 781 RAMASSER (*Gram.*)
- 783 RAMENER (*Gramm.*)
- 788 RANCUNE (*Gramm.*)
- 791 RANIMER
- 796 RAPPORT (*Gram.*)
- 808 RAPPORTER (*Grammaire*)
- 816 RASSURER (*Gram.*)
- 829 RATTACHER (*Gram.*)
- RATTEINDRE (*Gramm.*)
- 830 RAVAGE (*Gramm.*)
- 832 RAVIR
- 838 RÉALISTE (*Philos.*): from Chambers, REALISTS, but condensed.
- RÉALITÉ (*Gram.*)
- 849 RECHERCHER (*Gramm.*)
- 859 RÉCONCILIER (*Gramm.*)
- 862 RECONSULTER (*Gramm.*)
- 865 RECRIER (*Gramm.*)
- 870 RECUEILLEMENT (*terme de Grammaire*)
- RECUEILLIR (*terme de Grammaire*)
- 872 RECULER
- 873 RÉDACTEUR (*Gramm.*)
- RÉDACTION (*Gramm.*)
- 875 REDEVABLE (*Gramm.*)
- REDEVANCE (*Gramm. & Jurisprud.*)
- 876 REDIRE (*Gramm.*)
- REDITE (*Gramm.*)
- 882-3 RÉDUIRE (*Gramm.*)

Vol. XIV
- 33 REGNER (*Gram.*)
- 52 RELACHER (*Gram.*)
- 64 RELEVER (*Gram.*)
- 101 REMPORTER (*Gramm.*)
- 102 REMUNERATEUR (*Gramm. & Théol.*)
- RENAISSANT (*Gramm.*)
- RENAITRE (*Gramm.*)
- 105-6 RENCONTRE (*Gram.*)

108 RENFERMER (*Gramm.*)
110-11 RENOM (*Gram.*)
123 RENVERSER (*Gram.*)
RENVOI (*Gram.*) . . . Je hais la méthode de Wolf, elle fatigue par la multitude des *renvois*, & elle en devient d'une obscurité profonde & d'une sécheresse dégoûtante, par une affectation barbare & gothique de démonstration rigoureuse & de briéveté. En l'introduisant en Allemagne, cet homme fameux y a éteint le bon goût, & perdu les meilleurs esprits . . .
124 RENVOYER (*Gram.*)
REPAITRE (*Gram.*)
130 REPENTIR (*Gram.*)
136 REPLI (*Gram.*)
140 REPOSER (*Gram.*)
147 REPRESENTER (*Gramm.*)
REPRIMANDER (*Gramm.*)
REPRIMER (*Gramm.*)
149 REPROCHE, REPROCHER (*Gramm.*)
166 REQUISITOIRE (*Gram. & Jurisprud.*): the sting in the article was removed by Le Breton (Gordon & Torrey, p. 72).
171 RESIGNATION, s.f. (*Gramm.*) entiere soumission, sacrifice absolu de sa volonté à celle d'un supérieur. Le chrétien se *résigne* à la volonté de Dieu; le philosophe aux lois éternelles de la nature.
192 RESSOURCE (*Gram.*)
RESSOUVENIR (*Gram.*)
199 RETARDER (*Gram.*)
RETATER (*Gram.*)
200 RETENTIF (*Gram.*)
202 RETENTIR, RETENTISSEMENT (*Gram.*)
RETENUE (*Gram.*)
206 RETIRER (*Gram.*)
206-7 RETOUR (*Gram.*)
208 RETOURNER (*Gram.*)
RETRACTATION (*Gram.*)
217 RETRANCHER, v. act. (*Gramm.*) . . . Toutes les religions ont droit de *retrancher* de leur communion ceux qui ne pensent pas orthodoxement, & qui ont de mauvoises moeurs; mais les excommuniés n'en sont pas de moins bons citoyens, auxquels le souverain doit toute sa protection.
223 REVANCHE (*Gram.*)
224 REVEILLER (*Gram.*)
227 REVENIR (*Gram.*)
229 REVERENCE, s.f. (*Gram.*) . . . Portez aux magistrats la *révérence* qu'on doit à ceux qui sont chargés du dépôt des lois

& du soin de rendre la justice . . .
235 REVETIR (*Gram.*)
236 REVIVRE (*Gram.*)
237 REUNIR (*Gram.*)
271 RICHE (*Gram.*)
    RICHE COMPOSITION (*Peinture*)
290 RIGIDE (*Gram.*)
    RIGORISTE (*Gram.*)
    RIGOUREUX (*Gram.*)
    RIGUEUR (*Gram.*)
311 ROBUSTE, adj. (*Gramm.*) qui est fort, vigoureux. On dit une plante *robuste*, un homme *robuste*, une santé *robuste*. Hobbs (*sic*) ayant remarqué que l'homme étoit d'autant plus méchant qu'il avoit plus de force & de passion, & qu'il avoit moins de raison, a défini le méchant, *puer robustus*, un enfant *robuste*; définition courte, laconique & sublime.
320 ROGNER (*Gram.*)
328 ROIDE (*Gram.*)
    ROIDEUR (*Gram.*)
    ROIDIR, v.act. (*Gram.*) . . . Il est naturel à l'homme, que la nature a créé libre, de se *roidir* contre l'autorité; c'est la raison qui lui en fait connoître les avantages, qui le soumet au poids de la chaîne, & qui l'empêche de la secouer.
360 RONFLER
    RONGER (*Gramm.*)
421-2 ROYAUTÉ s.f. (*Gramm.*) dignité du roi. Les Grecs & les Romains autrefois, aujourd'hui tous les peuples républicains sont ennemis de la *royauté*. La *royauté* n'est pas un métier de fainéant; elle consiste toute dans l'action.
428 RUDE
429 RUDIMENT, s.m. . . . j'ai déjà dit au *mot* MÉTHODE, ce que je pense sur cette sorte d'ouvrages . . .
433 RUGIR, RUGISSEMENT (*Gram.*)
    RUINE (*Peinture*)
434 RUMEUR (*Gram.*)
440 RUSE (*Gram.*)
528 SAISIR (*Gram.*)
542 SALETÉ (*Gram.*)
    SALEUR (*Gram.*)
571 SALIR (*Gram.*)
583-4 SALUER (*Gramm.*)
589 SALUTAIRE
606 SANCTIFIANT (*Gram.*)
617-18 SANGLANT (*Gram.*)

625 SANGUINAIRE (*Gram.*)
723 SAVOURER, v.act. (*Gramm.*) c'est goûter avec grand plaisir dans les organes de cette sensation. Je *savoure* la douceur de ce mets. Il se dit au figuré: cet homme est heureusement né, la peine l'affecte peu, il *savoure* le plaisir.
751 SCÉLÉRAT, adj. qui se prend aussi substantivement (*Gram.*) celui qui est né malfaisant, & qui s'est rendu coupable de quelques grands crimes.
  SCÉLÉRATESSE (*Gram.*)
814 SCRUPULE (*Gram.*)
851 SÉANCE, s.f. (*Gram.*) . . . Les ducs & pairs ont droit de *séance* à la grand'chambre, & ils entendent mal leur intérêt & celui de la nation de n'en pas user plus souvent.
  SÉANT (*Gram.*)
861 SECOUER (*Gram.*)
  SECOURS (*Hist. ecclés. mod.*): attack on *convulsionnaires*.
876 SECTAIRE (*Gram.*)
844 SECURITÉ (*Gram.*)
885 SEDENTAIRE (*Gram.*)
887 . . . SEDUCTEUR (*Gram.*): a 4-lined addition to an article by Jaucourt.
899 SEIN (*Gram.*)

Vol. XV
57 SENTENTIEUX (*Gram.*)
  SENTEUR (*Gram.*)
96 SÉRIEUX (*Gram.*)
117 SERREMENT (*Gram.*)
  SERRER (*Gram.*)
121 SERVICE (*Gram.*)

122 SERVIR (*Gram.*)
186 SIGNALEMENT (*Gramm.*)
187 SIGNALER (*Gramm.*)
191 SILENCE
192 SILENCIEUX (*Gram.*)
204 SIMPLE, adj. (*Gramm.*)
  SIMPLE, s.m. (*Gramm.*)
  SIMPLE (*Métaphysique*)
205 SIMPLIFIER (*Gramm.*)
206 SIMULATION (*Gram. & Jurispr.*)
  SIMULTANÉE, adj. (*Gram.*) . . . Il se passe souvent dans la vie, dans la même maison, dans le même appartement des scènes *simultanées*. Pourquoi ne les rendroit-on pas sur le théâtre? cf. *Entretiens sur le Fils naturel* (AT, Vol. VII, p. 116).

247-8 SOBRE (*Gramm.*)
251 SOCIAL, adj. (*Gramm.*) mot nouvellement introduit dans la langue pour désigner les qualitées qui rendent un homme utile dans la société, propre au commerce des hommes: des vertus *sociales*.
307 SOIN (*Gram.*)
326 SOLLICITER (*Gram.*)
    SOLLICITUDE (*Gramm.*)
359 SONNANT (*Gramm.*)
    SONNER (*Gramm.*)
    SONNERIE (*Gramm.*)
381 SORTIE (*Gram.*)
382 SORTIR (*Gram.*)
384 SOUBRETTE, s.f. (*Gram.*) C'étoit autrefois une femme attachée au service d'une autre. Il n'y a plus de *soubrette* dans nos maisons; mais elles sont restées au théâtre, où elles sont communément méchantes, bavardes, sans décence, sans sentiment, sans moeurs, & sans vertu; car il n'y a rien dans la société qui ressemble à ce personnage. Cf. *Entretiens sur le Fils naturel* (AT, Vol. VII, pp. 90-1).
387 SOUDAIN (*Grammaire*)
395 SOUDOYER (*Gram.*)
    SOUFFLER
397 SOUFFRANCE (*Gramm.*)
404 SOULAGER (*Gram.*)
411-12 SOUPLE (*Gram.*)
422 SOUTENIR (*Gram.*)
427 SPADASSIN (*Gramm. Escrim.*)
432-4 ? . . . SPARTE: addition (nearly 4 columns) to Jaucourt's article.
442 SPECIEUX (*Gram.*): on relations with J. J. Rousseau?
478 SPIRITUALITÉ (*Gramm.*)
    SPIRITUEL (*Gramm.*)
    SPIRITUEUX (*Gram.*)
479 SPLENDEUR (*Gram.*)
    SPLENDIDE (*Gram.*)
481 SPONTANÉE
486 STABILITÉ (*Gram.*)
565 SUBIR (*Gram.*)
    SUBJUGUER
570 SUBMERGER (*Gram.*)
572 SUBSÉQUENT (*Gram.*)
. . . SUBSIDE, *terme de droit*: the first 8 paragraphs of Chambers, SUBSIDY = paragraphs 2-9 of this article. Then comes

the following passage in italics (p. 573a): Un homme de mérite a rassemblé sous un même point de vue l'apologie d'un des meilleurs auteurs politiques de nos jours, & la critique de quelques-uns de nos articles de finance. Son ouvrage, publié par lui-même, pouvoit certainement lui faire plus d'honneur, & nous causer plus de peine (s'il étoit si pénible de reconnoître ses erreurs), que n'en peuvent jamais attendre de leurs injurieuses & pauvres productions une infinité d'hommes obscurs, qui depuis 20 ans jusqu'à ce jour, depuis le plat Ch . . . jusqu'à l'hypocrite abbé de S...[84], se sont indignement déchaînés contre nous.

Celui qui a écrit les observations suivantes, homme d'un caractere bien différent, nous les a envoyées à nous-même, pour en faire l'usage qui nous conviendroit, & nous les imprimons.

M. de Voltaire s'est tout nouvellement chargé de nous venger des autres. Il a dit dans une de ses lettres à-propos de la brochure de cet abbé de S . . . 'Quel est celui qui s'est occupé à vuider les fosses d'un palais où il n'est jamais entré . . . Tel misérable petit architecte qui n'est pas en état de tailler un chapiteuu, ose critiquer le portail de S. Pierre de Rome'.[85] Nous voudrions bien que ces comparaisons flatteuses, plus méritées de notre part, nous honorassent autant qu'elles doivent humilier nos ennemis.

Pesselier's article begins at this point (p. 573b) and continues to p. 582a. The following notes to it must be ascribed to Diderot:

(c) (to Pesselier's text: '. . . les espérances qu'on avoit de la continuation d'un dictionnaire qui auroit honoré la nation, sont malheureusement aujourd'hui très foibles'.) L'auteur ne parloit pas sans beaucoup de vraisemblance. Les jésuites existoient encore lorsqu'il écrivoit.

(d) Un ministre auquel un étranger demanderoit pourquoi il n'y a pas au moins dans la capitale une salle où l'on puisse représenter convenablement les chef-d'œvres du théàtre françois répondroit-il en disant qu'autrefois une populace d'importuns se mêloit à un sénat romain, qu'Athalie avoit un panier, & que ces grossieretés ridicules sont abolies?

(e) Nous ne pouvons nous dispenser de remarquer ici que nous ne sommes point du tout de l'avis de l'auteur de ces considérations. S'il y eut jamais un besoin d'opinion, c'est la dentelle, par exemple; cependant qu'il calcule le prix énorme du chanvre manufacturé de cette maniere, le tems & le nombre des mains

---

[84] Chaumeix and Abbé Saas (for their attacks on the *Encyclopédie* see *Essays*, pp. 286-299, 315-319).

[85] See the letter to Damilaville of 15 October 1764 (Best. 11304).

employées, & il verra combien ce besoin d'opinion rend à la terre.

(f) On conçoit que l'on satisfait mal à la question, en citant d'*Amboise*, *Richelieu* ou *Mazarin* : on peut faire de grandes choses, sans être un *bon ministre*. Celui qui auroit vendu le royaume pour acheter la tiare, celui qui sacrifioit tout à son orgueil & à sa vengeance, celui qui faisoit servir son pouvoir à son insatiable avarice, ne méritent point le titre de *bon ministre*.

(g) Si le bon, l'adorable Henri IV s'aigrissoit souvent contre le vertueux *Sully*, quel souverain pourra se promettre d'être plus accessible que lui *aux calomnies travaillées de mains de courtisan*?

(h) On sait jusqu'où la fureur du peuple poussa l'atrocité après la mort de *Colbert*, qu'on ne nomme aujourd'hui que pour en faire l'éloge.

(i) Je ne trouve dans l'histoire de France que *Sully* qui ait constamment voulu le bien; mais il étoit parvenu dans ces tems orageux qui forment les ames vigoureuses & sublimes : il avoit partagé les malheurs de son maître; il étoit son ami, & il travailloit sous les yeux & pour la gloire de cet ami.

(k) Si le maître ne s'étoit pas trompé dans son objet, c'est-à-dire s'il n'eût pas pris pour la gloire ce qui n'en étoit que le fantôme, *Colbert* auroit préféré l'utilité à la splendeur.

590 SUBSTITUER (*Gram.*)
594 SUBTERFUGE (*Gram.*)
    SUBTILITÉ (*Gram.*)
596 SUCCÉDER (*Gram.*)
606 SUCCINCT (*Gram.*)
607 SUCCOMBER
634-5 ? SUFFISANTE RAISON (*Métaphys.*)
645 SUINTEMENT, SUINTER (*Gram.*)
649 SUITE (*Gram.*)
653 SUIVANTE (*Littérat.*)
    SUIVRE (*Gram.*)
661 SUPERBE (*Gram.*)
    SUPERFICIEL (*Gram.*)
    SUPERFLU (*Gram.*)
671 SUPPLANTER (*Gram.*)
688 SURETÉ (*Gram.*)
690 SURMONTER (*Gram.*)
691 SURNAGER (*Gram.*)
693 SURPASSER (*Gramm.*)
696 SURSAUT (*Gramm.*)
697 SURVENIR (*Gram.*)
    SURVIVANT (*Gram.*)
    SURVIVRE

698 SUSCEPTIBLE (*Gram.*)
SUSCITER (*Gram.*)
700 SUSPECT (*Gram.*)
SUSPENDRE (*Gram.*)
701 SUSPICION (*Gram.*)
705 SUSTENTATION (*Gram.*)
750 SYNDERESE (*Gram.*)
819 TACITURNE (*Gram.*)
857 TAILLE, se dit de la hauteur & de la grosseur du corps humain . . .
859 TAIRE (*Gram.*)
863 TALENT (*Gram.*)
887 TANIERE, s.f. (*Gramm.*) . . . Il se prend aussi quelquefois au figuré, & l'on appelle *taniere*, la demeure d'un homme vorace, solitaire & méchant.
904 TARDER (*Gram.*)
TARDIF (*Gram.*)
914 TARIR (*Gramm.*)
935 TATER (*Gram.*)

Vol. XVI
52 TÉMÉRITÉ (*Morale*)
128 TENDANT
130 TENDRE, v.act. (*Gram.*)
140 TENTATIVE (*Gram.*)
142 TENU (*Gram.*)
TENUE (*Gram.*)
160 TERMINER (*Gram.*)
162 TERNIR (*Gram.*)
251 THÉOLOGIEN (*Gram.*): cut down to one line by Le Breton (Gordon & Torrey, p. 95).
274 THÈSE (*Gram.*)
318 TIC, s.m. (*Gram.*) . . . Wasp a le tic de juger de tout, sans avoir jamais rien appris.
TIÈDE (*Gram.*)
339 TIRADE, s.f. (*Littérat.*) expression nouvellement introduite dans la langue, pour désigner certains lieux communs dont nos poëtes, dramatiques sur-tout, embellissent, ou pour mieux dire, défigurent leurs ouvrages . . . (24 lines in all), cf. *Entretiens sur le Fils naturel* (AT, Vol. VII, p. 106).
344-5 TIRER (*Gram.*)
402 TOMBER (*Gram.*)
TOME (*Gram. & Littérat.*)
446 TOUCHER, v.act. (*Gram.*) . . . il est dangereux de *toucher*

aux choses de la religion, des moeurs & du gouvernement.
476 TOURMENT (*Gram.*)
478 TOURNER, v.act. & neut. . . . La terre *tourne* autour du soleil, hérésie autrefois, fait d'astronomie démontré aujourd'hui.
531 TRAINER (*Gram.*)
533 TRAITÉ (*Gram.*)
536 TRAITEMENT (*Gram.*)
TRAITER (*Gram.*)
TRAITRE (*Gram.*)
538 TRANCHANT (*Gram.*)
544 TRANCHER (*Gram.*)
546 TRANSCRIRE (*Gram.*)
TRANSFERER (*Gram.*)
553 TRANSGRESSER (*Gram.*)
554 TRANSIR (*Gram.*)
556 TRANSMETTRE (*Gram.*)
566-7 ? TRAPPE, abbaye de la (*hist. ecclés.*): this follows on TRAPPE, *moines de la* (*Géog. mod.*) by Jaucourt; there is a reference to the senseless austerities of these monks in a letter of Diderot to Sophie Volland (7 October 1762; Roth, Vol. IV, p. 188).
570 TRAVERSER (*Gram.*)
587 TREMPER (*Gram.*)
602 TRESSAILLIR, v.n. (*Gram.*) éprouver une émotion subite & légere: on *tressaillit* de peur & de joie; l'homme le plus intrépide qui regarde sa fin d'un air tranquille, ne peut fixer long-tems son attention sur cet objet, sans *tressaillir*; combien notre éducation est mauvaise de ce côté! pourquoi nous effrayer sans cesse sur un événement qui doit un jour avoir lieu? pourquoi nous surfaire à tout moment le prix d'une vie qu'il faut perdre? ne vaudroit-il pas mieux nous en entretenir avec mépris dès nos plus jeunes ans? nous *tressaillons* de frayeur quand on nous montre la mort de près; on pourroit nous apprendre à *tressaillir* de joie en la recevant; quels hommes que ceux qu'on auroit instruits à mourir avec joie!
617 TRIBADE (*Gram.*)
689 TROISIÈME (*Gram.*)
693 TROMPER (*Gramm.*)
698 TRONQUER (*Gram.*)
712 TROUBLE (*Gram.*)
718 TROUSSER (*Gram.*)
737 TUER (*Gram.*)
TUER, DÉTRUIRE (*Peinture*)
792 VACILLANT, VACILLATION, VACILLER (*Gram.*)

798 VAIN (*Gram.*)
    VAINQUEUR (*Gram.*)
810 VALABLE (*Gram.*)
825 VALOIR (*Gram.*)
836 VAQUER (*Gram.*)
873 VÉHÉMENT (*Gram.*)
    VÉHICULE (*Gram.*)
822 VELLÉITÉ, s.f. : the definition and the opening lines of this article come straight from Chambers, VELLEITY, but not the passage which follows : Si on examinoit bien toute sa vie, on trouveroit que la cause pour laquelle on a eu si peu de succès, c'est qu'on n'a presque point eu de volonté; mais qu'excité par le désir de la chose, retenu par la paresse, la pusillanimité, la vue des difficultés, on n'a eu que des demi-volontés. Les Italiens ont un proverbe qui contient le secret de devenir pape; & ce secret est de le vouloir.

Vol. XVII
5 VENIR (*Gram.*)
53 VERBEUX (*Gram.*)
   VERBIAGE (*Gram.*)
68 VÉRIFIER (*Gram.*)
   VÉRITABLE (*Gram.*)
163 VERSER, v. act. (*Gram.*) . . . Les évangélistes n'accusent pas unanimement Hérode d'avoir *versé* le sang des innocens.
182 . . . VERTU; addition of 6 lines.
222 . . . VÉTÉRAN : addition of 2 paragraphs.
246 VICTORIEUX (*Gram.*)
267 VIGILANT, VIGILANCE (*Gramm. & Morale*) . . . Sans la *vigilance*, le philosophe bronchera quelquefois; le chrétien ne fera pas un pas sans tomber.
272 VIGUEUR, s.f. (*Gramm.*) Lorsque les lois sont sant *vigueur*, les mauvaises actions sans châtimens, les bonnes sans récompense; il faut que l'anarchie s'introduise, & que les peuples tombent dans l'avilissement & le malheur. Quelques actions de *vigueur* de la part d'un prince intelligent & ferme, suffisent pour relever un état chancelant . . .
VIL, adj. (*Gram.*) c'est celui qui a quelque mauvaise qualité, ou qui a commis quelque mauvaise action, qui marque dans son ame de la pusillanimité, de l'intérêt sordide, de la duplicité, de la lâcheté; il y a des vices qui se font abhorrer, mais qui supposant quelque énergie dans le caractère, n'avilissent pas. Comme ce sont les usages, les coutumes, les préjugés, les superstitions, les circonstances même momentanées qui décident de

la valeur morale des actions, il y a telle action *vile* chez un peuple, indifférente ou même peut-être honorable chez un autre; telle action qui étoit *vile* & qui a cessé de l'être; la morale n'est guere moins en vicissitude chez les hommes, & peut-être dans un même homme, que la plupart des autres choses de la nature ou de l'art; *multa renascentur, multa cecidere cadentque quae nunc sunt in honore.* C'est ce qu'on peut dire des vertus & des vices nationaux, comme des mots. Tacite nous apprend que les Romains regardoient les Juifs, le peuple de Dieu, celui qu'il s'étoit choisi, pour lequel tant de miracles s'étoient opérés, comme la partie la plus *vile* des hommes.

  VILAIN (*Gram.*)
339 VISÉE (*Gramm.*)
  VISER (*Gramm.*)
355 VISITE (*Gramm.*)
373 ULCERER
376 ULTRAMONTAIN, adj. & subst. (*Hist. mod.*): the words in square brackets are added to Chambers, ULTRAMONTANE: Les opinions des *ultramontains,* c'est-à-dire des théologiens & des canonistes italiens, [tels que Bellarmin, Panorme, & d'autres qui prétendent que le pape est supérieur au concile général, que son jugement est infaillible sans l'acceptation des autres églises, &c.,] ne sont point reçues en France.

379 UNANIME (*Gram.*)
  UNANIMITÉ (*Gram.*)
426 VOILER (*Gram.*)
443 VOLATIL (*Gram.*)
  VOLATILISATION, VOLATILISER (*Gram. Chimie*)
  VOLATILITÉ (*Gram.*)
454 VOLONTAIRE (*Gram. Morale*)
457 VOLUBILITÉ (*Gram.*)
463 VOMIR (*Gram.*): censored by Le Breton (Gordon & Torrey, p. 107).
471 VOQUER
471-2 VORACE, VORACITÉ (*Gram.*)
473 VOULOIR, v. act. (*Gramm.*): . . . quand les rois *veulent,* ils ordonnent, & à des gens bassement disposés à leur obéir aveuglément; ils ne peuvent donc être trop attentifs à ne *vouloir* que des choses justes . . .
  VOULOIR, s.m. (*Gram.*)
476 VOYAGE (*Gram.*)
494 URGENT (*Gram.*)
522 USER (*Gram.*)
574 VUIDER (*Gram.*)

576 VULGAIRE, adj. (*Gram.*) . . . penser comme le *vulgaire*, sur le vice, sur la vertu, sur la religion . . .
689 ZAHORIE (*Gram.*)

It will be noticed what a high proportion of the articles in lists VIII and X—i.e. of articles not included in the Assézat-Tourneux edition which are expressly attributed to Diderot by Naigeon or which, although not reproduced or mentioned by Naigeon, may reasonably be attributed to him cover the part of the alphabet from R to Z. In the course of a most interesting and valuable discussion of the methods by which the two editors made their selection of articles, Professor Proust[86] gives high marks to Tourneux who was responsible, after the death of Assézat, for Vol. XVII. 'Le tome XVII est . . . un modèle de prudence . . . Du moins Tourneux a-t-il limité les risques en ne reproduisant qu'un tout petit nombre d'articles depuis *Raison* justqu'à *Zend-Avesta*'. Yet, with due respect to the invaluable contribution made by Tourneux to eighteenth-century French studies, can one avoid the conclusion that, in a rather different way from Assézat, he made a mess of the task of assembling Diderot's contribution to the last four and a half volumes of the *Encyclopédie*? The 324 pages to which he confined that contribution are distinguished by a considerable number of sins of commission and an even greater number of sins of omission. Such clear errors of attribution as RAISONNEMENT, REPRÉSENTANTS, SENSATIONS, SENTIMENT INTIME, SOCIÉTÉ, SPINOSA, THÉOCRATIE, VÉRITÉ and VRAISEMBLANCE account for nearly a third of these pages. If we confine ourselves to the list of articles for which Diderot's authorship is vouched for by Naigeon we find that Tourneux left out RÉCOMPENSE, RÉFUGIÉS, RESSENTIMENT, RESSUSCITER, REVE, REVENANT, REVER, RIGORISME, SCHOOUBIAK, SPÉCULATION, SPINOSISTE, SUBIT, SUCCÈS, SURPRISE, SYNCRÉTISTES, VEILLE, . . . VICE, VINDICATIF, VOLONTÉ, VOLUPTUEUX and VULNÉRABLE. With one exception, these are short or even very short articles, and yet several of them are of the highest significance for an understanding of Diderot's

---

[86] pp. 119-27.

development as a writer and thinker.

One thing that Professor Proust has firmly established is that, even allowing for his trials and tribulations in collecting articles from the other contributors and for the work which he had to put in on the volumes of plates, the publication of which extended down to 1772, Diderot was not totally submerged by his labours on the *Encyclopédie* for some twenty-five years of his life. His total contribution to the work was nothing like as great as has often been imagined; in this period he must have had a good deal of time left over for his own writings—and for those of other people.

Yet there is another side to the medal. If one cuts down too drastically Diderot's contribution to the *Encyclopédie* which was, when all is said and done, his main preoccupation throughout this period and especially down to 1765, one breaks the continuity of his development as writer and thinker. In the years between 1750 and 1770 he wrote a good deal. but published relatively little. Some part of the evidence for his outlook and interests in these years is hidden away in odd corners of the *Encyclopédie*. Fortunately some of these short or very short articles were rescued from the work by Naigeon; if we follow cautiously in the same direction, we may rescue quite a lot more, some of them reprinted by Assézat and Tourneux, and others ignored. If we put all these together we find that they fit in with what we know of Diderot's ideas at this period of his life and also help to enrich our knowledge of it.

We see, for instance, in articles like OUTRER, SOUBRETTE, SIMULTANÉE, note (d) to SUBSIDE, and TIRADE, that he was still anxious to get across his ideas on the theatre. More important, we see that in the 1750s and 1760s Diderot was far more interested in political questions than has generally been imagined. In his notes to SUBSIDE we see a man far from ignorant of the past history of France, and particularly of the development of Absolutism. Doubt surrounds the authorship of such general political articles as INDÉPENDANCE, OLIGARCHIE, PAIX, POLITIQUE, POUVOIR, PROPRIÉTÉ, PROTECTION and SOUVERAINS; but one thing which strikes very forcibly the student of the unsigned articles in the last ten volumes of the *Encyclopédie* is that Diderot definitely took sides—as he was later to do at the time of Maupeou's *coup d'état*—in the struggle between Parlements and Crown, the main feature of France's history in the 1750s and 1760s. In *IMPROBATION, MAGISTRAT, MAGISTRATURE and OBVIER, reproduced in the Assézat-Tourneux edition, we find a discreetly worded, but none the less clear support of the Parlements' political claims. With these four articles go several other short ones, unmistakably by Diderot, which this edition left out: MORGUE, PARLEMENTAIRE, REVERENCE and SÉANCE. The article RÉQUISITOIRE, emasculated by Le Breton, shows with what mixed feelings Diderot and other *philosophes* looked upon the *cours souveraines* of France; yet in the *Encyclopédie* the attitude which he was to take up in the crisis of 1771 is already foreshadowed.

We owe to Naigeon the knowledge that Diderot was the author of RÉFUGIÉS, but other unsigned articles attacking religious intolerance drive the lesson home— . . . INTOLÉRANT, MASSACRE, OBÉISSANCE, PACIFICATION, PACIFIQUE and PERSÉCUTER, reproduced in the Assézat-Tourneux edition, are matched by others which are not—for instance, RETRANCHER. Diderot's hatred of all forms of religious asceticism is poured forth in VOLUPTUEUX among other unsigned articles. His love of sly digs at religious orthodoxy comes out in the cheeky article, IMPIE, or in the pinprick in ORIGINE.

Most important of all perhaps are those short articles which reveal clearly—at any rate to the modern reader who knows his Diderot—his materialism and determinism. Three brief articles linked by cross references (the first two mere additions to articles from Chambers)—MATÉRIALISTES, NATURALISTE and SPINOSISTE— form an obvious group. Articles in the Assézat-Tourneux edition which are expressly attributed to Diderot by Naigeon—INVOLONTAIRE, LAIDEUR, MALFAISANT, MODIFICATION, NAITRE and PRODUIRE, —go together with other articles which, while guaranteed by Naigeon, did not have the honour of being included in that edition: INCORPOREL, OPERATION, RECOMPENSE, RESSUSCITER, REVENANT, SUCCES, . . . VICE and VOLONTÉ. To these may be added a few others which are not attested by Naigeon: MACHINAL

in the Assézat-Tourneux edition and JAMAIS, PARFAIT, RESIGNA-
TION, VELLÉITÉ and VIL which are not.

In the last resort, it is clear, the problem of the unsigned articles in the *Encyclopédie* is insoluble. We shall no doubt never know who actually wrote several hundred articles in it. On the other hand it is possible to restore to their rightful owners—to men like D'Holbach, Saint-Lambert, Turgot and Polier de Bottens—quite a number of articles which have been wrongly attributed to Diderot. It is also possible to take away from Diderot quite a number of articles even if we do not know who wrote them. With the assistance of the editorial asterisk (though even that presents such problems as that it often covers mere compilation from Chambers or other sources) we can make some fairly reliable attributions for the first eight volumes; for unsigned articles in this part of the *Encyclopédie* we have relatively little to go on except analogy with other writings of Diderot. For the last nine volumes, however, we can rely, at any rate for more or less philosophical articles, on a great deal of assistance from Naigeon. Yet even so the declared limits which he set to his reproduction of articles by Diderot leave us with the gruesome task of trying to sort out for ourselves, by the light of nature, what other unsigned articles may be assigned to Diderot.

If one thinks of the problem in the light of the projected new edition of the complete works of Diderot, one is struck by its resemblance to another tricky problem, the exact degree of Diderot's participation in successive editions of Raynal's *Histoire philosophique et politique des établissements et du commerce des Europèens dans les deux Indes*. In both cases the editor or editors of the complete works of Diderot will have a good deal of solid information on which to rely in attributing part of the work to Diderot; but with both works there is an area of doubt which nothing in the manuscript material available in Paris and Leningrad can remove.

So far as Diderot's contribution to the *Encyclopédie* is concerned, a new edition of his collected works would certainly leave out a great many articles included in Vols. XIII-XVII of the Assézat-Tourneux edition; it would put in their place those unsigned articles for the authorship of which Naigeon vouches. But should an editor stop there? He can surely go a little beyond where Professor Proust stops, so as to include the other Diderot articles for which Naigeon was prepared to vouch, and then move cautiously beyond that point, relating certain anonymous articles in the *Encyclopédie* to the other writings of Diderot and also bearing in mind Naigeon's testimony as to the large number of 'grammatical' articles contributed by him.

Inevitably we are left with a considerable number of doubtful cases—particularly in the important field of political ideas, where, as we have seen, it is difficult either to attribute to Diderot or to remove from the canon of his writings some significant articles. Certainly any editor is going to have a difficult task if he should venture beyond the cautious limits set by Professor Proust. However, that is not our problem here. The aim of this chapter has not been to solve an insoluble problem, but merely to carry the discussion a little further, adding fresh articles to the list of those which can in all certainty be attributed to Diderot, making a number of suggestions as to others which with varying degrees of certainty may be attributed to him, and bringing together what information is available concerning articles which are definitely known to be by other hands.

Bibliography

MANUSCRIPT SOURCES

Bordeaux Bibliothèque de la Ville, MS. 828, Vol. XX. Papers of the Académie des Sciences, Belles-Lettres et Arts.
Geneva Bibliothèque Publique et Universitaire: Ms. fr. 916; Archives Tronchin 198, 210, 211.
London British Museum, Sloane MS. 4053. Royal Society, Archives.
Paris Archives Nationales. o^1 406, 408, 412, Maison du roi; U 1051, accounts of the *Encyclopédie*; Y 5072, Châtelet de Paris; 86 AP, Jaucourt family papers; Minutier Central, Études I, XXVII, XC, C, CXVII. Bibliothèque de la Société de l'Histoire du Protestantisme Français, MS. 790, Jaucourt family papers. Bibliothèque Nationale, MS. fr. 22069, Luneau de Boisjermain and the *Encyclopédie*; Ms. fr. 24416, Bouhier correspondence; Nouv. acq. fr. 3345, Malesherbes papers; Nouv. acq. fr. 24013. Bibliothèque Victor Cousin, MSS. Vols. II, V.

PRINTED SOURCES

Album Studiosorum Academiae Lugduno Batavae, The Hague, 1875.
Les Archives de la Bastille, ed. F. Ravaisson, Paris, 1866-1904, 19 vols.
Autographes de Mariemont, ed. M. J. Durry, Paris, 1955-1959, 4 vols.
BACHAUMONT, *Mémoires secrets pour servir à l'histoire de la République des Lettres en France de 1762 jusqu'à nos jours*, London, 1777-1789, 36 vols.

BARBIER, *Chronique de la Régence et du règne de Louis XV*, Paris, 1866, 8 vols.
BARRIÈRE, P., *L'Académie de Bordeaux centre de culture internationale au XVIIIe siècle (1712-1792)*, Bordeaux-Paris, 1951.
BARTHOLMESS, C., *Famille de Jaucourt*, Paris, 1841.
DE BOISSY, J. F., *Lettres*, ed. C. E. Engel, Neuchâtel, 1941.
BOULANGER, *L'Antiquité dévoilée*, Amsterdam, 1766.
BROWN, J. E., 'Goldsmith's Indebtedness to Voltaire and Van Effen', *Modern Philology*, 1926.
BUFFIER, CLAUDE, *Cours de Sciences sur des principes nouveaux*, Paris, 1732.
CANDAUX, J. D., 'Trois lettres de Voltaire au chevalier de Jaucourt', *BSHPF*, 1962.
CORDA, A., *Catalogue des Factums et d'autres documents judiciaires antérieurs à 1790*, Paris, 1890-1905, 7 vols.
CRANE, R. S., and FRIEDMAN, A., 'Goldsmith and the *Encyclopédie*', *Times Literary Supplement*, 11 May 1933.
CRU, R. LOYALTY, *Diderot as a Disciple of English Thought*, New York, 1913.
DIDEROT, *Correspondance*, ed. G. Roth, Paris, 1955- (in course of publication).
——, *Mémoires pour Catherine II*, ed. P. Vernière, Paris, 1966.
——, *Œuvres*, ed. J. A. Naigeon, Paris, 1798, 15 vols.
——, *Œuvres complètes*, ed. J. Assézat and M. Tourneux, Paris, 1875-1877, 20 vols.
——, *Salons*, ed. J. Seznec and J. Adhémar, Oxford, 1957-1967, 4 vols.
DIECKMANN, H., 'Diderot membre honoraire de la Société d'Antiquaires d'Écosse', *Cahiers Haut-Marnais*, 1951.
——, *Le Philosophe. Texts and Interpretation*, Saint Louis, 1948.
——, *Inventaire du Fonds Vandeul et inédits de Diderot*, Geneva-Lille, 1951.
——, 'L'Encyclopédie et le Fonds Vandeul', *RHL*, 1951.
——, 'The Sixth Volume of Saint-Lambert's Works', *Romanic Review*, 1951.
BOCCAGE, MME DU, *Recueil des Œuvres de*, Lyons, 1770, 3 vols.
DU BOIS, L. P., *Histoire civile, religieuse et littéraire de l'abbaye de la Trappe*, Paris, 1824.
DU PONT DE NEMOURS, P. S., *L'Enfance et la jeunesse de Du Pont de Nemours racontées par lui-même*, ed. H. A. Du Pont de Nemours, Paris, 1906.
DUTENS, L., 'Lettre à M. De *** sur les différentes éditions de l'*Encyclopédie*', *Journal encyclopédique*, 15 June 1771.
——, 'Lettre au sujet de l'*Encyclopédie d'Yverdon*', *Journal*

encyclopédique, 15 March 1772.
Edinburgh Review, Edinburgh, 1755-1756.
Encyclopaedia Britannica, Edinburgh, 1768-1771, 3 vols.; 2nd edition, Edinburgh, 1777-1784, 10 vols.; 3rd edition, Edinburgh, 1788-1797, 18 vols.; *Supplement*, 1801, 2 vols.
Encyclopédie méthodique, ou par ordre de matières ... proposée par souscription, n.p., 1782.
——, *Philosophie ancienne et moderne*, ed. J. A. Naigeon, Paris, 1791-1797, 3 vols.
Abbé de Feller, *Dictionnaire historique*, 2nd edition, Augsburg-Liège, 1791.
Formey, *Souvenirs d'un Citoyen*, Berlin, 1789, 2 vols.
Frederick II, *Œuvres*, ed. J. D. E. Preuss, Berlin, 1846-1856, 31 vols.
Garrick, David, *Letters*, ed. D. M. Little and G. M. Kahrl, London, 1963, 3 vols.
——, *Private Correspondence*, London, 1832, 2 vols.
Gentleman's Magazine, London, 1735-1807.
Gibbon, *Autobiography*, ed. O. Smeaton, London, 1911.
Goldsmith, *Works*, ed. J. W. M. Gibbs, London, 1884-1886, 5 vols.
Gordon, D. H. and Torrey, N. L., *The Censoring of Diderot's Encyclopédie and the Re-established Text*, New York, 1947.
Grosclaude, P., *Malesherbes témoin et interprète de son temps*, Paris, 1961.
Guhrauer, G. E., *Gottfried Wilhelm Freiherr von Leibnitz*, Breslau, 1842, 2 vols.
Hardy, S. P., *Mes Loisirs*, ed. M. Tourneux and M. Vitrac, Paris, 1912, Vol. I.
Hébrail, J. and de La Porte, J., *La France littéraire*, Paris, 1769, 2 vols.
Hecht, J., 'La vie de François Quesnay' in *François Quesnay et la Physiocratie*, Paris, 1958, 2 vols.
Hedgcock, F. A., *David Garrick and his French Friends*, London, 1912.
Hermand, P., 'Sur le texte de Diderot et sur les sources de quelques passages de ses Œuvers', *RHL*, 1915.
——, *Les Idées morales de Diderot*, Paris, 1923.
Histoire de l'Académie royale des Sciences et des Belles-Lettres, Berlin, 1772.
Huard, G., 'Les planches de l'Encyclopédie et celles de la *Description des Arts et Métiers*' in *L'Encyclopédie et le progrès des sciences et des techniques*, Paris, 1952.
Journal encyclopédique, Liège, 1756-1759; Bouillon, 1760-1793.

LAUNAY, M., 'Madame de Baugrand et Jean Romilly, horloger, intermédiaries entre Rousseau et Diderot', *Europe*, 1963.
LE GRAS, J., *Diderot et l'Encyclopédie*, Amiens, 1928.
LEIGH, R. A., 'Les amitiés françaises du Dr. Burney', *Revue de littérature comparée*, 1951.
London Magazine or Gentleman's Monthly Intelligencer, London, 1732-1785.
LOUGH, J., 'The Encyclopédie in Eighteenth-Century Scotland', *MLR*, 1943.
——, (ed.) *The Encyclopédie of Diderot and D'Alembert. Selected Articles*, Cambridge, 1954 (revised edition, 1969).
——, *Essays on the Encyclopédie of Diderot and D'Alembert*, London, 1968.
LOUIS, A., *Éloges lus dans les séances publiques de l'Académie royale de Chirurgie de 1750 à 1792*, ed. E. F. Dubois, Paris, 1959.
LUNEAU DE BOISJERMAIN: see the appendix to Chap. V. pp. 153-158.
MABLY, *Entretiens de Phocion*, Amsterdam, 1763.
MACCABEZ, E., *F. B. de Félice (1723-1789) et son Encyclopédie (Yverdon, 1770-1780)*, Bâle, 1903.
MALESHERBES, *Mémoires sur la Librairie et sur la liberté de la presse*, Paris, 1809.
MARMONTEL, *Mémoires*, ed. M. Tourneux, Paris, 1891, 3 vols.
MAY, L. P., 'Documents nouveaux sur l'*Encyclopédie*. L'histoire et les sources de l'*Encyclopédie*, d'après le registre de déliberations et de comptes des éditeurs, et un mémoire inédit'. *Revue de Synthèse*, 1938.
MAYER, J., *Diderot homme de science*, Rennes, 1959.
MICHAUD, J. F. and L. G., *Biographie universelle*, Nouvelle édition, Paris, 1843-1865.
MONTESQUIEU, *Œuvres complètes*, ed. A. Masson, Paris, 1950-1955, 3 vols.
Monthly Review, London, 1749-1789.
MORELLET, *Mémoires*, Paris, 1821, 2 vols.
MORNET, D., 'Les Enseignements des bibliothèques privées (1750-1780)', *RHL*, 1910.
MORTIER, R., *Diderot en Allemagne (1750-1850)*, Paris, 1954.
NAIGEON, J. A., *Mémoires historiques et philosophiques sur la vie et les ouvrages de D. Diderot*, Paris, 1821.
NANGLE, B. C., *The Monthly Review. First Series, 1749-1789: index of Contributors and Articles*, Oxford, 1934.
NAVES, R., *Voltaire et l'Encyclopédie*, Paris, 1938.
PALISSOT, *La Dunciade*, London, 1771, 2 vols.
PERRET, J. P., *Les Imprimeries d'Yverdon au XVIIe et au XVIIIe*

siècle, Lausanne, 1945.
POWELL, L. F., 'Johnson and the *Encyclopédie*', *Review of English Studies*, 1926.
PROUST, J., *Diderot et l'Encyclopédie*, Paris, 1962 (second edition, 1967).
——, 'La Documentation technique de Diderot dans l'*Encyclopédie*', *RHL*, 1957.
The Record of the Royal Society for the Promotion of Natural Knowledge, London, 1940.
ROGER, J., *Les Sciences de la vie dans la pensée française du XVIIIe siècle*, Paris, 1963.
ROUSSEAU, *Œuvres complètes*, ed. B. Gagnebin and M. Raymond, Paris, 1959- (in course of publication).
SAINT-AMANS, *Notice biographique sur M. de Vivens*, Agen, 1829.
SAINT-LAMBERT, *Œuvres philosophiques*, Paris, 1797, 6 vols.
SCHOLES, F. A., *The Great Dr. Burney*, Oxford, 1948, 2 vols.
SCHWAB, R. N., 'The Extent of the Chevalier de Jaucourt's Contribution to Diderot's *Encyclopédie*', *MLN*, 1957.
——, 'The Chevalier de Jaucourt and Diderot's *Encyclopédie*', *Modern Language Forum*, 1957.
——, 'Un encyclopédiste huguenot: le chevalier de Jaucourt', *BSHPF*, 1962.
SCOTT, W. R., *Adam Smith as Student and Professor*, Glasgow, 1937.
SEGUIN, J. P., 'Courte histoire des planches de l'*Encyclopédie*' in *L'Univers de l'Encyclopédie*, Paris, 1964.
MARQUIS DE SÉGUR, *Le Royaume de la Rue Saint-Honoré, Madame Geoffrin et sa fille*, Paris, 1897.
SELLS, A. LYTTON, *Les sources françaises de Goldsmith*, Paris, 1924.
SEVESTRE, E., *L'Enquête gouvernementale et l'enquête ecclésiastique sur le clergé de Normandie et du Maine*, Paris, 1918.
SMITH, ADAM, *Letters on Justice, Police, Revenue and Arms*, ed. E. Cannan, Oxford, 1896.
THIELEMANN, L., 'Diderot's Encyclopedic Article on Justice: its sources and significance', *Diderot Studies IV*.
TRONCHIN, H., *Le Conseiller François Tronchin et ses amis Voltaire, Diderot, Grimm, etc.*, Paris, 1895.
——, *Un Médecin du XVIIIe siècle, Théodore Tronchin*, Paris, 1906.
TROUSSON, R., 'Diderot et Homère', *Diderot Studies VIII*.
TURGOT, *Œuvres*, ed. G. Schelle, Paris, 1913-1923, 5 vols.
VENTURI, F., *Le Origini dell'Encyclopedia*, Florence, 1946 (second edition, Turin, 1963).

PIETRO and ALESSANDRO VERRI, *Carteggio*, ed. F. Novati and others, Milan, 1923-1942, 12 vols.
VOLTAIRE, *Correspondence*, ed. Theodore Besterman, Geneva, 1953-1966, 107 vols.
——, *Lettres inédites aux Tronchin*, ed. B. Gagnebin, Geneva-Lille, 1950, 3 vols.
——, *Œuvres complètes*, ed. L. Moland, Paris, 1877-1885, 52 vols.
YOUNG, ARTHUR, *Political Arithmetic*, London, 1774.
——, *Rural Economy*, London, 1770.

Index

NOTE. Articles from the *Encyclopédie*, which are printed in small capitals, are listed in alphabetical order. Where it is known, the name of the author or authors is given in parentheses; where the attribution is not absolutely certain, the name is followed by a question mark.
Articles are also listed under the name of their author or authors; a name in brackets after an article indicates that it was the work of more than one contributor. A question mark precedes those articles whose attribution is not absolutely certain.
* in front of an article stands for Diderot's editorial asterisk, whether he was responsible for the whole or only for a small addition.

*ABAREMO-TEMO, 172
*ABARNAHAS, 172
*ABSENT (D'Alembert, Toussaint), 172, 216
ACCOUCHEMENT (Louis), 186, 189
*ACOUSMATIQUES, 168
ACRIDOPHAGES (Chambers), 179, 188
ACTE (Mallet), 186, 189
ACTION (Yvon), 186n.
Adams, 118
ADORATION (*Théol.*), 179
ADORATION (*Hist. mod.*), 179
ADORER (*Théol.*), 179
ADULTÈRE (Yvon), 186n.
AEDES, 179
*AFFECTION (*Physiol.*), 169
AFFINITÉ (*Jurisprud.*), (Toussaint?) 179, 189
AGIR (Yvon), 186n.
AGRICULTURE (Diderot), 181, 189
*AGUAPA, 172
*AIGLE, 169, 208
AIGU (La Chapelle), 186, 189
AIGUILLE (Diderot), 186n.
Aiguillon, Mme d', 41
*AIR, 169
*AIUS LOCUTIUS, 213
ALCORAN (Mallet), 187, 189
*ALECTO, 169

Alembert, Jean Lerond d', 1, 7-8, 12, 13, 23, 43-44, 48, 55, 56, 57, 75, 91, 94, 95, 98, 100, 103, 174n.
Discours préliminaire, 6, 9, 10, 12, 15, 20-21
*ABSENT (Toussaint), 172, 216
CONTINGENCE, 187, 188
ERUDITION, 15n.
NATURE (*Philos.*), 126n.
NATURE, *lois de la*, 126n.
*ALLEMAGNE, 172
*ALSACE (d'Hérouville de Claye), 172
*ALUN, 172
*AME (Yvon), 172
*AMENTHÈS, 169
*AMER, 170
*AMITIÉ (Yvon), 186n.
AMOUR (Yvon), 14, 186n.
*ANAGRAMME, 159
ANATOMIE (Diderot), 186
A New and Complete Dictionary of Arts and Sciences, 18, 21
A New and Universal Dictionary of the Arts and Sciences, 18
A New Complete Dictionary of Arts and Sciences, 21
A New Royal and Universal Dictionary of the Arts and Sciences, 21
*ANGLETERRE, 172

*ANIMAL, 172-173
Année littéraire, 125
Annual Register, 9
ANTÉDILUVIENNE (Diderot), 189
ARABES (Diderot), 189
*ARBRE (Daubenton, L. J. M.), 16n.
ARCANE (*Chimie*) (Diderot?) 211-212
ARCHONTES (Mallet?), 179, 189
ARDOISE (Diderot) 186n.
*ARISTOCRATIE (Mallet), 173
*ARITHMETIQUE (*Machine*), 170
*ARITHMETIQUE POLITIQUE, 173, 188
ART (Diderot), 189
ARTISAN (Diderot?), 204
ARTISTE (Diderot?), 204
*ASCHARIOUNS, 168
ASIATIQUES (Diderot), 189
ASSAISONNEMENT (Diderot?), 204
*ASSAZOÉ, 173
ASSEZ, SUFFISAMMENT (Diderot?), 204
ASSURÉ, SUR, CERTAIN (Diderot?), 204
ASSURER, AFFIRMER, CONFIRMER (Diderot?), 204
ATHÉES (Yvon), 183, 185
ATTACHER, LIER (Diderot?), 204
ATTÉNUER, BROYER, PULVÉRISER (Diderot?), 204
Aumont, Arnulphe d'
   DIGESTEUR, 176
AUSTERE, SEVERE, RUDE (Diderot?), 204
AUTORITÉ POLITIQUE (Diderot), 190, 204
AUTORITÉ *dans les discours et dans les écricts* (Diderot?), 204
AXIOMES (Yvon), 184
Ayloffe, Sir Joseph, 7-8, 9
*AZARECAH, 168
*AZUR FACTICE, 173

*BACCHIONITES, 168
Bachelier, 115-116
Bacon, Francis, 18
*BARAICUS, 170
Baraton de Dame, 119
*BARBARIE, 173
Barbeyrac, Jean, 36
Barbier, 122, 165
Barruel, Abbé Augustin, 2
Bartholmess, Christian, 60-61

BAS (*métier à*) (Diderot), 191
*BASSESSE, ABJECTION, 168, 201n.
*BATRACHITE, 173
BATTE (Diderot?), 204
Beauzée, Nicolas, 201
*BELBUCH, 168
Bénard, Robert, 128
BENIN, 179
Bentley, Richard, 29
Besenval, Pierre Victor, Baron de, 40
*BETE, ANIMAL, BRUTE, 169
*BEURRE, 159
Bewley, William, 9n.
BIBLIOMANE, 179
BIBLIOTHÈQUE (Diderot?), 204
Bibliothèque raisonnée, 36
Bochart, Nicolas, 61, 62
Boerhaave, Hermann, 27, 33-34, 38, 56, 59
*BOIS SACRÉS, 168n.
Boissy, Jean François de, 5
Boitel de Richeville, 115-116
Boswell, James, 13
Boucher d'Argis, Antoine Gaspard
   INTENDANS & COMMISSAIRES DÉPARTIS (with another), 79, 88, 213
   MAGISTRAT (*Jurisprud.*), 206
Bouchu, Etienne Jean
   FORGES (GROSSES), 184
Bouhier, Jean, 37n.
Boulanger, Nicolas Antoine, 186n.
   CORVÉE, 185
   DÉLUGE, 185
Bourk, Comte de, 119
BOURREAU (Diderot?), 204
*BRACHMANES, 168
*BRAMINES, 168
Branche-Godart, Mme, 118
Brayer, 118
Briasson, Antoine Claude, 3-5, 48, 51-53, 71-76, 91-95
   lawsuit with Luneau de Boisjermain, 96-158
British Magazine, 9
BROCHURE (Diderot?), 204
Broglie, Mme de, 45, 69
Brosses, Charles de, 101
   FÉTICHISME, 162n.
Buffier, Father Claude, 181, 184, 185, 186

INDEX 241

Buffon, Georges Louis Leclerc, Comte de, 13, 40, 75, 126, 171, 172-173, 177
Burlamaqui, Jean Jacques, 181
Burmann, Peter, 29
Burney, Charles, 2n., 9 n., 16-17
BUT, VUE, DESSEIN (Diderot?), 204

CALICUT (Diderot?), 204
Cambridge, University of, 28-31
Camille Massimo, Marquis de, 115
*CAPUCHON, 204
CARAÏBES (Diderot?), 204
Carmichael, John, 27, 30
CARPOCRATIENS (Diderot?), 212
Casteliau, William, 21
CATHÉDRALE (*Hist. ecclés.*) (Mallet?) 179, 189
Catherine the Great, 49-50, 84
Caveirac, Abbé Jean Novi de, 207, 209
Caze, 31, 35, 40, 69
CEILAN (Diderot?), 204
CENTON (Chambers), 179, 188
*CERF, 173
*CERTITUDE (de Prades), 159-160, 216
CHALCÉDOINE (Diderot?), 212
CHALDÉENS (Diderot), 190
Chambers, Ephraim, 17, 18, 19, 21, 55, 126n., 142, 159-160, 173, 179-182, 184, 185, 188, 191, 203-213, 215, 217, 222, 226, 227, 231
Chambon, Théodore, 63-68
CHAMPIGNON (Jaucourt), 58n.
*CHANGEMENT, VARIATION, VARIÉTÉ, 169
Chappe, Abbé, 50
*CHARIDOTES, 169
*CHARITÉ, 205
Châtelet, Mme Du, 38-39
Chaumeix, Abraham Joseph de, 222
*CHAVARIGTES, 168
*CHEF-D'OEUVRE (*Arts & Mét.*), 173
*CHEVEUX, 173
CHINE, LA (*Géog.*) (Diderot?), 212
*CHINOIS (PHILOSOPHIE DES), 168, 212
CHRISTIANISME, 179
CITATION (*Théol.*) (Mallet), 184
Clarke, Samuel, 19
Clisson, Mlle, 118

Closier, 119
*COACTIF, 173
*COACTION, 173-174
COLIQUE DE POITOU (Jaucourt), 46
CONCOURS, 184
Condillac, Abbé Étienne de, 185
Condorcet, Antoine Nicolas, Marquis de, 12
*CONJECTURE, 169
*CONSERVATION, 169
CONSOLATION (Diderot?), 204
*CONTINENCE, 169
CONTINGENCE (D'Alembert), 187, 188
Cooke, Rev. Thomas, 21
*COQ (*Mythol.*), 169
CORDELIER (Diderot?), 204
Cornuet, 119
CORVÉE (Boulanger), 185
*COTERIE, 168
Cottin de Fontaine, 119
Cramer, Gabriel, 110
*CRAPAUD, 174
Craven, William, 3
Critical Review, 9
Croker, Temple Henry, 19
*CYNIQUE, (*Secte*), 168
*CYRENAÏQUE (*Secte*), 168

Daily Advertiser, 8
Damilaville, Etienne Noël, 25, 209, 222
VINGTIEME (Diderot) 186n.
Daubenton, Louis Jean Marie, 75, 126-127, 177
*ARBRE, 16n.
Daubenton le jeune, 127-128
David l'aîné, 3-5, 48, 51-53, 71-76, 91-95, 97n.
DÉFICIENT (*Arithmétique*), (Diderot?), 212
Deleyre, Alexandre
ÉPINGLE (Diderot?), 14
DÉLUGE (Boulanger), 185
Descartes, René, 177
Desevelinge, 118
Desmaizeaux, Pierre, 36
Dessaint, J. B. jr., 62
Dictionnaire de Trévoux, 15
Diderot, Denis, 1, 2, 7, 8, 12, 14-15, 16, 18, 23, 25, 43-44, 47n., 48-

50, 66, 67, 69, 75, 91, 95, 148-149
contribution to *Encyclopédie*, 159-232
articles with asterisk listed, 168, 169-171, 172-178
unsigned articles wrongly attributed to him, 179-186, 188-189
unsigned articles to be attributed to him with certainty, 186n., 189-200
unsigned articles to be attributed to him with varying degrees of probability, 204-228
criticisms of *Encyclopédie*, 139-142
earnings from *Encyclopédie*, 103-104
part in Luneau de Boisjermain lawsuit, 97-158
Prospectus, 20, 99-101, 162
quarrel with Le Breton, 76-89, 99, 126, 128-131
other mentions of articles
AGRICULTURE, 181, 189
*ANAGRAMME, 159
*ARBRE (Daubenton, L. J. M.), 16n.
*BEURRE, 159
*CERTITUDE (de Prades), 159-160, 216
*ENCYCLOPÉDIE, 18, 22, 168, 204
MALFAISANT, 203, 231
*MARBREUR DE PAPIER, 164
MENACE, 87
MODIFICATION, 203, 231
?PRÉSOMPTUEUX, 184
PYRRHONIENNE, PHILOSOPHIE, 79
SARRASINS, PHILOSOPHIE DES, 79, 86
SOCRATIQUE, PHILOSOPHIE, 88
SPINOSISTE, 203
VICE (Jaucourt), 203
VOLONTÉ, 203
VOLUPTUEUX, 203
ZENDA VESTA, 100n.
DIEUX (Diderot?), 204
DIGESTEUR (D'Aumont), 176
DISTINCTION, 179
Donne, John, 185
Douchet, Jacques Philippe Auguste, 201
*DRANSES, 168

Du Boccage, Mme Anne Marie 42n.
Du Pont de Nemours, Pierre Samuel, 27
Durand, Laurent, 3-5, 48, 51-53, 71-76, 91-95, 97n.
Dutens, Louis, 5n., 57
Duval, 118
Duval de Lepinois, 115
Dyche, Thomas, 17
*DYDIME, 174-175

*ÉCLAIRÉ, 168
*ÉCLECTISME, 168
Edinburgh Review, 13-14
*EGAGROPILES, 175
*EGYPTIENS (PHILOSOPHIE DES), 168
*ELEATIQUE (SECTE), 168
Encyclopaedia Britannica, 1-2, 12, 14, 21-23
Encyclopédie
Discours préliminaire, 6, 9, 10, 12, 15, 20-21
Prospectus, 20, 99-101, 162
accounts of, 71-76, 91, 103-104, 142-153
Arrêts du Conseil: (1752), 216n.
(March 1759), 107n., 115, 121-122, 137
(July 1759), 107n., 115, 116, 122-125, 146-147
attitude to politics, 2, 10-11, 230
religion, 2, 12, 24
censored by Le Breton, 27-28, 71, 76-89, 128-131, 190n., 193n., 200n., 205, 206, 208, 210, 213, 218, 224-225, 228
contributors, 101-104, 150-151
cost of, 108-112
crisis of 1759, 91-95, 120-125
Diderot's criticisms of, 139-142
distribution of last ten volumes, 131-139
English translation, 7-8
Geneva folio reprint, 49, 50, 110, 140, 142n., 153
London quarto edition, 3-7, 75
Luneau de Boisjermain lawsuit, 96-158
plates, 19-21, 105n., 108-112, 123-124, 125-128, 145-146

INDEX

reception in England, 1-24
subscribers, 105-120
Supplément, 58, 115, 163, 179
unsigned articles, 103, 159-232
*ENCYCLOPÉDIE, 18, 22, 168, 204
Encyclopédie d'Yverdon, 16, 57, 58, 115
*ENTREPRISE, 175
*ÉPÉES, 175-176
*ÉPICURÉISME, 168
ÉPINGLE (Deleyre; Diderot?), 14
*ÉPREUVE, ESSAI, EXPÉRIENCE, 204n.
Ermengard de Beauval, Marie Jean François, 59-60
ERUDITION (D'Alembert), 15
*ESCULAPE, 170
Esprit de l'Encyclopédie, 8, 10
Esterhazy, Prince d', 119, 138
ETERNITÉ (Jaucourt, Formey; Diderot?), 212
*ETHIOPIENS, 168
ETYMOLOGIE (Turgot), 187, 189
EVIDENCE (Quesnay), 187, 189
*EXHUMER, 176
EXISTENCE (Turgot), 187, 189
EXPANSIBILITÉ (Turgot) 187, 189

*FACE, 169
FALBALA (Marquise de Jaucourt?), 44-45
FAMILIARITÉ (Saint-Lambert), 180, 187
*FAMILISTES, 176
FANTAISIE (*Morale*) (*Saint-Lambert*), 179, 180, 189
*FANTOME, 169
FASTE (*Morale*) (Saint-Lambert), 180, 189
Faulche, Samuel, 131, 135, 149
Félice, Barthélemy de, 57-58
Feller, François Xavier de, 2n.
FERMETÉ (Voltaire), 180
FERMETÉ & CONSTANCE (Saint-Lambert), 180, 189
FERMIERS (Quesnay), 16, 189n.
FÉTICHISME (de Brosses), 162n.
FEU (*Physiq.*) (D'Alembert), 176n.
*FEU (*Pompe à*) (Perronnet), 176-177
*FIGER (SE), 177
Findlater, James Ogilvy, Earl of, 3
FINESSE (Marmontel), 187n.

FINESSE (Voltaire), 187n.
FLATTERIE (Saint-Lambert), 180, 187, 189
Flinne, J. T. de, 118
FOIBLE (Diderot?), 204
FOIRE (Turgot), 187, 189
FONDATION, (Turgot), 180, 187, 189
FONTANGE (Marquise de Jaucourt?), 44-45
Fontenelle, Bernard Le Bovier de, 33, 181, 183
*FORDICIDIES, 168
FORGES (GROSSES) (Bouchu), 184
Formey, Jean Henri Samuel, 55-56, 68
ETERNITÉ (Jaucourt; Diderot?), 212
FORTUNE, 180
FORTUNE (Jaucourt), 180n.
FRAGILITÉ (*Morale*) (Saint-Lambert), 179, 180, 189
Frazé, Pierre, 118
Frederick the Great, 55, 56
FRIVOLITÉ (Saint-Lambert), 179, 180, 189
Fromagil, 119

Gaillon, 118
GALANTERIE (*Morale*) (Diderot?), 204
Garrick, David, 3n., 16
GAZETIER (Diderot?), 212
GÉNIE (Saint-Lambert), 161, 179, 180, 189
Gentleman's Magazine, 5, 7-8, 9
Geoffrin, Mme Marie Thérèse Rodet, 90-95
*GÉOMÉTRIE SOUTERREINE, 177
George III, 2, 3
Gerbier, Pierre Jean Baptiste, 97n., 113, 135, 141
Gibbon, Edward, 15, 16
Gillaboz, 118
Gilly, Simon, 41, 69
Girard, Abbé Gabriel, 201n., 205, 207
*GIROVAGUE, 177
GLORIEUX, 180
*GOG & MAGOG, 177
Goldsmith, Oliver, 9, 15-16
Goussier, Louis Jacques, 75, 145 150-151

GOUVERNEMENT (Jaucourt), 47
GRAINS (Quesnay) 16, 189n.
Granet, 68
GRAVE, 180
GRAVITÉ, 180
*GRECS (Philosophie des), 168
Grenaud, 115-116
Grimm, Friedrich Melchior, 3n., 44, 48, 50-51, 52, 59, 80-81, 82, 85, 86, 92, 93, 107, 122, 128, 165, 179-182, 186n., 187
GRONDEUR, 180
Gua de Malves, Abbé de, 76
Gulston, Joseph, 3

HABITUDE (Diderot?), 204
Harris, John, 17
Haller, Albert de, 57-58
*HAMBELIENS, 168
HAMMON (Mallet), 180, 189
*HARMONIE, 169
HAWAMAAL (D'Holbach), 187, 188n.
Hébert, Nicolas, 119
Heiss, Baron de, 119
HÉLAS (Diderot?), 205
Helvétius, Claude Adrien, 55
*HERACLITISME, 168
HÉRALDIQUE (Art) (Jaucourt; Diderot?), 212-213
HÉROÏSME (Diderot?), 205
Hérouville de Claye, Comte d'
*ALSACE, 171
*HÉSITATION, 169
Heubens, 117
*HIERACITES, 169
Hillou, 115
Hinde, M., 21
Hirzel, Hans Caspar, 16
HISTOIRE (Voltaire), 10
*HOBBISME, 168
Holbach, Charles Marius d', 165
Holbach, Paul Thiry, Baron d' 48, 66, 67, 93n., 128, 165, 231
  HAWAMAAL, 187
  ?JAKUTES, 181, 188n.
  ?KING, 181, 188n.
  ?LAO-KIUN, 181, 188n.
  MADRÉPORES, 188
  ?MARABOUS, 182, 188n.
  NGOMBOS, 182
  ?ODIN, 182, 188n.
  ?OFAVAI, 182, 188n.
  OMBIASSES, 188
  OVISSA, 188
  ?PARÉAS, 182, 188n.
  PAVÉ DES GÉANTS, 188
  ?PIACHES, 183
  ?PRASSAT, 184, 188n.
  PRETRES, 161, 165, 184
  REPRÉSENTANTS, 161, 165, 185
  SAMBA-PONGO, 188
  THÉOCRATIE, 161, 165, 185
  TOPILZIN, 188
  ?ULEMA, 186, 188n.
HONNETE (Saint-Lambert), 187, 189
HONNEUR (Morale) (Saint-Lambert), 187, 189
*HOPITAL, 205
HOTEL-DIEU (Diderot?), 205
*HUMAINE ESPECE, 177
HUMANITÉ (Diderot?), 205
HUMBLE (Diderot), 205
Hume, David, 13
HUMILITÉ (Diderot?), 205
HYLOPATHIANISME (Diderot?), 205
HYPOCRITE (Diderot?) 205

IDENTITÉ, 180
IGNORANCE (Métaphys.) (Diderot?), 205
ILIADE, 180
ILLIMITÉ (Diderot?), 205
ILLUSION (Diderot?), 205
*IMAGINAIRE, 169
IMAGINATION (POUVOIR DE L') (Diderot?), 205
*IMBIBER, 171
IMMATÉRIALISME (Yvon), 160, 180, 189
IMMOBILE (Diderot), 190
IMMONDE (Diderot?), 205
IMMORTALITÉ (Diderot), 190
*IMPARFAIT, 215
*IMPARTIAL, 169
*IMPERCEPTIBLE, 169
*IMPÉRISSABLE, 169
IMPIE (Diderot), 191-192, 230
IMPLORER (Diderot?), 213
IMPORTANCE (Diderot), 190
IMPOT en faveur du Théâtre (Diderot?), 213

INDEX

IMPRESSION (Diderot?), 205
*IMPROBATION, 230
IMPURETÉ (Diderot?), 205
INCOGNITI (Diderot?), 205
INCOMMODE (Diderot?), 205
*INCOMPRÉHENSIBLE, 170
*INCONSEQUENCE, INCONSEQUENT, 170
INCORPOREL (Diderot), 192, 231
INCORRIGIBLE (Diderot?), 213
*INCROYABLE, 170
*INCULTE, 177-178
*INDÉCENT, 170
*INDÉCIS, 170
INDÉPENDANCE (Diderot?), 205, 230
INDIENS (Diderot), 190
*INDISPOSÉ, 178
*INDISTINCT, 170
INDOLENCE (Diderot?), 205
INDUCTION, 181
INDULGENCE (Diderot?), 205
INFIDÉLITÉ (Diderot?), 205
*INFUS, INFUSE, 178
INGÉNUITÉ (Diderot?), 205
INJURE, TORT (Diderot?), 205
*INNÉ, 170
INQUIÉTUDE (Diderot?), 205
INSENSÉ (Diderot?), 205
INSENSIBILITÉ (Diderot?), 205
*INSÉPARABLE, 170
INSERTION DE LA PETITE VÉROLE (Diderot?), 205
INSTINCT (Charles Georges Leroy), 187, 189
*INTEMPÉRIE, 171
INTENDANS & COMMISSAIRES DÉPARTIS (Boucher d'Argis and another) 79, 88, 213
INTÉRÊT (Morale) (Saint-Lambert), 161, 181, 189
INTERLOCUTEUR (Diderot?), 213
INTERMEDE (Diderot?), 205
INTERMÉDIAIRE (Diderot), 192
*INTERMINABLE, 178
INTOLÉRANCE (Diderot), 190, 207, 209
INTOLÉRANT (Jaucourt; Diderot?), 206, 230
INTRÉPIDITÉ (Diderot?), 206
INTRIGUE (Diderot?), 206
INVECTIVE (Diderot?), 213
INVÉTÉRÉ (Diderot?), 213

INVINCIBLE (Diderot?), 206
INVIOLABLE (Diderot?), 206
INVISIBLE (Diderot), 190
INVOLONTAIRE (Diderot), 190, 231
*IONIQUE, secte, 168
*IRASCIBLE, 170
*IRRÉGULARITÉ, 178
*IRRELIGIEUX, 170
IRRÉSOLUTION (Diderot?), 206
*ISOLÉ, ISOLER, 170

Jacobinism, 1, 2
JAKUTES (D' Holbach?), 181, 188n.
JAMAIS (Diderot?), 213, 231
JANSÉNISTE (Mode) (Diderot?), 206
*JAPONAIS, PHILOSOPHIE DES, 168
Jaucourt, Armand Henri de, 59, 61
Jaucourt, Arnail François, Marquis de, 27
Jaucourt, Élisabeth Sophie Gilly, Marquise de 37n., 41, 46
Jaucourt, François de, 69
Jaucourt, Isabelle de, 27, 30, 32-33, 39, 41, 43, 69
Jaucourt, Louis, Chevalier de, 80, 92, 99-100, 101, 104, 110, 142, 148-149, 164, 201
biographical sketch, 25-70
CHAMPIGNON, 58n.
COLIQUE DE POITOU, 46
ÉTERNITÉ (Formey; Diderot?), 212
FORTUNE, 180n.
GOUVERNEMENT, 47
HERALDIQUE (Art) (Diderot?), 212-213
INTOLÉRANT (Diderot?), 206
JEU (Droit naturel & Morale) (Diderot?), 206
LABARUM, 50
LEYDE, 33
LIBERTÉ CIVILE, 181
LIBERTÉ NATURELLE, 181
LIBERTÉ POLITIQUE, 181
?MONT-FAUCON, 182
NATURELLE, loi, 181
POITOU, COLIQUE DE, 46
?POLI, CIVIL, 183
PRUSSE (Diderot), 217
?PUISSANCE LÉGISLATIVE, EXÉCUTRICE & DE JUGER, 185

RELIGION PROTESTANTE, 27-28
SEDUCTEUR (Diderot?), 220
SOUVERAINETÉ, 88
SPARTE (Diderot?), 221
SUPERSTITION, 67
THÉOLOGIE SCHOLASTIQUE, 79
THÉOLOGIE, *Réflexions sur la*, (Morellet), 79
TOLÉRANCE, 79
TRAITE DES NEGRES, 37
TRAPPE, *Moines de la*, 63-64, 66, 225
TYRANS, LES TRENTE, 185
TYRANNICIDE, 185
TYRANNIE, 185
VICE (Diderot), 197-198, 229
VOORHOUT, 33-34
Jaucourt, Louis Pierre, Marquis de, 41-47, 50, 69
Jaucourt, Marie de Monginot, Marquise de, 26, 27, 30, 31, 35, 37, 52
Jaucourt, Marie Josèphe de, 26-27
Jaucourt, Pierre Antoine I, Marquis de, 26, 30, 31, 35, 37
Jaucourt, Pierre Antoine II, Marquis de, 27, 37, 45
Jaucourt, Suzanne Marie de Vivens, Marquise de, 32-33, 41-47, 54
?FALBALA, 44-45
?FONTANGE, 44-45
JÉSUITE (Diderot), 190
Jesuits, 10, 60-62, 186n.
JÉSUS-CHRIST (Diderot), 190
JEU (*Droit naturel & Morale*) (Jaucourt; Diderot?), 206
Johnson, Samuel, 2n., 13, 16
Joly de Fleury, Jean Omer, 120
*JOQUES, 168
JORDANUS BRUNUS (Diderot), 190
Jossan, Daudet de, 115
*JOUER (*Gramm.*), 178
*JOUER (*Gram. Mathémat. pures*), 178
JOUISSANCE (Diderot), 190
*JOURNEE DE LA SAINT-BARTHÉLEMY, 170, 207
JUDAÏSER (Diderot?), 213
JUDAÏSME (Diderot?), 206
*JUIFS, *Philosophie des*, 168, 206
Jussieu, Bernard de, 127

JUSTE, INJUSTE, 181

KIJUN (Polier de Bottens), 187-188
KING (D'Holbach?), 181, 188n.

LABARUM (Jaucourt), 50
Labat, Jean Louis, 28, 68
LABEUR (Diderot?), 206
LABORIEUX (Diderot?), 206
LABOURAGE OU AGRICULTURE (*Hist. anc.*), 181
LABOUREUR (Diderot?), 206
La Chapelle, Abbé de
    AIGU, 186, 189
La Colonge, de, 117
La Condamine, Charles Marie de, 118
La Court, de, 115
La Ferté-Imbault, Mme de, 91, 94
LAIDEUR (Diderot), 190, 231
Lalande, Joseph Jérôme de, 58, 115, 116n.,
Lallemant de Betz, 119, 138
La Londe de Sainte-Croix, 117
Lambert, 118
Lamoignon de Blancménil, Guillaume de, 146
Lancry de Rimberlieu, Charles de, 59-60
Landais, 119
Landois, Paul, 75
LANGRES (Diderot?), 206
LANGUEUR (Diderot?), 206
Lansegue, Marquis de, 115
LAO-KIUN (D'Holbach?), 181, 188n.
LAQUAIS (Diderot?), 206
Laurès, 118
La Vallière, Duc de, 114
Lawson, Isaac, 69
Le Breton, André François, 3-5, 48, 51-53, 61, 68, 71-76, 91-95
  censors *Encyclopédie*, 27-28, 71, 76-89, 128-131, 190n., 193n., 200n., 205, 206, 208, 210, 213, 218, 224-225, 228
  lawsuit with Luneau de Boisjermain, 96-158
LEÇON (Diderot?), 206
Le Duc de Tournelle, 118
Lefranc de Pompignan, Jean Jacques, 46, 114, 123-124

INDEX

LÉGÈRETÉ (Diderot?), 206
LÉGISLATEUR (Saint-Lambert), 161, 181, 189
LÉGISLATION (Diderot), 190
Leguay, 115-116
Le Guelinel, Robert Jacques François, 63-68
LEIBNITZIANISME (Diderot), 190
Leibniz, Gottfried Wilhelm, 36, 37n.
Lemaire, 118
Lemonnier, Dr., 119
Leroy, Charles Georges
  INSTINCT, 187, 189
  PIÉGE, 187
LESTE (Diderot?), 206
Lesure, Jean, 119
Lesure, Nicolas Rémy, 119
Letourneur, Pierre, 59
Levesque de Pouilly, Jean Simon, 182
LEYDE (Jaucourt), 33
LIAISON (*Métaphysique*), 181
LIBERTÉ (*Morale*) (Naigeon, Yvon), 160, 181, 189, 206
LIBERTÉ CIVILE (Jaucourt) 181, 189
LIBERTÉ NATURELLE (Jaucourt), 181, 189
LIBERTÉ POLITIQUE (Jaucourt), 181
LIBERTINAGE (Diderot?), 206
LIBRAIRIE (Diderot?), 206
LICENCE (Diderot?), 206
LIGATURE, 181
LITURGIE (Polier de Bottens), 188
LIVRE (*Littér.*) (Chambers, Diderot), 213
LOCKE (Diderot), 190
LOCUTIUS (Diderot?), 213
LOGIQUE, 181
LOGOMACHIE (Polier de Bottens), 188
LOI NATURELLE (*Morale*), 181
LOISIR (Diderot), 190
London Magazine or Gentleman's Intelligencer, 5, 9
LOUANGE (*Morale*) (Saint-Lambert), 181, 189
LOUER (Diderot?), 206
Louis XV, 134, 135, 138-139
Louis XVI, 135
Louis, Antoine
  ACCOUCHEMENT, 186, 189

LUBRIQUE, LUBRICITÉ (Diderot?), 206
LUL (Diderot?), 213
Luneau de Boisjermain, Pierre Joseph François, 49, 58, 84-85, 87, 88, 92
  lawsuit with publishers, 96-158
LUXE (Saint-Lambert), 161, 181-182, 189
LUXURE (Diderot?) 213

Mably, Abbé Gabriel Bonnot de, 63, 66
MACARIENS (Diderot), 190
MACÉRATION (Diderot?), 206
MACHER (Diderot?), 206
MACHIAVÉLISME (Diderot), 190
MACHIAVÉLISTE (Diderot?), 206
MACHINAL (Diderot?), 206, 231
Maclaine, Archibald, 11-12
MADRÉPORES, (D'Holbach), 188
MAGICIENS (Polier de Bottens), 188
MAGIE (Polier de Bottens), 188
MAGISTRAT (Diderot?), 206, 230
MAGISTRAT (*Jurisprud.*) (Boucher d'Argis), 206
MAGISTRATURE (Diderot?), 206, 230
MAGNANIME (Diderot?), 206
MAGNIFIQUE (Diderot?), 206
MAGOT (Diderot?), 213
Maignan de Savigny, 118
MAINTIEN (Diderot?), 206
MALABARES (Diderot), 190
MALACHBELUS (Polier de Bottens), 188
MALADROIT, MALADRESSE (Diderot?), 206
MALE (Diderot?), 207
Malebranche, Nicolas, 183, 184, 185
MALEBRANCHISME (Diderot?), 190
MALÉDICTION (*Gram.*) (Diderot?), 207
MALÉDICTION (*Jurispr.*) (Diderot?), 207
MALÉFICE, 181, 182
Malesherbes, Chrétien Guillaume de Lamoignon de, 90, 91, 107n., 122-123, 146
MALFAISANT (Diderot), 191, 203, 231
MALICE (Diderot?), 207
MALIGNITÉ (Diderot?), 207
MALINTENTIONNÉ (Diderot?), 207
Mallet, Edme, 8, 174
  ACTE, 186, 189
  ALCORAN, 187, 189

?ARCHONTES, 179, 189
*ARISTOCRATIE, 173
?CATHÉDRALE (*Hist. ecclés.*), 179, 189
CITATION (*Théol.*), 184
HAMMON, 180, 189
Malluet, 119
MALVEILLANCE & MALVEILLANT (Diderot?), 207
MANES (Polier de Bottens), 182
MANICHÉISME (Yvon), 160, 182, 184, 189
MANIERES (Saint-Lambert), 182, 189
MANIERES, FAÇONS (Diderot?), 207
MANSTUPRATION (Ménuret de Chambaud), 182, 189
MAOSIM (Polier de Bottens), 188
MARABOUS (D'Holbach?), 182, 188n.
*MARBREUR *de papier*, 164
Maréchal, 118
Marel, 118
Maret, Hugues, 182
MARIAGE (Ménuret de Chambaud), 182
Marlborough, Charles, Duke of, 55
Marmontel, Jean François, 51, 94, 95, 101
FINESSE, 187n.
Marshall, J., 21
MASSACRE (Diderot?), 207, 209, 230
Masson, Arthur, 14-15
MATÉRIALISTES (Diderot?), 213-214, 231
Maudave, de, 119, 138
Maupeou, René Nicolas, 141, 142n.
MÉCONNAISSABLE (Diderot?), 207
MÉCONTENT (Diderot?), 207
MÉDISANCE (Diderot?), 207
MÉDITATION (Diderot?), 207
MÉFIANCE (Diderot?), 207
MÉGARIQUE (Diderot), 190
Meister, Jean Henri, 93-95
MÉLANCOLIE (Diderot?), 207
MÉLANGE (Diderot?), 214
MELER (Diderot?), 214
MENACE (Diderot), 87, 191
MÉNAGERIE (Diderot?), 214
MENÉE (Diderot?), 207
MENTION (Diderot?), 207
MENSONGE OFFICIEUX (Diderot?), 207
Ménuret de Chambaud, Jean Joseph

MANSTUPRATION, 182, 189
MARIAGE, 182
MÉPRIS (Diderot?), 207
MERCENAIRE (Diderot?), 207
MESSIE (Polier de Bottens), 188
MÉTAPHYSIQUE (Diderot), 192
MÉTEMPSYCOSE (Diderot?), 207
MÉTHODE (Diderot?), 214, 220
Michel, 119
Middleton, Rev. Erasmus, 21
Mills, John, 71
MINCE (Diderot?), 214
MISÉRABLE (Diderot?), 207
MISÈRE (Diderot?), 207
MODICITÉ, MODIQUE (Diderot?), 207
MODIFICATION (Diderot), 191, 203, 231
MOEURS (Diderot?), 207
MOMERIE (Diderot?), 207
MONT-FAUCON (Jaucourt?), 182
Montesquieu, Charles de Secondat, Baron de, 23, 40-41, 54, 101, 208
Montmort, Pierre Rémond de, 37n.
Monthly Review, 1, 6, 9-12, 19-20, 24
Moreau, 116-117, 125
Morel de Villiers, 117
Morellet, Abbé André, 92, 95, 164n.
THÉOLOGIE, *Reflexions sur la* (Jaucourt), 79
MORGUE (Diderot?), 214, 230
MORIGENER (Diderot?), 214
MOSAÏQUE & CHRÉTIENNE (PHILOSOPHIE) (Diderot), 190
MOTIF (Diderot?), 207
Mouchy, Maréchal de, 114
MULTIPLICITÉ (Diderot?), 214
MULTITUDE (Diderot), 191
MUNIFICENCE (Diderot?), 207
MUTUEL (Diderot?), 214

Naigeon, Jacques André, 51, 82
attribution of articles by, 162n., 167-171, 181, 182, 183, 184 185, 188, 189-202, 203, 204, 206, 211, 229-232
LIBERTÉ (*Morale*) (Yvon), 160, 181, 189, 206
NAITRE (Diderot), 191, 231
NATAL (Diderot), 190
NATIF (Diderot), 207

INDEX

NATURALISTE (Diderot), 190, 231
NATURE (*Philos.*) (D'Alembert), 126n.
NATURE, *lois de la* (D'Alembert), 126n.
NATUREL (Diderot?), 207
NATURELLE, *loi* (Jaucourt), 181
NÉANT (Diderot), 190
NÉCESSAIRE (Diderot?), 207
NÉCESSITANT (Diderot?), 207
NÉCESSITÉ, 182
Neret, 119
NGOMBOS (D'Holbach), 182, 188
NIAIS (Diderot?), 207
NIGRO-MANTIE (Diderot?), 207
Noailles, Maréchal de, 41-42, 114
Noailles, Marquis de, 114
NOCTAMBULE (Diderot?), 208
NOMMER (Diderot?), 208
NONCHALANCE (Diderot?), 208
NOURRICE (Diderot?), 208
Nourse and Saillant, 4n.
Vaillant, 4-5, 145-146
NOVATEUR (Diderot?), 215
NU (Diderot?), 208
NUIRE (Diderot?), 208

OBÉISSANCE (Diderot?), 208, 230
OBJECTER (Diderot?), 208
OBLAT (Diderot?), 215
OBSCÈNE (Diderot?), 208
OBSCUR (Diderot?), 208
OBSCURITÉ (Diderot?), 208
OBSTINATION (Diderot?), 208
OBTENIR (Diderot?), 208
OBVIER (Diderot?) 208, 230
OCCASION (Diderot?), 208
OCCULTE (Diderot?), 215
OCCURRENCE (Diderot?), 208
ODIEUX (Diderot?), 208
ODIN (D'Holbach?), 182, 188n.
ODYSSÉE, 182
OFAVAI (D'Holbach?), 182, 188n.
OFFENSE (Diderot?), 208
OFFICIEUX (Diderot?), 208
OH (Diderot?), 208
OINDRE (Diderot), 191
OLIGARCHIE (Diderot?), 208, 230
Olimpies, d', 118
OMBIASSES (D'Holbach), 188
OMPHALOMANCIE (Diderot?), 208
ONOMANCIE (Diderot?), 208

ONTOLOGIE (Diderot?), 208
OPÉRATION (Diderot), 192-193, 231
OPHIOMANCIE (Diderot?), 208
OPPOSER (Diderot?), 208
OPPRESSEUR (Diderot?), 208
OPPRESSION (Diderot?), 208
OPPROBRE (Diderot?), 208
OPULENCE (Diderot?), 208
ORIENTALE, PHILOSOPHIE (Diderot), 190
ORIGÉNISTES (Diderot?), 208
ORIGINAIRE (Diderot?), 208
ORIGINAL (Diderot?), 209
ORIGINALITÉ (Diderot?), 209
ORIGINAUX (Diderot?), 208
ORIGINE (Diderot?), 209, 230
ORIX (Diderot?), 215
ORNEMENT (Diderot?), 209
OSÉE (Diderot?), 209
OUBLI (Diderot?), 209
OUBLIER (Diderot?), 209
OUTRAGE, OUTRAGEANT, OUTRAGER (Diderot?), 215
OUTRANCE (Diderot?), 215
OUTRÉ (Diderot?), 215
OUTRER (Diderot?), 215, 230
OUVRIR (Diderot?), 215
OVISSA (D'Holbach), 188

PACIFICATION (Diderot?), 209, 230
PACIFIQUE (Diderot?), 207, 209, 230
PAIN BÉNI (Diderot?), 209
PAIN CONJURÉ (Chambers), 182, 188
PAIX (Diderot?) 209, 230
PALE (Diderot?), 209
PALIBOTRE (Diderot?), 215
PALINODIE (Diderot?), 209
Palissot de Montenoy, Charles, 46-48, 51-52
PAMILLIES (Diderot?), 209
PAN (Diderot?), 209
Panckoucke, Charles Joseph, 49, 50, 110, 140, 142n., 153
PAPE, 88
PAPEGAI (Diderot?), 209
PARAITRE (Diderot?), 209
PARCOURIR (Diderot?), 209
PARDONNER (Diderot?), 209
PARÉAS (D'Holbach?), 182, 188n.
PARFAIRE (Diderot?), 215
PARFAIT (Diderot?), 215, 231

Parlement, Paris, 120-122, 143, 165
PARLEMENTAIRE (Diderot?), 215-216, 230
Parlements, 230
PARLER (Diderot?), 209
PARMÉNIDENNE, PHILOSOPHIE (Diderot), 190
PAROLE (Diderot?), 209
PAROLE ENFANTINE (Diderot?), 209
PARTICULIER (Diderot?), 209
PARTIR (Diderot?), 209
PARTISAN (Diderot?), 209
PARVENIR (Diderot?), 209
PASQUIN (Diderot?), 209
PASQUINADES (Diderot?), 209
PASSAGER (Diderot?), 209
PASSANT (Diderot?), 209
PASSE-DROIT (Diderot?), 209
PASSIONNER (Diderot?), 209
PASSIONS, 182-183
PATIENCE, 183
Paulmy, Marquis de, 114
PAVÉ DES GÉANTS (D'Holbach), 188
Pechin, 115
PÉCUNE (Diderot?), 209
PÉDALIENS (Diderot?), 209
PEINE (Diderot?), 209
PÉNÉTRATION (Diderot?), 209
PÉNÉTRER (Diderot?), 209
PÉNIBLE (Diderot?), 210
PERDRE (Diderot?), 210
Perein, Jean, 61, 62
PERFECTIONNER (Diderot), 191
PERFIDE (Diderot?), 210
PERIPATETICIENNE, PHILOSOPHIE (Diderot), 190
PÉRIR (Diderot?), 210
PERPÉTUER (Diderot?), 210
PERPLEXE (Diderot?), 210
PERQUISITION (Diderot?), 216
Perronet, Jean Rodolphe
*FEU (Pompe à), 176-177
PERSÉCUTER (Diderot?), 210, 230
PERSES (Diderot), 190
PERSISTER (Diderot?), 210
PERSONNAGE (Diderot?), 210
PERSONNALISER (Diderot?), 216
PERSUASION (Diderot?), 210
PERTURBATEUR (Diderot?), 216
PERVERS (Diderot?), 210

PESER les malades (Diderot?), 210
Pesselier, Charles Étienne
SUBSIDE (Diderot), 222-223
PETIT (Diderot?), 210
Petit, Dr., 118
PETIT-MAITRE (Diderot?), 210
PETITESSE (Diderot?), 210
PHÉNICIENS (Diderot), 190
Philippe, Don, of Parma, 117, 137
PHILOSOPHE, 160, 183
PHILOSOPHIE, 183
PHYSIONOMIE (Diderot?), 210
PIACHES (D'Holbach?), 183, 188n.
PIÉGE (Charles Georges Leroy), 187
PINDARIQUE (Diderot?), 210
PIQUANT (Diderot?), 210
PIRE (Diderot?), 210
PITOYABLE (Diderot?), 210
PLAISIR, 183
PLASTIQUE, 183
PLATONISME (Diderot), 190
POITOU, COLIQUE DE (Jaucourt), 46
POLI, CIVIL (Jaucourt?), 183
Polier de Bottens, Antoine Noé de, 231
KIJUN, 187-188, 189
LITURGIE, 188, 189
LOGOMACHIE, 188, 189
MAGICIENS, 188, 189
MAGIE, 188, 189
MALACHBELUS, 188, 189
MANES, 182, 189
MAOSIM, 188, 189
MESSIE, 188, 189
POLITESSE (Diderot?), 210
POLITIQUE, 183, 230
POLITIQUE ARITHMÉTIQUE (Chambers), 173, 188
POLITIQUE, GRACE, 183
POLYANDRIE (Diderot?), 210
POLYTHÉISME (Yvon), 160, 183, 189
Pompadour, Mme de, 90
POMPE (Diderot?), 210
POPLICAIN (Diderot), 190
POPULAIRE (Diderot?), 210
POSSIBLE, 183
POSTÉRITÉ (Diderot?), 210
POUVOIR (Diderot?), 210, 230
Prades, Abbé Jean Martin de, 102, 163

INDEX

*CERTITUDE, 159-160, 216
PRASSAT (D'Holbach?), 184, 188n.
PRATIQUER (Diderot?), 210
PRÉADAMITE (Diderot?), 210
PRÉCAUTION (Diderot?), 210
PRÉCIEUX (Diderot?), 210
PRÉDESTINATIENS, 184
PRÉDILECTION (Diderot?), 210
Préménil, de, 117
PRÉMOTION PHYSIQUE, 184
PRÉOCCUPATION, 184
PRÉPOSÉ, PRÉPOSER (Diderot?), 216
PRESCIENCE, 184
PRÉSOMPTION, 184
PRÉSOMPTUEUX (Diderot?), 184, 210
PRESSENTIMENT (Diderot), 193
PRESSENTIR (Diderot?), 210
PRETRES (D'Holbach), 161, 165, 184
PRÉVALOIR (Diderot?), 210
Priestley, Joseph 9n.
PRIER (Diderot?), 216
PRIEZ-DIEU (Diderot?), 216
PRINCIPES, PREMIERS, 184, 185
PRIVILÈGE (*Gouv. Comm. polit.*), 184
PRIVILÈGE (*Gramm.*) (Diderot?), 216
PROBABILISTE (Diderot?), 216
PROBABILITÉ (Diderot?), 160, 171, 216
PROBITÉ, 184
Proctor, Rev. Percival, 21
PRODUCTION (Diderot), 190, 191n., 201
PRODUIRE (Diderot), 191, 231
PROIE (Diderot?), 210
PROMESSE, 184
PROMETTRE (Diderot?), 210
PROMISSION (Diderot?), 210
Pronnais, Anne Antoine de, 59-60
PROPAGATION DE L'ÉVANGILE (Diderot?), 210-211
PROPHÈTE, PROPHÉTIE, 184
PROPHÉTIE, 184
PROPOSITION (*Poésie*) (Diderot?), 211
PROPRIÉTÉ (*Droit naturel & politique*) (Diderot?), 211, 230
PROPRIÉTÉ (*Métaphysique*), 184
PROSTITUER (Diderot?), 211
PROTATIQUE (Diderot?), 211
PROTECTION (Diderot?), 211, 230
PROVENIR (Diderot?), 211
PROVIDENCE, 184

PROVINCIAL (Diderot?), 217
PRUDE (Diderot?), 211
PRUDENCE, 185
Prunelé, de, 68
PRUSSE (Jaucourt, Diderot), 217
PSYCHOLOGIE, 185
PUBLICAINS (Diderot?), 211
PUÉRILITÉ (Diderot), 190
PUISSANCE, 185
PUISSANCE LÉGISLATIVE, EXÉCUTRICE & DE JUGER (Jaucourt?), 185
PURITAINS (Diderot?), 211
PYRRHONIENNE, PHILOSOPHIE (Diderot), 79, 190
PYTHAGORISME (Diderot), 190
Quesnay, François, 164n.
    ÉVIDENCE, 187, 189
    FERMIERS, 16, 189n.
    GRAINS, 16, 189n.
Quinquet, Mme, 118
QUODLIBÉTAIRE (Diderot?), 217
QUOTIDIEN, JOURNALIER (Diderot?), 211

RACONTER (Diderot?), 217
RAFFINEMENT (Diderot?), 217
RAISON (Diderot?), 211
RAISONNABLE (Diderot?), 217
RAISONNEMENT, 185, 229
RALENTIR (Diderot?), 217
RALLUMER (Diderot?), 217
RAMASSER (Diderot?), 217
RAMENER (Diderot?), 217
RANCUNE (Diderot?), 217
RANIMER (Diderot?), 217
RAPPORT (Diderot?), 217
RAPPORTER (Diderot?), 217
RASSURER (Diderot?), 217
RATTACHER (Diderot?), 217
RATTEINDRE (Diderot?), 217
RAVAGE (Diderot?), 217
RAVIR (Diderot?), 217
Raynal, Abbé Guillaume, 231-232
RÉALISTE (Diderot?), 217
RÉALITÉ (Diderot?), 217
Réaumur, René Antoine Ferchault de, 13, 125-126
RECHERCHER (Diderot?), 217
RÉCOMPENSE (Diderot), 193, 229, 231
RÉCONCILIER (Diderot?), 217

RECONSULTER (Diderot?), 217
RÉCRIER (Diderot?), 217
RECUEILLEMENT (Diderot?), 217
RECUEILLIR (Diderot?), 217
RECULER (Diderot?), 217
RÉDACTEUR (Diderot?), 217
RÉDACTION (Diderot?), 217
REDEVABLE (Diderot?), 217
REDEVANCE (Diderot?), 218
REDIRE (Diderot?), 218
REDITE (Diderot?), 218
RÉDUIRE (Diderot?), 218
Rees, Abraham, 17, 21
RÉFUGIÉS (Diderot), 193, 229, 230
REGARDER (Diderot?), 211
REGNER (Diderot?), 218
RELACHER (Diderot?), 218
RELEVER (Diderot?), 218
RELIGION PROTESTANTE (Jaucourt), 27-28
REMORDS (Diderot), 193-194
REMPORTER (Diderot?), 218
REMUNERATEUR (Diderot?), 218
RENAISSANT (Diderot?), 218
RENAITRE (Diderot?), 218
RENCONTRE (Diderot?), 218
RENFERMER (Diderot?), 218
RENOM (Diderot?), 218
RENVERSER (Diderot?), 218
RENVOI (Diderot?), 218
RENVOYER (Diderot?), 218
REPAITRE (Diderot?), 218
REPENTIR (Diderot?), 218
REPLI (Diderot?), 218
REPOSER (Diderot?), 218
REPRÉSENTANTS (D'Holbach), 161, 165, 185, 229
REPRÉSENTER (Diderot?), 218
REPRIMANDER (Diderot?), 218
REPRIMER (Diderot?), 218
REPROCHE, REPROCHER (Diderot?), 218
REQUISITOIRE (Diderot?), 218
RESIGNATION (Diderot?), 218, 231
RESSENTIMENT (Diderot), 194, 229
RESSOURCE (Diderot?), 218
RESSOUVENIR (Diderot?), 218
RESSUSCITER (Diderot), 190n., 194, 229, 231
RÉSURRECTION (Diderot?), 190, 211
RETARDER (Diderot?), 218

RETATER (Diderot?), 218
RETENTIF (Diderot?), 218
RETENTIR, RETENTISSEMENT (Diderot?), 218
RETENUE (Diderot?), 218
RETIRER (Diderot?), 219
RETOUR (Diderot?), 219
RETOURNER (Diderot?), 219
RETRACTATION (Diderot?), 219
RETRANCHER (Diderot?), 219, 230
REUNIR (Diderot?), 219
REVANCHE (Diderot?), 219
REVE (Diderot), 194-195, 229
REVEILLER (Diderot?), 219
REVENANT (Diderot), 195, 229, 231
REVENIR (Diderot?), 219
REVER (Diderot), 195, 229
REVERENCE (Diderot?), 219, 230
REVETIR (Diderot?), 219
REVIVRE (Diderot?), 219
Rey, Marc Michel, 73
Reybaz, Étienne Salomon, 56, 69, 110
Reynolds, Sir Joshua, 16
Riballier, Ambroise, 119, 138
Richard, Father, 119, 124
RICHE (Diderot?), 219
RICHE COMPOSITION (Diderot?), 219
RIGIDE (Diderot?), 219
RIGORISME (Diderot), 195, 229
RIGORISTE (Diderot?), 219
RIGOUREUX (Diderot?), 219
RIGUEUR (Diderot?), 219
Robinet, Jean Baptiste René, 163
ROBUSTE (Diderot?), 219
ROGNER (Diderot?), 219
ROIDE (Diderot?), 219
ROIDIR (Diderot?), 219
ROMAINS, PHILOSOPHIE DES (Diderot), 190
ROMANCE (Diderot?), 211
Romilly, Jean, 56-57, 69
Romilly, Jean Edme, 57
  VERTU (Diderot?), 226
Rondel de Bériac, 119
RONFLER (Diderot?), 219
RONGER (Diderot?), 219
Rose, Dr. William, 10n.
Rousseau, Jean Baptiste, 23
Rousseau, Jean Jacques, 13, 17, 23, 27-28, 45-46, 57, 222

INDEX

Royal Magazine, 9
Royal Society, 53, 54-55
ROYAUTÉ (Diderot?), 219
Royer, 118
RUDE (Diderot?), 219
RUDIMENT (Diderot?), 214, 220
Ruffhead, Owen, 10-11
RUGIR, RUGISSEMENT (Diderot?), 220
RUINE (*Peinture*) (Diderot?), 220
RUMEUR (Diderot?), 220
RUSE (Diderot?), 220

Saas, Abbé Jean, 222
SACCAGER (Diderot), 195
Saint-Florentin, Louis Phélypeaux, Comte de, 69, 133, 134, 136-139, 152
Saint-Lambert, Jean François, Marquis de, 80, 101, 164n., 231
  FAMILIARITÉ, 180, 189
  FANTAISIE, 179, 180, 189
  FASTE, 180, 189
  FERMETÉ & CONSTANCE, 180, 189
  FLATTERIE, 180, 187, 189
  FRAGILITÉ (*Morale*), 179, 180, 189
  FRIVOLITÉ, 179, 180, 189
  GÉNIE, 161, 179, 180, 189
  HONNETE, 187, 189
  HONNEUR (*Morale*), 187, 189
  INTÉRÊT (*Morale*), 161, 181, 189
  LÉGISLATEUR, 161, 181, 189
  LOUANGE (*Morale*), 181, 189
  LUXE, 161, 181-182, 189
  MANIERES, 182, 189
  TRANSFUGE (*Art milit.*), 188, 189
SAISIR (Diderot?), 220
SALETÉ (Diderot?), 220
SALEUR (Diderot?), 220
SALIR (Diderot?), 220
SALUER (Diderot?), 220
SALUTAIRE (Diderot?), 220
SAMBA-PONGO (D'Holbach), 188
SANCTIFIANT (Diderot?), 220
SANGLANT (Diderot?), 220
SANGUINAIRE (Diderot?), 220
Saone, Marquis de la, 115-116
SARRASINS, PHILOSOPHIE DES (Diderot), 79, 86, 190
Sartine, Gabriel de, 119, 134, 136-139, 141, 142n.

SAVOURER (Diderot?), 220
SCANDALEUX (Diderot?), 211
SCÉLÉRAT (Diderot?), 220
SCÉLÉRATESSE (Diderot?), 220
SCEPTICISME (Diderot), 190
SCHOLASTIQUE (Diderot), 190
Schorne, Abbé de, 61
SCHOOUBIAK (Diderot), 195-196, 229
Scotland, Society of Antiquaries of, 15
Scott, George Lewis, 55
SCRUPULE (Diderot?), 220
SCYTHES, PHILOSOPHIE DES (Diderot), 190
SÉANCE (Diderot?), 220, 230
SÉANT (Diderot?), 220
SECOUER (Diderot?), 220
SECOURS (*Hist. ecclés. mod.*) (Diderot?), 220
SECTAIRE (Diderot?), 220
SECTES DU CHRISTIANISME, 79
SECURITÉ (Diderot?), 220
SEDENTAIRE (Diderot?), 220
SEDUCTEUR (Jaucourt; Diderot?), 220
SEIN (Diderot?), 220
SEMI-PÉLAGIENS, 185
Sénac, Jean Baptiste, 69
SENS COMMUN, 184
SENSATIONS, 185, 229
SENSORIUM (Chambers), 188
SENTENTIEUX (Diderot?), 220
SENTEUR (Diderot?), 220
SENTIMENT INTIME, 184, 185, 229
SÉRIEUX (Diderot?), 220
SERREMENT (Diderot?), 220
SERRER (Diderot?), 220
Servan, Joseph Michel Antoine, 165
SERVICE (Diderot?), 220
SERVIR (Diderot?), 221
S'Gravesande, Willem Jacob, 36
SIGNALEMENT (Diderot?), 221
SIGNALER (Diderot?), 221
SILENCE (Diderot?), 221
SILENCIEUX (Diderot?), 221
Silhouette, Étienne de, 41-42
Simand, 119
SIMPLE (Diderot?), 221
SIMPLIFIER (Diderot?), 221
SIMULATION (Diderot?), 221
SIMULTANÉE (Diderot?), 221, 229

Sloane, Sir Hans, 36, 68
Smith, Adam, 3, 13-14, 16
Smollett, Tobias, 9
SOBRE (Diderot?), 221
SOCIAL (Diderot?), 221
SOCIÉTÉ, 185, 229
SOCRATIQUE, PHILOSOPHIE (Diderot), 88, 190
SOIN (Diderot?), 221
SOLLICITER (Diderot?), 221
SOLLICITUDE (Diderot?), 221
SONNANT (Diderot?), 221
SONNER (Diderot?), 221
SONNERIE (Diderot?), 221
SORTIE (Diderot?), 221
SORTIR (Diderot?), 221
SOUBRETTE (Diderot?), 221, 230
SOUDAIN (Diderot?), 221
SOUDOYER (Diderot?), 221
SOUFFLER (Diderot?), 221
SOUFFRANCE (Diderot?), 221
SOULAGER (Diderot?), 221
SOUPLE (Diderot?), 221
SOUTENIR (Diderot?), 221
SOUVERAINETÉ (Jaucourt), 88
SOUVERAINS (Diderot?), 211, 230
SPADASSIN (Diderot?), 221
SPARTE (Jaucourt; Diderot?), 221
SPECIEUX (Diderot?), 222
SPÉCULATION (Diderot), 196, 229
SPINOSA, PHILOSOPHIE DE, 185, 229
SPINOSISTE (Diderot), 196, 203, 229, 231
SPIRITUALITÉ (Diderot?), 222
SPIRITUEL (Diderot?), 222
SPIRITUEUX (Diderot?), 222
SPLENDEUR (Diderot?), 222
SPLENDIDE (Diderot?), 222
SPONTANÉE (Diderot?), 222
SPONTANÉITÉ (Diderot), 196
Squire, W., 21
STABILITÉ (Diderot?), 222
Stanhope, Philip, Earl, 55
Starhemberg, Count, 117, 136
STOÏCISME (Diderot), 190
Stoupe, Jean Georges Antoine, 100-101, 106
Strube de Piermont, Frédéric Henri, 181
Suard, Jean Baptiste, 3n., 94

SUBIR (Diderot?), 222
SUBIT (Diderot), 196, 229
SUBJUGUER (Diderot?), 221
SUBMERGER (Diderot?), 221
SUBSÉQUENT (Diderot?), 222
SUBSIDE (Pesselier, Diderot), 222-223, 230
SUBSTITUER (Diderot?), 223
SUBTERFUGE (Diderot?), 223
SUBTILITÉ (Diderot?), 223
SUBVENIR (Diderot?), 211
SUCCÉDER (Diderot?), 223
SUCCÈS (Diderot), 196-197, 229, 231
SUCCINCT (Diderot?), 223
SUCCOMBER (Diderot?), 223
SUFFISANTE RAISON (Diderot?), 223
SUICIDE, 185
SUINTEMENT, SUINTER (Diderot?), 223
SUITE (Diderot?), 223
SUIVANTE (Diderot?), 224
SUIVRE (Diderot?), 224
Sully de Bellegarde, 117
SUPERBE (Diderot?), 224
SUPERFICIEL (Diderot?), 224
SUPERFLU (Diderot?), 224
SUPERSTITION (Jaucourt), 67
SUPPLANTER (Diderot?), 224
SURETÉ (Diderot?), 224
SURMONTER (Diderot?), 224
SURNAGER (Diderot?), 224
SURPASSER (Diderot?), 224
SURPRISE (Diderot), 197, 229
SURSAUT (Diderot?), 224
SURVENIR (Diderot?), 224
SURVIVANT (Diderot?), 224
SURVIVRE (Diderot?), 224
SUSCEPTIBLE (Diderot?), 224
SUSCITER (Diderot?), 224
SUSPECT (Diderot?), 224
SUSPENDRE (Diderot?), 224
SUSPICION (Diderot?), 224
SUSTENTATION (Diderot?), 224
SYNCRETISTES (Diderot), 197, 229
SYNDERESE (Diderot?), 224

TACITURNE (Diderot?), 224
TAILLE (Diderot?), 224
TAIRE (Diderot?), 224
TALENT (Diderot?), 224
TANIERE (Diderot?), 224

INDEX

TARDER (Diderot?), 224
TARDIF (Diderot?), 224
TARIR (Diderot?), 224
TATER (Diderot?), 224
TÉMÉRITÉ (Diderot?), 224
TENDANT (Diderot?), 224
TENDRE (Diderot?), 224
TENIR (Diderot?), 211
TENTATIVE (Diderot?), 224
TENU (Diderot?), 224
TENUE (Diderot?), 224
TERMINER (Diderot?), 224
TERNIR (Diderot?), 224
The Complete Dictionary of Arts and Sciences, 18-21
The Modern Dictionary of Arts and Sciences, 21
THÉOCRATIE (D'Holbach), 161, 165, 185, 229
THÉOLOGIE, Réflexions sur la (Jaucourt, Morellet), 79
THÉOLOGIE SCHOLASTIQUE (Jaucourt), 79
THÉOLOGIEN (Diderot?), 224-225
THÉOSOPHES (Diderot), 190
THÈSE (Diderot?), 225
Thibault, Pierre Charles Emmanuel, 61-62
Tholiez, Abbé J.P., 119
Thomas, Antoine Léonard, 94
THOMASIUS (Diderot), 190
TIC (Diderot?), 225
TIÈDE (Diderot?), 225
TIRADE (Diderot?), 225, 230
TIRER (Diderot?), 225
Titelouze de Gournay, de, 118
TOLÉRANCE (Jaucourt), 79
TOMBER (Diderot?), 225
TOME (Diderot?), 225
TOPILZIN (D'Holbach), 188
TORTURE (Chambers), 185, 188
TOUCHER (Diderot?), 225
TOURMENT (Diderot?), 225
TOURNER (Diderot?), 225
Toussaint, François Vincent, 183, 207
 *ABSENT (D'Alembert), 172, 216
 ?AFFINITÉ (Jurisprud.), 179, 189
TRAINER (Diderot?), 225
TRAITE DES NEGRES (Jaucourt), 37
TRAITÉ (Diderot?), 225

TRAITEMENT (Diderot?), 225
TRAITER (Diderot?), 225
TRAITRE (Diderot?), 225
TRANCHANT (Diderot?), 225
TRANCHER (Diderot?), 225
TRANSCRIRE (Diderot?), 225
TRANSFERER (Diderot?), 225
TRANSFUGE (Art milit.) (Saint-Lambert), 188, 189
TRANSGRESSER (Diderot?), 225
TRANSIR (Diderot?), 225
TRANSMETTRE (Diderot?), 225
TRAPPE, abbaye de la (Diderot?), 63-64, 66, 225
TRAPPE, moines de la (Jaucourt), 63-64, 66, 225
TRAVERSER (Diderot?), 225
Trembley, Abraham, 55
TREMPER (Diderot?), 225
TRESSAILLIR (Diderot?), 225-226
TRIBADE (Diderot?), 226
TROISIÈME, (Diderot?), 226
TROMPER (Diderot?), 226
Tronchin, François, 28
Tronchin, Jean, 30-31, 34-35, 68
Tronchin, Théodore, 28-29, 32, 33-40, 43n., 45-46, 56, 57, 68, 69
TRONQUER (Diderot?), 226
TROUBLE (Diderot?), 226
TROUSSER (Diderot?), 226
TUER (Gram.) (Diderot?), 226
TUER, DÉTRUIRE (Diderot?), 226
Turgot, Anne Robert Jacques, 80, 101, 164n., 231
 ÉTYMOLOGIE, 187, 189
 EXISTENCE, 187, 189
 EXPANSIBILITÉ, 187, 189
 FOIRE, 187, 189
 FONDATION, 180, 187, 189
TYRAN, 185
TYRANS, LES TRENTE (Jaucourt), 185
TYRANNICIDE (Jaucourt), 185
TYRANNIE (Jaucourt), 185

ULCERER (Diderot?), 227
ULEMA (D'Holbach?), 186, 188n.
ULTRAMONTAIN (Diderot?), 227
UNANIME (Diderot?), 227
UNANIMITÉ (Diderot?), 227

URGENT (Diderot?), 228
USER (Diderot?), 228

VACILLANT, VACILLATION, VACILLER, (Diderot?), 226
VAIN (Diderot?), 226
VAINQUEUR (Diderot?), 226
VALABLE (Diderot?), 226
VALOIR (Diderot?), 226
Vandeul, Marie Angélique de, 82
VAQUER (Diderot?), 226
VÉHÉMENT (Diderot?), 226
VÉHICULE (Diderot?), 226
VEILLE (Diderot), 197, 229
VELLÉITÉ (Diderot?), 226, 231
VELOURS (Diderot), 197
VENIR (Diderot?), 226
VERBEUX (Diderot?), 226
VERBIAGE (Diderot?), 226
VÉRIFIER (Diderot?), 226
VÉRITABLE (Diderot?), 226
VÉRITÉ, 186, 229
Verri, Alessandro, 51
Verri, Pietro, 51
VERSER (Diderot?), 226
VERTU (J. E. Romilly; Diderot?), 226
VÉTÉRAN (Jaucourt; Diderot?), 226
VICE (Jaucourt, Diderot), 197-198, 203, 229, 231
VICTORIEUX (Diderot?), 226
VIGILANT, VIGILANCE (Diderot?), 226-227
VIGUEUR (Diderot?), 227
VIL (Diderot?) 227, 231
VILAIN (Diderot?), 227
VINDICATIF (Diderot), 198-199, 229
VINGTIEME (Damilaville, Diderot), 186n.,
VISÉE (Diderot?), 227
VISER (Diderot?), 227
VISITE (Diderot?), 227
Vivens, François, Chevalier de, 41, 54
VOILER (Diderot?), 227
VOLAGE (Diderot?), 211
VOLATILISATION, rot?), 227
VOLATILITÉ (Diderot?), 227
Volland, Sophie, 48-49, 66, 83, 87, 99, 193, 205, 209, 225
VOLONTAIRE (Diderot?), 228
VOLONTÉ (Diderot), 199-200, 203, 206, 229, 231
Voltaire, François Marie Arouet, 13, 23, 25, 28, 37, 38-39, 40, 47, 50, 53, 60, 69, 101, 122, 222
  FINESSE, 187n.
  HISTOIRE, 10
VOLUBILITÉ (Diderot?), 228
VOLUPTUEUX (Diderot), 200, 203, 229, 230
VOMIR (Diderot?), 228
VOORHOUT (Jaucourt), 33-35
VOQUER (Diderot?), 228
VORACE, VORACITÉ (Diderot?), 228
VOULOIR (Diderot?), 228
VRAISEMBLANCE, 186, 229
VOYAGE (Diderot?), 228
VUIDER (Diderot?), 228
VULGAIRE (Diderot?), 228
VULNERABLE (Diderot), 200, 229

Williams, Thomas, 19

Young, Arthur, 16
Young, Edward, 59
Yvon, Abbé Claude, 102-103, 160n., 163
  ACTION, 186n.
  ADULTÈRE, 186n.
  AGIR, 186n.
  *AME, 172
  *AMITIÉ, 186n.
  AMOUR, 14, 186n.
  ATHÉES, 183, 185
  AXIOMES, 184
  IMMATÉRIALISME, 160, 180, 189
  LIBERTÉ (*Morale*) (Naigeon), 160, 181, 189, 206
  MANICHÉISME, 160, 182, 184, 189
  POLYTHÉISME, 160, 183, 189

ZAHORIE (Diderot?), 228
ZENDA-VESTA (Diderot), 100n., 190